Rethinking Multiculturalism

Cultural Diversity and Political Theory

Bhikhu Parekh

First published 2000 by
MACMILLAN PRESS LTD
Houndmills, Basingstoke, Hampshire RG21 6XS
and London
Companies and representatives
throughout the world

ISBN 0–333–60881–X   hardcover
ISBN 0–333–60882–8   paperback

A catalogue record for this book is available
from the British Library.

This book is printed on paper suitable for recycling and
made from fully managed and sustained forest sources.

10   9   8   7   6   5   4   3   2   1
09   08   07   06   05   04   03   02   01   00

Copy-edited and typeset by Povey–Edmondson
Tavistock and Rochdale, England

Printed and bound in Great Britain by
Creative Print & Design
(Wales) Ebbw Vale

For J.P.M.

Contents

Acknowledgements

I am deeply grateful to several good friends who very kindly read the first draft of this book and made most valuable comments. They are Michael Sandel, Homi Bhabha, David Miller, Will Kymlicka, Stuart Hall, Rainer Bauböck, Preston King, Tariq Modood, Peter Jones, Uday Mehta, Albert Weale and Jan Nederveen Pieterse. They read the text from different disciplinary and theoretical perspectives and made sure that I took full account of them. Michael Sandel has placed me under an additional debt, and I like to hope that the book measures up to his confidence in it.

The book was originally intended as a short introduction to multiculturalism and part of the excellent series edited by Peter Jones and Albert Weale. I am grateful to them from releasing me from that commitment and generously allowing it to be published independently. Steven Kennedy has borne with its slow progress with an exemplary blend of patience and pressure, and no author could have wished for a better editor. Michael Aronson at Harvard University Press was most encouraging and I am grateful to him for many valuable suggestions. I thank Amalendu Misra for his useful comments and irreplaceable help with the typing and other matters relating to the preparation of the text.

During the years that the book has been in gestation, I have had the good fortune of discussing many of its ideas with several friends and colleagues and benefiting from their comments. They include Joe Carens, Nathan Glazer, Charles Taylor, Ben Barber, Fred Dallmayr, Paul Thomas, Jim Tully, Terence Ball, Andrew Mason, John Stone, Steven Lukes, Luc Ferry, Seyla Benhabib, Leroy Rouner, Ashutosh Varshney, Ferran Requejo, Shlomo Avineri, Dan Avnon, Avner de Shalit, Pratap Mehta, Pierre Birnbaum, Alan Montefiore, Catherine Audard, Matthew Festenstein, Pravin Patel, Upendra Baxi, Joe McCarney, Thomas Pantham, Gurpreet Mahajan, Muhammed Anwar, Rajeev Bhargava, Sudipta Kaviraj, Noel O'Sullivan, Ashis Nandy,

Dhirubhai Sheth, Sarah Spencer, Scott Appleby, and the late and much missed Richard Ashcraft. Various chapters were tried out at international conferences or academic seminars in Cambridge, Oxford, London, Toronto, Montreal, Paris, Vienna, Harvard, Berkeley, Philadelphia, Barcelona, Madrid, Amsterdam, Berlin, Trinidad, Durban, Tokyo, Delhi, and Bombay. I thank the participants for their comments, and like to hope that they will find the book genuinely multicultural in its orientation and range of cultural sensibilities.

The book began just after I had completed three years as Vice-Chancellor of the University of Baroda, India and five as Deputy Chair of the Commission for Racial Equality, UK, and was both prompted and enriched by my experiences there. During the final phase of the book I was privileged to chair the Commission on the Future of Multi-Ethnic Britain, an independent body set up to analyse the state of race relations in Britain and propose an agenda of action to help Britain and hopefully other European societies feel at ease with and profit from their cultural diversity. The experience of working with distinguished fellow commissioners drawn from different walks of life proved invaluable, and I thank them all for their shrewd insights into the practical dilemmas and creative tensions of multicultural society. I am also grateful to several scholars and activists who gave evidence to the Commission or participated in its seminars, especially Joe Raz, Anne Phillips, John Solomos, Ceri Peach, Steven Vertovec and Lord Lester.

I dedicate this book to a very dear friend without whose affection and commitment it would never have seen the light of the day.

BHIKHU PAREKH

Introduction

The last four decades of the twentieth century witnessed the emergence of a cluster of intellectual and political movements led by such diverse groups as the indigenous peoples, national minorities, ethno-cultural nations, old and new immigrants, feminists, gay men and lesbians, and the greens. They represent practices, life-styles, views and ways of life that are different from, disapproved of, and in varying degrees discouraged by the dominant culture of the wider society. Although they are too disparate to share a common philosophical and political agenda, they are all united in resisting the wider society's homogenising or assimilationist thrust based on the belief that there is only one correct, true or normal way to understand and structure the relevant areas of life. In their own different ways they want society to recognize the legitimacy of their differences, especially those that in their view are not incidental and trivial but spring from and constitute their identities. Although the term identity is sometimes inflated to cover almost everything that characterizes an individual or a group, most advocates of these movements use it to refer to those chosen or inherited characteristics that define them as certain kinds of persons or groups and form an integral part of their self-understanding. These movements thus form part of the wider struggle for recognition of identity and difference or, more accurately, of identity-related differences.

Their demand for recognition goes far beyond the familiar plea for toleration, for the latter implies conceding the validity of society's disapproval and relying on its self-restraint. Rather they ask for the acceptance, respect and even public affirmation of their differences. Some of these groups want the wider society to treat them equally with the rest and not to discriminate against or otherwise disadvantage them. Some go further and demand that it should also respect their differences; that is, view them not as pathological deviations to be accepted grudgingly but as equally valid or worthy ways of organizing the relevant areas

1

of life or leading individual and collective lives. While acceptance of differences calls for changes in the legal arrangements of society, respect for them requires changes in its attitudes and ways of thought as well. Some leaders of the new movements go yet further and press for public affirmation of their differences by symbolic and other means.

In the eyes of their champions, these and related demands represent a struggle for freedom, self-determination and dignity and against contingent, ideologically biased and oppressive views and practices claiming false objectivity and universal validity. For their critics the demands represent moral and cultural laissez-faire, a relativist rejection of all norms and concern for truth, a shallow, self-indulgent and ultimately self-defeating celebration of difference for its own sake; in short, the ethics and politics of the unregulated will. The debate between the two in their extreme as well as moderate forms constitutes the substance of the discourse surrounding the politics of recognition.

Although the politics of recognition has its own autonomous logic, it is also closely related to the older and more familiar politics of social justice or economic redistribution. The latter was never merely about redistribution and had an implicit or explicit cultural agenda. Classical socialism was not just about better economic opportunities for the poor and underprivileged but also about creating a new culture and new forms of social relations. Marxism attacked capitalism in the name of a new civilization based on the kind of universalist identity represented by the proletariat. Although the new movements spearheading the politics of recognition sometimes appear to be exclusively preoccupied with the issues of identity and difference, their more articulate spokesmen appreciate that the latter cannot be dissociated from the wider economic and political structure. Identities are valued or devalued because of the place of their bearers in the prevailing structure of power, and their revaluation entails corresponding changes in the latter. Women, gays, cultural minorities and others cannot express and realize their identities without the necessary freedom of self-determination, a climate conducive to diversity, material resources and opportunities, suitable legal arrangements, and so on, and all these call for profound changes in all areas of life.

Although these new movements are sometimes subsumed under the capacious term multiculuralism, the latter in fact refers to only some of them. Multiculturalism is not about difference and identity *per se* but about those that are embedded in and sustained by culture; that is, a body of beliefs and practices in terms of which a group of people understand themselves and the world and organize their individual and collective lives. Unlike differences that spring from individual choices, culturally derived differences carry a measure of authority and are patterned and structured by virtue of being embedded in a shared and historically inherited system of meaning and significance. To highlight this distinction between the two kinds of differences, I shall use the term diversity to refer to culturally derived differences. Multiculturalism, then, is about cultural diversity or culturally embedded differences. Since it is possible to welcome other kinds of differences but not those derived from culture, or vice versa, not all advocates of the politics of recognition need be or, as a matter of historical fact, are sympathetic to multiculturalism. Although part of the politics of recognition, multiculuralism is a distinct movement maintaining an ambivalent relationship to it.[1]

Cultural diversity in modern society takes many forms of which three are most common.[2] First, although its members share a broadly common culture, some of them either entertain different beliefs and practices concerning particular areas of life or evolve relatively distinct ways of life of their own. Gays, Lesbians, those following unconventional lifestyles or family structures, and so on belong to the first category, and miners, fishermen, jet-set transnational executives, artists and others to the latter.[3] They all broadly share their society's dominant system of meaning and values and seek to carve out within it spaces for their divergent lifestyles. They do not represent an alternative culture but seek to pluralize the existing one. For convenience I shall call it subcultural diversity.

Second, some members of society are highly critical of some of the central principles or values of the prevailing culture and seek to reconstitute it along appropriate lines. Feminists attack its deeply ingrained patriarchal bias, religious people its secular orientation, and environmentalists its anthropocentric and technocratic bias. These and other groups represent neither subcultures, for they often challenge the very basis of the existing culture, nor distinct cultural communities living by their values and views of the world, but intellectual perspectives on how the dominant culture should be reconstituted. I shall call this perspectival diversity.

Third, most modern societies also include several self-conscious and more or less well-organized communities entertaining and living by their own different systems of beliefs and practices. They include the newly arrived immigrants, such long-established communities as Jews, Gypsies and the Amish, various religious communities, and such territorially concentrated cultural groups as indigenous peoples, the Basques, the Catalans, the Scots, the Welsh and the Quebecois. I shall call this communal diversity.

Although these three kinds of diversity share several common features and sometimes overlap in practice, they differ in important respects. Subcultural diversity is embedded in a shared culture which it wishes to open up and diversify and not replace with another. This does not mean that it is shallower or more easy to accommodate than other types of diversity. Single-sex marriages, cohabitation and gay parenting deeply offend and often provoke strong reactions among many members of society. However, their challenge is limited in scope and is articulated in terms of such values as personal autonomy and choice that are derived from the dominant culture itself. Perspectival diversity represents a vision of life the dominant culture either rejects altogether or accepts in theory but ignores in practice. It is more radical and comprehensive than subcultural diversity and cannot be so easily accommodated. Communal diversity is quite different. It springs from and is sustained by a plurality of long-established communities, each with its own long history and way of life which it wishes to preserve and transmit. The diversity involved here is robust and tenacious, has well-organized social bearers, and is both easier and more difficult to accommodate depending on its depth and demands.[4]

The terms 'multicultural society' and 'multiculturalism' are generally used to refer to a society that exhibits all three and other kinds of diversity, one that displays the last two kinds, or to that characterized by only the third kind of diversity. Although all three usages have their advantages and disadvantages, the third has on balance most to be said for it, and that is how I shall generally use the term. Since the first two kinds of diversity are to be found in most societies throughout history, the first two usages are so wide as to deprive the term of focus and even render it useless. Furthermore, since communal diversity is logically distinct and raises questions that are unique to it, it constitutes a coherent and self-contained object of investigation, and deserves a name specific to it. Although feminism, gay liberation, environmentalism and so on overlap with it, their basic concerns are different.

Our narrow usage also has a historical basis for the terms 'multicultural' and 'multiculturalism' and the movement associated with them first appeared in countries which found themselves faced with distinct cultural groups. These societies had long assumed that they had a single national culture into which all their citizens should assimilate. They now found that they included groups, either long-established or new arrivals, who would not or whom it could not assimilate and whose presence therefore faced them with new and unfamiliar challenges. As a nation of immigrants, the United States has long insisted on the 'swift assimilation of aliens' into the 'language and culture that has come down to us from the builders of this republic' as Theodore Roosevelt put it.[5] Dominated by the idea of a single American identity and culture that constituted the core of 'Americanism' or 'American creed', the country offered a 'great asylum for diverse peoples' but 'has not always been a great refuge for diverse cultures [which] … at best have been kept marginal to the mainstream'.[6] For reasons that do not concern us here, the black struggle in the United States took a cultural turn in the 1960s, and many of its leaders insisted on the maintenance and recognition of their culture, partly as an affirmation of their distinct ethnic identity, partly in the hope that this would counter the educational underachievement and low self-esteem of their children, and partly to build a political and ideological basis in their struggle against white racism. They were joined by Puerto Ricans, Mexican Americans, native peoples, some sections of non-European immigrants, and others, who all insisted on affirming their cultural identity, declaring America multicultural, and championing the cause of multiculturalism.

Australia officially declared itself multicultural and committed itself to multiculturalism in the early 1970s because of its increasing 'Asianization' and the presence of 'nonassimilable types'. This was also broadly the case in Canada. Israel began to see itself as multicultural in the late 1960s because the oriental and sephardic Jews began to demand revision of its hitherto dominant self-definition and national culture. 'Where is the pride of the sephardics?' was one of the popular slogans of Black Panthers, a militant group among them. In Britain the sizeable presence of South Asians and Afro-Caribbeans in the 1960s, and their refusal, especially of the former, to assimilate, placed multiculturalism on the public agenda. In Germany multiculturalism appeared on the national agenda with the arrival of large bodies of immigrants from Turkey and elsewhere who 'no longer want to be assimilated as far giving up their cultural identity is concerned, especially because more and more come from other cultural spheres' as a prominent German politician put it. In all these societies multiculturalism became a politically and ideologically significant movement because of its rejection of the assimilationist demand of the wider society.

A multicultural society, then, is one that includes two or more cultural communities. It might respond to its cultural diversity in one of two ways, each in turn capable of taking several forms. It might welcome and cherish it, make it central to its self-understanding, and respect the cultural demands of its constituent communities; or it might seek to assimilate these communities into its mainstream culture either wholly or substantially. In the first case it is multiculturalist and in the second monoculturalist in its orientation and ethos. Both alike are multicultural societies, but only one of them is multiculturalist. The term 'multicultural' refers to the fact of cultural diversity, the term 'multiculturalism' to a normative response to that fact.

The failure to distinguish between a multicultural and a multiculturalist society has often led to an agonized but largely unnecessary debate about how to describe a society. In Britain the ethnic minorities, made up of several distinct cultural communities, comprise just over 6 per cent of the population. Although the country is clearly multicultural, the conservative opinion has systematically resisted the description. In its view Britain has over the centuries evolved a distinct culture which is integrally tied up with its national identity and should continue to enjoy a privileged status. To call it multicultural is to imply that its traditional culture should not be given pride of place, that the minority cultures are equally central to its identity, that they should be respected and even cherished and not encouraged to disappear over time, and that the ethnic minorities consist not of individuals but of organized communities entitled to make collective claims. Since conservatives reject all this, they refuse to call Britain multicultural; by contrast many British liberals, who endorse most of these implications, have no hesitation in accepting that description.

France has roughly the same percentage of ethnic minority population as Britain, and its composition too is broadly similar. Not just the conservative but even the liberal opinion there refuses to call it a multicultural society. The French political tradition is based on a strong notion of citizenship. To be a French citizen is to be integrated by an act of will into the French nation and to enjoy the same rights and obligations as the rest. The tradition recognizes only the citizens and has no space for the concept of minority; citizens can be *in a minority* on this or that matter but not *a minority* with its connotation of an organized, exclusive and more or less permanent status. Furthermore, the French nation is supposed to embody and protect the French culture, which its citizens are expected to accept as a condition of their citizenship.

Indeed, since the values of the French culture are believed to be not peculiarly French but universal in their validity, France feels justified in requiring its 'minorities' to abide by them. In such a view minority cultures have no claim to public recognition let alone acceptance. For both conservatives and liberals, France is not a multicultural society.[7]

In both Britain and France the terminological dispute arises from the confusion referred to earlier. Both societies are multicultural in the sense defined earlier, and the disagreement is about how to respond to that fact, some preferring a multiculturalist and others an assimilationist or monoculturalist response. Their normative difference should not be allowed to influence the description of empirical reality. Rather than debate whether Britain, France or any other society is 'really' or 'truly' multicultural, we should acknowledge their multicultural character and discuss whether or not they should remain so.

Although contemporary multicultural societies are not historically unique, for many premodern societies also included several cultural communities, four important facts distinguish them from their predecessors. First, in premodern societies minority communities generally accepted their subordinate status and remained confined to the social and even the geographical spaces assigned them by the dominant groups. Although Turkey under the Ottoman Empire had fairly large Christian and Jewish communities and granted them far greater autonomy than do most contemporary western societies, it was not and never saw itself as a multicultural society. It was basically a Muslim society which happened to include non-Muslim minorities, called *dhimmis* or protected communities. It followed Islamic ideals and was run by Muslims who alone possessed the full rights of citizenship, the rest enjoying extensive cultural but few political rights. The cultural and political climate in contemporary multicultural societies is quite different. Thanks to the dynamics of the modern economy, their constituent communities cannot lead isolated lives and are caught up in a complex pattern of interaction with each other and the wider society. And thanks to the spread of liberal and democratic ideas, they refuse to accept inferior political status and demand equal political rights including the right to participate in and shape the cultural life of the wider society. For its part the wider society, too, concedes the legitimacy of some of these demands and goes at least some way towards meeting them.

Second, thanks to colonialism, slavery, the Holocaust, and the enormous suffering caused by the communist tyrannies, we realize better than before that moral dogmatism and the concommitant spirit of aggressive self-righteousness not only lead to egregious violence but also blind us to its enormity and blunt our moral sensibility. Our understanding of the nature, sources and subtle forms of violence is deeper, and we appreciate that just as groups of people can be oppressed economically and politically, they can also be oppressed and humiliated culturally, that these and other forms of oppression reinforce each other, and that the concern for social justice needs to include not just economic but also cultural rights and well-being. Thanks further to the developments in the sociology of knowledge, psychoanalysis and cultural psychology, we appreciate better than before that culture deeply matters to people, that their self-esteem depends on others' recognition and respect, and that our tendency to mistake the cultural for the natural and to unwittingly universalize our beliefs and practices causes much harm and injustice to others. All this has led to a greater acceptance of cultural differences and a redefinition of the relation between politics and culture, making culture a politically relevant category and respect for an individual's culture an integral part of the principle of equal citizenship.

Third, contemporary multicultural societies are integrally bound up with the immensely complex process of economic and cultural globalization. Technology and goods travel freely, and they are not culturally neutral. Multinationals introduce new industries and systems of management and require the receiving societies to create the necessary cultural preconditions. World opinion demands subscription to the body of universal values embodied in the various statements on human rights, and imposes some degree of moral homogeneity. People travel for employment and as tourists, and both export and import new ideas and influences. Thanks to all this, no society can remain culturally self-contained and isolated. Indeed, the external influences are often so subtle and deep that the receiving societies are not even aware of their presence and impact. The idea of national culture makes little sense, and the project of cultural unification on which many past societies and all modern states have relied for their stability and cohesion is no longer viable today. Contemporary cultural diversity thus has an air of inexorability and unpredictability about it and confronts us as a shared universal predicament.

Fourth, contemporary multicultural societies have emerged against the background of several centuries of the culturally homogenising nation-state. In almost all premodern societies cultural communities were widely regarded as the bearers of collective rights and left free to follow their customs and practices. The modern state rested on a very different view of social unity. It generally recognized only the individuals as the bearers of rights and sought to create a homogeneous legal space made up of uniform political units subject to the same body of laws and institutions. It set about dismantling long-established communities and reuniting the 'emancipated' individuals on the basis of a collectively accepted and centralized structure of authority. Since the state required cultural and social homogenization as its necessary basis, it has for centuries sought to mould the wider society in that direction. Thanks to this, we have become so accustomed to equating unity with homogeneity, and equality with uniformity, that unlike many of our premodern counterparts we feel morally and emotionally disorientated by, and do not quite know how to accommodate, the political demands of a deep and defiant diversity.

Although contemporary multicultural societies are not unique, their historical context, cultural background and patterns of interaction between their constitutive communities are. Not surprisingly they raise questions either not faced by earlier societies or at least not in their current forms, and call for new concepts or radical redefinitions of old ones.[8] The questions relate to cultural rights of minorities, the nature of collective rights, why cultures differ, whether their diversity is a transitional or permanent phenomenon, whether and why it is desirable, whether all cultures deserve equal respect, whether they should be judged in their own terms or ours or by universal standards and how the last can be derived, and whether and how we can communicate across and resolve deep differences between cultures. They also include questions about the state's relation to culture, such as whether it should ignore or give public recognition to its various cultures, and if the latter whether it should privilege the dominant culture or treat them all equally; whether equality involves neutrality or evenhandedness; how the state can both respect cultural diversity and ensure political unity; and how it should determine the range of permissible diversity. Just as the state in a class-divided society might institutionalize and legitimize the rule of the dominant class, it might in a culturally divided society enshrine the domination of one cultural community, raising the question whether and how this danger can be avoided.

Multicultural societies also raise questions about the nature and task of political theory. Almost all past political theorists took the entire humankind as their intended audience and claimed universal validity for their visions of the good life, models of political unity, theories of rights, justice, political obligation, equality and so on. Once we appreciate that human beings are culturally embedded, that cultures differ greatly, and that the intended audience of political theory is not culturally homogeneous, such a view of its nature and task requires reconsideration. Even if the political theorist decided to confine himself to his own or his kind of society as John Rawls has done in his later writings, his problem would not end. He is located within and likely to be influenced by one of his society's several cultures, and his concepts, assumptions and answers might not carry conviction with those belonging to other cultural traditions, as Rawls's critics have shown to be the case with his political liberalism.

Since these and related questions are all in one form or another connected with culture, a theory of multicultural society cannot offer coherent answers to them without developing a well-considered theory of the nature, structure, inner dynamics and role of culture in human life. Much of traditional political theory either ignores the subject altogether or gives a misleading account of it. Broadly speaking it is dominated by two major strands of thought, one making human nature and the other culture the basis of political theory. Arguing rightly that political theory should be grounded in a theory of human beings, and wrongly equating the latter with a theory of human nature, the first group of writers, whom I shall call naturalists or monists, claimed to arrive at one true or rational way of understanding man and the world and leading the good life.[9] Some, such as the Greek and Christian philosophers, J. S. Mill and Hegel, took a substantive or 'thick' view of human nature, whereas Hobbes, Locke and Bentham opted for a largely formal or 'thin' view. Both alike, however, assumed that human nature was unchanging, unaffected in its essentials by culture and society, and capable of indicating what way of life was the best. Their thought therefore left little creative role for culture, seeing it as largely epiphenomenal, confined to the morally indifferent areas of customs and rituals, and making little difference to how moral and political life should be organized.

Culturalism or pluralism, which emerged as a reaction against naturalism and was shared in different degrees by some of the Sophists, Vico, Montesquieu, Herder, the German romantics and others, made the opposite move. It argued that human beings were culturally constituted, varied from culture to culture, and shared in common only the minimal species-derived properties from which nothing of moral and political significance could be deduced. Although culturalists were right to appreciate the importance of culture, they misunderstood its nature. Since they took an organic view of it, they ignored its internal diversity and tensions and could not explain how it changed and why its members were able to take a critical view of it. They split up humankind into different cultural units, and could not give a coherent account of how human beings were able to communicate across, and even evaluate the customs and practices of other cultures. In their own different ways culturalists ended up naturalizing culture, seeing it as an unalterable and ahistorical fact of life which so determined its members as to turn them into a distinct species.

Neither naturalism nor culturalism gives a coherent account of human life and helps us theorise multicultural societies. One stresses the undeniable fact of shared humanity, but ignores the equally obvious fact that human nature is culturally mediated and reconstituted and cannot by itself provide a transcendental basis for a cross-culturally valid vision of the good life; the other makes the opposite mistake. Neither grasps the two in their relationship and appreciates that human beings are at once both natural and cultural, both like and unlike, and like in unlike ways. If we are to develop a coherent conception of human beings, we need to subject each to a rigorous critique and break through their frozen polarity.[10]

*   *   *

This book falls roughly into three parts, the historical, the theoretical and the practical. The first part is concerned to trace the origins and elucidate the internal varieties of naturalism and culturalism. Its purpose is twofold; to undertake the kind of critique referred to earlier and highlight the continuing presence of the two traditions in many of the assumptions informing contemporary discussions of multicultural societies.[11] The historical part is not purely historical but theoretically structured, and not incidental or external but integral to the theory outlined in the second part. If it was to be done satisfactorily, it would have to include many more philosophers and discuss them in greater detail. Since that would have taken up the space needed elsewhere, the present arrangement seemed the best compromise.

In the first chapter I outline and trace the development of the naturalist tradition and distinguish and discuss its three major forms. Since liberalism is rightly assumed to be the most hospitable of all political doctrines to cultural diversity, I discuss at some length its monist tendencies. Although monism has been challenged from almost its very beginning by a variety of small traditions such as scepticism, relativism and moral pluralism, cultural pluralism did not really come into its own until the eighteenth century when historical, sociological and anthropological forms of thought placed cultural diversity at the centre of the philosophical agenda. Since Vico, Montesquieu and Herder show varying degrees of sympathy with it, I examine their ideas in the next chapter and tease out their insights and limitations. Realizing the limitations of monism and pluralism, many contemporary theorists of multicultural society, almost all liberal, have sought to rethink the place of culture in human life and given the debate a new orientation. Accordingly I critically examine the thought of Rawls, Raz and Kymlicka and conclude that, although it takes us in the right direction, it contains unresolved contradictions and is too committed to some form of liberal monism to provide a coherent response to cultural diversity.[12]

Having established the need for a theory of multicultural society, the second part of the book goes on to sketch the outlines of one. It critically examines the concept of human nature, shows that, though valuable, it is too thin to do the philosophical work expected of it, and outlines a culturally sensitive theory of human beings which includes human nature but also much else. In the remaining chapters in this part I discuss the nature, basis and structure of culture, how and within what limits it is possible to arrive at cross-cultural moral principles, how cultures can and should be judged, the basis and limits of respect for other cultures, and the reasons why cultural diversity should not be viewed as a brute fact to be reluctantly accepted and accommodated but as a positive value to be cherished and fostered. In the following chapters I concentrate on the specifically political questions raised by multicultural societies, and discuss how these societies can be held together, develop a common sense of belonging, and reconcile the demands of political unity and cultural diversity. I suggest that in order to do so we need to rethink the modern state and explore new kinds of political structures that might be better suited to contemporary multicultural societies.

The third part discusses the practical problems of multicultural societies, such as what differences to recognize, how to resolve disagreements inherent in the struggle for recognition, deal with practices that offend against some of the deeply held values of the majority community, and apply the principle of equality in a culturally sensitive manner. Since abstract theoretical discussions of these questions cannot capture their complexity I concentrate on concrete examples drawn from different societies. With all the good will in the world, a multi-cultural society is bound from time to time to throw up issues that divide it deeply and appear irresoluble. The Rushdie affair was one such and I discuss it at some length in the penultimate chapter to show why it got out of control, what kind of debate it provoked, and what it tells us about the nature and limits of political discourse in a multicultural society. In the concluding chapter I tease out the insights and errors of multiculturalism and restate my view of it.

In order to avoid likely misunderstanding, four general points need to be made. The dogmatism and intolerance I criticize in some traditions of western thought are to be found in the rest of the world as well, sometimes in even more acute and dangerous forms. The fact that I concentrate on the West should not be taken to imply that they are unique to it, or that I share Nietzsche's and Heidegger's simplistic view that the drive for cultural domination is deeply rooted in its very structure of thought. I do not discuss non-western traditions of thought for reasons of space, my own limited knowledge of them, and to give the book a clear focus.

Second, there is a recurrent tendency in some circles to equate multiculuralism with minorities, especially nonwhites, and to see it as a revolt of the restless natives asserting their dubious cultural values and demanding special rights. In this discourse multiculturalism is racialized and becomes a site for thinly veiled racist sentiments. This is most unfortunate. As I argue, multiculuralism is not about minorities, for that implies that the majority culture is uncritically accepted and used to judge the claims and define the rights of minorities. Multiculturalism is about the proper terms of relationship between different cultural communities. The norms governing their respective claims, including the principles of justice, cannot be derived from one culture alone but through an open and equal dialogue between them.

Third, it might be asked if the theory I sketch in the book is liberal in character or of some other ideological persuasion. The question is misconceived and arises from a misunderstanding of the nature of multicultural society. By definition a multicultural society consists of several cultures or cultural communities with their own distinct systems of meaning and significance and views on man and the world. It cannot therefore be adequately theorised from within the conceptual framework of any particular political doctrine which, being embedded in, and structurally biased towards, a particular cultural perspective, cannot do justice to others. This is as true of liberalism as of any other political doctrine. Liberalism is a substantive doctrine advocating a specific view of man, society and the world and embedded in and giving rise to a distinct way of life. As such it represents a particular cultural perspective and cannot provide a broad and impartial enough framework to conceptualise other cultures or their relations with it.[13]

It might be argued that since we live in a liberal society, we need to and may legitimately seek to develop a liberal theory of multicultural society. The argument excludes non-western societies, many of which are not liberal and some do not even aspire to be one, and we cannot exclude them from our theoretical inquiry. Even so far as western societies are concerned, they are multicultural and include cultures some of which are liberal and some others nonliberal or cut across and cannot be easily subsumed under either. Since the latter contest liberal principles, neither the society nor a theory of it can be constructed on these principles alone. To do so is both unjust, because it denies the legitimate claims of nonliberal cultures to participate in decisions relating to the political structure of the wider society, and risky because the resulting structure cannot count on their allegiance. Since liberalism is a powerful political and moral presence in western society, any theory of multicultural society must take full account of and critically engage with it, but it cannot remain confined to it.

This does not mean that we should not construct a liberal theory of multicultural society as Kymlicka and others have done, for it explores and deepens the theoretical resourses of liberalism and has a persuasive power over liberals, but rather that such a theory cannot provide an intellectually coherent and morally acceptable theoretical basis of multicultural society. We need to rise to a higher level of philosophical abstraction. And since we cannot transcend and locate ourselves in a realm beyond liberal and nonliberal cultures, such a basis is to be found in an institutionalised dialogue between them. Like Gadamer, Hebermas and other theorists of deliberative democracy, though along lines somewhat different to theirs, the theory I sketch is dialogically constituted. It stresses the centrality of a dialogue between cultures and the ethical norms, principles and institutional structures presupposed and generated by it.[14] Some of the principles and institutions the theory endorses are liberal, and hence it has a strong liberal orientation. However, since it also endorses others that are not strictly liberal and brings them into a creative interplay with liberal principles, it departs from liberalism in important respects.[15] It bypasses the debate between comprehensive and political liberalism, both of which take liberalism as the only valid basis of society and disagree about its extent or area of application, and stresses instead a shared commitment to dialogue in both the political and nonpolitical areas of life as the unifying focus and principle of society. Political dialogue has a distinct structure and is not as inconclusive and open-ended as is sometimes suggested. Commitment to it implies a willingness both to accept certain norms, modes of deliberation, procedures, and so on and to live with and act on such consensus as the subject in question allows.

Finally, since the problems thrown up by multicultural societies exercise the minds of not only political theorists but also ordinary citizens and political activists and leaders, this book is addressed to both. If these societies are to run smoothly the latter have to be brought in as serious dialogical partners, both to help them see their day-to-day problems from a deeper theoretical perspective and to learn from their practical experiences and insights. The fact that I have myself been involved for years in the public life of two multicultural societies and have run two of their major institutions provided a further reason for this approach. From time to time, especially in the last part, I therefore step back and forth between various audiences, confront each with the other's concerns, and switch idioms and levels of discourse. This has its obvious dangers, and I hope that I have managed to avoid at least some of them.

1

Moral Monism

The obvious fact that different societies understand and organize human lives differently and entertain different even conflicting conceptions of the good life has been noted and commented upon in all civilizations. In western thought, reflections on the subject go back to the ancient Greeks and have given rise to several responses, of which moral monism is one of the oldest and the most influential. Moral monism refers to the view that only one way of life is fully human, true, or the best, and that all others are defective to the extent that they fall short of it.[1] Since every way of life necessarily embodies several values, moral monism either argues that one value is the highest and others merely a means to or conditions of it, or more plausibly and commonly that although all values are equally important or some more than others, there is only one best or truly rational way to combine them. For the monist evil, like error, can take many forms, but the good, like truth, is inherently singular or uniform in nature. Even as the same proposition cannot be true in one place and false in another, the same way of life cannot be good for one person or society and bad for another. Although the monist considers only one way of life to be truly human, he is not committed to the view that all human beings or societies ought to live by it. He might believe that since they are unequally endowed intellectually and morally, those unable to lead the truly human life should be left free to live such inferior ways of life as are best suited to them. What he cannot concede is that the good life can be lived in several more or less equally worthwhile ways.

Although the monist has the theoretical resources to establish a hierarchy among different ways of life, it is not necessary that he should do so. He might agree with the Stoics that ways of life that fall short of the

16

highest are so imperfect and unworthy that there is no point in taking them seriously and establishing a moral hierarchy among them. Or, like the early Christian theologians, he might argue that the good does not admit of degrees and that ways of life are either good or bad and cannot be hierarchically graded. Or he might argue with the Gnostics and the Neo-Platonists that such a hierarchy should be avoided in order to discourage people from aiming at the next best way of life rather than the best itself. Although the monist need not grade ways of life, he cannot ignore important differences between them.

In order to show that one way of life is the best, the monist needs to ground it in something that all human beings necessarily share and is transcultural in nature. If some did not share it, they would not be bound by his preferred way of life, and if they shared it coincidentally it would lack a rational basis. The obvious candidate is human nature. The monist could also appeal to the structure of the universe, God, and so on, but in order that these can be shown to be binding on all human beings, they need to be mediated by human nature. He might define human nature strongly or weakly, as something that determines or only disposes humans to act in a certain way. And he might either give it a substantive content or only highlight its distinctive and largely formal features. Whatever his approach, and each has its strengths and limitations, the monist relies on a conception of human nature to deduce or justify a particular way of life.

If his conception of human nature is to do the required philosophical work, the monist needs to assume the following. First, the uniformity of human nature; that is, all human beings, however much they are divided by time and space, share a common nature consisting of certain unique capacities, dispositions and desires. The monist does not deny that they differ in important respects or that no two human beings are ever exactly alike, but insists that differences define their particularity not their humanity and do not penetrate or shape their shared nature. In his view differences are not autonomous, and only represent so many different ways of expressing or combining the shared universal features. Some men pursue wealth, others women, fame or learning. Although the objects of their desires differ, the underlying desire is the same, be it that for pleasure, status, recognition or pride. Like human desires human capacities too, in his view, have basically the same nature, structure and mode of operation. Reason, the allegedly highest among these, is the same in all human beings and functions or ought to function in an identical manner.

Second, the monist assumes the moral and ontological primacy of similarities over differences. Since only what human beings share in common is supposed to constitute their humanity, the monist argues that their similarities are ontologically far more important than their differences. Differences vary from individual to individual, do not affect let alone form part of their humanity, and are ultimately inconsequential. All human beings are human in exactly the same way, not each in his or her own way. Third, the monist insists on the socially transcendental character of human nature. Human nature inheres in human beings as their natural endowment. Although it can be developed only in society, it is deemed to be unaffected by the latter. For the monist human beings are therefore basically the same in different times and places, and their cultures or ways of life make at best only a minor difference. Fourth, the monist assumes the total knowability of human nature. For some monists human nature is relatively simple and consists of readily specifiable capacities and desires; for others it is complex and elusive but capable of being discovered by means of sustained philosophical, theological or scientific investigation. Finally, the monist takes human nature as the basis of good life or, what comes to the same thing, asserts the unity of good and truth. For the monist the content of the good life is determined in the light of the central truths about human nature, not merely because 'ought' implies 'can' but because the good lacks an ontological basis and remains purely subjective unless it is grounded in human nature. Since human nature consists of several different capacities and desires, the question arises as to which of them is central to it and should form the basis of the good life. The usual monist tendency is to stress the *differentia specifica* of the human species, be it the theoretical intellect, love of God, or the capacity for self-determination and autonomy.

Monism can take several forms. I shall briefly examine three of the most influential, namely the rationalist monism of Greek philosophy, the theological monism of Christianity, and the regulative monism of classical liberalism, and show how each has difficulty accounting for and coming to terms with moral and cultural diversity. Of the three the first advocates a substantive and comprehensive way of life, the second a substantive body of doctrines and a way of life based on them, and the third a relatively thin vision of the good life to which all ways of life are expected to conform. All three appeal to human nature but define it differently. The first takes a thick and largely secular, the second a thick and theologically grounded, and the third a relatively thin and secular view of it.

Greek monism

The tendency to argue that only one way of life is the best and that all others can be judged and even graded in terms of it goes back to Plato. For him the natural world was diverse and not uniform because God or the *demiurgus* would otherwise remain purely ideal in nature and lack perfection (Lovejoy, 1961, pp. 48–52). Each species had a distinct nature or rather embodied a distinct 'idea', and its characteristic mode of perfection consisted in realizing the latter and thereby contributing to the perfection of the cosmos. Different species formed a hierarchy based on the degree to which they realized the totality of goodness or the Idea of the Good.

For Plato, human beings were no different. Their characteristic mode of perfection consisted in realizing the potentialities of their nature and living up to the idea of man. While social customs and practices varied, human nature did not. This raised the question as to who was to discover it and how, for the person doing so was himself shaped by the customs and beliefs of his society, and the human nature he aimed to discover was itself overlaid with customs and hence opaque. Plato gave little attention to the question. He took the rather simple-minded view that human nature consisted of those capacities that were unique to humans, and that their discovery and the determination of their status called for a capacity for rational abstraction and critical reflection which a philosopher acquired after arduous training.

For Plato, human nature was composed of three basic elements, namely reason, spirit and desire. Reason was both theoretical and practical in nature. The former, which human beings shared in common with God, was equipped to acquire true knowledge of the universe, and the latter, which was unique to them, related to human conduct. The spirit was the source of psychological energy and expressed itself in emotions such as anger, indignation, pride, honour and ambition. Desires largely related to the objects of bodily and other needs. For Plato, reason was the highest of the three faculties. Desires were inherently unruly and required its directive and regulative control, and the spirit too had an irrational dimension and needed to be guided by reason. Of the two forms of reason, theoretical reason was higher because it was the source of the knowledge of the Idea of the Good without which practical life lacked coherence and direction. It also dealt with eternal and unchanging objects, was free of the constraints of space and time, and hence divine in nature. Plato argued that although all human beings shared a common nature and possessed all three faculties, they did so in different degrees and were unequally equipped to lead the highest form of life. Depending on which of the three elements was dominant in them, different human beings found their happiness in different forms of life. Although these forms of life were good *for* them and indeed the only forms of life possible for them, their *objective* moral worth could be rationally determined and hierarchically graded.

Plato graded all human activities and ways of life on the basis of the hierarchical theory of the human soul. The *bios theoretikos*, the way of life devoted to the contemplation and pursuit of theoretical knowledge, was the highest. The activities and ways of life in which the spirit was the dominant principle came second, and those devoted to the satisfaction of desires came last. Plato readily admitted that all ways of life involved all three faculties, for the philosopher practised moral virtues and had his share of desires, and the artisan thought about God and the meaning of life. His hierarchical distinction was based on which human faculty dominated and formed their organizing principle.

Plato's discussion of the ways of life was intended to be universally valid, applying not just to the Greeks but also to others. To be sure, he did not say much about the latter, but what he did say reflected his general view.[2] The Greeks were a superior people to the Egyptians and the Phoenicians for, unlike the latter who took an instrumental and practical view of knowledge, they desired and pursued it for its own sake and valued 'theory' or pure contemplation. Unlike many an Enlightenment writer nearly two millennia later, Plato freely acknowledged that the Greeks had learned and borrowed much from others, but insisted that they had invariably refined and improved upon it, and that their very willingness to learn from others and the desire to 'travel for the sake of theory' as Pythagoras had put it demonstrated their superiority (Halbfass, 1990, pp. 6f). The fact that the Greeks had established a regime of free enquiry conducive to intellectual and other pursuits whereas other societies only knew despotism and tyranny offered further evidence of Greek superiority. Such a distinction between the Greeks and non-Greeks implied that relations among the former were governed by different principles from those regulating their relations with non-Greeks. For Plato, all Greeks constituted a 'single people', were 'kindred', and 'by nature' friends. Regrettably they did fight among themselves, but this was a 'civil strife' not a war and subject to certain rules: they should not treat each other harshly or take fellow Greeks as slaves. By contrast non-Greeks were their 'natural enemies', and their relations with them were exempt from these constraints. Although opposed to wars for national glory and territorial expansion, Plato, like Aristotle after him, approved of those intended to rule over 'inferior' subjects (Tuck, 1999, p. 53; Aristotle, *Politics*, p. 12).

Like Plato, Aristotle was struck by the diversity of the natural world and explained it in terms of the principle of divine plenitude. Each species had a distinct 'nature' – the term he preferred to Plato's 'idea' – and took it to mean a dynamic and self-moving essence. All members of a species shared a common nature or essence, and their well-being and characteristic mode of perfection, as well as their distinct contribution to the harmony of the cosmos, consisted in realizing their species-potentialities.

Aristotle's view of human nature was somewhat different from Plato's. He did not assign the spirit a distinct status, and thought desires to be less chaotic and unruly than Plato did. However, he too believed that reason was the highest human faculty, and was both theoretical and practical in nature. Theoretical reason was divine and immortal and, although it was an integral part of human nature, it entered it 'from outside'. It was higher than practical reason because it was self-sufficient, free from worldly constraints, and enabled human beings to participate in God-like existence (*Ethics*, 1955, Book X, ch. VIII). Unlike the life of practical reason, which involved the development and exercise of moral and political virtues such as justice and courage and required other human beings, the life devoted to theoretical contemplation was self-contained and free from the contingent responses of other men. It dealt with immortal and unchanging objects, was most honourable and worthy, and offered the highest and lasting happiness. As Aristotle put it, 'That which is proper to each thing is by nature best and most pleasant for each thing. None of the other animals is happy since they in no way share in contemplation'.

Theoretical life was devoted to the study of theology or first philosophy, mathematics and physics, and of these the first was the highest. And even here, 'since pleasure is found more in rest than in movement', contemplating truths already attained was more pleasurable than inquiring after them (*Ethics*, 1995, Book X, ch. VIII). For Aristotle the best way of life was devoted to 'the worship and contemplation of God' (Ross, 1956, p. 234). Sometimes he gestured in a slightly different direction, arguing that, since human beings lived in society, they should also cultivate appropriate virtues and combine the contemplative with moral and political life. It is not clear whether he thought such a balanced life higher or lower than the purely contemplative (Ross, 1956, pp. 232–4; MacIntyre, 1985, pp. 137–53). In any case he was convinced that only the life in which contemplation played a dominant role was truly human and happy. Next in worth was the life devoted to moral and political virtues and practical wisdom, and included above all the life of the citizen. The life devoted to productive activities had the least worth. Since human beings were unequally endowed, Aristotle thought that only a small minority was capable of leading the highest life. Many more were capable of the next best life, most others fated to lead the third best, and some were only fit to be slaves. For Aristotle a properly constituted society should respect this hierarchy and create conditions in which each way of life received its due recognition and importance.

In spite of their important differences, both Plato and Aristotle were moral monists and shared all the five assumptions of moral monism stated earlier. They classified and graded different ways of individual and collective life in terms of which human faculties these exercised and cherished, and graded the ontological status and dignity of the latter in terms of their metaphysical view of man's place in the universe. For them, humans occupied an intermediate position between God and animals. Theoretical reason, which enabled them to participate in the divine, was the highest, and desire which drew them closer to the animals was the lowest.

The vision of the highest form of life advocated by Plato and Aristotle is underpinned by a number of beliefs concerning the nature of God, the inner human impulse or duty to become God-like, the constitution of human nature, the idea of the highest or purest pleasure, and so on. They do not offer convincing reasons for these beliefs and sometimes only reproduce the cultural biases of the Greek aristocracy. This is not to say that their views are indefensible, though some are, but rather that it is possible to take different and equally valid views on the nature of God and man, purity of pleasure, the nature of human happiness and so on, and arrive at very different ideas about the best way of life. For Plato and Aristotle the philosopher's way of life is higher than that of the artist, the poet, the priest and the citizen because theoretical reason is the highest faculty and its exercise the source of true and lasting happiness. On different assumptions to theirs, just as plausible as their own if not more so, their whole way of thinking appears self-serving and even incoherent.

As we saw earlier, moral monism disjoins reason and morality from culture, and Plato's and Aristotle's thought is a good example of this. It takes no account of the fact that different societies understand and structure human nature differently, cultivate different capacities and virtues, and assign different meanings and worth to human activities and relationships. To be sure Plato acknowledged the role of the 'type of human character' dominant in a society, and thought that it determines what kind of constitution suits it best. However, the character involved only refers to which of the three human faculties is predominant and has no cultural significance. Aristotle stressed the importance of social classes and relativity of the criteria of justice, but this, again, amounted to no more than recognizing the importance of economic interests. The closest either of them came to appreciating the importance of culture is their acknowledgment of the role of customs, which are but a small part of it. And even then they treat these as largely irrational outgrowths, spontaneous like natural vegetation, mute, passive and devoid of moral meaning and significance. Since both philosophers ignored the role of culture in shaping human beings, they were unable either to appreciate that the good life can be defined and lived in several different ways, or to guard against the influence of their culture on their own thought.

Christian monism

Like Plato and Aristotle, Christian theologians combined their even greater delight in the infinite diversity of the natural world with a commitment to moral monism. God could have easily created a uniform universe. The fact that He did not shows how great a value He placed on diversity (Lovejoy, 1961, pp. 64f). Augustine asked why God did not make all things similar and replied, *non essent omnia, si essent aequalia* (if all things were similar, all things would not exist). Thanks to God's infinite and overflowing love of His creation, He conferred the gift of actuality on all possible grades of goodness. He created diversity not as a vehicle of His self-realization, for He was already self-sufficient, but out of His love of his creation and as part of His design to create a perfect world. Each species in it was endowed with a unique nature, occupied a distinct place in the universe, and contributed to its perfection and harmony by attaining its own characteristic mode of perfection.

Aquinas developed this argument more fully. Existence was a form of goodness, and it was better to exist than to be merely possible. The divine will, which always chose the good, willed the existence of all possible grades of goodness. The perfection of the universe consisted in 'the orderly variety of things', each reflecting the likeness of God 'according to its measure'. In a profoundly significant remark he observed that the fact that an angel was better than a stone did not mean that two angels were better than one angel and a stone, for 'two natures are better than one'. A stone might benefit from being an angel but the universe did not, for although the universe with two angels contained a greater quantity of goodness than that with one angel and a stone, it was less 'excellent' (*ibid.*, pp. 75f). For Aquinas as for many other Christian theologians, diversity was an intrinsic good, an irreducible and autonomous value, and the perfection of the universe as of any social whole within it consisted not in the highest possible quantity of goodness in the abstract, but in the widest possible variety of the natures it contained. As we shall see later this idea was used by Vico, Herder and others to provide a theologically grounded theory of moral and cultural pluralism.

The celebration of diversity in Augustine, Aquinas and others was grounded in a particular view of the universe and suffered from its obvious limitations. The diversity they celebrated was that of types or species, each endowed with a distinct nature whose realization constituted its characteristic mode of perfection. All the members of a species therefore had an identical destiny, to realize the potentialities of their shared nature. Indeed, since each species contributed to the harmony and perfection of the universe only by remaining true to its unique nature, its members must conform to the uniform norms of their species-nature. So far as human beings were concerned, they were to aspire for the same kind of perfection. Since they were unequally endowed or differently circumstanced, they attained their characteristic mode of perfection in different degrees, but it was inconceivable that they could lead different and equally legitimate forms of good life.

Christian moral monism differed from the Greek in several important respects. It was theologically grounded, and went hand in hand with religious monism or the belief that Christianity alone represented the 'one and true' religion. While Plato and Aristotle claimed to demonstrate on philosophical grounds that a particular way of life was the highest, Christianity made it a matter of faith. Some of its theologians did, of course, seek to demonstrate its truths on rational grounds, but most realized that this could not be done. Some even welcomed this limitation because it showed that one accepted Christianity not as a matter of rational necessity but as an uncoerced act of faith. Plato and Aristotle had no interest in how the rest of humankind lived and whether or not it knew of their doctrines; for Christianity humankind had a vital common interest in salvation, and those knowing the way to achieve it had a duty of love to 'spread the good news'. This missionary work was theoretically facilitated by the fact that, unlike Plato and Aristotle for whom most of humankind was inherently incapable of leading the highest way of life, the Christian way of life was within the moral reach of all. Although Christian theologians admitted that some kind of moral life could be lived on the basis of natural reason alone, they insisted that it was inherently precarious because of the fallibility of natural reason, shallow because it lacked energy and depth which could only come from the love of God, and incomplete because morality was only a step towards the otherworldly life which alone represented the final human destiny. A truly moral life therefore needed a religious basis, and its quality was higher the truer the underlying religion. While Christianity thus accommodated moral diversity, it graded it hierarchically and remained as committed to moral as to religious monism. Christian monism introduced the ideas of moral universalism, missionary work and religious intolerance that were absent in its Greek counterpart.

Christian monism faced two problems, internal and external. Since its central doctrines could be interpreted in several different ways, its spokesmen had to decide whether to establish a theological orthodoxy or tolerate and even cherish hermeneutic pluralism. Secondly, Christianity was confronted with other religions such as Judaism and Paganism and later Islam, 'Hinduism' and others and, again, it had to decide whether to dismiss them as false or embrace religious pluralism. Although hermeneutic and religious monism do not entail each other, there is a tendency for them to go together, partly because intolerance and exclusivity in one area tend to encourage them in the other, and partly because the 'only true' religion cannot risk diversity of interpretations lest it should unwittingly come under the influence of other religions and compromise its absolute truth. Not surprisingly Christianity built up a powerful tendency towards hermeneutic and religious monism. No great religion, especially one as philosophically rich and universalist in its ambition as Christianity, can suppress all internal differences or dismiss other religions as false. Christian monism was therefore constantly shadowed by a pluralist impulse, and its history is marked by a tension between the two.

In the early years Christianity was widely seen by its followers as a strand of thought within Judaism. Some of them even thought that one could not become a Christian unless one was a Jew. After all Jesus himself was one, Judaism provided the context of everything he said and did as well as his sacrificial death, and he could not be accepted as a Messiah without also believing in the Mosaic covenant, the Davidian monarchy, and the divine inspiration of the Hebrew Scriptures. Other Christians took a looser view of the relation between the two, but even they thought that one could be both a Jew and a Christian. Not surprisingly early Christians observed many of the ritual precepts of the Law and frequented the Jerusalem Temple. The subsequent Christian decision to reject the practice of circumcision and some of the Jewish dietary taboos was largely designed to facilitate missionary work among non-Jews and not to signify a break with Judaism.

For reasons too complex to discuss here things began to change radically towards the end of the second century. Christianity made a clean break with Judaism, and a Christian who observed any of its ritual precepts was excommunicated. It was argued that Jesus had not only fulfilled Biblical Judaism but established a new religion, and that his followers were now God's chosen people. Christianity was the only true religion, it had supplanted and superseded Judaism, and a Jew who fully understood his faith had a duty to convert to it. Such a view was not easy to maintain, for several passages in the Book of *Leviticus* stated that the Law was a perpetual covenant, Jesus himself said that he had not come to abolish or even alter but fulfill the Law, and several passages in the Acts depicted the Apostles as attending Temple services, observing at least some Mosaic dietary regulations, and performing various other ritual acts after the death, resurrection and ascension of Jesus. Not surprisingly, Patristic writers devoted enormous intellectual energy to explaining all this away and insisting on a total rupture with Judaism. St Augustine played a decisive role in the process. Drawing on the scattered elements of Patristic thought, he worked out a position that was later incorporated into the Latin theological tradition and became part of the standard Catholic view.

For Augustine the Mosaic Law and all of Jewish history were significant only as a prelude to Christianity. Moses and other Old Testament prophets knew that the Law was grossly inadequate, a mere shadow of the true reality that was to come in the shape of Jesus. Christians were therefore the only true heirs of Moses, and the Jews who failed to covert to Christianity were guilty of apostasy. For Augustine the Hebrew scriptures themselves indicated that the Mosaic Law would be abrogated with the arrival of the Messiah and that its validity was historically limited. The Jews who continued to observe its precepts were spiritually blind, willful, 'carnal' (sticking to the letter of the Law and missing its deeper spiritual meaning) and idolatrous. They had become so degenerate that they had not only denied themselves the salvation offered by Jesus, but done the work of Satan by rejecting and crucifying him.

While denouncing the Jews and their religion, Augustine had to explain their part in the divine design (Augustine, 1967, pp. 218f; Hood, 1995, pp. 10–14). He was convinced that their providential role was to assist the spread of Christianity. Their status as homeless exiles and the destruction of their Temple offered the conclusive proof that God had rejected them in favour of Christians, whose church alone was the *Verus Israel*. They also served the purpose of vouchsafing the veracity of the claims of Christianity. If they did not exist, pagans would accuse Christians of inventing the Old Testament prophecies that pointed to Jesus as Messiah. Christians therefore had a duty to tolerate and even protect Jews not because they had given them their Messiah, let alone because every religion deserved to be tolerated, but because their existence furthered the cause of Christianity (Hood, 1995, pp. 10–15 and 110; Deane, 1963, pp. 72, 206–20).

For Augustine, Christianity was the only true religion, the Catholic church was its only authorized spokesman, and there was no salvation outside the Church (Gilson, 1959, pp. 165–84). Christians alone led a truly good life, and that too only if their faith was free of theological errors. It is hardly surprising that Augustine spent much of his active life fighting what he took to be the four great heresies of his age, namely Manicheism, Donatism, Pelagianism and Arianism, and laying the theological foundations of what he took to be the true interpretation of Christianity.[3] Surrounded by so many heresies, he could not avoid appreciating that sincere Christians 'accommodated the sacred words' to their understanding and 'found therein true albeit different meanings'. However, he was uneasy with the consequences of such hermeneutic pluralism and insisted that new meanings were to be accepted only 'if they ... are true', that is, in conformity with the views of the Catholic Church.

Armed with a doctrine claiming to offer the only true interpretation of Christianity, Augustine attacked non-Christians and heretics. Although he thought that the prevailing Roman way of life was not based on such low vices as greed and brute conquest but on the 'love of honours, power and glory' and created a free republic devoted to the pursuit of the common good, he was in no doubt that this *libido ista domination* was 'smoke without weight', a source of deep moral corruption, and had predictably led to Rome's ruin. Devoid of a true religion Rome was not a 'true commonwealth', lacked 'true justice', and offered not a genuine but only an 'allowable peace'. Like the individual, a society was to be judged by the object of its love, and only the Christian society which was based on the highest and noblest object of love in the shape of God was truly human. Augustine's rejection of Rome was so fierce that at every turn he juxtaposed 'your Virgil' with 'our Scriptures' and exuded the spirit of what one of his perceptive commentators calls 'Christian nationalism' (Brown, 1967, pp. 306f and 231).

In his early writings Augustine had argued that the state should do no more than maintain earthly peace, leaving the salvation of the soul to the Church and tolerating non-Christian ways of life. In his later writings he took the opposite view that the Christian ruler had a duty to cultivate Christian virtues among his subjects and use his power 'for the greatest possible extension of his worship' (Deane, 1963, ch. VI). The 'righteous persecution' of heretics and backsliders, which was designed to safeguard their own 'spiritual health' and save them from 'eternal death', was an act of love, like that of a father chastizing his undisciplined son. The ruler therefore had a duty to punish heretics with death, to ensure that no Christian was left outside the church, and peacefully to convert Jews and other non-Christians. If the latter persisted in their errors, they were to be tolerated but not accorded the full membership of society.

Unlike Augustine, Aquinas was more hospitable to some of pre-Christian thought. To be sure Augustine, too, had drawn philosophical inspiration from Plato, but he did not think much of his or Aristotle's political and social thought or of the Greek and Roman ways of life. Aquinas was sympathetic to and drew heavily on them. Rejecting the fear of the Franciscans and secular priests, the so-called Augustinians, that Aristotelian ideas would corrupt the Christian faith, he produced a brilliant and generous philosophical synthesis of Christian and pre-Christian ideas. However, thanks to his belief in the absolute truth of Christianity and his insistence on the need for its one true interpretation, he adopted a largely instrumental attitude to Aristotelian ideas, taking over only those that fitted into the Christian framework as propounded by the Catholic church. Even then his theology remained highly suspect in the eyes of the church for decades.

For Aquinas, as for Augustine, religion was the basis of the truly good life, Christianity was the only true religion, the Catholic Church was the only authorized custodian of it, and an unquestioning faith in it was the only way to salvation. Since true faith was the *sine qua non* of the good life, Aquinas insisted that all possible steps should be taken to safeguard its purity. It was 'a much graver offence to corrupt the faith than to forge money' and deserved harsher punishment. If heretics and blasphemers persisted in their errors, they could be put to death unless political expediency and the likely disorder dictated otherwise. The same treatment was to be meted out to apostates who 'could be constrained, even physically, to observe what once they accepted for ever'. As for unbelievers, they threatened the faith of 'simple people', for whom it was 'dangerous' to hear 'anything different from what they believe' and who should therefore be 'forbidden to communicate with unbelievers'. Since it was prudent to tolerate smaller evils in order to avoid greater ones, unbelievers should be isolated rather than persecuted; as Aquinas says quoting Augustine, 'if you do away with harlots, the world will be convulsed with lust'.

Aquinas's treatment of Jews was not very different from Augustine's (Aquinas, 1952, vol. 2, pp. 43f; Hood, 1995, pp. 76–105). He thought that although they rejected the Christian faith, they accepted its anticipation in the form of 'the figure of that faith in the Old Law'. This was both to their advantage and disadvantage, the former because they did receive some divine guidance, the latter because they chose to disregard it. Since Jews shared some of the Christian scriptures and corrupted the Christian faith by their 'false interpretation' of them, their unbelief was a 'more grievous sin than that of the heathens' who did not accept the Gospel. Thanks to their sin of deicide, Jews were 'destined to perpetual slavery', and sovereigns 'may treat their goods as their own property' provided, of course, that they did not deprive them of the basic necessities of life. Christians were not to socialize or discuss religion with them, and Jews were not to be allowed to exercise public or even private authority over Christians. Jews of both sexes should 'on all occasions be distinguished from other people by some particular dress', so that Christians may not inadvertently mistake them for one of them. As against many of his intolerant predecessors and contemporaries, Aquinas argued that the Jewish religious rites should be tolerated because they foreshadow the truth of Christianity and reassure its adherents that even 'our enemies bear witness to our faith'. Like Augustine, he saw Judaism as nothing more than a part of Christian prehistory, and Jews as a people whose theological *raison d'être* was to serve the cause of Christianity (Aquinas, 1952, vol. 2, pp. 432–40).

Aquinas was one of the first to formulate a coherent and influential Christian response to Islam. His *Summa Contra Gentiles* was a theological manual intended to guide Christian missionaries in Spain in their disputes with non-Christians. Since it was designed to convert the latter and since the arguments derived from the Bible were of no help, Aquinas based the work on allegedly neutral philosophical premises. They were, of course, nothing like that and largely presupposed the truth of the Christian faith. Aquinas had little interest in understanding Islam let alone entering into a dialogue with it. His main concern was to show that it was a false and immoral religion.[4]

Since the central doctrines of Christianity were deemed to be open to only one true interpretation, those disagreeing with it had no choice but to leave the Catholic fold and set up an alternative church and theology of their own. Luther and Calvin did not challenge the traditional belief that Christian doctrines were amenable to only one true interpretation, and simply replaced the standard Catholic view with their own. As Protestantism in turn gave rise to different sects, each of them made the same monist claim. Although Christianity became internally diversified, the monist claim of each group and the consequent doctrinal hostility to the rest did not encourage hermeneutic pluralism. The doctrinally closed, exclusive and dogmatic groups had little interest in a mutual dialogue or even tolerance, except among the dissidents at the periphery.

As far as other religions were concerned, Christians faced a problem. On the one hand they were convinced that theirs was the only true religion and that others were either false or inferior. On the other hand, they could not demonstrate such a claim and had the additional difficulty of explaining why God should be partial to them and condemn the rest to eternal damnation. By and large they stuck to religious monism and explained away the difficulties involved in terms of God's inscrutable will, circular philosophical arguments, and the symbolic significance of the greater worldly success of Christian societies. Some non-Christian religions were rejected as false, others presented as commendable anticipations of Christianity. In either case salvation of their adherents lay in converting to it.

Thanks to the Holocaust, the end of the European empires, the pluralist ethos of our times, and the self-assertion of non-Christian religions, some radical rethinking is taking place among Christian theologians and religious leaders, and there is a genuine desire to understand other religions better. Such movements had, of course, occurred in the past as well, but they were confined to a small minority of liberals and disapproved of by the religious establishment. When, for example, Chicago held the World Parliament of Religions in 1893 in order, among other things, to explore what the *Chicago Tribune* called the 'wells of truth outside', some religious leaders condemned it for 'coquetting' with 'false' religions, and the Archbishop of Canterbury refused to attend it on the ground that Christianity was 'the only true religion' and had nothing to gain from a dialogue with others (Eck, 1993).

This is no longer the case today. Some years ago the World Council of Churches set up a unit in charge of dialogue with other religions, and it has done valuable work. The Second Vatican Council set up a special secretariat in 1963 to deal with non-Catholics, and issued a sympathetic *Declaration on the Relationship of the Church to Non-Christian Religions*. The Declaration generously urged reverence for what is 'true and holy' in other religions and belatedly rejected the pernicious belief that Jews were guilty of deicide. It called their persecution immoral and insisted that they should 'not be spoken of as rejected or accused' (Ariarajah, 1991, pp. 129–30). In many countries there are also several church-inspired interfaith networks which organize dialogues between Christianity and other religions and explore areas of common theological and moral concerns. Indeed, it would not be an exaggeration to say that the initiative for the dialogue is almost invariably taken by Christians.

Contemporary Christian attitudes to other religions vary greatly, ranging all the way from their dismissal to their acceptance as equally worthy religions. The most influential and widely shared view, however, is to see them as valuable but wholly insufficient for salvific purposes, and hence inferior. The Second Vatican Council, which talked of 'sincere respect' for the goodness in other religions, insisted that all such goodness was necessarily inadequate. Pope Paul VI's *Ecclesium Suan* 'recognizes and respects' their moral and spiritual values but not their religious insights, and hopes that since there is 'but one true religion', those who 'seek God and adore him' will one day convert to Christianity (Ariarajah, 1991, p. 131). Even the currently fashionable talk of the Judeo-Christian tradition reflects the same attitude. While it shows respect for Judaism, it tends to see it largely as a precursor to and reaching its perfection in Christianity. Karl Rahner, one of the major influences on Catholic and even non-Catholic attitudes to other religions, expresses this with considerable theological sophistication. For him Christianity is the 'absolute religion ... which cannot recognize any other religion besides itself as of equal right'. Since God loves all human beings, His grace is given to non-Christians as well, but only on 'account of Christ'. They are 'anonymous Christians' and 'invisible members' of 'the only true Church' (D'Costa, 1986, p. 84, Ariarajah, 1991, pp. 201f).

Like every other religion claiming to be the only true religion, Christianity faces a problem.[5] It cannot abandon its claim to uniqueness, for that denies its historical and doctrinal identity; nor should it, for the claim is both true in the sense that Christianity does represent a distinct vision of God and human destiny and is consistent with the similar claims of other religions. Again Christianity may rightly claim that it is self-sufficient and has the resources to provide a worthy life, for the claim is eminently reasonable and intellectually defensible. This does, of course, deny its adherents access to the rich resources of other religious traditions, but if they are content with the kind of good it realizes, they are right to live by its truths.

While Christianity is right to claim uniqueness and even self-sufficiency, it is wrong to claim that it exhausts all possible forms of religious goodness, that there is no salvation outside of it, and that all other religions are misguided or inferior. Such a claim is inherently unsubstantiable as there is no non-circular way of comparing and grading the truths of different religions. The claim also has only a limited historical basis, for early Christians rarely made it, and it is, as we saw, largely a product of subsequent theological orthodoxy. In the New Testament Jesus said that Gentiles will share the kingdom of heaven and be judged on the same basis as the faithfuls. Peter told Cornelius that 'God has no favourites' and that 'whoever in every nation is God fearing and does what is right is acceptable to Him' (*Acts*). The monist Christian claim has also been a source of much intolerance and violence against Jews, Muslims, native Indians and others, and sits ill at ease with its commitment to love and non-violence.[6] Christian theology needs to find ways of both retaining its identity and uniqueness and opening up itself to the reality and value of religious plurality (Hick, 1973).

Monism of classical liberalism

In the formation of liberal thought many factors played an important part, of which three have received far less attention than they merit, namely Christianity, colonialism and the nation-state. Since liberalism developed within a cultural milieu suffused with centuries of Christian influence, it could hardly avoid being shaped by it. Some early liberals such as Locke, Montesquieu and Tocqueville thought that Christianity was the only religion to develop the liberal values of human dignity, freedom, equality and even dissent, and was alone worthy of a free man. In their view liberalism was a secular expression of and sustained by Christianity, which is why the expression 'spreading Christianity and civilization' (meaning liberalism) aroused no anxiety on either side. Other liberals such as Bentham, some leaders of the French enlightenment and the two Mills were either ambivalent or hostile towards Christianity and saw liberalism as its secular surrogate, playing broadly the same moral and social role that Christianity had played for centuries.

Whatever their attitude to Christianity, liberal writers freely borrowed or imbibed the latter's language, categories of thought, imagery, self-understanding and manner of relating to others ways of life and thought. Liberals represented the 'light', the rest lived in darkness; they had discovered the truly human way of life, others left much to be desired. Human history was a struggle between good and evil represented respectively by liberty, individuality and rationality on the one hand, and despotism, collectivism, blind customs and social conformity on the other. Like pre-Christian Europe, preliberal Europe lived in 'dark ages'. And just as non-Christian religions were pagan and devoid of true religious sensibility, nonliberal societies were benighted, backward, unconsciously yearning for liberal truths, made up of 'anonymous' liberals, and desperately in need of liberal missionaries.

Liberalism developed during the period of European colonial expansion, and some of its greatest thinkers such as John Locke and J. S. Mill were personally associated with it. Liberal writers had to take a principled stand on colonialism and show why the colonies were not free to lead their self-chosen ways of life. Colonialism thus could not and did not remain an external historical phenomenon which liberals could comfortably ignore.[7] It confronted them with theoretical problems and perplexities, and shaped the way in which they articulated their conception of the individual, the content of their principles, and the conditions and limits of their application (Gerth and Williams, 1948, pp. 71–2; Tuck, 1999, pp. 14–15 and 226f). This is not at all to maintain the absurd view that liberalism was nothing more than an ideological justification of colonialism, but rather that it did not develop in a historical vacuum and that its theoretical content and self-understanding cannot be fully comprehended without taking account of its complex relationship with the colonial experience and its subjugated 'other' (Mehta, 1999; Parekh, 1994b).

The third factor that played an important part in the development and articulation of liberalism had to do with the rise of the modern state. The latter was a historical fact by the time liberalism appeared on the scene. As I argue later, liberalism formed a close alliance with it and successfully shaped it in a particular direction. It is hardly surprising that a strong, united, powerful, territorially bounded and sovereign state became and has remained one of its central presuppositions. Almost all liberals assumed, often uncritically, that every society needed such a state, and even that the latter was one of the major distinguishing marks of a 'civilized' society. As liberalism gained intellectual and political ascendancy, it gave the state its modern character. It emphasized and institutionalized such ideas as the rule of law, equality of citizens, individuals as the sole bearers of rights and obligations, and the direct and unmediated relationship between the citizen and the state. In order to consolidate itself both politically and ideologically and to create an individualist moral and political culture, the state set about dismantling traditional institutions, communities and ways of life, with liberals providing the necessary ideological justification. Since these communities and the associated bodies of ideas offered strong resistance, liberal writers had to show why their vision of the good life was superior and deserved to be enforced. The resulting intellectual and political battles with their countrymen formed the domestic counterpart of the colonial experience, and provided yet another context that shaped the structure and content of liberal thought.

Even as liberals sought to civilize 'backward races' abroad, they used the state to civilize the 'reactionary' feudal and the 'backward' working classes at home. The two missions were closely related, required a similar strategy, and formed part of a common national project. A liberal state could not consistently claim to civilize backward races abroad while leaving their domestic counterparts untouched, and vice versa. It also could not mobilize the political and military power required to carry out its external civilizing mission unless its own people were internally united and enthusiastically shared that mission; conversely, the task of uniting them became easier if they were all inspired by a common external project and materially benefited from it. As with all revolutionary doctrines, the sense of mission became central to liberal self-understanding and deeply shaped its identity. Indeed, unless liberals were constantly engaged in distinguishing themselves from and subduing their ideological opponents at home and abroad, they felt they were in danger of losing or diluting their sense of what they stood for and why. J. S. Mill, Tocqueville and many others thought that a large empire was necessary to cultivate lofty sentiments, a global vision and a sense of personal and national pride among its citizens, and that these in turn were essential to sustain a vibrant and self-confident liberal culture at home and in the world at large.

Given the importance of these and other factors the presence of monism in liberal thought is hardly surprising. Classical liberalism drew on Greek rationalism and Christian universalism and arrived at a form of monism which, while sharing some features in common with both, is nevertheless distinct. Like the Greek philosophers classical liberals stressed the centrality of reason and arrived at a vision of the good life based on such values as critical rationality, choice and personal autonomy. Unlike them, however, they defined reason in more modest and largely practical terms and stressed its universality. Like the Christian thinkers they therefore argued that their vision of the good life was within the moral reach of all human beings. However, unlike them and like the Greek philosophers, they argued that it could be rationally demonstrated and shown to be binding on all rational beings.

Some classical liberals took a formal and relatively minimalist view of human beings and prescribed not the highest but the minimally good way of life, not the moral maximum but the moral minimum. Others advanced a more substantive vision and came pretty close to the Greek philosophers. Locke is a good representative of the first and J. S. Mill of the second tradition. In their own different ways, both held up particular visions of the good life as universally binding and judged all societies and ways of life in terms of them.

Locke

Locke advanced a set of what he considered to be universally valid propositions about man and society. God created human beings and gave them the earth in common. God's gift entailed both rights and duties, the right to mix their labour with nature and use its products to satisfy their needs, and the duty to develop natural resources to the full and maximize the conveniences of life (Locke, *Second Treatise*, § 33–4). Since all men had identical faculties including and especially reason, and since they were all ontologically dependent on their creator and hence independent of one another, they were all equal. For Locke equality implied that all human beings had equal dignity and rights, that no authority was legitimate unless it was based on their uncoerced consent, that each should exercise his rights with a due regard for others, and so on. As rational beings, humans were expected to govern their affairs rationally. Since the use of force signified rejection of reason, whoever used it without due authorization opted out of the human community and could be punished and treated like an animal.

Locke had no doubts about how the rational person should live, and how rational society should be organized. The former possessed such qualities as industry, energy, enterprise, self-discipline, civility, acknowledgment of others as one's equals and all that followed from it, control of passions, obedience to the law, and reasonableness. A truly rational society established the institution of private property and encouraged industry and accumulation of wealth. The duty to be fruitful and multiply 'contains in it the improvement too of arts and sciences', and hence a rational society encouraged these as well. As for its political structure, it had a clearly defined territorial boundary, a cohesive, centralized and unified structure of authority entitled in peace and war to speak and act in the name of the community, and the will to persist as an independent polity that made it 'too hard' for its neighbours to attack and overrun it (Locke, *Second Treatise*, § 108; Tully, 1993, p. 165). A rational society was governed not by customs and traditional practices but by general and 'positive laws' enacted by the supreme legislature. Political power in it was institutionalized, subject to clearly stated procedures and checks, and separated into legislative, executive and federative powers. Locke's conception of the truly rational man and society informed his theory of education, and his attitudes to the poor and the working classes in England and the Indian ways of life in the 'new world'. Since his attitude to the latter shows most clearly the limitations of his approach to cultural diversity, I will concentrate on it.

English colonization of America was not without its internal critics. These, many of them clergymen, argued that England was wrong to violate Indians' rights to their land and way of life. Land was their 'rightful inheritance', and depriving them of it was an act of injustice. Since it was also the basis of their way of life, the injustice amounted to 'impiety' and was most 'displeasing before God' as the Rev. Roger Williams, the minister of Salem, put it. Although the critics were a small and uninfluential minority, they raised important issues which the defenders of colonialism could not ignore.

Locke justified English colonialism in terms of his vision of the good life. Since Indians roamed freely over the land and did not enclose it, it was free, empty, vacant, wild, and could be taken over without their consent. Whilst some Indians did not enclose their land in Locke's sense, coastal Indians who lived in villages and engaged in nonsedentary agriculture did. Locke argued that enclosure was not enough, for their practice of letting it rot and compost every three years for soil enrichment showed that they did not make a rational use of it. In Locke's view, the trouble with Indians was that they lacked the desire to accumulate wealth, engage in commerce and produce for an international market, and hence to exploit the earth's potential to the fullest. In this regard English settlers were vastly superior and had a much better claim to the land. Locke acknowledged that the principle of equality required that Indians should not starve or be denied their share of the earth's proceeds. Since English colonization increased the conveniences of life, lowered prices, created employment, and thus benefited Indians as well, Locke thought that it did not violate the principle of equality.

Vacant lands in Locke's sense existed in several parts of Europe as well, but he would not allow their colonization because they fell within the boundaries of established political societies, whose independence and territorial integrity demanded respect under international law. Locke had to show why the Indian vacant land was not part of their territory, and hence unavailable for colonization. He argued that although Indians called themselves nations or political societies, these were nothing of the kind. They had no centralized and unified structure of authority, were not governed by positive laws, lacked a collective sense of identity, did not have clearly bounded territories, did not speak 'one language' and so on. Locke could not see how such a loosely held collection of individuals could be said to be 'one society', let alone a political one (Tully, 1993, pp. 151f).

Although Indians did not constitute a political society in Locke's sense, he could not deny that they had developed at least some kind of civil structure. Rather than argue that it was a less-advanced political society, he insisted that it represented a more advanced stage of the state of nature. The distinction was crucial, for it enabled him to draw a qualitative distinction between Indian and European societies and to argue that relations between the two were governed not by the law of nations, which demanded respect for their territorial and cultural integrity, but by the law of nature which only enjoined respect for Indians as individuals. Since Indians were unable to raise themselves to the level of the 'civilized part of mankind', English colonialism was in their interest. Locke was prepared to admit that Indians might not see things this way, but was convinced that in the long run they would 'think themselves beholden' to the English. If the obstinate Indians resisted, they would have behaved irrationally, forfeited their liberty in an 'unjust war', and could 'be destroyed as a lion or tiger' or taken as slaves.

It never occurred to Locke that the very idea of owning land appeared odd and sacrilegious to those who saw themselves as inseparable from and defined their collective identity in terms of it. For him, enclosure had to involve unambiguous physical demarcation, an informal, notional and relatively permeable boundary would not do. Locke insisted that labour, too, had to be of a particular kind to qualify as such, and dismissed planting, hunting, trapping, fishing and non-sedentary agriculture as 'spontaneous provisions' or products of 'unassisted nature' and, except for the very last step of picking or killing, not forms of labour at all. For Locke, land must not be wasted, but again he defined 'waste' in extremely narrow and utilitarian terms, considering land used for hunting, roaming for fun, or chasing animals as a waste. Cultivation, too, was narrowly defined to mean 'improvement', and the latter in turn had to produce a maximum yield, with the result that the Indian practice of not exploiting land to the fullest, letting it 'rest and breathe for a while', and allowing animals their share of access to it was dismissed as irrational and wasteful. Locke insisted that the right to property must be based on labour, be it one's own or one's servants'. This culturally biased argument took no account of the basis of the Indian claim to their land, which was that they had lived on it for generations, that their gods and dead spirits inhabited it, that their customs were interwoven with it, and so on. For Indians it was not their land because they laboured on it; rather they laboured on it because it was their land, which they owed it to their ancestors to keep in good condition. Locke's conception of political society displayed a similar cultural bias. He uncritically universalized the emerging European, especially English, state, and condemned other societies for failing to be like it (Tully, 1993).

Locke's whole approach to the Indian way of life was based on the belief that there was only one proper or rational way to organize personal and collective life, and that those that differed from it were defective and deserved neither respect nor even a patient and sympathetic exploration from within. He uncritically assumed that reason was the highest human faculty and formed the basis of the good life, that it was inherently calculating and result-orientated, that the earth's resources should be exploited to the full, that the desire to accumulate wealth signified rationality and civilization, that life must be lived with utmost moral seriousness, and so on. This is a coherent and in parts an attractive view of life but not the only one, and Locke says nothing to show that it is. Reason is certainly an important faculty but not the highest, and can be defined and exercised in several different ways. The references to God's injunction to develop the earth's resources to the full have no meaning outside a particular interpretation of the Christian tradition. And there is no obvious reason why only the life devoted to the pursuit of wealth, power and satisfaction of ever-increasing desires should be considered truly rational or human.

Locke never asked if the Indian way of life might not represent a different view of human flourishing and contain elements missing in his own and from which he might learn something. Even when he noticed that Indians led peaceful and contented lives, were 'free of hurry and worry' as a contemporary missionary put it, did not quarrel over property, settled disputes peacefully, did not commit offences, and managed to do without a centralized coercive apparatus, the qualities he himself admired in other contexts, he dismissed them as deficiencies born out of a lack of ambition and drive. Convinced of the absolute superiority of his preferred way of life, he was unable to view Indian society with critical sympathy, distinguish its good and bad features, and use it to interrogate his own.

J. S. Mill

Although Mill shared many of Locke's views, his liberalism differed from Locke's in several important respects. Locke was a natural-law theorist, Mill a qualified utilitarian. Locke's liberalism was largely deontological, Mill's teleological. Locke's had a religious basis and was a form of secularized Christianity; Mill's was secular and intended to provide a secular alternative to it. Like all contractualist writers, Locke was primarily concerned to show the necessity and value of civil society and explore the kind of moral qualities and virtues individuals needed to sustain it; that is, he began with civil society and defined and structured moral life in terms of it. Being a perfectionist and a teleologist Mill proceeded in the opposite direction, aiming to show the kind of life human beings ought to lead and exploring the type of society that was most conducive to it. In this respect he was following the lead of the Greek and Christian philosophers, for all of whom reflections on the nature and destiny of man were their starting point and provided the guiding principles of their social and political thought. Not surprisingly liberalism in Mill's hands no longer remained minimalist and advocated a substantive vision of the good life.

Mill's theory of man is too well-known to need elaboration. Man is the highest being on earth and should lead a life worthy of his status. His 'destiny' and 'comparative worth as a human being' consists in perfecting himself, in becoming the 'highest' or the 'best thing' he is capable of becoming (Mill, 1964, pp. 116f). Such a fully human life has two related components. First, it involves all-round development of his intellectual, moral, aesthetic and other capacities and growing up to his fullest stature. A person whose life is a 'complete and consistent whole' has a fullness of life about him, is both a 'noble and beautiful object of contemplation', and makes the human race 'infinitely worth belonging to'. Mill calls this the Greek ideal of self-development and thinks that it is not only better than but includes all that is worthy and valuable in others:

> It may be better to be a John Knox than an Alcibiades, but it is better to be a Pericles than either: nor would a Pericles, if we had one in these days, be without *anything* good which belonged to John Knox. (Mill, 1964, p. 120)

Second, a fully human life involves individuality, self-determination or autonomy, the terms Mill uses either interchangeably or to emphasize different aspects of a common ideal. The goal is to become the author of one's life such that ideally there is little about oneself beyond the unalterable that one has either not created or reflectively endorsed. It involves making one's own choices and decisions, forming one's own desires, beliefs, opinions and values, making sure that they are 'properly one's own', critically examining the rationale of inherited beliefs, and revising them where necessary. 'One whose desires and impulses are not his own has no character, no more than a steam-engine has a character' (*ibid.*, p. 118).

Given his view of man, Mill was most sensitive to the value of diversity, choosing as the epigraph for his *On Liberty* Humboldt's remark stressing 'the absolute and essential importance of human development in its rich diversity'. For Mill the diversity of individual character, lifestyles, and tastes was both inescapable and desirable, the former because each individual was unique, the latter both intrinsically and instrumentally. Diversity added richness and variety to the human world and made it aesthetically pleasing. It stimulated imagination, creativity, curiosity and love of difference. Since mankind 'speedily became unable to conceive diversity when they have been for some time unaccustomed to see it', it was 'good that there should be differences even though not for the better'. Diversity also led to progress because it created a climate conducive to the emergence of exceptional and original minds, provided new sources of inspiration, and encouraged a healthy competition between different ways of thought and life. Furthermore, since no way of life developed all human potentialities, no type of character all desirable traits and no system of morality all virtues, each needed others to balance and complement it and to guard it against the all too familiar tendency to mistake a partial truth for the whole. There was a role in society for both secular and religious moralities, for left to itself the former lacked a feel for the great virtues of self-sacrifice and the latter encouraged submissivenes and passivity. For similar reasons a society needed both rational and reflective as well as emotional and passionate individuals.

Mill insisted that, like individuals, societies too were unique. They had different histories and traditions, and their members differed in their temperament, character and level of mental development. In some societies people were dreamy and affectionate, in others intensely worldly and practical; in some trustful, in others suspicious and even cynical; some had an advanced moral and political culture, others were primitive. Just as no way of life suited all individuals, none fitted all societies, and each had to discover by trial and error one most appropriate to it. Although a universally valid legal and political philosophy was possible, its application must be mediated by a 'philosophy of national character'.

Mill set so much store by diversity that he almost turned it into the master key to progress (Mill, 1964, pp. 129f). For centuries Europe had remained stagnant, decadent, mired in dogmas, but had now decisively turned the corner. For Mill, Europeans avoided the 'Chinese' fate because of their 'remarkable' diversity of character and culture. In Europe individuals, classes and states cherished their differences, struck out diverse paths of development, and resisted attempts at assimilation. As a result they never entirely lost their vibrancy and creativity, for if one society was passing through a bad period, it could always draw inspiration from the liveliness of some others. Mill's explanation raised more questions than it answered. He did not clearly explain why Europe declined for centuries and passed through the dark ages, and why and when its people began to develop the love of diversity. He did not explain either why the presence of different classes should by itself cultivate and sustain the love of diversity when similar social differences in India, China and elsewhere allegedly did not.

Since Mill considered diversity so important, he was deeply disturbed by the tendency towards social homogenization and cultural assimilation that he found dominant in his age. Thanks to such factors as increased communication, uniform education, disappearance of ranks and varied neighbourhoods, social levelling and the ascendancy of public opinion, people read, saw, desired and listened to the same things, feared and hoped for the same objects, enjoyed the same rights and liberties, and developed the same character. No class was strong and distant enough to have the will to resist mass opinion and nurture nonconformity. The greatness of England was 'now all collective', and its individual citizens were all small. 'But it was men of another stamp than this that made England what it has been, the men of another stamp will be needed to prevent its decline'. Mill was convinced that England and indeed every other European society as well as the United States required a radical cultural change. They needed to encourage differences of tastes, beliefs, opinions, character and lifestyles even if these sometimes appeared pointless, and to cherish eccentricity even if it occasionally took wild and strange forms. The earlier hierarchical society which once stood against homogenization had irretrievably disappeared, and the task had now fallen on intellectuals and the cultural elite.

Mill made out a far more powerful case for diversity than most of his predecessors and gave liberalism a new orientation. He was able to do so because he appreciated the immense richness and complexity of human nature and the inability of any way of life to embody more than a small part of it. This enabled him to argue that the good life could be lived in several different ways, that each profited from a dialogue with the rest, and that it was wrong to construct an ideal mode of human existence on the basis of 'some one or some small number of patterns'. These are profound insights which no theory of cultural diversity can afford to ignore.

In spite of its obvious strengths, Mill's case for diversity is inadequate.[8] It rests on the assumption that human beings are naturally unique and that human uniqueness somehow underwrites moral and cultural diversity. Although the assumption is not totally mistaken, it is too simplistic to form the basis of a theory of diversity. Mill does not ask why and in what respects human beings are unique, the depth and extent of their uniqueness, under what social conditions it can be nurtured, and so forth. Furthermore, the assumption sits ill at ease with his repeated complaint against the increasing homogenization of his age, for the latter would seem to imply that the natural uniqueness of human beings is powerless before the pressure of public opinion and cannot be depended upon to sustain diversity.

Even if Mill were able to give a coherent account of human uniqueness, his theory of diversity would remain inadequate because of its limited range and content. For him each individual must lead a life of excellence. The form of excellence varied from individual to individual but not the moral imperative to pursue excellence itself. Anyone who was content to drift through life, ignored his higher capacities, or failed to approach life with the requisite degree of intellectual and moral seriousness betrayed the dignity of the human species. Furthermore, it was not enough to pursue excellence. Excellence had to have a specific content, namely, to develop all one's powers into a 'complex and consistent whole'. No 'portion of human nature' that one possessed should remain uncultivated, for then one wasted rare human passions and capacities and led a truncated and one-sided life, which is why Mill considered John Knox's life inferior to that of Pericles. Again, for Mill the desirable way of life should be freely determined by the individual on the basis of a careful assessment of available alternatives and aim at constant self-creation. This ruled out a wide variety of ways of life, such as the traditional, the community-centred and the religious as well as those that were not grounded in self-knowledge, did not set much store by an energetic and go-ahead spirit, or preferred contentment, weak ambition, humility and self-effacement to their opposites. Since Mill's theory of diversity was embedded in an individualist vision of life, he cherished individual but not cultural diversity, that is diversity of views and lifestyles within a shared individualist culture but not diversity of cultures including the nonindividualist.

Mill naïvely assumed that different ways of life and types of character can all happily coexist, that the social structure is neutral between them, and that the best of them will win out in the end. Ways of life compete for power and resources, and the success of some often spells the disintegration of others. Furthermore, every social structure tends to value and throw its weight behind some of them rather than others. Diversity cannot therefore be left to the vagaries of the cultural marketplace, which might not encourage it at all as Mill thought to be the case in contemporary Britain. Since Mill does not analyse the social conditions necessary for the flourishing of diversity, and since he does not want the state to play a cultural role, he has no way of guarding against such a possibility and is reduced to vague and sentiment exhortations about cultivating eccentricity and difference.

Like Locke and others, Mill had difficulty appreciating the role of culture and finding a secure space for it in his theory of man. He started with a particular view of man and derived from it his preferred conception of the good life. Culture matters to him only as a context or raw material to be taken into account in deciding how best to realize a transculturally valid vision of the good life, not as an independent factor that might shape the nature and content of that vision itself. For him all societies have an identical destination. Since they are unique and unequally endowed, their paths, pace and degrees of achievement vary, but not their ultimate goal. This is why he argues that 'philosophy of national character' mediates only the application and not the character and content of the truly human life.

The limitations of Mill's theory of diversity are strikingly evident in the fact that he saw no difficulty in justifying colonialism and dismantling the traditional cultures of subject societies. Since they allegedly did not cherish autonomy, individuality, go-ahead character, restless energy, ambition and constant progress, they were 'backward' societies with 'no history' and had to be civilized. And since their members were in a state of 'nonage', the civilizing mission had to be undertaken by a 'superior people'. Like Locke, Mill insisted that these societies, which included 'dark Africa' and the 'whole East', had no right to territorial integrity. The right to one's way of life and to territorial non-intervention only belonged to those who were 'mature' enough to think and judge for themselves. Since backward societies allegedly lacked that capacity, the right was 'either a certain evil or at best a questionable good for them'. A 'parental despotism' by outsiders was necessary to kick-start their history, and bring them to a take-off point from where they could be relied upon to continue their progress unaided (Mill, 1964, pp. 199, 224, 377, 378, 382).

As human beings their members had equal *moral* claims to the pursuit and protection of their individual interests, but as collectivities they had no *political* claim to independence and self-determination. Mill condemned both the racial arrogance of and the misuse of political power by the colonial government, so much so that many of his countrymen called him unpatriotic and some of his obituarists could barely restrain their relief at his death. However, like Locke, the natives were for him equal individual objects of moral concern, not self-determining collective subjects entitled to equal respect for their ways of life.

For Mill, great empires served three important liberal goals. They carried liberal ways of life and thought to backward parts of the world. They made the world safe for liberal societies by eliminating potential threats. And finally, by fostering national pride, self-confidence, sense of greatness, lofty sentiments and a high sense of moral purpose, they inspired their citizens to pursue great ideals and scale yet greater heights of intellectual and moral excellence from which both the country and the entire humankind benefited. The linkage between liberal values and national power and greatness is to be found in the writings of many other liberals as well, including James Mill, Tocqueville and T. H. Green.

Mill maintained that just as a civilized nation had a right to rule over primitive or semi-civilized societies, a more civilized group within it had a right to 'absorb' and dominate inferior groups. He had no doubt that the Breton and the Basque and the Scottish Highlanders and the Welsh stood to benefit greatly by becoming absorbed respectively into the French and the English ways of life and gaining access to the latter's artistic, philosophical and other achievements. Indeed, he could not understand why small and backward cultural communities should wish to remain within the 'narrow mental orbit' of their cultures rather than stay 'in tune' with the great intellectual and moral currents of the age. As he put it (1964, p. 363),

> Nobody can suppose that it is not more beneficial to a Breton, or a Basque of French Navarre, to be bought into the current of ideas and feelings of a highly civilized and cultivated people – to be a member of the French nationality, admitted on equal terms to all the privileges of French citizenship, sharing the advantages of French protection, and the dignity and prestige of French power – than to sulk on his own rocks, the half-savage relic of past times, revolving in his own little mental orbit, without participation or interest in the general movement of the world. The same remark applies to Welshman or the Scottish Highlander as members of the British nation.

Mill welcomed the 'blending' or 'admixture of nationalities' because, like a 'crossed breed of animals', the new group was likely to 'inherit the special aptitudes and the excellences' of the original groups (1964, p. 304). However, that happened only if the culturally superior group remained the dominant partner. If there was any danger of the inferior group acquiring ascendancy by virtue of its greater numerical strength or power, that would constitute a 'sheer mischief to the human race and one which civilized humanity with one accord should rise to prevent'. This is why, when Lord Durham's Report on Canada rejected the 'backward' French Canadians' 'vain endeavour' to preserve their cultural identity and insisted that their true interests lay in being subjected to the 'vigorous rule of an English majority', Mill enthusiastically welcomed it, calling it an 'imperishable memorial of that nobleman's courage, patriotism and enlightened liberty' and urging 'all legitimate means' to assimilate the French Canadians, (*ibid.*, p. 377).

The thought of Locke and Mill, like that of Christian thinkers, displays a strange blend of moral egalitarianism and political and cultural inegalitariansim: equality of human beings but inequality of cultures, respect for persons but not their ways of life, rejection of racism but advocacy of cultural domination, equal concern for all as individuals but not as self-determining collective subjects. The process of reasoning involved in each case is the same. Human beings are considered to be equal because they share a common nature, and the latter implies that the good life is the same for them all. The shared human nature is the basis of *both* equality and moral uniformity or monism. All human beings are entitled to equal respect by virtue of being human. However, precisely because they are human their ways of life must conform to the required model and, if they do not, others may legitimately control and guide them. This form of reasoning underlies the thought of many other liberal and nonliberal writers including Tocqueville, Kant, Hegel and Marx.[9]

Critique of Monism

In earlier sections I have discussed three major traditions of moral monism and argued that none of them is able to redeem its promise to show that there is only one correct or best way to understand human existence and lead the good life. This is not because the thinkers involved were not rigorous enough, after all they were some of the finest minds of their age, but because their enterprise was philosophically flawed. Human beings are culturally embedded, and a culture not only gives a distinct tone and structure to shared human capacities but also develops new ones of its own. Since cultures mediate and reconstitute human nature in their own different ways, no vision of the good life can be based on an abstract conception of human nature alone. Furthermore, as I have indicated from time to time and shall argue fully later, moral life is necessarily embedded in and cannot be isolated from the wider culture. A way of life cannot therefore be judged good or bad without taking full account of the system of meaning, traditions, temperament and the moral and emotional resources of the people involved. An attempt to prescribe one in the abstract would necessarily be based not on what human beings are like, but on what they should ideally be like, and would have no relevance for nor carry conviction with any community.

The very idea that one way of life is the highest or truly human is logically incoherent (Berlin, 1969, pp. 145ff; Gray, 1995a, pp. 38–76). It rests on the naive assumption that valuable human capacities, desires, virtues and dispositions form a harmonious whole and can be combined without loss. Human capacities conflict for at least three reasons, namely intrinsically and because of the limitations of the human condition and the constraints of social life: the first, because they often call for different even contradictory skills, attitudes and dispositions and the development of some of them renders that of others difficult if not impossible; the second, because human energies, motivations and resources are necessarily limited and one can cultivate only some of the valuable human capacities; and the third, because every social order has a specific structure with its inescapable tendency to develop some capacities rather than others and allow only certain ways of combining them. Since human capacities conflict, the good they are capable of realizing also conflicts. Like human capacities, values and virtues too conflict. Justice and mercy, respect and pity, equality and excellence, love and impartiality, moral duties to humankind and to one's kith and kin, often point in different directions and are not easily reconciled. In short every way of life, however good it might be, entails a loss. And since it is difficult to say which of these values are higher both in the abstract and in specific contexts, the loss involved cannot be measured and compared, rendering unintelligible the idea of a particular way of life as representing the highest good. As Raz observes, 'what one loses is of a different kind from what one gains … and quite commonly there is no meaning to the judgement that one gains more than one loses' (1994, p. 179).

The idea that different ways of life can be graded is equally untenable. It presupposes that a way of life can be reduced to a single value or principle, that all such values or principles can in turn be reduced to, and measured in terms of, a single master value or principle, and that the good can be defined and determined independently of the agents involved. No way of life can be based on one value alone. It necessarily involves a plurality of values, which cannot all be reduced to any one of them and which can be combined in several different ways. Furthermore, the values realized by different ways of life are often too disparate to be translated into a common and culturally neutral moral language, let alone measured on a single scale. And since a way of life is meant to be lived, it cannot be abstracted from the capacities, traditions, dispositions and historical circumstances of its members (Walzer, 1983, pp. 312f).

Moral monism also runs the constant danger of grossly misunderstanding other ways of life and spells a hermeneutic disaster. Since its approach to them is primarily judgmental, it has only a limited interest in understanding them. And to the extent that it seeks to understand them, its focus is on explaining why they are similar to or different from its preferred way of life. Such a biased frame of reference, and the consequently skewed angle of vision, necessarily prevents the monist from appreciating their specificity and complex internal structures. Since many of these ways of life are generally too weak or diffident to talk back, or since the monist is too impatient to listen to their protest, he is rarely compelled to reconsider the theoretical apparatus he brings to his study of them. The standard Christian and liberal accounts of non-Christian religions and nonliberal ways of life respectively provide good examples of this.

Moral monism suffers from other defects as well. It views differences as deviations, as expressions of moral pathology. For Plato and Aristotle non-contemplative and non-Greek ways of life had little to recommend themselves. For Augustine and Aquinas, non-Christians and even those Christians who disagreed with the official interpretations of their central doctrines were all wrong and had nothing of value to contribute. For many liberals, non-liberal ways of life are irrational, tribal or obscurantist; and for Marxists religious, traditional and national ways of life are worthy of destruction. Since moral monism cannot see any good outside its favoured way of life, it either avoids all but minimum contact with them or seeks to assimilate them by peaceful or violent means. Plato and Aristotle favoured the first approach because they considered the barbarians congenitally defective and incapable of education. Christians, liberals and Marxists favoured the second approach because they thought that the divinely revealed or rationally excogitated truths were within the moral reach of all. The ease with which these and other groups have justified or condoned egregious violence against alternative ways of life, often in the name of human equality and universal love, should alert us to the dangers of all forms of monism.[10]

2

Forms of Pluralism

The previous chapter outlined some of the major forms of monism, and argued that monism is a deeply flawed response to moral and cultural diversity. Although it was frequently challenged on ontological and epistemological grounds, a systematic moral and political critique of it was not mounted until the seventeenth century. Such influential writers as Vico, Montesquieu, Herder and Montaigne stressed the inescapability and sometimes the desirability of cultural plurality, and highlighted the importance of culture in their accounts of human beings. I shall briefly discuss how the first three writers, who represent very different approaches to culture and its diversity, went about laying the philosophical foundations of pluralism and what theoretical lessons we can learn from their insights and limitations.

Vico

Vico, whose life spanned the last three decades of the seventeenth and the first four of the eighteenth century, was one of the first to take a historical view of human beings and emphasise the uniqueness of every society. Thanks to their varying geographical circumstances, history and forms of self-understanding, different societies organized themselves on different principles. They developed different human capacities, needs, ideals of human excellence, forms of cognition, modes of imagination and systems of belief, and threw up different forms of artistic and literary activities. They asked different questions about human life and the world and answered these in their own unique manner. Like many other historically oriented thinkers before and after him, Vico assumed that every society was informed by a single vision of the world and that all its various parts stood in 'necessary harmony'.

For Vico, every society was a distinct cultural community, a 'nation', the term he was one of the first to use in its modern sense. Different societies represented different and often incompatible forms of thought and life. The values and ideals of one could not be combined with those of another, and the kinds of virtues, literature, arts and heroism that flourished in one society were often impossible in another. Homer and Achilles were only possible in ancient Greece and could not be reproduced elsewhere. What was true of societies was also true of historical epochs. Great achievements of one age were sometimes lost for ever, and historical development entailed both gains and losses (Berlin, 1991, pp. 123ff).

Since human societies were vastly different, Vico argued that understanding them was an exceedingly complex activity. A good deal of their inner life was lived in the imagination and based on unarticulated assumptions and unreflective judgement. They were structured by customs and conventions and driven by deepest fears and hopes, whose internal rationality was often missed by outsiders. For Vico it was a pernicious rationalist fallacy to think that we could understand a society fully in terms of a universally shared human nature or by rational analysis. Human nature was a product of history not a transhistorical substance, and was differently developed and expressed in different epochs and societies. As for reason, it only dealt with the universals, with what was common to different societies, and was ill-equipped to appreciate their specificity. It also sought order, regularity, patterns of development and causal uniformity, and was unable to understand or even feel at ease with the necessarily complex, vague, fluid and largely unconscious structure of social experiences. Since every society was an integrated whole and informed by certain general principles, reason did help us understand it, but only to a limited degree. The general principles of a society were deeply embedded in its beliefs and practices and not amenable to easy identification. We need to feel our way into its inner structure and grasp its ethos and complexity by means of emotional sympathy, self-transcendence and a historically attuned imagination.

Although Vico showed great sensitivity to and highlighted the nature and significance of cultural diversity, he found it difficult to explain why every society was or should be an integrated and harmonious whole, why societies differed and threw up different forms of cognition, imagination and literary and artistic activity, how we can feel our way into and judge other societies if they are wholly different from ours. Not surprisingly he could not resist turning to the rationalist oversimplification and the familiar philosophical strategies of the monist tradition that he had elsewhere castigated.[1] He introduced the concept of human nature which, although less substantive than Plato's and less essentialist than Aristotle's, was not purely formal either. He argued that as members of a common species all human beings shared several properties in common. They had identical passions, common vices in the form of 'ferocity, avarice and ambition', and common capacities such as reason, imagination and common sense or 'judgement without reflection'. They also shared 'a common mental language' or 'mental vocabulary' lying at the basis of and differently expressed in different languages, which was why the proverbs and maxims of different societies conveyed 'substantially the same meanings' and were easily intelligible to outsiders (Vico, 1984, para 161). While these and other human characteristics, which constituted the naturally and universally shared minimum, remained constant, the rest were a product of history.

For Vico, human beings began their history equipped with a shared nature. During the course of their development they acquired new capacities and suitably modified their original nature. In his view human history passed through three distinct ages, each signifying new human capacities, dispositions, forms of government and social structure (*ibid.*, paras 31f). During the earliest and most primitive 'age of gods', human reason was undeveloped, fear was a dominant passion, ideas of causality were inchoate and confused, and human beings ascribed all agency to gods whose oracles and auspices it was the job of wise elders to decode and enforce. During the 'age of heroes', human spirit or sense of honour was a most highly developed and admired human capacity, might was right, and heroic men, deriving their authority from their superior valour, ruled over the rest with 'pitiless cruelty'. The 'age of men' marked the third and final stage. Reason here was fully developed, human beings acquired the consciousness of belonging to a common species, recognized themselves as 'equal in human nature', and aimed to create a society based on reason and tolerance (*ibid.*, paras 927, 929). Vico did not date the three ages and seems to have thought that the last age had begun in Europe with the rise of the Roman Republic.

Vico considered all societies in a given age to share common features. He neither explained why this should be so, nor appreciated that if that was the case societies were not as distinct and unique as he had argued and did not call for the powers of empathy and imagination on which he had laid so much stress. Vico also needed to explain why all societies passed through the same three ages. Not surprisingly he turned them into part of a teleological pattern, each age being a stage in the increasing realization of the 'true and proper nature of man' or 'rational humanity' (*ibid.*, para 973). The age of men was the final stage and contained all that was necessary for the fullest development of human capacities. Vico's teleology needed a guiding principle and since he rejected the Aristotleian belief in an abiding human essence, he turned to God. Human history was not internally driven by the demands of human nature as the contemporary Aristotelians argued, but piloted by an 'intelligible substance' as part of a 'divine design' (*ibid.*, para 1096).

For Vico the fullest realization of rational humanity represented the highest stage of human development. Broadly speaking it consisted in the harmony of reason and religion. Reason was a most valuable faculty because it offered knowledge of the secular world, challenged dogmas and superstitions, and regulated desires and passions. However it suffered from two basic limitations. Since it had a critical orientation, it encouraged scepticism or the 'barbarism of reflection' and led to such widespread differences of views that 'scarcely any two human beings were able to agree' (*ibid.*, para 1106). Secondly, since human actions were motivated by feelings and passions which reason had no power to activate and mobilize, it was incapable of generating action let alone inspiring virtuous deeds and sacrifices of self-interest. No society could therefore be based on reason alone. Religion rectified its limitations and was its indispensable ally. It revealed profound moral and spiritual truths which reason could not itself discover but whose point it saw when presented with them. It also mobilized moral and spiritual feelings and provided a counterweight to natural human passions. 'If religion is lost among the peoples, they have nothing left to enable them to live in a society' (*ibid.*, para 1109). Left to itself, however, religion had a tendency to encourage superstitions and blind dogmas, promote oppressive social structures, and stifle free inquiry. Reason and religion thus complemented each other. Only a society that harmonised them realized the human potential and ensured both stability and virtue.

Vico used his vision of a fully developed rational humanity to judge different religions, societies and historical epochs. Pagan religions were false because they were full of irrational beliefs and discouraged reason. For broadly similar reasons medieval Catholicism represented a period of barbarism. Since they did not appreciate the importance of religion, Vico did not think much of Socrates and Athenian rationalism either (Lilla, 1993, pp. 227f). Islam was a 'false' religion because it was dogmatic, oppressive and hostile to rational inquiry. Christianity was the only 'true' religion because, among other things, it rested on an 'infinitely pure and perfect idea of God', articulated a noble and non-instrumental vision of the highest good, contained truths so profound that they attracted the 'most learned philosophers of the gentiles', and reconciled the 'wisdom of revealed authority with that of reason'. Although the ages of gods and heroes had great achievements to their credit, some of them beyond the reach of the modern age, they were both inferior to the latter. They did not value reason and equality, grasp the unity of the human species, and develop refined and rational religions. Vico admitted that the modern age carried individualism and rationalism too far and fostered a spirit of scepticism that subverted long-established customs and unreflective common sense. Indeed since he considered imagination to be a source of religion and thought that reason tended to stifle it, he wondered if the modern age would be able to nurture religion. However, he was moderately optimistic that unless 'extraordinary causes' intervened, it stood a reasonably good chance of doing so and achieving the right balance between reason and religion.

In the modern age Vico thought that Europe was superior to all other societies. It possessed the only true religion, had long developed the capacity for rationality, cherished the values of universal brotherhood and independent inquiry, and so forth. Japan was in transition from the second to third age and had all the ferocity and inequality of the former. China and India were better, but they had defective religions and underdeveloped rationality. Only Europe abounded in 'all the good things that made for the happiness of human life, ministering to the comforts of the body as well as to the pleasures of mind and spirit'. Since Europe represented the most developed society, it had a right to guide the rest of the world. 'Natural order' required that those who cannot pursue their own good should be guided and governed by those who can, and that the affairs of the world should be in change of the 'naturally fittest'. If some societies are factious, disorderly or devoid of regener-

ative resources, 'providence decrees ... that they become subject to better nations', if not voluntarily then by conquest (*ibid.*, para 1105). Vico
thought this to be the case with non-European societies whose good lay
in European colonization.

Although Vico hoped to lay the foundations of a pluralist moral and
political theory, his success was considerably limited. He appreciated
that different ages threw up different kinds of good life, but was convinced that in any given age only one way of life was truly human, that
all others could be graded in terms of it, and that those who had realized or approximated it had a right and a duty to guide and even govern others. Unlike most monists he appreciated that all progress
involved loss and that some of the great achievements of the past were
beyond our reach, but he was in no doubt that losses were offset by
gains and that overall there was considerable progress. Unlike monists,
again, he valued cultural diversity, but only as an inescapable transitional stage to a culturally homogeneous world. Cultural diversity characterized the undeveloped ages of humankind and declined as society
reached the higher stage. Vico had no monist illusions about achieving
a perfect and frictionless society, but equally he had no doubt either
about creating one that was as flawless and harmonious as humans can
hope to achieve. Like many a monist, again, he more or less uncritically
universalized his religion, age and society, and set them up as universal
norms. He offered no good non-circular reasons for the view that
Christianity was the only true religion. And he considered the modern
age the highest stage of human development only because he judged it
in terms of such values as reason, equality, material comfort, mastery
of nature and progress that were derived from it.

Montesquieu

Although Montesquieu, whose *Persian Letters* was published just
before and *The Spirit of the Laws* 23 years after Vico's *Scienza Nuova*
(1744), shared the latter's sensitivity to cultural diversity, he differed
from him in several respects. Unlike Vico he was interested in both
European and non-European societies. And in each case he was primarily interested in their social and political institutions rather than
their arts, forms of literature, systems of philosophy and modes of

thought. His approach was more sociological than psychological. And although he repeatedly invoked a view of human nature, he did not assign it the central explanatory role that Vico did.

For Montesquieu, cultural diversity was a pervasive and inescapable feature of human life. No two societies were alike. Each had different customs, practices, manners, system of laws, structure of family and forms of government, and each encouraged different passions, moral virtues, traits of temperament, forms of excellence and conceptions of the good life. Even when they had similar customs and laws, these had different effects and played quite different roles. Although all human beings shared a common nature, Montesquieu thought that each society also developed distinct human capacities, desires, and so forth, and gave rise to a second 'national' nature. Its members grew up with it, and were as much home with their socially derived as with their natural or biological nature. Thanks to the diversity of national natures 'it is a great piece of luck if those [laws] of one nation can suit another'. Although all societies pursued certain common goals, each had 'nevertheless an object which is peculiar to it'.

For Montesquieu, cultural diversity raised two questions, explanatory and normative; the former concerned with the reasons why different societies threw up different customs and practices, the latter with how to judge these. To explain a practice was to show that it was not accidental or absurd but rational, necessary, natural or intelligible, the expressions Montesquieu used interchangeably. Explanation was a non-judgmental activity, concerned neither to 'censure' nor to 'justify' but only to understand and explore the rationale of the *explicandum*. Since moral judgement distorted explanation, one must approach one's subject matter without moral preconceptions and prejudices. This did not at all mean that one should not judge it, but rather that this was a different kind of activity and had a different focus and logic. Montesquieu was so fastidious about this distinction that he patiently demonstrated the rationality of such practices as slavery and polygamy, inviting the criticism that he had in effect justified them. His reply to the charge was unequivocal. 'In all this I only give their reasons, but do not justify their customs' (1959, vol. I, p. 253).

Montesquieu explained social structures and practices in terms of what he called physical and moral causes (*ibid.*, pp. 293ff; Shklar, 1987, pp. 67–110). The former were independent of human agency and included such things as the size, terrain and location of the country, the nature of the soil, economic resources and, above all, the climate (Montesquieu, 1959, vol. I, p. 229). The latter referred to human actions and institutions, especially forms of government, laws and religion. Thanks to the interplay of the two sets of causes, every society developed a distinct national 'genius' or spirit which, though derivative in nature, exercised an independent influence on and integrated social institutions and practices into a coherent whole (*ibid.*, p. 293). The national spirit could be changed by modifying the underlying moral causes, but only up to a point, with the greatest of effort, and only by acting in harmony with its overall character. Since society was an integrated whole, changes in one area had profound and unpredictable consequences for the rest. Even if a practice was immoral or unacceptable, the reformer should approach it with 'trembling hand'. The question is 'not whether it was right to establish it but whether it has been established'.

For Montesquieu, the climate exercised a decisive influence in backward societies. In hot countries girls matured early and were ready for marriage long before they had developed their reason. They also got old quickly and earlier than men did. Since people there had fewer and easily satisfied wants, it cost them little to maintain a large family. For these and related reasons it was 'extremely natural' that polygyny was widely practised in these climates (*ibid.*, p. 251). In cold countries the situation was very different, and hence polygyny was unnecessary and strongly disapproved of. Montesquieu did not explain why women and not men matured and got old early in a hot climate, why polygyny did not obtain in all hot countries, and why these societies opted for polygyny rather than monogamy accompanied by easy divorce or any one of a number of other possible forms of marriage. Even as polygyny was 'natural' and 'tolerable' in a hot climate, so was slavery. Extreme heat rendered men so 'slothful' that only the fear of chastisement led them to perform laborious tasks. Although slavery was 'against nature', it was in these climates 'founded on a natural reason' (*ibid.*, p. 240). Like slavery, despotism, for Montesquieu the most inhuman form of government, was also rational in a hot climate: 'Even liberty appeared intolerable to peoples who were not accustomed to enjoy it. Thus is pure air sometimes harmful to those who have lived in swampy countries'.

The influence of climate could be countered by moral causes, especially religion and laws, for Montesquieu two of the most powerful human institutions. Moral causes shaped the national spirit and, through that, human character and conduct. A decadent society could only be regenerated by 'men of genius', those 'capable of penetrating' the prevailing national spirit and devising and persuading their fellow citizens to accept a new set of religious and political institutions. For Montesquieu the law-givers of classical Greece and Rome, great religious leaders, and some of the enlightened monarchs of Europe belonged to this category

Montesquieu was concerned not only to explain but also to judge a society's beliefs and practices. He thought he needed universal standards to do so. He could not judge a society in terms of its own standards because it was an integrated whole and its values, being of a piece with its practices, could not provide the required principles of criticism, nor in terms of those of his own society because their validity was limited to it and carried no conviction with outsiders. Although Montesquieu is not entirely clear, he derived the universal moral standards from three interrelated sources, namely the 'nature of things', 'laws of human nature', and a sociological analysis of human experience (*ibid.*, pp. 1–5).

Briefly the nature of things or the 'necessary relations' between them referred to principles that were inherent in the constitution of the world and obliged all moral beings by their rational necessity. These included such principles as that kindness deserved gratitude, that those who harmed others deserved to be harmed themselves, and that promises should be kept. The principles bound all intelligent beings including God, and would have been obligatory on human beings even if they had been constituted differently.

Laws of human nature were derived 'entirely from our frame and existence', and bound us only because we are constituted in a certain way (*ibid.*, p. 3). For Montesquieu all human beings naturally desired to preserve themselves, live in society and pursue happiness, and loved their family. His conception of self-preservation was much deeper than that of Hobbes and involved not just staying alive but absence of terror, or an oppressive and pervasive sense of fear, vulnerability and unpredictability. The sense of security, for Montesquieu the basis of the human sense of liberty and a deep human need, was a product of settled and general laws, and ruled out despotism or subjection to the arbitrary will of another. For Montesquieu human beings were also endowed with the unique capacity of reason, and hence capable of understanding and controlling the natural and social worlds, critical self-reflection, and so on. Although reason was a most valuable capacity, it had its limits. It could never suppress or eliminate basic human passions and must come to terms with them. It was also unable by itself to generate action and depended on natural and socially acquired passions and virtues. Unlike many a monist, Montesquieu took a plural view of human capacities and insisted that reason must retain a measure of scepticism about itself and avoid degenerating into rationalism.

Human experience was Montesquieu's third source of moral standards. In his view, although the nature of things and human nature yielded important moral principles, these were few and highly general and did not cover many an area of human life. He also thought that since moral principles were meant to be lived, they needed to be discussed not only in general philosophical terms but also in the light of their social consequences and the kinds of social relations they fostered. For these and related reasons Montesquieu analysed different societies to see what kind of collective and personal life was created by different moral principles and practices. Sometimes his analysis only confirmed the principles he had derived from human nature; on other occasions it generated new ones.

Based on his views of the nature of things, human nature and the historical experience of humankind, Montesquieu arrived at a distinct vision of the good life and a body of universal moral standards. Security, liberty, stable family, healthy relations between the sexes, self-restraint, mildness of passion, industry and avoidance of strong convictions and dogmatism were all universally desirable qualities, and so too were equality, a sense of justice, love, humanity, personal autonomy, the spirit of free inquiry, toleration, settled and general laws, checks and balances in personal, familial and political areas of life, and constitutional restraints on political power. For Montesquieu religion was the necessary basis of social life. It underpinned morality, fostered virtues, regulated natural passions, and provided motives for disinterested action. Since its value was almost entirely practical, it was to consist of little more than a body of moral values backed up by the belief in a benevolent God. It should be free from mysterious and mystical elements and avoid dogmas. It should not be contemplative and indifferent to worldly success, nor politically ambitious, excessively demanding, and impatient of normal human passions and ambitions. Islam did not meet most of these conditions whereas Christianity, the 'only true' religion, did. Unfortunately, it too had contemplative, mystical, dogmatic, ascetic and other dimensions, and these could and should be removed by suitable interpretation. Like Locke, Montesquieu was most anxious that Christianity should be rendered intellectually 'reasonable' and morally respectable (1959, vol. 2, pp. 27–41).

Given his conservative liberalism, Montesquieu was greatly sympathetic to the modern commercial society, which in his view created the necessary conditions of the good life as he defined it (*ibid.*, pp. 316f; Pangle, 1973, pp. 200ff). It increased human mastery over nature, multiplied wants, stimulated reason, and awakened the latent energies of the human mind. It gave pride of place to worldly pursuits and discouraged the pursuit of military glory and salvation after death. It weakened the hold of religion, reduced it to morality, demoted the contemplative life in favour of the practical, and used religion to subserve worthwhile social ends (Montesquieu, 1959, vol. II, pp. 30, 33). The commercial society also bred moderation, discouraged strong convictions and passions, and cultivated 'softness' of manners and feelings. It brought different societies together, increased their mutual knowledge and interdependence, and developed the spirit of shared humanity. It liberated the arts and the sciences from parochialism and censorship, loosened the rigorous regime of virtues common in earlier societies, and encouraged personal autonomy. Thanks to commerce, nations grew more and more similar to each other, acquired more or less the same needs, tastes and desires, and constituted a 'single State of which all societies are members' (*ibid.*, vol. I, pp. xx, 23). Since different societies were dominated by different spirits, commercial society could not take the same form in all of them. However, since it had its own 'laws' and 'spirit', Montesquieu thought that it would eventually overcome national spirits and shape all societies in a common mould. The government could facilitate this by playing an active role. 'To maintain the spirit of commerce it is necessary ... that this spirit alone rule and is not frustrated by another spirit, and that all laws favour it.'

For Montesquieu the commercial society was not free of defects. It promoted greed, discouraged virtues that went beyond 'exact justice', vulgarised the arts, created a climate in which everything was only done for money, and so forth (1959, vol. I, p. 317). However, he thought that although not perfect, the commercial society was on balance better than all past societies and most in harmony with our knowledge of human nature and life. Montesquieu thought that it should be extended throughout the world, especially to non-European societies where it would do much to ameliorate their despotic harshness and foster a new rational spirit.

Limitations

Montesquieu remarked in the Preface to *The Spirit of the Laws* that he was motivated by the 'love of all', one of the highest virtues for him, and that his main concern in the book was to help every society to understand itself better and to love itself more (lxvii–lxix). He went further than almost all earlier writers in his openness to the infinite diversity of human life. No social practice or belief shocked or offended him or was beyond his comprehension. He was convinced that since they were all human creations, they demanded and deserved sympathetic exploration and explanation. He rose above his own and his society's prejudices and tried to make sense of such practices as polygyny, polyandry, matriarchy and even incest. He showed that what appeared bizarre and incomprehensible at first glance made perfect sense when located in its context, and that hasty negative judgements should be avoided. Even his discussion of 'savages' and 'barbarians' was generous, admiring their spirit of equality, respect for the old, warm-heartedness, and love of tradition.[2]

Although Montesquieu was anxious to understand every society in its own terms and develop the pluralist moral and political theory that this required, his success was far more limited than he thought and deserved. This was due to two closely related factors, his Eurocentrism and his residual monist belief that his preferred vision of the good life was alone truly human. As a European himself and because Eurocentrism was in the air, Montesquieu could hardly avoid it altogether. However, someone of his intellectual stature and imaginative power could have resisted its influence if his vision of the good life had led him to be critical of the prevailing European way of life. His vision in turn would have been more robust and pluralist if he had not remained narrowly Eurocentric. The mutually reinforcing influence of the two deeply distorted his analyses of both European and non-European societies. Since the latter more clearly highlights his limitations, I will concentrate on it.

Montesquieu's thought is marked by a fairly neat contrast between Europe, the 'beautiful part of the world', and non-Europe or the 'other parts of the earth' (Richter, 1977, p. 229). Europe invented liberty and had a 'genius for it', the rest of the world had known nothing but 'servile spirit' (Montesquieu, 1959, vol. I, p. 269). In the whole of Asian history 'it is impossible to find a single passage which discovers freedom of spirit'. Africa was in the 'same servitude', and so were America before its European colonization and Persia in 'all periods of its history'. Despotism, a form of government in which 'a single man, unrestrained by law and other rules, dominates by his will and caprices', reigned supreme outside Europe. As a result people there were like 'beasts' or 'animals' who knew nothing but 'instinct, obedience and punishment', and whose lives revolved 'around two or three ideas' (Richter, 1977, p. 196, 214).

Montesquieu had no historical excuse for such a strange view of a large part of humankind, for it was widely challenged at the time by several writers and missionaries (Richter, 1977, p. 334). They had shown that the Ottoman Empire was free of European feudalism and hereditary aristocracy, had no state-supported church, was remarkably tolerant, administered justice impartially, and that the Sultan could be reprimanded and even arrested for abusing his power. They had shown, too, that India and China were not despotic in Montesquieu's sense, and that their rulers respected personal and religious liberties and derived their authority from long-established moral and social traditions which regulated their exercise of power. Montesquieu either ignored all this or dismissed it as biased.

Montesquieu's view of non-European societies was not easily reconcilable with his own theory of human nature either. Since human beings 'naturally' desired liberty and security, abhorred terror and violence, and loved their families, they should be expected to find despotism outrageous and even revolt against it. Montesquieu, who seems to have anticipated this criticism, contended that their acceptance of despotism was 'easily understood' (*ibid.*, pp. 216f). First, although despotism was against human nature, the latter was subject to the influence of and could be distorted by climate and other factors. The hot climate rendered men so feeble and passive that they lost their desire for liberty and security or at least the willingness to fight for them. This is strange, for if a desire can be lost either wholly or for all practical purposes, it can hardly be considered natural. Besides, if human nature is subject to climatic and other sources of distortion, it is not clear how Montesquieu is able to discover its true and undistorted form, and what evidence he can offer in support of his view other than that it is to be found in

Europe. Second, he argued that despotism was the simplest and easily comprehended form of government and came naturally to all societies unless they were raised above their primitive state by a 'masterpiece of legislation' provided by law-givers of genius. He does not explain why he thinks despotism to be the most easily understood form of government when it goes against what he takes to be the most basic human desires and needs, and why men of genius appear only in Europe. In the ultimate analysis Montesquieu's 'East', like that of J. S. Mill, is an ahistorical and ideological abstraction born out of a Eurocentric world-view and designed to subserve his polemics against the absolutism of Louis XIV.

Montesquieu's Eurocentrism distorted both his choice and explanation of his subject matter. Since he took European institutions and practices as norms, he largely concentrated on those aspects of non-European societies that differed from them, such as despotism, polygamy, the harem, and unusual religious practices and social customs. In so doing he exoticized these societies and implied that they shared little in common with their European counterparts. Although he offered a sympathetic account of them, it had the paradoxical effect of deepening their pathology, for to argue that unacceptable practices were natural or rational for these societies was to suggest that nothing better could be expected of them.

So far as Montesquieu's explanatory framework is concerned, it is striking that he stressed the role of physical causes, especially the climate in explaining non-European societies and that of moral causes in accounting for their European counterparts. People outside Europe were deemed to be passive, devoid of a sense of agency, mired in nature, and helpless victims of the imperatives of their geography (Montesquieu, 1959, vol. I, pp. 224f). They rarely threw up wise rulers let alone moral and religious geniuses capable of changing their national spirit. Not surprisingly, they had no history and the study of their institutions did not call for a historical approach. The opposite is the case with Europe where, according to Montesquieu, nothing was immutably dictated by nature and all institutions developed over time as a result of human activity. Unlike the East, Europe had a history and its institutions and practices could only be explained in historical terms.

A trivial but eloquent example highlights Montesquieu's asymmetrical approach to the two societies. Since excessive heat enfeebled Eastern people, they greatly yearned for repose. The Buddha was no exception. The poor man took his own desire for repose as his starting point, defined his vision of salvation in terms of it, and encouraged indolence among all under his unfortunate influence: 'his teaching which originated in the laziness produced by the climate' further encouraged it, and by so doing caused 'an infinite number of further evils' (Richter, 1977, p. 260). As if this absurdity was not enough, Montesquieu argued that the entire Indian philosophy, which allegedly cherished *le néant* (non-being) as the highest mental state, was only a reflection of the Indian climate. Montesquieu nowhere advanced such grotesque explanations in his accounts of Christianity or great European philosophical systems.

Since Montesquieu did not think much of non-European societies, his appreciation of their ways of thought and life was limited. Unlike many an extreme Eurocentrist, he readily acknowledged that some of their practices and beliefs were commendable, but insisted that they were also to be found in Europe. His moral values were all European and helped him decide what was good or bad elsewhere. If there was goodness outside Europe, it had to be of the European variety. It never occurred to him that other societies could nurture different kinds of goodness which might have no analogues in Europe and could enrich its understanding of the nature and possibilities of human existence. This is in start contrast to his attitude to Britain and France, the two European societies he most admired and knew well. He argued that for historical reasons they had developed along different lines, that one was strong in areas whether the other was weak, and that they had much to gain from a sympathetic dialogue. Montesquieu did not extend this appreciation of diversity outside Europe.

Montesquieu's anonymously published *Persian Letters* is a good example of the strengths and limitations of his approach to cultural diversity. Applying what one commentator has called the double optic of cultural relativism, it was an attempt to see the French and Persian societies from each other's point of view. Consisting of letters between two Persian visitors to France and their friends, servants, eunuchs and wives at home about their observations on various aspects of French society, the book is designed to show how the latter appeared to outsiders and how in turn it transformed their perceptions of their own society. Montesquieu shows great skill and imaginative freedom in exploring both an unfamiliar society from within and his own from outside. By asking apparently innocent questions the Persian visitors highlight the oddity and even the absurdity of several French practices, such as the absence of divorce, the Pope's wealth, priestly celibacy, the inquisition, dull theological tomes that numb religious sensibility, and some of the conventions of the bourgeois society. In order to enhance the power of their criticism and to prevent culturally conditioned responses to it, Montesquieu deculturalizes some of these practices by giving them Persian or neutral names, calling the rosary 'little wonder beads' and the priest a 'dervish'.

Although Montesquieu succeeds in mocking and problematizing several areas of French life, his Persian visitors are too dazzled by it to mount a radical critique of it or highlight its central assumptions and legitimizing myths. By and large they only criticize what was being currently questioned either widely or in small but influential circles. And while some of their other criticisms amuse the reader, they only reveal their ignorance and reflect more on them than on their target. Neither of the two visitors pokes fun at or challenges the dominant ideas of individualism, liberty, rationalism, progress, colonialism, French obsession with national glory and grandeur, universalist claims of French civilization, and basic Christian beliefs (cf. Richter, 1977, p. 35).

By contrast, Montesquieu uses the Persian visitors to cast their society in an irredeemably bad light. He makes such silly generalizations as that 'hardly a soul' laughs in Turkey, that friendship is 'unknown' in Persia and Turkey, and that Orientals are humourless, untrustworthy and cheats. He takes the harem as the paradigmatic institution of Persian society, and thinks that its goings-on reveal the latter's true nature. He presents only a few aspects of Persian society with sympathy and none with admiration. It is for him not a human society with all its virtues and vices but, as Judith Shklar puts it, a 'nightmare territory of the mind in which all the worst human impulses govern' (Shklar, 1987, p. 46).

Not surprisingly, Rica, one of the two Persian visitors, is charmed by Regency Paris and decides to settle there. Uzbek, the other visitor and the main character in the book who at first sees only the follies of 'profane' Europe, later comes to see his own irrationalities with which he cannot cope and returns home to hold together his fast disintegrating harem and lead a miserable life. Since Montesquieu was convinced that what was natural to man must ultimately prevail, liberty triumphs over despotism even in Uzbek's harem. Uzbek discovers that he was wrong to think that his wives were his passive and obedient servants. As Roxana writes in a letter to him,

I may have lived in slavery, but I have always been free: I have reformed
your laws by those of nature and my spirit has never lost its independence
... I have profaned virtue by allowing that name to be applied to my submission to your whims ...You believed me to be deceived, and I deceived
you. (Letter, CLXI)

It is striking that Montesquieu takes the collapse of the harem to signify the moral bankruptcy of the wider Persian society. In the ultimate
analysis *Persian Letters* remained too one-sided to realize
Montesquieu's intention to make it a genuine exercise in intercultural
dialogue.

Even as Montesquieu's Eurocentrism limited his ability to appreciate the inner lives of non-European societies, his narrow vision of the
good life prevented him from appreciating the value of moral and cultural diversity within Europe itself. As we saw he warmly welcomed
the fact that, thanks to the rise of commercial society, the European
and indeed all other societies were becoming culturally homogenized
with men and even women everywhere acquiring basically the same
desires, passions, traits of temperament and emotional dispositions
and sharing a single vision of the good life (Pangle, 1973, pp. 207ff).
Montesquieu was so keen on this that he urged governments to facilitate the process by appropriate policies and laws. He did have mild
regrets about the increasing disappearance of national diversity, especially in France whose national spirit he greatly cherished, but he
either accepted the outcome as the inevitable price of progress or
vaguely hoped that something of each country's national genius
would somehow survive the logic of the commercial spirit at least in
an attenuated form.

Montesquieu welcomed the cultural and moral homogenization of
Europe and the world at large because he thought it realized what he
took to be a truly human life, one characterized by moderation, scepticism, industry, self-limiting rationality, thrift, competitive spirit, mild
passions, love of life, absence of strong emotions and convictions, a
rationally domesticated and socially subordinated religion, pursuit of
worldly success, and the spirit of free enquiry. Montesquieu's vision of
the good life is attractive and coherent but also suffers from important
limitations. It is spiritually and morally shallow, narrow in its sympathies, and excludes or marginalizes many a valuable human capacity,
emotion and ideal. It is hostile to the deeply religious, contemplative,
heroic, non-competitive, adventurous, traditional and other ways of

life, and the virtues and habits of mind associated with them. It is also antipathetic to strong convictions and passions, a sense of the mystery of human life, contentment, piety, a measure of scepticism about the pleasures of life, and so forth. Montesquieu sympathetically explains why human societies differ in their structure and organization and patiently explores the internal rationale of even their most outrageous practices, but never relents in his judgement that they are all inferior to the extent that they fall short of his vision. His thought has ample space for social but not cultural and moral diversity, for a wide variety of customs and practices but not for the view that human existence can be conceptualized and the good life lived in several different and worthy ways.

Herder

Although Herder lacked Vico's sense of history and Montesquieu's sense of geography, he surpassed both in his appreciation of the wholeness and diversity of cultures. He rejected the monist view that cultures were so many different byproducts of a universally shared human nature, and argued that the latter was a 'pliant clay' differently moulded by different cultures (Herder, 1969, pp. 185–6). For Herder neither the abstract individual of the contractualist imagination, nor human nature as proposed by the classical Greek and Christian philosophers, but the cultural community was the starting point of moral and political philosophy (*ibid.*, p. 186).

For Herder every culture was uniquely associated with the experiences of a *volk*, its progenitor and historical bearer, and expressed the way in which its members understood and imaginatively interpreted these experiences. The community's natural environment played an important part in shaping its culture, not in a directly causal manner as Montesquieu had thought but by structuring its world of experiences which the creative human imagination interpreted and ordered. Unlike Montesquieu, Herder did not assign much importance to great lawgivers. Their ability to rise above and give their society's culture a new direction was limited, both because they were themselves profoundly shaped by it and because culture was too subtle and complex to be amenable to such alteration. For Herder culture was a product of the largely unconscious collective efforts of the relevant *volk*, and like all creative acts there was always an element of mystery as to why it developed in the way and took the form it did. Intellectuals and creative writers played an important part in the process, but it largely consisted in giving the community's deepest yearnings a concentrated and articulate expression.

For Herder nature had put 'tendencies towards diversity in our hearts' (1969, p. 186). Each culture had a 'singular, wonderful, inexplicable, ineradicable' identity, embodied a distinct vision of human life, realized different human capacities, cultivated different virtues and temperaments, and had its own unique 'core of happiness', 'centre of gravity', 'spirit', 'ethos' or 'atmosphere'. It was a self-contained and integrated whole and moved according to its own internal principles (Clark, 1969, pp. 329f; Herder, 1969, p. 181). Under the influence of Leibnitz's metaphysics, Herder understood cultures in the image of monads. They were windowless and self-sufficient, viewing the world from within their own perspectives and possessing sufficient inner strength and vitality to resist and refract external influences. Each had its own *telos* and developed in a direction dictated by it. 'The future determines the present, and the present determines the past, as the purpose determines the constitution of the means to be used.'

For Herder, culture was inextricably bound up with language, the point ignored by Montesquieu and only incidentally referred to by Vico. Every cultural community had a language of its own and was a distinct linguistic community. As against the dominant Enlightenment view that language was a means of communication or a vehicle for expressing already formed ideas, Herder insisted that it was the very basis and medium of thought (1969, p. 132). 'Every nation speaks in the manner it thinks and thinks in the manner it speaks.' Its language was the repository of its thoughts, feelings, memories, hopes and fears, and moulded its speakers' minds and hearts in a specific direction. To speak it was to participate in a way of life, to experience and view the world in a particular manner, to be bound to fellow-speakers by the indissoluble and intangible bonds of shared memories, sentiments, traditions and pride (*ibid.*, p. 181).

Since a cultural community profoundly shaped its members, it created the 'whole structure of man's humanity'. To be human was to grow up within a particular cultural community and become a particular kind of person. The abstract and universally shared human nature, which supposedly underlay and remained unchanged across cultures as the Enlightenment thinkers had argued, was a fiction.[3] The Enlightenment view assumed that the human mind could be separated from the body and consisted of discrete faculties such as reason, will and instincts. For Herder the mind did not think or will, only the whole human being did, and that too from within a cultural community. The will could not be free or unfree, only the human being could be. Reason was not transcendental in nature but culturally embedded, and its mode of functioning was closely bound up with the cultural tradition (Clark, 1969, p. 122).

For Herder, the influence of culture permeated the individual's ways of thinking, feeling and judging, food, clothes, bodily gestures, way of talking, manner of holding himself or herself together, pleasures, pains, values, ideal, dreams, nightmares, forms of imagination, and aesthetic and moral sensibilities. Human beings felt at home and realized their potential only within their own culture and were awkward and profoundly disorientated outside of it, which was why Europeans, who displayed great civic virtues at home, often behaved with uncharacteristic brutality when travelling or living abroad. Not surprisingly every community 'holds firmly' to its culture and seeks to transmit it across generations 'without any break'. Its commitment to its culture was based not on rational conviction or utilitarian considerations but 'prejudice', an unquestioning and grateful acceptance of its inheritance accompanied by pride and confidence in its value. Prejudice 'returns people to their centre [and] attaches them more solidly to their roots'. Since no man could be human outside his cultural community, membership of it was a basic human need just as much as food and physical security.

All cultures, for Herder, were unique expressions of the human spirit, incommensurable and, like flowers in the garden, beautifully complementing each other and adding to the richness of the world.[4] He had an almost mystical belief in the principle of variety and a religious reverence for diversity. Like many Christian theologians, he thought that God had so created the world that it realized the plenitude of His being, and like Leibintz he insisted that the principle of sufficient reason ruled out the possibility of any two cultures being alike. Unlike many an earlier writer, including Montesquieu who located moral and cultural diversity within the framework of and subjected it to the constraints of different forms of moral universalism, Herder insisted that all morality was concrete and contextual. Far from transcending culture, moral life was embedded in and inseparable from it. It derived its ideals and values from the wider culture, and drew its energy and vitality from the latter's myths, fables, stories, heroes, poetry, rituals, proverbs, and the emotions and memories evoked by its language. A morality for 'all times and places' was but a 'foam', ephemeral and devoid of depth and substance.

Herder was anxious to avoid thoroughgoing relativism and tried to find such space as he could for common humanity and universal morality.[5] Human beings, he argued, belonged to a single species and shared in common certain physical, emotional and cultural needs and such capacities as rationality, imagination and, above all, the capacity to create and sustain cultures. Each cultural community differently developed these needs and capacities, and also cultivated new ones. Since the shared humanity was culturally reconstituted, it was not homogeneous but internally differentiated. Like common humanity, universal morality was embedded not in a body of abstract principles and norms but in empathetic identification with others and the willingness to treat them the way one would like to be treated oneself. For Herder, we should respect other cultures not because some moral law or principle so requires, but because they mean as much to their members as ours does to us, and we should understand them in their own terms both because we cannot otherwise understand them at all, and because this is how we want others to treat us. Slavery was 'foul' not because all human beings were abstractly equal, but because 'snatching' people away from their natural and social habitat produces 'frenzy', 'rootlessness' and 'despair' and we would not ourselves like to be so treated (1968, pp. 76f). Herder thought that unlike the abstract and 'impotent' moral injunctions of the Kantian variety, such a culturally grounded moral attitude had the power to motivate human beings, for it drew on their attachment to their own culture and required nothing more than empathy and reciprocity.

For Herder all cultures were equal not because they were equally good, though he sometimes said so, but because they meant much to their members and best suited their needs. Each culture tended to think itself superior to others, and was wrong to do so. 'The Negro is as much entitled to think the white man degenerate as the white man is to think of the Negro as a black beast.' The distinction between civilized and uncivilized ways of life was at best a matter of degree, and the fact that some cultures were less developed did not mean that the people involved were inferior. Every group of human beings had an equal potential for perfection 'including the Eskimos and the native Indians',

and they were all equally human. Herder was highly critical of
and other Enlightenment thinkers for their preoccupation with race and
implicit or explicit endorsement of racism. ' "Race" is an ignoble
word', and no nation should be allowed to rule over others by virtue of
its alleged innate superiority (Clark, 1969, p. 322; Herder, 1969,
pp. 319f).

Each culture, according to Herder, was valuable because of what it
was, and not as a stepping stone to an allegedly higher culture or as a
stage in a grand historical teleology. Its sole concern should be to be
true to itself and live by its own highest values, and it must be judged
by its own standards. To judge it by the standards of another was to
imply that it should be something other than what it is, and that did it
grave injustice and invariably led to a 'most distorted caricature'. Since
each culture was bound up with the life of a particular *volk* and
enriched the world, to destroy it or violate its integrity was a sacrilegious act. Herder condemned the ancient Romans in the strongest possible terms for destroying native civilizations, and criticized Christian
missionaries for converting by force or financial and other inducements
the helpless subjects of the great European empires.

A cultural community, or a nation as he sometimes called it, was an
'extended family' representing one language, one culture, one people
and 'one national character', and should at all cost avoid dilution and
loss of its internal coherence. Since it flourished only when it had its
own state, we should avoid 'a wild mixing of various nationalities
under one sceptre'. The nation was prior to the state and sustained it by
providing it with moral unity and solidarity. In its absence the state
remained an inherently fragile and artificial machine relying solely or
heavily on crude physical force to maintain itself. Herder was a liberal
and thought, like Mill, Tocqueville and others, that liberalism required
a strong spirit of nationhood and cultural unity. A strong nation meant
a weak state, the necessary precondition of individual liberty.

For Herder the coherence and vitality of a culture was the greatest
collective asset, which its members had a duty to safeguard. The duty
was entailed by the elementary sense of gratitude for what their culture
had done for them, by self-interest for, if their culture disintegrated,
their own lives would lack wholeness and stability, and by the duty to
God to cherish the variety of His cultural creations and participate in
His self-expression. Although Herder was unclear as to what loyalty to
culture entailed, he seemed to have in mind the duty to safeguard its

alues and ideals against internal and external
. This did not mean that one should not criticize
hat it should be done with great care and sensitiv-
ⱱn principles, and only to help it realize its poten-

f culture was a remarkable intellectual achievement.
⸺ ⸺ced and in parts anticipated by Vico, Montesquieu and others, it highᴜ.ghted aspects of culture that were largely ignored in the traditional discussion of the subject, and encouraged folk studies, philology, comparative philosophy, historical study of law, ethno-sociological study of language, and sympathetic explorations of premodern European and contemporary non-European societies. Herder was one of the first to insist on the close relation between culture and language, and to argue that language was not just a means of communication and self-expression but an embodiment and vehicle of culture. Seeing culture as a communal creation, he shifted the focus from high culture and traced the countless ways in which it was nourished by popular culture. He rightly insisted that cultures were not results of geographical circumstances and stages of mental development as Montesquieu and Vico had respectively argued, nor functional responses to life's needs as Montaigne had hinted, but products of human imagination, creativity and the search for self-understanding. Cultural diversity was a permanent feature of human life and could never disappear as long as human beings remained what we have always known them to be, playful, curious, inventive, capable of dreaming dreams and probing the limits of their knowledge and experience.

Like Vico and Montesquieu but at a deeper level than both, Herder highlighted the inadequacy of the traditional conception of human nature. He insisted that since human beings were culturally embedded, human nature was not a uniform substratum underlying and remaining unaffected by culture as most monist philosophers since Plato had imagined. However, since only humans create cultures and communicate across cultural boundaries, he argued that we could not dispense with the concept of human nature altogether in favour of radical cultural relativism. Although he failed to establish a coherent relation between human nature and culture and to develop a culturally sensitive theory of human nature, he was one of the very few writers to wrestle with the question. Unlike most of his predecessors and contemporaries, he saw each culture not only from the standpoint of its members but also from a wider human perspective, and stressed the aesthetic and moral value of a culturally diverse world.

Despite its many original insights, Herder's theory of culture remains unsatisfactory. Like Vico, Montesquieu, Burke and many other writers on the subject, he makes the all too familiar mistake of seeing culture as a tightly knit and tensionless whole informed and held together by a single overreaching principle or spirit. No culture save perhaps the most primitive is or can be like that. It is divided along class, gender, regional and generational lines and is made up of several historically inherited and ill-coordinated strands of thought, each struggling to claim its ownership. It also includes economic, political, religious and other institutions, each with its own history, momentum and logic, and all collectively making the whole more like a patchwork or a mosaic than a neat pattern. Since all cultures are ridden with varying degrees of incoherence and tension, they neither match Herder's idealized account of them nor posses the kind of cohesion and constitutive power he ascribes to them.

While appreciating the diversity *of* cultures, Herder is antipathetic to that *within* it. Indeed the very ground on which he champions the former, namely that every culture is a distinct and harmonious whole, requires him to ignore or suppress its internal differences and diversities. He cherishes a culturally plural *world* but not a culturally plural *society*. This was why he attacked the cosmopolitan German intellectuals and aristocrats for their fondness for the French culture and language, and excluded them from his definition of the German *Volk*. Only the *burghers*, who included the farmers, the merchants and the artisans, were the 'true' German people entitled to speak in their name and set their cultural tone. Herder's theory of culture is not only externally but internally exclusive, and is obsessed as much by the internal as by external enemies.

This damages his case for cultural diversity. As he understands it, different cultures represent different expressions of the human spirit and, like flowers in the garden, form a harmonious whole. Such aestheticization of diversity renders it mute and passive and eviscerates its creative potential. Like flowers in the garden, Herder's cultures exist side by side with nothing to say to each other. Indeed, being self-contained and integrated wholes, they not only do not need each other but suffer from a close contact. This was why Herder was haunted by the fear of cultural miscegenation, including even the borrowing of foreign words and manners. Other cultures are not options for Herder, and do not increase the range of one's choices. They are not to be used to interrogate and highlight the strengths and limitations of one's culture either. And obviously one is not expected to learn anything from them. It is difficult to see what purpose cultural diversity serves other than as an object of aesthetic contemplation, an important but a limited value.

Even the aesthetic case for cultural diversity runs into obvious problems. Unlike flowers in the garden or paintings in an art gallery, cultures never stay in their assigned places. They compete, conflict and threaten each other and we need to decide which ones to support, how and why. During Herder's own lifetime European powers were busy 'civilizing' the rest of the world, and Christian missionaries converting the 'heathens'. His response was muddled. Sometimes he condemned colonialism as a 'treason against the majesty of Nature', which intended each nation to remain separate and independent (1968, pp. 77f). On other occasions he justified it on the ground that this was the only way 'childlike' and 'less-advanced societies' could be improved, provided that the colonial rule was 'benevolent' and did not undermine indigenous religions and cultures. Herder did not explain how he judged some societies inferior and how they could be 'civilized' without changing their cultures. Not surprisingly he despaired of finding an answer, and took comfort in the belief that since God was at work in history and realized Himself through the multiplicity of cultures, he would somehow ensure their survival or create new ones and continue to underwrite cultural diversity. He did not ask why God created a world of intercultural conflict in the first instance, and instructed his Christian followers to engage in active proselytization which Herder saw as a grave threat to non-Christian cultures.

The way in which Herder defends cultural diversity creates yet another problem for him. In his view each culture is valuable and worth cherishing because it contributes a distinct tune to the universal symphony. This implies that if a cultural community wishes to enjoy others' respect, it should fiercely strive to remain unique and guard against all external influences. This leads to an absurd and obsessive preoccupation with difference, and discourages a judicious examination of what aspects of one's culture are worth preserving and why. Herder also has considerable difficulty explaining why each culture is unique. Following Montesquieu he sometimes accounts for it in terms of climate and physical geography, which was why he argued that the 'national character' of the Jews had stemmed from their Palestinian origins and remained unchanged during their diasporic existence, and that it was 'good' for them to return to their original home. Such a naive view is open to the objections we raised against Montesquieu. More often Herder explains cultural differences in terms of human creativity, and argues that there is always an element of mystery as to why human beings interpret and imaginatively reconstitute their experiences in certain ways. Although this is a more promising line of inquiry, he finds it difficult to resist the essentialist language of his age and contends that the uniqueness of a culture springs from the unique 'soul', 'spirit' or 'genius' of the *Volk* that created it. He does not explain how the community comes to develop a particular 'soul' in the first instance. And it also goes against his view that it is the culture, especially the language, that shapes and nurtures the soul of the community.

Despite his intentions to the contrary, Herder's theory teeters over the edge of cultural relativism.[6] Since human beings are for him not just culturally constituted in the very core of their being, he cannot adequately explain how they can understand other cultures or meaningfully communicate across cultural boundaries. They must have at least some capacity to rise above their deepest cultural prejudices, which is ruled out by his theory of the culturally constituted self. Herder rightly talks of empathy and imaginative identification with other cultures, but neither is possible if one's imagination and identity are culturally suffused and lack openness to others.

A similar difficulty bedevils his moral theory. He insists that one should not judge other cultures by one's standards but theirs. Since moral life is for him deeply embedded in the highly intricate structure of the wider culture, its standards are obviously too elusive to be identified with ease and confidence. Furthermore, since a culture is an organic whole for Herder, he cannot explain why its practices get out of step with its values in the first instance, and why we should criticize the practices and not the values themselves unless we have already used *our* standards to condemn the practices. If a culture practises slavery without internal protest, the latter obviously meets its standards, and Herder gives no grounds for condemning it. He can show that *we* should not take its members as slaves, for we should respect their freedom just as we want them to respect ours, but not why *its members* should not take some of them as slaves. That requires some minimally common standards that are neither theirs nor ours but shared by both. Herder is unable to provide a theoretical basis for such a universal morality. He cannot avoid invoking it, but it is no more than a personal preference that sits ill at ease with the general thrust of his moral theory.

Since Herder sees cultures as self-contained wholes that are corrupted by external influences, his defence of culture subtly slides into that of the nation, and his plea for cultural integrity is really one for cultural nationalism with all its attendant problems including its inability to provide a coherent and realistic theory of the state. Herder deeply distrusts the state, and thinks that the only way to minimize its role and power is to rely on the solidarity of the organic and close-knit cultural community (Herder, 1969, p. 324). This view makes sense if we assume that the nation is a morally homogeneous entity agreed on all the essentials of the good life and that it is a prepolitical fact which has somehow developed by its own efforts. Neither assumption is justified. As we shall see, no nation or culture is homogeneous and free of deep conflict and contestation. And it is not a prepolitical given but a political construct defined, consolidated and sustained by the political process. Herder was so committed to the spontaneous harmony of interests and views brought about by culture that he had neither a theory of the will nor, as Kant astutely observed, that of evil. Naïvely imagining like many a cultural nationalist that a unified culture made coercion redundant, he did not appreciate the role of the state either in the constitution and consolidation of culture or in containing and managing endemic social and economic conflicts.

Misunderstanding culture

We have discussed three major theorists of cultural diversity who, in their own different ways, sought to break with the long and enormously powerful tradition of moral monism and lay the foundations of a pluralist alternative. More than almost all their predecessors they appreciated that human beings were born within and profoundly shaped by their cultural communities, and that different cultures differently reconstituted the shared human nature and gave rise to human beings who were at once both similar and different. The three writers and others like them gave difference an ontological status and dignity missing in their monist counterparts. They were therefore able to argue that moral life could not be separated from the wider culture and elevated to a transcendental realm of its own as monists had insisted. Since each culture represents a distinct way of life, it needs to be approached with sensitivity and empathy and calls for great powers of imagination, a concept the three writers placed at the centre of their moral and social epistemology and which was largely ignored by the monists. Their appreciation of cultural plurality enabled them to raise novel questions such as how we could understand and judge other cultures, why cultures were different, whether the differences were a transient phenomenon or a permanent feature of human life, and why cultural diversity was an important value. The three writers wrestled with these and related questions with considerable skill, gave the discussion of cultural diversity a new orientation, and offered insights no theory of it can ignore.

Since Vico, Montesquieu and Herder were pioneers of a new tradition of thought, they got things wrong from time to time. And since they were reacting against the powerful monist tradition, which they did not subject to a systematic critique and whose continuing hold on their thought they did not therefore fully appreciate, they either fell under its spell in certain crucial areas (Vico and Montesquieu) or rejected far more of it than was justified (Herder). It would be helpful to highlight several common and interrelated mistakes they all made and which prevented them from offering a coherent theory of cultural diversity. The mistakes are by no means unique to them and tend to occur in many a contemporary discussion of the subject as well. For analytical convenience and because we are likely to succumb to their seductive appeal unless we clearly identify and distinguish them, I shall state these mistakes schematically and give them occasionally infelicitous names.[7]

- First, the three writers we have discussed took culture to be an integrated and organic whole, and ignored its internal diversity and tensions. We might call this the fallacy of holism.
- Second, they assumed that cultures were self-contained units, had distinct spirits, ethos or organizing principles, and could be easily individuated and distinguished from each other. We might call this the fallacy of distinctness.
- Third, they tended to take a static view of culture. While appreciating that culture was the product of a long historical process, they thought that it was from now onwards to be preserved more or less intact. This was as true of Herder who insisted on preserving the

authenticity of the current German culture, as of Vico and Montesquieu who thought that the culture of their age represented the highest human achievement and marked the end of history. We shall call this a positivist, historicist or end-of-history fallacy.

- Fourth, they saw each culture as an unique and organic expression of the spirit, soul, national character, level of mental development or the deepest yearnings and instincts of the relevant community. They homogenized both the culture and the community, took a quasi-anthropomorphic view of the latter, and found it difficult to explain how the community required a particular character in the first instance, why its culture changed over time, why it was internally contested, why cultures shared some of their important features in common, and so forth. We shall call this the fallacy of ethnicization of culture.

- Fifth, all three theorists and many others took a highly conservative attitude to culture. Since culture was assumed to be an integrated whole, even the smallest changes in it were deemed to be fraught with unpredictable consequences. Reforms were therefore either to be avoided or undertaken with the greatest of care. We could call this the fallacy of closure.

- Sixth, all three writers, especially Herder and his fellow-romantics, saw culture as a kind of self-acting collective agent which 'dictated', 'required' or 'expressed itself' in a particular body of beliefs and practices and followed its own internal laws and logic. For them each culture had a dominant spirit or organizing principle, which constituted and disposed its more or less passive members to act in certain ways. Not surprisingly, their theories of culture left only a limited space for freedom, even Montesquieu allowing creative intervention only to men of genius. We shall call this the fallacy of cultural determinism.

- Seventh, all three writers dissociated culture from the wider political and economic structure of society. Vico and Herder made only passing references to the role of social and economic factors. Even Montesquieu, who was more sensitive to their influence, did not appreciate that despotism was tied up with the prevailing form of land ownership and the economic system in general, and that polygyny was closely related to the pattern of power relations between the sexes and their respective places in the production process. None of the three writers and their successors appreciated the ideological and political dimensions of culture and the highly complex ways in which dominant interests define, constitute and enforce it. Since every culture represents a particular way of looking at the world and structuring human relations, it tends to legitimize and sustain a particular kind of social order. Itself a system of power, it is interlocked with other systems of power, and can never be politically neutral. Far from being a transparent and univocal system of meaning claiming the spontaneous allegiance of its members, every culture is subject to contestation, and its dominant meaning tends to reflect the balance of power between its different groups. In ignoring the politics and economics of culture, the three writers misunderstood the process of its creation and consolidation and the basis of its power. We might call this the fallacy of cultural autonomy.

These and other mistaken beliefs informing the thought of the three writers and others whom we have not discussed are interrelated. The belief that a culture is an integrated whole encourages the view that cultures can be neatly individuated, and conversely they can be easily distinguished only if each is assumed to be a self-contained whole. The two beliefs are in turn closely tied up with cultural conservatism. Since a culture is supposed to be thoroughly integrated and distinct, any change in it is fraught with large and unexpected consequences and likely to dilute its identity. Once a culture is viewed as an integrated and self-contained whole, its development can only be explained by reifying it and endowing it with a collective spirit possessing the power of independent and autotelic agency. Such a view in turn makes culture an autonomous area of life, and overlooks its embeddedness in the wider economic and political structure. And once we see cultures as more or less closed worlds, we get caught up in the interminable and irresoluble debate about how to judge them. 'Our' standards do not apply to them, 'theirs' might be difficult to discover or accept, and common standards are either impossible in such a fragmented world or beyond our ethnocentric grasp. The task facing a theorist of cultural diversity is how to account for the importance, power and coherence of culture without committing these and related mistakes.

3

Contemporary Liberal Responses to Diversity

We have discussed two major traditions of thought and concluded that neither provides a coherent theory of cultural and moral diversity. Monists take no account of the role of culture in shaping human beings and defining the nature and content of the good life, and have little appreciation of the sources and significance of cultural diversity. As for their pluralist critics they either take a radically culturalist view of human beings and see them as wholly constituted by their culture, or see culture as a kind of superstructure resting on and interacting with an unchanging and identical human nature. In the former case they cannot explain how cultures come into being, change, communicate with, learn from and judge each other, and generally end up embracing relativism. In the latter case they face considerable difficulty relating human nature and culture, and advance weaker forms of monism or relativism or, more often, an uneasy blend of the two.

In recent years several political philosophers, almost all liberal, have offered theories of moral and cultural diversity that seek to avoid these mistakes. They appreciate both the shared human nature and the cultural embeddedness of human beings, and redefine liberalism to make it more hospitable to diversity than their classical predecessors without compromising its commitment to certain universal principles. I shall examine the thought of John Rawls, Joseph Raz and Will Kymlicka to see how they go about the task and with what results.[1] I take these three writers because they are among the most influential, stress different liberal principles, and concentrate on different kinds of diversity. Rawls is primarily interested in the problems thrown up by moral diversity or different conceptions of the good, Kymlicka in those thrown up by cultural diversity or different ways of life, and Raz in both.[2]

Rawls

Rawls's *A Theory of Justice* was his first systematic attempt to deal with the question of moral plurality. In his view plurality was both inescapable and desirable, the former because human beings arrived at different and equally plausible conceptions of the good life in the course of exercising their rational powers, the latter because they possessed different talents and opportunities and needed others to 'bring forth a part' of themselves which they 'have not been able to cultivate'. Rawls asked how such men and women could create a society that was just, stable and respected deep moral differences (Rawls, 1971, pp. 4f).

Rawls's answer is too well-known to need elaboration. Since major social economic and political institutions or what he called the basic structure of society profoundly affected citizens' exercise of their rights, liberties and prospects in life, Rawls insisted that they were the 'primary subject' of justice. The principles governing them should be arrived at rationally and settled once and for all, and not left to the democratic political process which might not produce a consensus or one likely to last for generations, or which might 'bend justice' to volatile public opinion and 'unreason'. Rawls relied on such devices as the veil of ignorance and reflective equilibrium to arrive at his two principles of justice, the lexical priority between them, and the list of primary goods or those basic liberties, conditions and opportunities which every 'rational man' wants irrespective of his conception of the good life. He claimed that such a society was stable because its members endorsed the principles of justice as the expression and realization of their moral nature, and it respected their deep moral differences because it only demanded what they agreed upon and left them free to pursue their self-chosen conceptions of the good.

Within about a decade of the publication of *A Theory of Justice* Rawls, who now better appreciated the extent and depth of moral differences or the 'fact of pluralism' in contemporary western societies, noticed a 'serious problem' with it. He dealt with it in number of important articles and later in his *Political Liberalism* (1993a). In *A Theory of Justice* the just society depended for its stability on a shared theory of the human person or human nature, what Rawls now calls a comprehensive philosophical doctrine. Although this Kantian doctrine is coherent and defensible, which is why Rawls continues to subscribe to it, he thinks that one might also hold others that are equally plausible. Since differences between comprehensive doctrines cannot be philosophically resolved, and since using the power of the state to suppress all but one is unjust, Rawls argues that the account of stability given in *A Theory of Justice* was 'unrealistic' and must be 'recast' (Rawls, 1993, pp. xvi–xvii). He abandons the project of grounding the principles of justice in a comprehensive doctrine and prefers to make them free-standing, a view he calls a political as different from a metaphysical conception of justice. Although this strategy is not new to him, for it was also proposed by Michael Oakeshott in his *Harvard Lectures* (1993) and informed his *On Human Conduct* (1972), Rawls adds several new elements to it.[3]

Since the political conception of justice is free-standing and does not need the support of a well-considered philosophical doctrine, Rawls is led to revise his earlier view of the nature and role of political philosophy. The political philosopher does not offer a philosophical defence of the principles of justice as Rawls had argued in *A Theory of Justice*. His aim is 'practical not metaphysical', to offer a conception of justice that makes no claim to truth and only provides a 'workable and shared basis' of co-operation between citizens holding different comprehensive doctrines. Thanks to this 'method of avoidance' as Rawls calls it, or the doctrine of epistemic abstinence as Raz baptizes it, his theory of justice 'stays on the surface, philosophically speaking'.

Since Rawls's main concern is to provide a workable basis of social cooperation for liberal democratic societies, he turns to them to tease out the 'fundamental ideas' implicit in their 'political culture'. In making this move Rawls assumes that political cultures of democratic societies are substantially alike, that they are more or less homogeneous, and that their fundamental ideas can be identified with relative ease and without much disagreement. He also assumes that the democratic public culture is neutral between and capable of providing a 'nondoctrinal basis' for a society divided by comprehensive doctrines. He does not explain how this can be reconciled either with the obvious fact that every culture embodies a particular conception of the human person and the concomitant view of the good, or with his own view that the democratic public culture represents a Kantian conception of the person.

For Rawls the ideas of free and equal persons and society as a system of voluntary cooperation between them are central to the political culture of democratic societies. In deriving the principles of justice from the political culture of democratic societies, Rawls implicitly limits their moral validity to the latter and risks giving a relativist account of them.[4] He also needs to show that the principles are not just a brute fact of contemporary life but have a genuine normative force. Since he wants to take them off the political agenda, he also needs to give good reasons why future generations should remain bound by them. Not surprisingly he offers a philosophical defence of them, arguing that citizens are free and equal persons because they all possess two crucial moral powers, namely the sense of justice and the capacity to form, revise and pursue a conception of the good. Whatever one may think of such a defence, Rawls implicitly concedes that democratic public culture is *not* self-validating and that the role of the political philosopher is not as marginal and uncritical as he suggests.

Political liberalism or the political conception of justice then is Rawls's new answer to the fact of pluralism. It is limited to the political realm defined broadly to include the basic structure of society. It is free-standing in the sense that it does not presuppose, and is presented and defended independently of, a comprehensive doctrine including comprehensive liberalism. It is autonomous in the sense that all its relevant categories and principles are derived from within it. It does not talk of human beings but of citizens, not of human reason but of public reason or reason of citizens, not of human person but of a political conception of the person, not of human powers but powers of the citizen. It cherishes personal autonomy but limits its exercise to the political realm. The index of primary goods is also derived from within the political conception of justice. Citizens conduct their common affairs according to their public reason. Since as citizens they are committed to justifying their actions and proposals to each other, they only appeal to the ideals and principles embodied in the political conception of justice or to political values. They accept the burdens of judgment, and acknowledge that others might reach different conclusions on the basis of the same evidence and arguments and sincerely disagree on important issues. They eschew all appeals to comprehensive doctrines except when their society is badly ordered, and then too only to strengthen or better realize its shared political values, or when they are discussing such non-political issues as man's relation to nature, the environment and the animal welfare.

For Rawls the general ideas underlying the political conception of justice help us decide what comprehensive doctrines are reasonable or unreasonable. Although he equivocates on this point and sometimes seems to confuse unreasonable individuals with unreasonable comprehensive doctrines, his general position seems to be that those doctrines that accept the idea of free and equal persons, the free-standing status of the political realm, the burdens of judgment, and so on are reasonable; those that do not are 'unreasonable and irrational, and even mad'. Although Rawls occasionally suggests that the latter may be disallowed altogether, he generally prefers to 'contain' them as one does with 'war and disease' (Rawls, 1993a, pp. xvii and 64).

Although the political conception of justice is supported by the democratic public culture and the kinds of philosophical reasons Rawls gives for them, he thinks that it does not by itself solve the problem of social stability unless it enjoys the broadbased support of reasonable comprehensive doctrines. It is not entirely clear why he considers such additional support necessary. He seems to think that since citizens do as a matter of fact hold comprehensive doctrines and since these matter much to them, the political conception remains precarious without their positive or at least negative support. If this is so, then it is an exceedingly risky strategy to formulate the political conception of justice without first identifying and analysing the kinds of comprehensive philosophical doctrines to be found in contemporary democratic societies, and showing that they provide it with an overlapping consensus and that, when they do not, they are mistaken. Rawls does not do this partly because he assumes that most citizens of liberal democratic societies are unlikely to entertain comprehensive doctrines that go against their public culture, and partly because he thinks that such doctrines can be legitimately disallowed (*ibid.*, pp. xvi, 64, 177, 190, 209).

Rawls's political liberalism claims to solve the problem of how citizens holding different comprehensive doctrines and conceptions of the good can create a polity that is just, stable and leaves 'enough space' for diversity. Judged by his own three criteria, his claim is only partly sustainable.

Rawls's first claim that his political liberalism provides a sound basis for a just polity rests on three assumptions. First, justice is the first virtue of society and agreement on it is the necessary precondition of political stability. Second, Rawls's two principles of justice are the only ones consistent with the basic ideas of free and equal citizens and society as a system of voluntary cooperation. While Rawls is all too willing to acknowledge a plurality of the conceptions of the good, he does not think that it might also extend to principles of justice. Third, the principles are free-standing and do not presuppose comprehensive liberalism.

As for Rawls's first assumption the question of justice neither arises nor can be settled in a historical and cultural vacuum. It is only when people live together over a period of time and develop common interests, common language and culture, habits of cooperation and at least some degree of mutual commitment that they are in a position even to debate and arrive at a shared conception of justice. This is particularly the case with deeply divided societies whose members not only cannot agree on the nature, criteria and limits of justice but find the very discussion of them yet another source of tension.[5] The vital need in such a society, as indeed in every other, is to get people to talk to one another, encourage the spirit of accommodation at all levels, contain their conflicts, avoid contentious issues especially of a moral kind, and in the meantime maintain peace and order by getting them to agree on a minimum structure of authority. Once they build up common interests, values and sentiments, agreement on the principles of justice becomes both less urgent and easier to secure. Paradoxical as it may seem, a society so devoid of other resources as to depend exclusively on the principles of justice to hold it together is the least likely to agree on them. Justice is not the first virtue of society because it presupposes and is embedded in a cluster of other virtues and because it is only one of the several preconditions of social and political stability.[6]

Since Rawls's second assumption has been much discussed, a few brief remarks should suffice. Although freedom and equality are central to democratic culture, they do not imply either Rawls's difference principle or that the basic structure of society should itself be made a matter of justice. As a matter of fact, many citizens of democratic society are so deeply imbued with the narrow notions of desert and merit that they do not share Rawls's view that all social and economic inequalities should be judged on the basis of what they do to the worst off, that one's undeserved natural talents should not be basis of claims to reward, and so on. Rawls gives excellent reasons in support of his principles of justice, but they are his reasons and do not correspond to the settled convictions of many of his fellow citizens. In a society as divided as he takes it to be, people's beliefs vary greatly. No reflective equilibrium, whether it is defined in introspective individualist terms that Rawls generally favours or in participatory political terms where it is embedded in public deliberation, can order our intuitions into a coherent pattern without excluding some and radically reinterpreting many others.

Even if we ignored current popular prejudices and reasoned solely on the basis of the abstract principles of freedom and equality, it is not clear that Rawls's two principles are the only ones possible. Free and equal citizens could just as plausibly arrive at more egalitarian principles, or at a different set of primary goods that might not be amenable to the kind of individualist redistribution that Rawls's principles presuppose. These goods include such things as a secure job, the necessary basis of self-respect which Rawls ignores, the spirit of social solidarity, a common sense of belonging, a culture of mutual concern and responsibility rather than only rights, and a planned and cooperative economy as an expression of human freedom and a way of reducing the contingency of economic life, all of which entail a very different form of social cooperation to Rawls's and give justice a less decisive political role than he does.

Rawls' third assumption that his political liberalism does not presuppose comprehensive liberalism is unconvincing. His political liberalism is largely only the old comprehensive liberalism restricted to the political realm. This is why the principles of justice as outlined in *Political Liberalism* are substantially the same as in *A Theory of Justice*. The fact that political liberalism is conceptually and substantively parasitic upon comprehensive liberalism is evident at several levels. When Rawls says that citizens have or should be assumed to have two moral powers and that they should act justly because this reflects and fulfills their moral nature, he is advancing a distinctly liberal conception of man. Human beings possess or are capable of acquiring a wide variety of powers, such as the capacity to love, to subordinate their interests to those of others, and to die for a worthy or an ignoble cause. The decision as to which of these powers should be deemed to be essential to human beings and socially cultivated cannot be morally and philosophically neutral. The two powers that Rawls emphasizes and institutionalizes presuppose a distinctly liberal perspective, and do not enjoy any or at least such enormous importance in the thought of Plato, Aristotle, Augustine, Burke, Rousseau, Mill, Hegel or Marx. Again, Rawls's belief that our natural talents are undeserved rests on a particular comprehensive doctrine. For the Hindus, the Buddhists, the Jains and others, they are products of the agent's meritorious deeds in his or her past life, and hence amply deserved. Furthermore, the very idea that we can and should first agree on the principles of social cooperation and use these to judge and delimit the acceptable range of the conceptions of the good presupposes a conception of man and society and a view of moral life that are integral to comprehensive liberalism and not to be found in other traditions of thought. While requiring others to abstract away their comprehensive doctrines, Rawls unfairly retains and capitalizes on his own.

As for Rawls's claim that his political liberalism ensures social stability, especially in the strong sense in which he uses the term, it is unconvincing. His political liberalism begins by excluding what he calls unreasonable men or those holding unreasonable comprehensive doctrines. Although Rawls is right to argue that every society is likely to contain such groups and that its survival requires their coercion, his political liberalism has limited resources to cope with them. Unlike the classical contractualists who excluded only those who refused to be incorporated into civil society and accept its authority, Rawls excludes all those who reject the 'essentials' of democratic society. Sometimes he seems to go even further and excludes those who refuse to share his principles of justice, argue in the required manner, and fail to display openness to other points of view. The excluded or marginalized group is thus fairly large and covers not only the Fascists, the racists and the fundamentalists of different persuasions but also the sexists, conservative critics of liberal democracy and those with strong religious convictions. It also includes some groups of Marxists who, though wedded to the ideas of freedom and equality, believe that the capitalist society undermines them and that its overthrow requires an interregnum of authoritarian rule. Unless these and other groups are clearly defined and distinguished, Rawls's society runs the danger of arbitrarily blocking out large areas of dissent and creating pockets of deep discontent.[7]

Even so far as reasonable comprehensive doctrines are concerned, Rawls is too optimistic to presuppose their overlapping consensus on his political conception of justice. Some might accept his principles of justice but define and prioritise them differently. Yet others might feel that Rawls unduly restricts the range of political discourse and that appeals to nonpolitical values should be allowed, especially if they happen to think that their society is deeply ill-ordered, not at all an eccentric or perverse view of some contemporary democracies. Even the comprehensive liberals might find Rawls's principles too conservative or too socialist, as has been argued by some of his liberal critics, and might not find sufficient reasons within their comprehensive doctrine to endorse them.[8]

A widespread consensus among comprehensive doctrines then might not be available and yet it is badly needed to make political liberalism viable. Rawls's society has no choice but to *create* one. Since liberal values are embodied in the basic structure of society and enjoy enormous power and prestige, Rawls hopes that all, or at least most, comprehensive doctrines would over time adjust to and be informed by political liberalism. Since the latter is grounded in comprehensive liberalism, this would mean the dominance of the latter over other comprehensive doctrines. Rawls's political liberalism is, or could be seen by some as, not a principled and self-limiting moral position but a political device with a large hidden agenda.

Rawls suggests that public institutions including the state should actively encourage citizens to reinterpret their comprehensive doctrines in the light of the political conception of justice. He is right to point to the inevitable and desirable interplay between public principles and comprehensive doctrines. This is how, for example, the *Koran* is currently reinterpreted, as the Bible once was, in the light of the democratic principles of equality of the sexes and freedom of conscience. Such an exercise, however, also has its dangers. It can easily violate the integrity of the texts and the tradition, charter them in the service of political and ideological fashions, encourage the government directly or indirectly to influence scholarly inquiries, and create a climate hostile to intellectual dissent. Since Rawls argues that, when all or most comprehensive doctrines are so reinterpreted as to endorse the political conception of justice, we have 'the deepest and the most remarkable basis of social unity', his thought is particularly open to this danger. The ethos of political liberalism could easily penetrate religious and philosophical doctrines, pressure them to understand and articulate themselves in standard liberal idioms, and all but eliminate nonliberal forms of thought. Locke did this when he turned Christianity into a 'reasonable' doctrine by stripping it of its theological mysteries, reducing its highly complex ethic to a simplified morality of bourgeois reciprocity, and turning churches into voluntary associations. J. S. Mill did the same with Christianity and indeed religion in general. Rawls's thought offers little protection against this persistent liberal tendency.

Rawls's third claim that his society leaves enough space for moral and cultural diversity is only partly true. Since his political liberalism does not require agreement on comprehensive doctrines, use education as a tool of cultural engineering, and expect all citizens to lead their personal lives autonomously as Raz and Kymlicka do, it is more hospitable to moral and cultural diversity than theirs. It also, however, contain elements that considerably restrict the space for diversity.

Although Rawls's political liberalism is limited to the political realm, its moral and cultural reach is extensive. Being embodied in the basic structure of society, it enjoys institutional protection, enormous political and economic power, and considerable moral and cultural prestige. After all Rawls makes the basic structure of society the primary subject of justice precisely because it profoundly shapes the rights, liberties and life-chances of its citizens. Although other ways of life are not prohibited, they live in the overpowering shadow of political liberalism and suffer from obvious structural advantages. When their members enter the political realm, they are required to deliberate in terms of the standard liberal values. If they do not, they are accused of behaving as bad citizens, and even risk being branded unreasonable. Since Rawls takes certain matters 'off the public agenda once and for all' he drastically restricts the scope of the normal political processes (Rawls, 1993a, p. 152). Although advocates of radical social change are at liberty to speak and even perhaps agitate, they cannot hope to change the already settled principles of political liberalism. Full-blooded and intellectually consistent communitarians are in a similar predicament, for the constraints they might wish to impose on civil liberties and rights are constitutionally ruled out. Religious persons are at an even greater disadvantage. Although Rawls equivocates, he seems to require that they should not speak in their native conceptual language, invoke their sincerely held beliefs, and appeal to their deeply held values. If some of them were to do so and take, say, a rigid anti-abortionist stand, they risk being branded 'cruel and oppressive' (*ibid.*, 1993a, pp. 243–4). Such persons are likely to feel deeply alienated and unjustly treated, and might reject the society that has no space for them.

Rawls's society is inhospitable to diversity in another area as well. Like many liberals he is sensitive to moral but not cultural plurality, and takes little account of the cultural aspirations of such communities as the indigenous peoples, national minorities, subnational groups, and the immigrants. Although these groups make different demands, they all seek cultural autonomy in one form or another, and hence some departure from the conventional liberal preoccupation with a homogeneous legal and political structure. Quebec wants an asymmetrical

Canadian federation and the right to redefine and reprioritize the basic liberal liberties in order to promote the collective goal of preserving its cultural identity. Indian Muslims demand respect for their personal law and reject the idea of common civil laws for all Indian citizens. The demands of indigenous peoples are too well-known to need elaboration. Since Rawls's political liberalism is largely individualist, and meant to be uniformly applied throughout society, it has no resources to accommodate these and other demands for differential treatment.

Rawls's society, then, does not leave enough space for diversity. He regrets this, but insists that no society can accommodate all ways of life. Although he has a point, there is all the difference in the world between discouraging a few eccentric or perverse and a large number of fairly mainstream ways of life, and it is the latter that is the case with Rawls's society. He says that this is a result of current historical conditions, and that not the principles of justice but history is against them (*ibid.*, pp. 197–9). This is a weak reply. Not history but the structure of Rawls's society, which embodies and throws its very considerable weight behind the liberal culture, is responsible for some of the damage done to other ways of thought and life. Besides, history is not an impersonal and transcendental entity operating behind our backs. We can regulate it and, if we choose not to, the responsibility for the consequences is ours. If valuable ways of life and thought are likely to disappear or be put under intolerable pressure, we must ask if we are happy with this outcome and the increasingly homogeneous world it creates, and, if not, what we can and should do to nurture them.

Raz

Since Rawls is primarily interested in moral diversity, he pays little attention to ethnic, cultural and other forms of diversity, the politics of recognition and difference, and more generally to the nature and importance of culture. Although Raz shows greater sensitivity to these questions in his *The Morality of Freedom* (1986), they are not central to his thought and his discussion of them is hurried and sketchy. He takes the Aristotlean view that the pursuit of human well-being is the *telos* or at least the inspiring principle of human life, and consists in successful pursuit of worthwhile goals over a lifetime. The kinds of goals available to individuals and the value they assign them are shaped by the social forms or practices of their society (pp. 308f). One can only think of pursuing a legal career in a society governed by law, and marriage as different from merely living together is an option only in a society in which the institution of marriage is established. This is not to say that the social structure determines individual choices, for individuals have the capacity to reflect critically on and imagine new variations of the prevailing social forms, but rather that their choices are channelled and structured by their society. The nature and content of personal well-being is thus contextual in nature and varies from society to society.

Since different societies encourage different kinds of choices and different forms of well-being, Raz's view points to some form of relativism and the consequent impossibility of comparing and judging them. He is not entirely happy with this and hints at a universal theory of human well-being. Human beings, he says, are genetically endowed with certain capacities, and many of these are accompanied by 'innate drives for their use' (*ibid.*, p. 375). These include the desires to exercise their bodies, stimulate their senses, engage their imagination and affection, and occupy their minds. Culture consists in 'training and channeling' these desires. While different societies do so differently, none can ignore them altogether without damaging human well-being, and hence they can be 'evaluated and compared' in terms of this transcultural test. Sometimes Raz suggests that autonomy, too, is a universal component of human well-being and offers yet another way of judging and comparing societies. Since he does not fully develop his theory of human well-being and self-consciously limits himself to modern western societies, we shall ignore it.[9]

For Raz modern western liberal society is based on the idea of personal autonomy in the sense that its major social, economic and other institutions as well as interpersonal relations call for autonomous choices. Its members have come to be so constituted that autonomy is an integral and deeply valued part of their self-conception, and they feel alienated from their lives and lack a sense of integrity if their choices are not their own. 'The value of personal autonomy is a fact of life' for them, and it is simply not open to them to opt for a different way of life. Furthermore, since all major institutions of society are based on individual choice 'we can prosper in it only if we can be successfully autonomous' (*ibid.*, pp. 369–70, 391, 394). The value of autonomy is structurally derived, a functional requirement of modern society, and 'does not depend on choice'.

Raz takes a less extreme view of autonomy than Mill, and extends it to a much larger area of life than Kant. By autonomy Raz means a continuous process of self-creation by means of small and large decisions concerning significant areas of one's life (pp. 369, 370, 408). To be autonomous is to be part-author of one's life and control its direction and development at least to some degree. Although autonomy involves choice, not all choices are autonomous. For Raz a choice is autonomous if it satisfies the following conditions. First, it should be free in the sense of being uncoerced and unmanipulated. Second, it should be deliberate and based on a careful assessment of relevant reasons. Third, it should relate to important matters such as marriage, occupation, social relations, forms of life and long-term projects. Fourth, the choice should be genuine in the sense of being made between significantly different and equally valuable options. If one of the options is such that the agent cannot possibly reject it, then it is not a genuine option, as for example is the case with a choice between good and evil, the latter not being an option for a moral person. Finally, the choice should be revisable or revocable, for it is always possible to make a mistake or be ignorant of important options or to discover new reasons against one's initial choice.

Raz's case for autonomy is twofold. First, it is central to western self-understanding, and for western people an intrinsic value. It is not an intrinsic value *per se* or universally but only for western people because of the way they have come to be historically constituted. Second, autonomy is necessary in order to succeed in modern society and also has an instrumental value. Although there is something to be said for both these arguments, neither is strong enough to make a convincing case for autonomy. As for the first argument, some, perhaps many, individuals in the west do value autonomy but others do not, as is evident in the popular support for Fascist and right-wing movements, collectivism, religious fundamentalism and bizarre religious cults. Indeed, the ease with which millions including intellectuals, scientists and philosophers in Germany, Italy and elsewhere surrendered their critical faculties and supported the murderous policies of megalomanic dictators only a few decades ago refutes Raz's reading of the modern western character. The self-understanding of the modern western individual is too complex and multistranded to permit simplistic generalizations and provide the basis of a coherent political theory. Hegel, Marx, Nietzsche, Habermas and others offer very different analyses of modernity to Raz's, each capturing some important features of it and overlooking others.

Furthermore, even when people in the west value autonomy, they do not do so in all areas of life or do so equally. They might value it in matters relating to marriage and occupation but not their moral values, religion or politics, in one or all of which they might be happy to continue with what they have inherited from their parents or derived from their ethnic or other communities. Again, the fact that they have acquired love of autonomy does not mean that they should retain it. It is a product of history and can be undone over time if they are so minded. They must therefore be given good reasons to cherish it other than that it is part of their history. Indeed if they are condemned to be autonomous, their autonomy is in no way superior to the heterenomous lives of traditional societies, and there is nothing moral or noble about it. It is self-contradictory to plead for autonomy if the latter itself is not an inescapable necessity.

Raz's second argument fares no better. It views autonomy as a functional requirement of modern society, no different from such socially necessary and amoral skills as literacy and numeracy, and cannot give it the status of a moral value that Raz is anxious to give it. The argument is also empirically false. For Raz, Asian immigrants to Britain do not value autonomy, yet their material success is remarkable. Indeed they have prospered precisely because they do not set much store by autonomy and draw on the ample resources of a flourishing and tightly knit community with its readily available network of social support. As for personal well-being, Asians do have their share of unhappiness, but no more and perhaps less than their white fellow-citizens. They do lose something for belonging to cohesive communities, but they also benefit from it, and it is difficult to say that the trade-off involved is on balance disadvantageous or unwise. What is true of British Asians is equally true of immigrants in the USA and elsewhere, and of many East Asian societies which have prospered economically without valuing autonomy.

Since Raz thinks that autonomy is central to modern western society, he asks what we should do with such groups as immigrants, indigenous people and religious communities who do not set much store by it. He is convinced that their culture is inferior and harms its young members (*ibid.*, pp. 423f. Since Raz has only shown that autonomy is a deeply cherished western and not a universal value, his judgment rests on a cultural preference and cannot claim wider validity. As for harming the young, since neither the parents nor the children value autonomy, their culture does not violate their integrity and moral self-respect as they define it. If the children can prosper in the wider western society – as I have showed they can – no material harm is done to them either.

Since Raz thinks that nonliberal cultures are inferior and harm their children, he concludes that they deserve no respect, the only question being whether they should be tolerated. He urges toleration if they are viable, do not harm outsiders and offer their members an adequate and satisfying life. Not being used to autonomy, their members lack both the capacity for it and a supportive cultural context, and would not be able to lead a rewarding life if wrenched from their communities. If, however, nonliberal groups are unviable, survive only because of the pressure of their leaders, and offer very little education or opportunity to their children to thrive outside their community, they should be assimilated, by force if necessary.

In *The Morality of Freedom*, then, Raz is unable to offer a convincing moral account of how best to deal with nonliberal ways of life. He considers them inferior and harmful on the basis of a view of personal autonomy which he does not show to be either a universally desirable value or even the constitutive value of liberal society. Raz's approach is also static. He says that if nonliberal ways of life are viable, and so on, they should be tolerated; if not, they should be assimilated. He does not appreciate that their viability is a function of the wider society's attitude to them. As he himself says, individual choices are shaped by the kinds of alternatives offered and the value placed on them by the prevailing social forms. Since Raz's society attaches little value to nonliberal ways of life, and even positively disapproves of them, it does much to undermine them. It is therefore somewhat disingenuous to blame them for the non-viability and use it as an excuse for dismantling them.

In several interesting articles published after *The Morality of Freedom* and collected in his *Ethics in the Public Domain* (1994), Raz addresses the subject of cultural diversity much more explicitly and from a somewhat different angle. In *The Morality of Freedom*, he had assumed that western society was liberal in character and had asked how it should treat nonliberal groups believed to be largely peripheral to it. These groups are now seen as an integral part of society which, although liberal, is also multicultural. The question therefore is not how a liberal society should treat its peripheral nonliberal minorities but how it can be truly multicultural and provide adequate spaces for them without undermining its own integrity. Thanks to this highly original reformulation, Raz is now concerned to develop not so much a liberal theory of minority rights as a liberal theory of multiculturalism (1994, ch. 8).

In *The Morality of Freedom*, Raz had argued that human beings were socially embedded, and assumed that society had a single culture. He now argues that they are culturally embedded and that society might contain several cultures. Drawing on his earlier view that human well-being is socially structured, and developing it in a somewhat different direction, he now argues that culture performs two vital functions. It structures its members' perceptual and moral world, gives meaning to their activities and relationships, helps them make sense of themselves, enables them to make intelligent choices, and in these and other ways provides the necessary basis of their freedom and autonomy. The second function is related not so much to autonomy as to human well-being. Culture gives its members a sense of rootedness and a focus of identification, and defines their identity. It also relates them to those sharing a common identity, facilitates social relations, bonds generations, and gives its members access to a rich world of personal relationship. In these and other ways culture promotes human well-being and is the indispensable basis of the good life. Raz argues that since liberals value human well-being, they should also value cultural membership (1994, pp. 177–9).

The two basic functions of culture do not necessarily coincide. A culture might promote human well-being but not autonomy, as is the case with many a traditional and hierarchical society. Or it might encourage such an extreme view of autonomy that it is unable to provide a sense of community, a focus for collective identification, a world of rich and deep personal relationships, and even integenerational bonding. This is what some think has happened to liberal society. Raz is aware of the tension between the two dimensions of culture, and thinks that no culture should be judged by either alone. It is enough if a culture promotes at least some degree of autonomy and well-being. Even repressive cultures mean much to their members and deserve to be tolerated. However, they should not be so repressive as to deny their members adequate opportunities to develop themselves and express important aspects of their nature. They should not deny them the right of exit either, because such a right respects their freedom and prevents the culture from becoming internally oppressive. Furthermore, although a culture need not be liberal in the sense of cherishing autonomy, it should embody values we can respect and whose point we can appreciate. Since it exists among other cultures, it should also be willing to tolerate and live amicably with them (*ibid.*, p. 181).

When cultures meet these minimum conditions, they deserve equal respect and support, Raz argues. Since human beings are culturally embedded and depend on their culture for their freedom, identity and well-being, they have a right to maintain and transmit it to succeeding generations. And since different cultures embody and realize different values, 'none of them can be judged superior to the others', though, of course, they might be criticized and compared in specific respects. In a multicutlural society the state belongs to them all, and the fact that some of them are in a minority should make no difference to their claims on it. They should all enjoy their fair share of public support and resources. Children should be educated in the languages and cultures of their communities if their parents so desire. Customs and practices of different communities should be respected and as far as possible accommodated. There should be generous public assistance for communal charities, libraries, museums and artistic groups. And the public media such as the radio and the television should reflect the multicultural composition of the wider society (*ibid.*, pp. 189–90; 154-6).

Although Raz's new and essentially sound approach represents a considerable advance over classical liberalism and points in the right direction, it still remains trapped in his earlier assumptions and does not allow him to exploit his valuable insights fully. His liberal theory of multiculturalism requires all cultures to respect the values inherent in his thinned-down liberalism. Since he grounds the values in the historical character of the modern western individual, he is unable to show why they are morally binding on nonliberals who have not autonomously chosen them and find Raz's demand an unacceptable form of moral coercion. Furthermore, the values he insists upon are not as minimal and unproblematic as he imagines. He requires that nonliberal cultures should allow their members full development and self-expression, give them adequate opportunities for participation in the wider economic and political life, grant them the right of exit, and should not oppress them. The concepts of full development and self-expression are vague, and it is not clear who is to define them and how. Oppression, too, is not easy to define once we go beyond such patently repressive practices as slavery, forced marriages, genital mutilation and untouchability. And it is not clear what full participation in the economic and political life means and why it is important. If Asian shop-keepers encourage their sons to acquire only the skills needed to run their parental business, and thus confine them to the ethnic economy, are they denying their sons 'full' participation in the economic life of the community? And should they be condemned if the sons are happy and able to lead a reasonably prosperous life? If a religious or socially 'conservative' community were to disapprove of and ostracize its members for engaging in of premarital or extramarital sex, cosmetic replacement of body parts, or usury, are they denying them full development and self-expression or even being repressive? This is not to say that every cultural practice should be tolerated or that all cultural communities deserve equal respect, but rather that some of Raz's criteria of the minimum that a culture should satisfy are either too vague to be helpful or too narrow to respect the integrity of other ways of life.

Raz's case for valuing culture is articulated almost entirely in terms of what it does to its members. The individual's own culture is all that matters to him or her, and it is of no consequence whether or not other cultures exist and flourish. If they do, they should respect them and get to know them out of 'duty' of citizenship; if they do not or die out, that is a fact of life and should cause them no anxiety. Raz establishes the value of one's culture but not of cultural diversity, and cannot explain if and why it should matter to us that other cultures should also flourish. In order to do that he needs to broaden his perspective and show why one needs not only one's own culture but also access to the resources of and a critical engagement with others. That calls for a deeper and richer theory of human freedom and well-being than he proposes.

Considering a culture only from the standpoint of its members also creates another problem. Cultures do not coexist peacefully. They compete, come into conflict, and struggle for domination and mastery. Since they are rarely equal numerically or in their political and economic power, moral and political status, and so on, the dominant culture has built-in advantages and tends over time to overwhelm the rest. The latter die out or decline not always because they have been worsted by better ones in a fair competition but because of their disadvantaged position and uneven playing fields. We might therefore sometimes need to protect dying cultures if they are valuable or disintegrating under severe external pressure, as in the case of declining monastic orders and indigenous communities. And even when we decide not to, we might give their members the necessary resources and encouragement to decide freely whether or not to retain their culture, or at least refrain from brainwashing them into taking a contemptuous view of it. All this requires the dominant culture to curtail its assimilationist zeal, welcome differences, make spaces for others to flourish, create a climate in which they do not feel under siege or denigrated, and be willing when necessary to allocate a greater share of public resources to them. We cannot ask it to do this on the ground that it should respect the rights of other cultures, for the latter entails no such thing. We might more persuasively ask it to do so on grounds of justice, but that only requires it to create level playing fields and not to restrain its assimilationist zeal, cherish differences, or even to allocate additional resources to minority cultures. We need to go further and make a positive case for cultural diversity, showing how and why it is worth cherishing, and that it benefits not just minorities but society as a whole.

Another difficulty arises from the way in which Raz conceptualizes the role of culture. He holds a basically liberal view of human well-being and autonomy, and discusses culture in largely functional terms. Hence he asks such questions as why culture is important, what functions it performs, and why one should have access to one's culture. This is also why he says that one's love of one's culture should be 'rational and valid' and based on the 'right reasons' (1994, p. 184). This is one way of relating to one's culture but not the only one. For some people their culture is a trust to be cherished, for others an inheritance to be enjoyed and suitably adjusted to changing circumstances, for yet others too constitutive of their identity to permit the kind of detachment that Raz's view requires. Raz uncritically universalizes the liberal view of culture and ignores the different ways in which human beings are shaped by and relate to their culture. Furthermore, to say that one should love one's culture for the right reasons or that one's love should be rational and valid implies that one's relation to one's culture is external and contingent and that one's love of it is conditional, a reward for its good points. To love a culture (or anything or any one) for the good in it is to love the latter not the culture itself, and entails the untenable view that one could or even should transfer one's love to another if that seemed better. Obviously love of one's culture should not blind one to its faults, but that is very different from making it a function of its desirable qualities.[10]

Kymlicka

Will Kymlicka first dealt with the question of liberal response to cultural diversity in his *Liberalism, Community and Culture* (1989) and has more recently returned to it in his *Multicultural Citizenship: A Liberal Theory of Minority Rights* (1995). Although there are important differences of emphasis between the two books, I shall ignore them and concentrate on his basic thesis.

Since liberalism is differently defined by different writers, Kymlicka begins by identifying what he takes to be its basic principles. For him human beings have an essential interest in leading a good life. This involves two things. First, they should lead their lives from the inside, that is, in accordance with their beliefs about what gives value to life. Second, since they are fallible and might later find their beliefs mistaken, they should be free to question and revise them. The two together constitute autonomy (1995, p. 81).

Kymlicka's view of autonomy is more modest than those of Mill, Kant and even Raz, and has nothing to do with the ambitious goals of self-creation, self-authorship, or self-legislation. Unlike them, he does not argue that autonomy is desirable because it expresses our moral nature or leads to individuality, progress, discovery of moral truths, or happiness, but rather that it is a necessary condition of the good life. Unlike them, again, he does not see the need to invoke a conception of human nature either to ground autonomy or to give it content. He is content to argue that human beings wish to and should be able to lead the good life and that this requires autonomy. Among liberal writers including Raz, Kymlicka's liberalism wisely carries the lightest philosophical baggage.

For Kymlicka, commitment to autonomy is the basis of liberal political theory. Since the good life requires that individuals should be able to live according to their beliefs without fear of punishment, the liberal insists on civil and personal liberties, constitutional government and freedom of conscience. They should also have the opportunity to acquire information about different ways of life and the ability to examine them critically, and hence the liberal concern for education, freedom of expression, freedom of the press, and so on. Since all individuals share an interest in the good life, they should be treated with equal concern and respect and enjoy equal rights. For Kymlicka, individuals alone are the moral agents, and the bearers of rights and obligations. Societies have 'no moral status of their own' and are to be judged in terms of their contribution to the good life of their members.

Like Raz, Kymlicka asks how the capacity for autonomy is developed, and introduces the concept of culture as its necessary basis. His arguments here are broadly similar to those of Raz (Kymlicka, 1995, pp. 85ff). For him human beings are 'cultural creatures', not in the communitarian sense of being constituted by their cultures but in the sense that cultures are essential to their development as human beings. This is so for two reasons. First, culture defines and structures their world, helps them make intelligent judgments about what is valuable, suggests worthwhile roles, provides them with meaningful options, guides their decisions concerning how to lead their lives, provides a secure background necessary for developing their capacity for choice, and in these and other ways constitutes the inescapable context of their freedom and autonomy. Second, culture gives them a sense of identity, provides an unconditional and non-achievement-orientated source of identification and belonging, facilitates mutual intelligibility, promotes social solidarity and trust, reinforces intergenerational bonds, and conduces to human well-being. The first argument stresses the autonomy-building role of culture, the second its contribution to human well-being and creation of stable communities (*ibid.*, pp. 84ff).

Although both functions are important, they do not necessarily coincide. Some cultures might promote human well-being more than autonomy; others might do the opposite. Unlike Raz who values both, though with a slight bias towards autonomy, Kymlicka insists that autonomy is the central liberal value and that a culture should be judged primarily in terms of its ability to provide its members with meaningful and worthwhile options and cultivate their capacity for individual autonomy (*ibid.*, p. 101). Although he does not explicitly say so, he implies that, other things being equal, a culture that encourages autonomy and choice is better or richer than, and in that sense superior to, one that does not. In order to maintain the climate of choice a culture should remain open to the influence of others, and should impose neither censorship nor prohibitive costs on those of its members who disapprove of its established beliefs and practices and wish to live differently.

Kymlicka uses the term culture in a narrower sense than Raz. For him it refers to 'an intergenerational community, more or less institutionally complete, occupying a given territory or homeland, sharing a distinct language and history' (*ibid.*, p. 18). It provides its members with a meaningful way of life across the 'full range of human activities, including social, educational, religious, recreational and economic life, encompassing both public and private spheres', and is 'institutionally embodied – in schools, media, economy, government, etc' (*ibid.*, p. 76). Kymlicka thinks that 'societal culture', one common to all its members and embodied in its major institutions, is a modern phenomenon and intimately linked with the modern economy and democracy. Accordingly, he uses the terms 'culture', 'cultural community', 'societal culture', 'nation' and 'people' interchangeably. Kymlicka says in effect that membership of a nation or a national community is the necessary basis of autonomy and a fundamental human interest. This is why in his view people prefer closed borders and forego their own greater freedom of movement in order to ensure the 'continued existence of their nation' and the opportunity to live within 'their own national culture'. As he says, quoting Yael Tamir, 'most liberals are liberal nationalists' (*ibid.*, p. 93). The freedom they demand is not the freedom to move beyond one's history and culture, but rather to move within it. And the autonomy they seek refers not to the opportunity to explore and experiment with other cultures but to question the beliefs and practices of their own. For Kymlicka, liberals expect the state to protect not only the individual rights but also the national culture.

If a society happens to be culturally homogeneous, all its members enjoy the benefits of a stable cultural community. The problem arises when it is multicultural for the majority community then exercises its cultural rights but minorities do not. One could ask them to assimilate as the classical liberals had done, but Kymlicka rightly rejects that view on both theoretical and practical grounds. His theoretical argument is twofold. Since culture is vital to human development, minorities have a right to their culture. Secondly, the principle of justice requires that minorities and majority should enjoy equal cultural rights and be able to exercise these equally effectively. Kymlicka here takes over the Rawlsian theory of justice, extends it to relations between cultures, and makes it the basis of his theory of multiculturalism. At the practical level he argues that enforced assimilation never works and tends to lead to the psychological and moral disorientation of those subjected to it.

For Kymlicka, cultural minorities are of different kinds. Some are territorially concentrated, others are not. Some are voluntary immigrants, some reluctant refugees, yet others are forcibly brought to the country. Kymlicka thinks that the cultural claims of these and other groups have different moral weights. National minorities have the strongest, and voluntary immigrants the weakest claim; the rest fall in between. A national minority or a minority nation refers to a group that is territorially concentrated, was previously self-governing and later incorporated, is institutionally complete, shares a common language and culture, and is in general a distinct cultural unit with a strong sense of collective identity. Such groups as the Indians, the Puerto Ricans, the Chicanos and the native Hawaiians in the United States, the Quebecois and the aboriginal communities in Canada, and the Maoris in New Zealand belong to this category. For Kymlicka, a minority nation is logically no different from the majority nation. Both alike have societal cultures, are territorially concentrated, institutionally more or less complete, and have a strong sense of nationhood. Relations between them are like those between two independent states and should be settled by peaceful negotiations (*ibid.*, p. 167). National minorities, argues Kymlicka, should have a right to maintain themselves as distinct cultural units and enjoy self-government. Since they are vulnerable to majority domination, ensuring them equality might require placing restrictions on the majority, such as limiting the movement of its members and capital. National minorities should also enjoy the rights to make their own cultural and language policies, restrict the sale of land, and so forth.

Since culture is only valuable as a condition for the development of autonomy, Kymlicka insists that minority nations should be required to be internally liberal as otherwise they would undermine the very basis of their right to collective autonomy. They should ensure basic civil and political liberties, equality between the sexes, the right of exit, and so on. If they do not, the wider liberal society has a 'right and a responsibility' to speak out against their illiberal practices, encourage internal liberal opinion, and in general to put pressure on them to mend their ways (*ibid.*, pp. 168, 171). While it should appreciate that it might not fully understand minority cultures, that liberality is a 'matter of degree', and that liberal institutions 'can only really work if liberal beliefs have been internalized', it cannot remain inactive when basic liberal values are involved. It should not use force because that amounts to 'paternalistic colonialism' and even 'aggression' in such a quasi-international context, except when there is a gross and systematic violation of basic rights as in the case of slavery and genocide (*ibid.*, pp. 167ff).

For Kymlicka, immigrants are at the other end of the moral spectrum. They are ethnic not national minorities, are neither territorially concentrated nor institutionally complete, and their culture is now cut off from its natural moorings and cannot be reproduced in their new environment. Since they have come to better their prospects, it is also in their interest to integrate into the new society. Kymlicka is not content to say that for these and other practical reasons immigrants are unable to exercise, and should therefore desist from asserting, their right to their culture. He advances the strange theoretical argument that they have in fact waived that right by voluntarily leaving their country of origin. The latter is their cultural home, and leaving it implies that they have chosen to live by the culture of their adopted country. Since culture is for Kymlicka a primary good, it is difficult to see how one can abandon one's right to it any more than to one's life or liberty. Even if the receiving country had made this clear in advance, the question would remain whether it was right to do so. Besides in these days of mass migration, it makes little sense to say that one's culture is confined to one's country. Here as elsewhere Kymlicka reflects the long-familiar liberal tendency noted earlier to draw a sharp contrast between ethnic groups and nations and privilege the latter. He also draws too neat a distinction between immigrants and citizens. The former are not casual visitors but have come to settle, and are what I might call probationary citizens or citizens-in-waiting. They are not therefore qualitatively different from, and may rightly make the same cultural and other claims as, other citizens.

Kymlicka argues that while immigrants can claim polyethnic rights such as the right not to be discriminated against, to be exempted from laws that unjustly disadvantage them, and to maintain their languages, they cannot claim national rights to self-government and cultural autonomy. Since they have waived their right to their culture, liberal society is right to 'compel' them to respect liberal principles:

> I do not think it is wrong for liberal states to insist that immigration entails accepting the legitimacy of state enforcement of liberal principles, so long as immigrants know this in advance, and nonetheless voluntarily choose to come. (*ibid.*, p. 170)

In contrast to new immigrants, such older groups as the Amish, the Mennonites and the Hasidic Jews who might have been allowed to maintain their illiberal institutions have a strong claim to maintain these. We might regret the tacit or explicit assurances given to them in the past, but should continue to respect these unless they follow grotesquely unjust or inhuman practices.

Kymlicka asks how a multinational and polyethnic society is to be held together. Polyethnicity is easily dealt with by integrating ethnic minorities into the national culture. Multinationality poses problems. The majority and minority nations do not share a common culture, and often not even a common language. Their historical memories too are different and often divisive. They might sometimes share common values, but these are not enough to overcome their deep differences. If they loved and took pride in their diversity, that would help. But it is never enough and is in any case put under constant strain by endless negotiations about such matters as constitutional arrangements, distribution of powers and resources and the range of permissible diversity. For Kymlicka, the only hope for such a society lies in developing a 'fairly strong sense' of mutual identification between its major groups and encouraging them to wish to continue to live together (*ibid.*, p. 191). If it manages to do this it has a future; if not it will break up.

Kymlicka's liberal theory of multiculturalism which I have briefly outlined above has the same logical structure as Raz's. He defines liberalism in terms of certain capacities and values and argues that culture plays a vital role in fostering them. Liberalism both grounds and regulates respect for culture, showing why the latter deserves respect and within what limits. There are also, however, important differences between Raz and Kymlicka arising out of their different conceptions of culture and autonomy. Kymlicka equates cultural community with national community, ties liberalism and nationalism fairly closely, and is a liberal nationalist in a way that Raz is generally not. Since Kymlicka thinks in nationalist terms, he divides cultural groups into national and non-national or ethnic groups, and assigns them different degrees of moral importance, rights and status. This mode of thinking is largely alien to Raz. Kymlicka is therefore far more concerned about national minorities such as the indigenous peoples and the Quebecois than Raz is. So far as immigrants are concerned, Kymlicka is less tolerant of their claims to cultural autonomy than Raz is. However, this has nothing to do with the logic of his liberalism and is a consequence of his contingent and detachable view on the nature of immigration. Since Kymlicka defines autonomy in less austere terms than Raz, his liberalism has a greater space for diversity. However, unlike Kymlicka, Raz is prepared to admit that well-being is as important as autonomy and that the good life can be lived in a non-autonomous culture. In spite of his stronger notion of autonomy, Raz's liberalism is therefore more tolerant of certain kinds of cultural diversity than Kymlicka's.

Like any such theory, Kymlicka's theory of multicultural society aims to provide a set of general principles for assessing the claims of and regulating the relations between different cultural groups within society. It is therefore best judged in terms of the coherence of these principles. As we have seen, Kymlicka's liberalism is articulated in terms of three basic propositions, namely that human beings have an essential interest in leading the good life, that the latter should be lived from within, and that its ends and projects should be revisable. He is ambiguous about the philosophical status of these propositions. Sometimes he says that they represent basic liberal beliefs; at other times he takes them to be general truths about human life and argues or implies that, because liberalism is based on them, it is truer or rationally more defensible than other political doctrines. In the first case, liberal beliefs and values have no authority over nonliberal members of society. The only reason for asking nonliberals to respect these is that they represent the beliefs and values of the majority, a form of moral positivism that violates their integrity and makes a falsely homogenized majority the arbiter of moral values. In the second case, we are right to ask nonliberals to respect liberal values provided that Kymlicka's defence of them is coherent and convincing. I suggest that it is not.

Kymlicka's first proposition that human beings have an essential or vital interest in leading the good life is unproblematic and even 'banal' as he claims, if the 'good life' means a life one likes living and finds enjoyable. However, this is not how he generally defines it. Following Dworkin he takes it to mean a life that 'has all the things that a good life should have', one whose ends and projects one believes to be worth pursuing. It is not obvious that all human beings as a matter of empirical fact aim to lead such a life. Some are content to drift through life, or do not want 'all the things' that a good life should have, or prefer an unreflective and traditional life, or treat life as a perpetual gamble, or aim to get their way by whatever means they can without running into trouble. Perhaps, like Raz, Kymlicka thinks that such a life is too incoherent to succeed, in which case the point needs to be argued. It is more likely that he does not consider such a life worthy and thinks that human beings should lead the good life as he defines it. This is a strong normative assertion, and needs to be established. It is also a little odd to say that every one has an 'interest' in leading the good life, for interest cannot be defined and its content determined without some reference to the good life in the first instance.

His second proposition is more persuasive but not in the form in which he states it. The very idea of living one's life from the inside presupposes a distinction between inside and outside, and hence a particular manner of separating oneself from others, and that in turn rests on a wider theory of individuation and the concomitant view of moral agency. Many cultures do not draw such a distinction, and even in liberal societies it gets blurred in some of the most intimate areas of interpersonal relations. Furthermore, it is not clear why the good life should be lived from the inside. One might live by certain beliefs not because they are sincerely held, itself a problematic concept in view of the fact that we are not always entirely clear about the content of our beliefs and our reasons and motives for holding them, but for several different reasons. One might live in a certain way because one thinks that it will please God and, although one is unsure of His existence, one is not prepared to take the risk; or because one thinks that, in such momentous matters as how to live, it is better to trust traditional wisdom even when one has some doubts about it; or because one is socially required to do so and the idea of forming one's beliefs oneself has never crossed one's mind. These are not at all eccentric cases but true of many men and women in our own and other societies. Indeed, the idea of leading life from the inside is essentially Protestant, and played only a limited role in classical Athens and Rome, medieval Europe, Catholic Christianity and non-western civilizations. The interiorisation of morality that it presupposes is conspicuous by its absence in some of these societies. 'Inside' and 'outside' are vague spatial metaphors and need to be more fully spelt out if they are to carry the weight Kymlicka places on them.

A similar difficulty bedevils Kymlicka's third proposition that one's beliefs should be revisable. Admittedly, he does not say, like J. S. Mill, that they should be periodically revised and their grounds brought to consciousness, but rather that the possibility should be kept open and that one should hold one's beliefs in that spirit. Since we are fallible beings and our self-understanding is subject to change, Kymlicka is right to stress this point. However, precisely because we are fallible, we might sometimes decide to commit ourselves irrevocably to a certain way of life, values, persons, projects or relationships by taking vows and pledges or making firm resolutions in order to resist life's unavoidable temptations, to build up resistance to periodic doubts, or to avoid being confused by too many counter-arguments or paralyzed by the infinite openness of options. We might find good reasons to give up some of these commitments in future, but that is very different from saying that we had an open mind about them when we made them or during the time we held them. Beliefs vary greatly in their nature, demands and what they mean to us. To say that they should all be revisable is to miss their crucial differences and to ignore the complex ways in which we navigate our way through life.

Kymlicka's defence of the basic liberal principles, then, is unlikely to convince nonliberals, who could therefore legitimately complain of moral intolerance when asked to live by them. And even if they accepted the principles on prudential grounds, they would not sincerely believe in them and lead the required liberal life from the inside. Unable to lead the good life as Kymlicka defines it, they could rightly complain that their essential human interests are being systematically violated. Kymlicka faces a further difficulty. Since he justifies liberal political institutions and practices on the basis of his three principles and ties the two too closely, he is unable to give nonliberals good reasons for respecting these institutions and practices. This was one of the major reasons why Rawls decided to separate the two and restrict liberalism to the political realm. Kymlicka is right to argue that Rawls's project fails, but wrong to think that the project itself is inherently misconceived or that his own comprehensive liberalism provides a theoretically more satisfactory alternative.

As we saw in our discussion of Raz, individuals relate to their cultures in many different ways. They may see it as an ancestral inheritance to be cherished and transmitted, or as a sacred trust to be preserved in a spirit of piety and gratitude, and so forth. Many of these cultural communities are not averse to self-criticism and change, but they do so in a spirit of humility rather than self-creation, and in terms of the central values and principles of their culture rather than some allegedly transcultural norms autonomously derived by an unanchored and self-sufficient reason. Kymlicka takes no account of these and other ways of relating to one's culture and sets up the liberal view as a universal model. He expects Amerindians, Inuits, Orthodox Jews and others to view and relate to their cultures in the same way that the liberal does to his, and defends them only to the extent that they behave as respectable liberals. As he puts it, 'I have defended the right of national minorities to maintain their culturally distinct societies, but only if, and in so far as, they are themselves governed by liberal principles' (*ibid.*, p. 153). Since Kymlicka does not appreciate them in their own terms, he does not respect them in their authentic otherness. While defending them he also subtly subverts their inner balance and identity and transforms them into something they are not. If we are to be fair to both liberal and nonliberal cultures, we need a theoretical framework capable of appreciating and accommodating *plural* understandings of culture.

Like Raz, Kymlicka gives a coherent account of the value of culture but not of cultural diversity. He shows why human beings need a stable culture but not why they also need access to other cultures. His main argument for cultural diversity is that it increases our range of options. This implies that other cultures are important to us only as possible objects of choice and have no value or lose it when no longer options for us. I shall later explore the difficulties of such an instrumental approach to cultural diversity. Even in Kymlicka's own terms, his argument for cultural diversity amounts to little. He says that we are deeply shaped, though of course not determined, by our culture, and that our primary concern should be not to explore and experiment with other cultures but to evaluate our own cultural beliefs and practices and in general to move around within them. This means that other cultures can have little real meaning for us as options or even as dialogical interlocutors. It is only when we are culturally self-critical and feel the need for alternative perspectives that other cultures begin to mean something to us. Like Raz, the kind of case Kymlicka makes for one's own culture renders it difficult for him to make one for cherishing others.

As we saw earlier, Kymlicka establishes a hierarchy of minority cultural rights. National minorities enjoy the more or less full complement of cultural rights. Such involuntarily brought and territorially dispersed groups as the American blacks and the indentured Indians in the Caribbean, Fiji and South Africa have fewer but fairly substantial rights. Refugees enjoy still fewer but considerable cultural rights because human beings should not be required to 'give up their culture in order to avoid dire poverty', and because we, who are partly responsible for their predicament, should compensate for this by allowing them to recreate their societal cultures. Immigrants who come voluntarily have the fewest rights.

It is difficult to see what general principles inform this hierarchy of rights. Kymlicka appeals to such disparate criteria as territorial concentration, history of independent existence, institutional completeness, past commitments, consent, the level of poverty in the immigrant's country, and the receiving country's degree of responsibility for it. Some of these criteria are highly contentious and do not admit of agreed answers; for example, the third and the last. They also conflict and we need to find ways of striking a judicious balance between them, a question on which Kymlicka offers no guidance. He seems to think that a more fully worked-out theory of justice than his would do the job. I doubt it because no theory of justice can deal with heterogeneous and mutually irreducible claims. Indeed one might even wonder if many of these criteria are a matter of justice at all. Except in the cases of conquest and colonization, national boundaries, for example, are generally not a matter of justice, and nor therefore are the claims of immigrants or even refugees and asylum-seekers, which are best dealt with in terms of the principles of humanity and generosity (Carens, 1997; Forst, 1997).

General comments

Three contemporary thinkers discussed above have perceptively reinterpreted, refined or even redefined liberalism to make it more hospitable to cultural and moral plurality. I have argued that although their thought marks a considerable advance over that of their classical predecessors and opens up new lines of inquiry, it remains inadequate. In each case the nature of and the reasons for their inadequacy have been indicated. It would be useful to highlight several common tendencies in their and other liberal writings which prevent liberals from developing a coherent and persuasive response to cultural and moral diversity.

- First, although liberals have begun to appreciate the cultural embeddedness of human beings, they still have considerable difficulty overcoming the traditional transcultural view of them. For Hobbes, Locke, Bentham, even J. S. Mill and others, human beings are naturally endowed with certain wants, needs and capacities, and social life either merely realizes these or at best adds new ones to them. Although Raz, Kymlicka and even Rawls rightly challenge this view and appreciate the profound ways in which culture shapes, structures, reconstitutes and channels human wants and capacities, they still remain too deeply committed to it to exploit their insights fully. Take their account of autonomy. As they understand it, culture helps individuals develop their capacity for autonomy, which then transcends it and views it and the wider world untainted by its provenance. This is a misleading account of the relation between the two. Although human beings are not determined by their culture in the sense of being unable to take a critical view of it and appreciate and learn from others, they are not transcendental beings contingently and externally related to it either. Their culture shapes them in countless ways, forms them into certain kinds of persons, and cultivates certain attachments, affections, moral and psychological dispositions, taboos and modes of reasoning. Far from being purely formal and culturally neutral, their capacity for autonomy is structured in a particular way, functions within flexible but determinate limits, and defines and assesses options in certain ways. Although Raz appreciates this more than most other liberals, the ghost of a transcultural and culturally untainted power of autonomy continues to shadow even his thought. Liberals cannot take a transcultural view of human powers and expect culture to play an obligingly passive role in developing them.

- Second, directly or indirectly and subtly or crudely, liberals continue to absolutize liberalism. Hence their persistent tendency to make it their central frame of reference, divide all ways of life into liberal and nonliberal, equate the latter with illiberal, and to talk of tolerating and rarely of respecting or cherishing them. The crudity of this distinction would become clear if someone were to divide all religions into Christianity and non-Christianity and equate the latter with anti-Christianity. If liberals are to do justice to alternative ways of life and thought, they need to break away from this crude binary distinction. They cannot do so unless they stop absolutizing the liberal way of life and making it their central point of comparison. And that in turn requires them to accept the full force of moral and cultural pluralism and acknowledge that the good life can be lived in several different ways, some better than others in certain respects but none is the best. Once they do so, their perspective undergoes a profound change. They would deabsolutize though not relativize liberal ways of life and thought, see these as both valuable and limited, and take a critical view of them. The spirit of critical self-understanding opens up a vitally necessary theoretical and moral space for a critical but sympathetic dialogue with other ways of life, now seen not as objects of willing or grudging tolerance but as conversational partners in a common search for a deeper understanding of the nature, potentialities and grandeur of human life.

- Third, in their discussions of how to treat the so-called nonliberal ways of life, liberal writers adopt one of two strategies. Some, mostly of teleological persuasion, confront nonliberals with a full-blooded liberal vision and attack them for failing to measure up to it (Barry, 1991, pp. 23–39). Others, many but not all of whom are deontological liberals, thin down liberal principles to what they take to be their minimum content, and make tolerance of nonliberal cultures conditional upon their acceptance of it. As seen earlier the first strategy is incoherent, rests on circular reasoning, and has been a source of much violence and moral arrogance. Although the second is better, it too is flawed. If the minimum that the liberal insists upon is essentially liberal in nature and cannot be shown to be morally binding on all, it cannot be demanded of nonliberals without violating their moral autonomy. If, on the other hand, it is universally binding, then there is nothing particularly liberal about it except the contingent historical fact that liberals happened to appreciate its importance more than others. In other words liberals need to rise to a higher level of abstraction than they have done so far, and distinguish between a universal and a liberal moral minimum, insisting on the former in all circumstances and on the latter when it does not violate the universal minimum and can be shown to be central to a liberal society's historically inherited cultural character.

Liberals often argue that since the modern western society is liberal, it is entitled to ask its members to live by basic liberal values. Even if we accepted this premise, deep disagreements would remain concerning what these values are, and we would get caught up in an interminable and unnecessary quasi-theological controversy concerning what a 'truly' liberal society stands for, what its 'real' identity consists in, what principles it 'cannot' betray, and so on. There is no obvious reason, however, why we should accept the liberal premise in the first instance. Modern western society includes nonliberal groups such as conservatives, socialists, communists, Marxists, religious communities, indigenous peoples, long-established ethnic communities and newly-arrived immigrants who cannot be excluded from its self-definition by an ideologically biased act of linguistic appropriation. Although all its institutions are touched by the liberal spirit, some are not and cannot be fully liberal; for example religion, the family, and perhaps schools. The fact that its political and economic institutions and some of its social practices are liberal does not make its entire way of life liberal any more than the fact that the state is largely secular entitles us to call the whole society secular. Again, liberals are not and perhaps cannot be liberal in all areas of life, and entertain and live by nonliberal ideas, a mixture of liberal and nonliberal ideas, or even by instincts, faith and habits in matters relating to intimate interpersonal relations, moral values, ethnic, political or national loyalties, and religious beliefs. In short as is only to be expected in a society with a long and rich history, contemporary western society is characterized by an interplay of several mutually regulating and historically sedimented impulses, some liberal, some nonliberal, some others a mixture of both, yet others too complex to fall into either category. Its members harbour and sometimes feel attached to all of these, and attempts to simplify their identity by purging it of all but the liberal impulses deprive them of their history, do injustice to their complex self-understanding, arouse avoidable hostility against liberalism, and rarely succeed.[11]

To call contemporary western society liberal is not only to homogenize and oversimplify it but also to give liberals a moral and cultural monopoly of it and treat the rest as illegitimate and troublesome intruders. When one then goes on to say that *because* the society is liberal, it should or should not allow certain practices or be guided by certain principles, one is guilty of bad logic and even bad faith. One abstracts a particular, albeit an extremely important aspect of modern society, turns it into its sole defining feature, and uses it to delegitimize other moral sensibilities and reshape the entire society in its image. One also gives the liberal the double advantage of setting nonliberals the challenging task of defending their principles to his satisfaction while more or less exempting himself from it. Earlier writers called contemporary western society open, free, public, civil or humane rather than liberal. These terms are ideologically less narrow and biased, and socially more inclusive. They too, however, are not free of difficulties, and that only goes to show both the danger and the futility of bringing the entire society under a single description. Paradoxical as it may seem, it is the glory of liberal (that is, tolerant, open and free) society that it is not, and does not need or even seek to become, exclusively or entirely liberal (that is, committed to a strong sense of autonomy, individualism, self-creation, and so on). Liberal writers misunderstand its inner logic and strength when they seek to turn it into one.

4

Conceptualizing Human Beings

We have seen in the earlier chapters that neither naturalism nor cultur-alism is able to offer a coherent theory of moral and cultural diversity. They are one-sided extremes and feed off each other's exaggerations. Full-blooded naturalism insists that human beings are basically the same in all societies and that their differences are shallow and morally inconsequential. This provokes a legitimate reaction in the form of cul-turalism, whose similar exaggerations in turn lend credibility to natu-ralism. Each is partial and both undermines and reinforces the other. If we are to give a coherent account of moral and cultural diversity, we need to critique and open up each to make a secure space for the other, and to develop on that basis a more satisfactory theory of human beings. Raz, Kymlicka and others have paved the way and what follows is an attempt to build on their insights.

Human nature

The question whether human beings have a nature cannot be answered unless we are agreed on what we mean by human nature.[1] This is not easy. Some writers take a substantive or thick view, and others a largely formal view of it. Some take a teleological and others a mechanistic view. For some it determines, and for others it only disposes human beings to act in certain ways. Some define it to mean all that character-izes human beings including what they share in common with animals; for others it only refers to what is distinctive to them and marks them off as a distinct species. Given these and other differences, the best way to discuss whether or not human beings have a nature is to concentrate on the minimum on which different views agree or can be expected to agree. The teleological and the mechanistic views, for example, give very different accounts of human nature, but both are agreed that human nature is not inert or passive and that to have a nature is to be inclined to act in a certain way, which they then go on to interpret in their own different ways.

Such a minimalist view of human nature has several advantages. It encompasses a wide variety of views and does not arbitrarily exclude inconvenient ones. It is true that no view, however minimalist, can do equal justice to all of them, for it has to draw a line somewhere and cannot avoid some degree of selectivity. However, as long as the selectivity is based on good reasons and is not too narrow, it provides the only practical basis of discussion. Second, the minimalist view enables us to concentrate on the crucial questions raised by the concept of human nature without getting sidetracked into important but irrelevant questions about its content and mode of operation. Third, if we can show that the concept is problematic even in its minimalist sense, it is bound to be even more so when defined in stronger or more substantive terms.

Minimally, the term human nature refers to those permanent and universal capacities, desires and dispositions – in short, properties – that all human beings share by virtue of belonging to a common species. The properties are permanent in the sense that they continue to belong to human beings as long as they remain what they are, and that, if they were to undergo changes, human nature itself would be deemed to have changed. They are universal in the sense that they are shared by human beings in all ages and societies. This does not mean that there are no exceptions, but rather that those lacking them are to that extent defective or at least not normal. The properties are acquired by virtue of belonging to the human species and not socially or culturally derived. They belong to human beings 'by nature', as part of their inherited physical and psychological constitution, and constitute their species heritage. Although society might modify them and regulate their expression, it can never altogether eliminate them or alter their inherent tendencies. Finally, the properties are not inert and indeterminate but have a specific character or content and operate in a particular manner. To say that all human beings have a propensity or instinct to preserve themselves is to say that they tend to do all they can to avoid

death and life-threatening situations. And to say that they seek to realize themselves, posses an inherent love of God, strive for happiness,
have an inclination to do evil, or are naturally curious is to say that they
would, as a rule, be inclined to act in a manner intimated by these
impulses.

Human beings do seem to have a nature in this sense. They have a
common physical and mental structure and all that follows from it.
They share a common anatomy and physiological processes, stand
erect, posses an identical set of sense organs which operate in an identical manner, have common bodily-derived desires, and so forth. The
fact that they are embodied in a particular way is not an incidental biological fact devoid of larger significance, but structures their perceptions of themselves, the non-human species and the world at large and
shapes their self-understanding. Human beings also share a common
mental structure and possess capacities such as rationality, ability to
form concepts, to learn language and employ complex forms of speech,
self-consciousness, self-reflection, and so on. These capacities do not
remain isolated but inform all aspects of human life and give rise to,
and are in turn shaped by, new capacities, emotions and dispositions. If
some human beings do not happen to possess the latter, they nevertheless have the potential to acquire them. These include the capacity to
will, judge, fantasize, dream dreams, build theories, construct myths,
feel nostalgic about the past, anticipate future events, make plans, and
so on and on. At a different level human beings are also capable of a
vast range of moral and non-moral emotions such as love, hate, anger,
rage, sadness, sorrow, pity, compassion, meanness, generosity, self-
hatred, self-esteem and vanity, and of such dispositions as curiosity, the
tendency to explore new areas of experience, to seek human company,
to ask questions and to seek justification of their own and others'
actions. Although these capacities, emotions and dispositions are distinct and have their unique modes of operation, they are interrelated and
both partially presuppose and contradict each other. Human nature is
not made up of discrete, readily specifiable and mutually compatible
properties as many philosophers have thought, but a complex whole
composed of related but often dissonant capacities and dispositions
which cannot all be reduced to a single master or foundational capacity, desire or disposition. Reason itself takes several different forms, of
which theoretical and practical reasons are but two, and they are not all
reducible to so many different expressions of an allegedly generic and
neutral reason. And the fact that humans can reason does not by itself

explain why they can also construct myths, dream dreams and imagine wholly new experiences.

Thanks to their shared physical and mental structure, human beings also share certain basic needs and common conditions of growth. They require a prolonged period of nurture and all that that implies. They also need to acquire a large body of skills, abilities and dispositions as well as a reasonably coherent conception of the world in order to hold themselves together, build up a stable self, and cope with the inevitable demands of personal and social life. In order to acquire these, they require a stable natural and social environment, close personal relationships, a measure of emotional security, moral norms, and so forth.

Human beings also go through common life-experiences. They mature slowly, reach their peak and begin to suffer losses of or diminutions in their physical and mental powers, grow old, and die. They see their loved ones die, anticipate their own death, experience joys and sorrows and moments of elation and happiness as well as disappointments and frustrations, and undergo changes of mood. They fall in and out of love, are drawn to some and not to others, cannot realize all their dreams and satisfy all their desires, makes mistakes, possess limited sympathies, and fall prey to temptations. They carry a large and dimly grasped unconscious all through their lives, and sometimes not only cannot make sense of themselves but are positively puzzled by their thoughts and feelings.

Human beings, then, do seem to have a nature in the sense defined earlier – that is, capacities, emotions and dispositions which are universal, relatively permanent, acquired as part of their species-heritage or by nature, and which tend to generate certain kinds of actions. Since human beings have a certain physical and mental structure with in-built tendencies and limits, and since they go through common life experiences and life-cycles, it would be odd if they did not have a nature. If we encountered a 'human being' who was six inches or six meters tall, immortal, had unusual sense organs, never felt an emotion or fluctuations of moods, spoke a refined language at birth, never made a mistake or faced a temptation throughout his or her life, or possessed no sense of selfhood or subjectivity, we would feel profoundly disorientated in their presence and would consider that person either an aberrant member of our species or, more likely, that of another. To have a nature is to have a potency for action, a tendency to behave in a certain way, and to be subject to certain constitutional limitations. All these are true of human beings.

While acknowledging that human beings have a shared nature, we may legitimately question its conceptualization, interpretation, the explanatory and normative weight put upon it, and the ways in which it is related to culture in much of traditional philosophy. First, human nature does not exhaust all that characterizes human beings as a species. It refers to properties that inhere in or are internal to human beings and which they share in their unique isolation, excluding those that lie between or outside of them altogether. These latter include such fundamental facts as countless ties to the non-human world, being subject to ecological and other constraints, and being part of a universe structured in a certain way. They also include the fact that human beings must work to stay alive, that they are shaped by their geography, are born in a particular historical epoch and shaped by their history, live among other human beings who constrain them in various ways, and so on. These and other aspects of human existence are not internal to human beings but external or interpersonal, and form part not of human nature but of the human condition or predicament. Not surprisingly they receive little attention in many a discussion of human nature. Since they profoundly shape the context and conduct of human life and are inextricably tied up with what is internal to human beings, traditional accounts of human nature which generally ignore these cannot give an adequate account either of human beings in general or even of human nature. In other words, a conception or a theory of human beings must include, but not remain restricted to, a view of human nature.

Second, the traditional account of human nature is deeply ahistorical. It assumes that human beings begin their history endowed with a certain set of properties, and does not adequately explain how they come to acquire these in the first instance. It either leaves the question unanswered, or appeals to God with all the attendant difficulties in that, or more plausibly invokes natural evolution. This last explanation postulates a fairly neat division between evolution and history. In the former, nature holds sway, creates humans as we more or less know them today, and brings them to the threshold of history when they begin to take charge of their development.

But this is a misleading account of human nature. Evolution does not occur behind the backs of human beings, for they are active participants in it. As they acquire a posture broadly resembling their current one and some capacity to understand themselves and their world, they increasingly engage in a creative interaction with their natural environment and change it in harmony with their needs. As their environment is humanized, it provides a relatively safe island of stability which they strive to humanize yet further. In the course of this dialectic with nature, they change both themselves and their world, develop new forms of social organization, and acquire new capacities and dispositions. These historically acquired capacities and dispositions are institutionalized and reproduced during successive generations, and become part of their species heritage or nature.

Almost all distinctive human capacities and dispositions are products of such a dialectic. Our primitive ancestors possessed little of what we call reason. They had some capacity for a largely instrumental understanding of their environment, which gave them an advantage over animals, but more sophisticated forms of reason developed later as products of a semi-conscious dialectic between society and nature. This is also the case with such human capacities as willing, judging, formulating ideals, dreaming dreams of a perfect society and myth-making, as well as such motives as greed, striving for domination, and the desire for self-respect and social preeminence. What is distinctive to humans is not inherent in, nor entailed by, such primitive cognitive equipment as they acquired through their natural evolution. The equipment did start them off on their historical journey, but all that developed later was largely a human achievement. Much of human nature is thus not a product of nature but of human struggle. It is natural in the sense that it is acquired by virtue of belonging to the human species, but it is not natural in the sense that it is a result of the efforts of the species itself and forms part of its process of self-creation.

Third, contrary to what most philosophers have assumed, all attempts to discover human nature beyond what is inherent in their physico-mental structure are open to two great difficulties. Since human beings have always led organized lives, their nature has been so deeply shaped by layers of social influences that we have no direct access to it in its raw or pristine form, and cannot easily detach what is natural from what is manmade or social. Some of those who appreciated the difficulty mistakenly thought they could gain access to human nature by examining the behaviour of our humanoid ancestors, primitive people, children, civilized people in times of social disintegration, or what is universally common. Since our humanoid ancestors have left no records of their thoughts and feelings, we have no knowledge of their nature, and in any case there is no good reason to assume that we must necessarily share a common nature with them. So-called primitive peoples are socially organized and shaped, and do not reveal raw human nature. Children are subject to deep social influences from the moment of their birth and even perhaps conception. When societies disintegrate, their members' behaviour does not reveal raw human nature but their socially shaped character in a climate of chaos and uncertainty. And what is common to all mankind could as well be a result of common processes of socialization rather than an expression of a common nature. In short, human nature is not a brute and empirically verifiable fact, but an inference or a theory which we have no reliable means of corroborating (Geertz, 1973, pp. 35 f, 49 §).

Another great difficulty relates to the students of human nature, who are themselves deeply shaped by their society and remain prone to the understandable tendency to mistake the normal and the familiar for the natural. This tendency is further compounded by the fact that an appeal to human nature has unique explanatory and normative advantages. To say that a particular form of behaviour is natural is to forswear the need to look for further or another explanation. And to say that certain values or ways of life are alone consistent with human nature is to give them a moral finality and to delegitimize alternative values and ways of life. Even the most rigorous and scrupulous philosophers have sometimes availed themselves of the easy advantages offered by appeals to human nature, and argued on the basis of little hard evidence that human beings have an innate tendency to pursue knowledge, love God, maximize pleasure, seek self-realization, and so on and that only such a life gives them 'true' happiness or fulfilment and is worthy of them. This does not mean that we should not appeal to human nature or seek to discover it, but rather that all references to it should be subjected to the strictest scrutiny and viewed with a healthy dose of skepticism.

Fourth and finally, human beings are culturally embedded in the sense that they are born into, raised in and deeply shaped by their cultural communities.[2] Thanks to human creativity, geographical conditions, historical experiences, and so on, different societies develop different systems of meaning, ways of looking at the world, ideals of excellence, traits of temperament and forms of moral and social life, giving different orientation and structure to universally shared human capacities and desires and cultivating wholly new ones of their own. Although skin colour, gender, height and other physical features are universally shared, they are all differently conceptualized and acquire different meaning and significance in different societies. In some societies skin colour is given a deeper metaphysical meaning and made the basis of a differential distribution of power and status, in others it is not even noticed. In some societies male–female distinctions are drawn fairly sharply; in others they are seen as overlapping categories, each sex carrying a bit of the other within itself, so that these societies draw no rigid distinction between masculine and feminine qualities or even between homosexuality and heterosexuality. In some, sexuality is viewed as a natural bodily function like 'scratching an itch', as Bentham once put it, and subjected to the fewest constraints; in others it is invested with cosmic significance, viewed as a quasi-divine activity of generating life, and surrounded with mystique and taboos. Even something as basic and inevitable as death is viewed and experienced differently in different cultures. In some it is a brute fact of life, like the falling of leaves or the diurnal setting of the sun, and arouses no strong emotions; in some others it is a release from the world of sorrow and embraced with joy; in yet others it is a symbol of human weakness, a constant reminder of inadequate human mastery over nature, and accepted with such varied emotions as regret, puzzle, incomprehension and bitterness. Different cultures, again, take different views of human life and the individual's relation to his or her body, leading to very different attitudes to suicide and manners of committing it.

Differences at the level of human capacities, emotions, motivations, values, ideals of excellence and so forth are just as great and in some respects even greater.[3] Although all human beings have the capacity to reason, different cultures cherish and cultivate different forms of it. The Greek *logos*, the Roman *ratio*, the Cartesian *cogito*, the Hobbesian reckoning with consequences, the Benthamite arithmetical reasoning, the Hegelian dialectic and the Indian *buddhi* and *prajnà* represent very different forms of human reason. Some cultures disjoin reason and feeling whereas others find their separation incomprehensible. Some distinguish between theoretical and practical reason or between thinking and willing, whereas others believe that reason has both theoretical and practical impulses built into its very structure. Different cultures also encourage different emotions and feelings. Some develop the concept of conscience and know what guilt and remorse mean; others find these emotions incomprehensible. Some have a poorly developed sense of history and cannot make sense of the desire to gain historical immortality or leave a footnote or a paragraph in history. Some others lack a sense of tradition and cannot make sense of the desire to be worthy of one's ancestors, loyal to their memories, or to cherish their heritage. Although all human beings require a prolonged period of nurture, the mode of upbringing and periodization of life vary greatly. In some cultures children graduate into adulthood without passing through adolescence, in others they never outgrow the latter. Some stress sharp individuation, self-enclosure and a tightly centred self; others encourage overlapping selves, openness to others, and a loosely held self.

Different cultures, then, define and constitute human beings and come to terms with the basic problems of human life in their own different ways. Cultures are not superstructures built upon identical and unchanging foundations, or manifestations of a common human essence, but unique human creations that reconstitute and give different meaning and orientation to those properties that all human beings share in common, add new ones of their own, and give rise to different kinds of human beings. Since human beings are culture-creating and capable of creative self-transformation, they cannot passively inherit a shared nature in the same way that animals do.

We might press the point further. As members of a cultural community, human beings *acquire* certain tendencies and dispositions, in some cases as deep and powerful as those they are deemed to possess by nature. Human beings do seek to preserve themselves, but they might develop such a strong religious commitment or patriotic spirit that they think nothing of dying for their religion or their country. They have now acquired a 'second nature' which overrides their 'natural' nature. Since the willingness to die for one's religion or country is not universally shared, it is not a part of universal human nature. However, since it is part of their culturally derived nature, it constitutes their culturally specific or shared human nature. There is no reason why we cannot say with some Chinese philosophers that some components of human nature vary from culture to culture.

The same thing also happens at the individual level. Human beings might so shape themselves that a fierce sense of independence, an uncompromising commitment to integrity, or a passionate love of God or their fellow humans might become woven into their being and become an integral part of their nature. They then not only instinctively and effortlessly act on those inclinations but might even feel helplessly driven by them. These dispositions have the same force as the tendencies deemed to be inherent in their shared human nature, and are just as inseparable and ineradicable from their being. We often call them part of their character to emphasize the fact that they represent their achievements. However, character is not external to who they are, often has the same force as human nature, and constitutes *their* nature.

This means that human beings are articulated at three different but interrelated levels: what they share as members of a common species, what they derive from and share as members of a cultural community, and what they succeed in giving themselves as reflective individuals. All three are parts of their psychological and moral constitution and relate to three different dimensions of their being. What is more, since these are distinctive to them as human beings, they are all part of their human nature. It therefore makes perfect sense to talk of their distinct *individual* natures (as the Hindus and Buddhists do), their nature as members of particular *cultural communities* (as the traditional Chinese do), and their nature as members of the *human species* (as much western thought has done over the centuries). To equate human nature with only the last is to take too narrow a view of it. Worse, it ontologically and morally privileges the species nature and marginalizes the other two.

Basis of cultural diversity

In the light of our discussion the concept of human nature is valid and valuable. It highlights several important facts about human beings, such as that they belong to the natural world, share several features in common, do so not accidentally but by virtue of possessing a common species-derived physical and mental structure, and are constitutionally limited in countless ways and cannot make of themselves what they will. Although for these and other reasons it has a useful explanatory and normative role, its value is limited. Human nature is only a part of, and does not exhaust, the totality of all that human beings share in common. It is largely a product of human self-creation, and although it has a certain degree of permanence, it can be altered over a long period of time. As beings who constantly push against their inherited limits and sometimes succeed in stretching them, their nature is not static and finished but subject to further development. Human nature is also culturally reconstituted and diversified, and is additionally subject to such changes as self-reflective individuals succeed in introducing. All this means that human nature alone can never explain human behaviour or justify a way of life, and that any moral and political theory that does so is inherently flawed.

Human beings share a common nature, common conditions of existence, life experiences, predicament, and so on. They also, however, conceptualize and respond to these in quite different ways and give rise to different cultures. Their identity is a product of a dialectical interplay between the universal and the particular, between what they all share and what is culturally specific. The universally shared features do not impinge on human consciousness and behaviour directly and in their raw form; they are mediated by and acquire different meaning and significance in different cultures. Cultures, however, do not exist in a vacuum nor are they created *ex nihilo*. They are embedded in, and limited by, the universally shared features of human existence including human nature. To be human is to belong both to a common species and to a distinct culture, and one only because of the other. Humans belong to a common species not directly but in a culturally mediated manner. And they belong to a cultural community by virtue of belonging to a common species. They are therefore human in very different ways, neither wholly alike nor wholly different, neither wholly transparent nor wholly opaque to one another. Their similarities and differences are both important and dialectically related. No theory of human beings can give a full account of them unless it is accompanied by a theory of culture; the reverse is just as true.

When we understand human beings in this way, we do not automatically assume that others are either basically like us as the concept of human nature encourages us to do, or totally different as the concept of cultural determinism or culturalism implies. We approach them on the assumption that they are similar enough to be intelligible and make a dialogue possible, and different enough to be puzzling and make a dialogue necessary. We therefore neither assimilate them to our conception of human nature and deny their particularity, nor place them in a closed world of their own and deny the universality they share with us. By acknowledging their universality and particularity, we acknowledge the obligation to respect *both* their shared humanity and cultural differences. While rejecting the exaggerations and falsehoods of naturalism and culturalism, this view retains their valid insights and finds a secure space for culture within a wider theory of human beings.

As we have seen, much of the dominant tradition of moral and political philosophy gravitated towards monism because of the influence of the following five assumptions, namely:

- the uniformity of human nature;
- the ontological primacy of similarities over differences;
- the socially transcendental character of human nature;

- the total knowability of human nature; and
- human nature as the basis of the good life.

Taken together, these interrelated assumptions encourage a manner of thinking in which one cannot appreciate the depth and importance of cultural differences. Since human similarities alone are deemed to be constitutive of their humanity, their differences have no moral significance and dignity. And since the good life is taken to consist in living up to the demands of human nature, it is assumed to be the same for all and leaves no room for diversity. The fact that human beings entertain different conceptions of the good therefore appears unnatural, and is explained away in terms of such factors as human ignorance, intellectual and moral deficiencies, the hold of vested interests, and geographical and other circumstances.

In the light of our earlier discussion, each of these five assumptions is wholly or partially false. As for the first, we have already seen that the concept of human nature as it has been traditionally defined is too narrow and ahistorical to capture the full content of what constitutes human beings, or what I might call human identity. Furthermore, although human beings share in common certain capacities, desires, experiences, conditions of existence and so forth, they are also cultural beings whose cultures differently develop their universally shared capacities and cultivate additional ones that are unique to them. Their shared humanity and cultural differences interpenetrate and jointly create their human identity. This means that the second assumption is also false. Indeed, since human similarities and differences mediate each other and cannot be disengaged, the question of giving either of them ontological primacy makes no sense. The third assumption is false both because cultures transform and reconstitute human nature, and because human beings in turn constantly transform their cultures and themselves.

The fourth assumption ignores the enormously complex and elusive character of human beings. Different cultures reconstitute human beings in countless different ways, and we can hardly hope to know them all. The future, too, is not closed, and we cannot claim to know in what new directions human beings might develop. As for the last assumption, since human identity is composed of both universally common and culturally specific features, the good life cannot be defined in terms of the former alone. Furthermore, if it is to be morally relevant and practicable, a vision of the good life must take account of the capacities, desires and habits of thought and feelings of those to whom it is recommended. If it has no other basis than the abstractly shared universal properties, it can have no meaning for and carry no conviction with them.

Once we reject or reformulate these and related assumptions, we create a secure space for cultural diversity in our understanding of human beings without losing sight of their shared identity. As thinking beings who seek to make sense of themselves and the world, humans create a system of meaning and significance or culture and organize their lives in terms of it. And since they face different natural and social circumstances, are heirs to different traditions, think and dream differently, possess the capacities for creativity and imagination, and so on, the cultures they create are inescapably diverse in nature. Far from being an aberration or a source of puzzle, cultural diversity is an integral feature of human existence. This is not to say that it is underwritten by human nature as Vico, Herder and others argue and might not one day disappear, but rather that given the kinds of beings humans have made of themselves, cultural diversity has tenacious roots and that its unlikely disappearance would signify a radically new stage in their development.

Pluralist universalism

When we understand human beings along the lines I have suggested, the question whether there are universal moral values or norms and how we can judge other cultures appears in a different light. Broadly speaking, the question has received three answers; namely relativism, monism and minimum universalism.[4] Briefly and somewhat crudely, the relativist argues that since moral values are culturally embedded and since each culture is a self-contained whole, they are relative to each society and the search for universal moral values is a logically incoherent enterprise. The monist takes the opposite view that since moral values are derived from human nature, and since the latter is universally common, we can arrive at not only them but also the best way of combining them. The minimum universalist takes the intermediate position, arguing that we can arrive at a body of universal values but that they are few and constitute a kind of floor, or a moral threshold subject to which every society enjoys what Stuart Hampshire calls a 'licence for distinctness'.

In the light of our discussion, relativism and monism are incoherent doctrines. Relativism ignores the cross-culturally shared human properties and is mistaken in its beliefs that a culture is a tightly integrated and self-contained whole, can be neatly individuated, and determines its members. Monism rests on an untenably substantive view of human nature, ignores the impossibility of deriving moral values from human nature alone, fails to appreciate its cultural mediation and reconstitution, and so on. There is much to be said for minimum universalism. It takes a minimalist view of human nature, appreciates both the cultural embeddedness of human beings and their universally shared properties, recognizes that while values can claim universal validity a way of life cannot, and so on. However, it suffers from several limitations. It naively assumes that the minimum universal values do not come into conflict, and that they are univocal and self-explanatory and mean the same thing in different cultures. Since it sees them as a set of uniform, passive and external constraints and uses them as mechanical yardsticks to judge all cultures, it also ignores the fact that different cultures are bound to balance, prioritize and relate them to their thick moral structures in their own different ways. It would seem that a dialectical and pluralist form of minimum universalism offers the most coherent response to moral and cultural diversity. As we shall see there are universal moral values and there is a creative interplay between them and the thick and complex moral structures of different societies, the latter domesticating and pluralizing the former and being in turn reinterpreted and revised in their light, thus leading to what I might call pluralist universalism.

Unlike Plato's Ideas, moral values are not self-subsistent entities occupying a transcendental realm of their own. They refer to things we consider worth cherishing and realizing in our lives. Since judgments of worth are based on reasons, values are things we have good reasons to cherish, which in our well-considered view deserve our allegiance and ought to form part of the good life. Universal moral values are those we have good reasons to believe to be worthy of the allegiance of all human beings, and are in that sense universally valid or binding. Moral values are meant for beings like us and intended to regulate our lives. Reasons relevant to a discussion of them are therefore of several kinds, such as our assessment of our moral capacities, what we take to be our basic tendencies and limits, the likely consequences of pursuing different values, their compatibility, the ease with which they can be combined into a coherent way of life, and the past and present experiences of societies that lived by them.

Although we might try to arrive at universal values by analysing human nature, universal moral consensus and so on, as philosophers have done over the centuries, the more satisfactory way to arrive at them is through a universal or cross-cultural dialogue. Since we are culturally embedded and prone to universalizing our own values, we need the dialogue to counter this tendency and help us rise to the required level of intellectual abstraction. The dialogue also brings together different historical experiences and cultural sensibilities, and ensures that we appreciate human beings in all their richness and that the values we arrive at are as genuinely universal as is humanly possible. It subjects our reasons for holding them to a cross-cultural test and requires us to ensure that they are accessible and acceptable to members of very different cultures. The dialogue has the further advantages that it shows respect for other cultures, offers those involved a motive to comply with the outcome, and gives the values an additional authority derived from democratic validation and a cross-cultural global consensus.

Moral discourse is comparative in nature and involves showing why we should subscribe to one set of values rather than their opposites. We decide in favour of the former not because we can make out a conclusive and irrefutable case for them, for such certainty is rare in human affairs, but because arguments for them are stronger and more convincing than those for their alternatives. It is therefore not enough for critics to say that our arguments are not conclusive; they need to show that a much better or an equally good case can be made out for the opposite value. If they cannot, our decision stands. For example, although we can offer powerful arguments for the equality of the sexes and races, they are unlikely to be conclusive and incontrovertible. However, if we can show, as indeed we can, that those for equality are more coherent, consistent with known facts about human beings, and so on and thus much stronger than those for inequality, we would have said enough to establish that equality is to be preferred over inequality.

Moral values have no foundations in the sense of an indisputable and objective basis, but they do have grounds in the form of intersubjectively discussable reasons and are not arbitrary. And although our defence of them is never conclusive and immune to all conceivable objections, it is conclusive for all practical purposes if it withstands criticism and is stronger than the case that can be made out for opposite values. We can, therefore, legitimately ask others to agree to these values or show us why they find our reasons unconvincing. If they do neither, we can charge them with being unreasonable. Unreasonable people participate in a dialogue and demand reasons from others, but refuse to give or be guided by them when these do not justify their preferred conclusions. Since we are prone to the human frailty of assuming our values to be self-evident and defining reasons in an ethnocentric manner, we should be extremely wary about accusing others of unreasonableness. We should make every effort to enter into their world of thought and give them every opportunity to show why they hold the views they do. If they offer no reasons or ones that are flimsy, self-serving, based on crude prejudices or ignorance of relevant facts, they are being unreasonable and have in effect opted out of the dialogue.

We can all agree that human beings have several unique and worthwhile capacities, such as the ability to think, reason, use language, form visions of the good life, enter into moral relations with one another, be self-critical and achieve increasingly higher levels of excellence. Thanks to these, they understand, control and humanize their natural environment, rise above the automatic and inexorable processes of nature, carve out spaces of freedom, create a world of aesthetic, scientific, literary moral and other great human achievements, give depth and meaning to their lives, and introduce a novel form of existence in the world. As beings capable of creating meaning and values, they deserve to be valued themselves, and have *worth*. It is, of course, possible that their capacities and achievements are all trivial in the eyes of God or even perhaps a hitherto unknown species of unusual gifts currently inhabiting our planet or descending on it in the future, and that the high value we place on them only reveals our species-bias. However, that does not diminish their value in *our* eyes, for we have no other standards to judge them by than those derived from as detached and objective a perspective as we can bring to bear on ourselves. We cannot leap out of ourselves and pretend to be something else. Even if we believed in God and tried to look at ourselves from His point of view, we would have to rely on our own judgment as to who to accept as God and how to interpret His intentions. Since we value human beings because of their capacities, we reduce our species-bias by conferring value on apes and other higher forms of animal species that display some of these capacities.

Human beings, then, have worth because we have good reasons to value their capacities and achievements. Human worth is not a natural property like eyes and ears but something we confer upon ourselves, and hence a moral practice. Since human beings have worth, it extends to all that they deeply value and to which their sense of worth is inextricably tied. This is why we rightly confer value on objects of art, cultural and religious communities, pet animals, rare manuscripts and ancient buildings, and consider them worth preserving even, sometimes, at the cost of human life.

To say that human beings have worth or, what comes to the same thing, to adopt the moral practice of conferring worth on them, is to commit ourselves to treating them in certain ways. Negatively, we may not treat them as worthless or devoid of intrinsic value and use them as a mere means to our ends, kill them at will, torture them, use them for dangerous experiments, sacrifice them for causes they do not share, violate the integrity of their intimate relationships, and treat with contempt what they deeply value. Positively, we should cherish their sense of self-respect and self-worth, value their individual and collective achievements, encourage them to develop and express their capacities, and help create conditions in which they can lead worthy and meaningful lives.

Since human beings have unique and worthwhile capacities which make them superior to animals and the rest of the natural world, they can also be said to have *dignity* or its conceptual analogues in other languages. Unlike worth, dignity is an aristocratic or hierarchical concept and describes a privileged status. It makes sense only in relation to what is judged to be inferior, and implies that our treatment of human beings should not fall below the minimum required by their status. This is why every discussion of human dignity directly or indirectly contrasts humans with animals, emphasizes their superiority, and insists that they may not be treated as if they were animals or inanimate objects. This does not mean that animals are human playthings, but rather that we can give good reasons why they should be cared for and loved but not treated as our equals and endowed with equal worth, and that there is a great moral difference between swatting a fly or trampling on an insect and killing a human being. Dignity is not inherent in human beings, but is a status they confer on themselves in acknowledgment of their uniquely shared capacities, not a natural property but a moral practice regulating their relations with each other. It is not an individual but a collective status, for the individual acquires it by virtue of belonging to the human species and possessing certain species-specific capacities.

Since human dignity is human worth seen in a comparative perspective, it is not an independent source of moral principles but it does add a new dimension to moral life. Living in a world surrounded by non-human beings, it is an integral part of our self-consciousness to define our ontological status in relation to them. Our identity is constituted both by what we are and are not, and whatever else we are, we are not like trees and plants and worms and insects and all the rest of the natural world. This inescapable awareness of difference, constantly reinforced by our daily experiences and activities, is an integral part of our sense of self and forms the basis of our sense of dignity. Since the concept of human dignity is based on a sharp distinction between humans and non-humans, it is central to those traditions of thought such as the Greek, the Christian and the Islamic which set much store by that distinction, and is relatively muted in those such as the Hindu and the Buddhist in which the distinction is less sharply drawn. However, even the latter stress the special and superior status of humans, and rely on a weaker notion of human dignity.

It is true that some categories of humans such as the mad or mentally handicapped may lack some of the distinctively human capacities and would therefore appear to have less or no worth. However, they are rarely devoid of these capacities altogether, and are mad and handicapped in a way that only humans can be. Besides, they are also the sons, daughters, parents, friends and so forth of normal human beings, to whom they are deeply bonded and in whose worth they therefore participate. Furthermore, madness and idiocy are not easy to define. Once we start denying worth to certain kinds of persons, we run the risk of denying it, or encouraging others to deny it, to a wider class of human beings, and hence we have good reasons not to go down that route. Conferring dignity and worth on such persons also tests, affirms and intensifies our general commitment to human worth for, if we are able to value them, we are even more likely to value our more fortunate fellow-humans. For these and other reasons, we may rightly grant them equal worth.

Human beings possess not only certain distinctive capacities but also desires and needs. They wish to continue to live, desire food and physical wholeness, loathe disease and pain, and seek sexual satisfaction. Since they live in society they also develop such socially derived desires and fears as self-respect, good opinion of others, friendship, love, and fear of rejection and humiliation. As distinct centres of self-consciousness with an inescapable inner life of their own, they require at least some measure of inviolability and privacy. They are subject to changes of mood, frustrations, anxieties and so on, and cannot come to terms with these without a relatively secure personal space and at least some measure of control over their lives. Human beings require a long period of nurture and cannot grow into sane adults without a stable, loving and stimulating environment and a sense of belonging and roots. In order to feel secure, plan their lives and form stable relationships, they need a society free from an oppressive climate of terror and total unpredictability. They also need a conducive environment in which to acquire certain existentially indispensable capacities and skills without which they cannot hold themselves together, make sense of their lives, and find their way around in the wider society.

Since human beings require certain common conditions to grow and flourish, these conditions constitute their well-being and define the content of their fundamental interests. Although different societies entertain different conceptions of the good life and differently define human well-being, the shared human capacities, needs and so forth imply that some constituents of human well-being are common to them all. These include, for example, survival, means of sustenance, physical wholeness, good health, a stable, stimulating and loving environment, access to the cultural resources of their community, freedom from the arbitrary exercise of power, a measure of privacy and control of their lives, and opportunities for self-expression. Like dignity and worth, promotion of these interests is a moral practice we adopt because we have good reasons to believe that human beings should live rather than die, grow into intelligent adults rather than zombies, enjoy health rather than suffer from diseases, and so forth.

Since human beings have equal dignity and worth and require common conditions of well-being, their claims to the latter deserve equal consideration and weight. Equality is not an empirical fact, for empirically we are either similar or different not equal or unequal. Equality is a matter of moral judgment based on how we interpret and what weight we give to the similarities and differences. It is a moral practice we have good reasons to adopt, such as that there is a basic equality of worth, needs and so on among human beings, that the practice reinforces and nurtures our sense of dignity and worth, and that it enables each of us to lead a fulfilling personal life and contribute to the creation of a rich collective life. This does not mean that we might not admire some persons more, for that depends on their capacities and how they use them; nor that all should enjoy equal income and wealth, for human capacities vary and the incentive of inequality is often necessary to spur people to greater efforts; nor that all should enjoy equal political power, for that again is ruled out by the inequalities of talents and the needs of wider society. Equality requires, minimally, that we should acknowledge the equal dignity and worth of all human beings, accord them equal respect, and give equal consideration to their claims to the basic requirements of the good life.

It is then possible to arrive at a body of moral values which deserve the respect of all human beings. I have mentioned recognition of human worth and dignity, promotion of human well-being or of fundamental human interests, and equality, but this is only illustrative and does not exhaust the totality of possible universal moral values. The manner in which I have arrived at them is sketchy and needs to be tightened up considerably, but it should give some idea of how we might go about the task and why and how it involves appealing not just to human nature but also to the human condition, historical experiences and our judgment of the likely consequences of different forms of human relations and social life.

Although we can draw up a list of universal moral values, not all societies have the required moral, cultural, economic and other resources to live up to their demands. Furthermore, our case for them is not equally compelling because we can offer far more powerful arguments for some of them than for others. Not all values are equally central to the good life either. We should therefore identify those that are within the reach of all, central to any form of good life, and for which we can give compelling reasons. We should consolidate global consensus around them and allow their inner momentum to generate a movement towards an increasingly higher level of consensus. As individuals and groups in different societies appeal to them in their struggles for justice and as the rest of the world responds to them, the consensus deepens, the values become a widely accepted political currency, and acquire new adherents.

In this context, the 1948 United Nations Declaration of Human Rights provides a useful starting point.[5] It was born out of the kind of cross-cultural dialogue referred to earlier and has a genuinely universal feel about it, which is why people all over the world continue to appeal to it, and all subsequent global or continental statements on the subject, while modifying it in some respects, endorse its basic values. These include respect for human life and dignity, equality of rights, respect for personal integrity and inviolability, recognition of basic human worth, and protection of fundamental human interests. These general values in turn entail and are realized by such measures as the prohibition of torture, genocide and slavery, freedom of association, liberty of conscience, equality before the law, fair trial, popular accountability of political power, protection of privacy, and respect for the integrity of familial and other intimate relationships.

Although admirable, the UN Declaration is not free of defects. It retains a distinctly liberal bias and includes rights which, though admirable, cannot claim universal validity; for example, the rights to a more or less unlimited freedom of expression, to marriage based on the 'free and full consent' of the parties involved, and to relatively unlimited property. What is even more important, it takes a statist view of human rights and emasculates their universalist and critical thrust. The rights are addressed to the state which alone is deemed to have the obligation to respect and realize them. Strictly speaking, human rights as expressions of the minimum that is both due *to* and *from* all human beings are addressed to all human beings and impose on them a duty to respect them and do all they can to facilitate their realization. Since there are good reasons to respect the autonomy of the state, human rights are its primary but not exclusive responsibility. If a state is unable to secure the conditions of their effective exercise for lack of resources, civil wars or other reasons, outsiders have a duty to render it such help as it needs and that they can afford. Universal human rights imply universal human obligations including a duty to create a global regime of justice.

The UN Declaration also makes the mistake of confusing human rights with particular institutional structures. Since the latter cannot take root and function effectively unless they suit a society's traditions and moral and political culture, they necessarily vary from society to society. We must not, therefore, hold up liberal democracy as the only acceptable political form, and condemn political systems that do not allow multiple political parties, separation of powers, and so on. We might have good reasons to believe that the desired values are more likely to be realized under one set of institutions rather than another, but we should neither be too dogmatic about our views nor so identify the institutions and the values that the latter cannot be discussed and defended independently of them.

The minimum universal values which we may legitimately insist upon are by their very nature general and need to be interpreted, prioritized, adopted to, and in case of conflict reconciled, in the light of the culture and circumstances of each society. Respect for human life is a universal value, but different societies disagree on when human life begins and ends and what respect for it entails. Again, respect for human life sometimes conflicts with that for human dignity or justice, as when a dying man has lost all control over his bodily functions, or injustices cannot be redressed without recourse to violence. Respect for human dignity requires that we should not humiliate or degrade others or treat them in a cruel and demeaning manner. What constitutes humiliation or cruelty, however, varies with cultures and cannot be universally legislated. In some societies a person would rather be slapped on her face than coldly ignored or subjected to verbal abuse. In some, human dignity is deemed to be violated when parents interfere with their offsprings' choices of spouses; in others their intervention is taken as a sign that they care enough for their offsprings' dignity and well-being to press their advice on them and save them from making a mess of their lives. Different societies might also articulate, defend and rely on different mechanisms to realize universal values. Some might prefer the language of rights and claims and rely on the state to enforce these. Others might find it too individualist, aggressive, legalistic and state-centred and prefer the language of duty, relying on social conditioning and moral pressure to ensure that their members respect each other's dignity and refrain from harming each other's fundamental interests.

Universal values might also come into conflict with the freely-accepted central values of a cultural community. Women members of some indigenous and traditional communities freely commit themselves to vows of obedience and service to men in their lives and want to have nothing to do with equality. They might be brainwashed and we need to counter that, but should not assume that those who refuse to share our values are all victims of false consciousness. Torture is bad, but members of many religious sects and even some terrorist groups welcome it as a punishment or expiation for grave moral and spiritual or political lapses. Degrading human beings is bad, yet the training for priesthood in many Christian sects involves daily public exposure and humiliation of novices suspected of harbouring 'carnal' thoughts or reading prohibited literature. Human worth is a great value, but many religious groups and even some secular communities see fit to cultivate a feeling of personal and collective worthlessness. Indeed, it is difficult to think of a single universal value which is 'absolute' or inherently inviolable and may never in practice be overridden.[6] Since we rightly consider them as constitutive of the moral minimum due to and from human beings and assign them the greatest moral weight, we must require that the overriding factors be proportionate in their importance and of at least equal moral weight.

Since different societies may legitimately define, trade-off, prioritize, and realize the universal values differently, and even occasionally override some of them, the question arises of how we can prevent them from engaging in specious and self-serving moral reasoning and reinterpreting the values out of existence or emasculating their critical thrust. There is no foolproof way of doing so. All we can do is ask their spokesmen to justify their decisions when they appear unacceptable to us. If they can provide a strong and reasonably compelling defence, we should respect their decisions. If not, we should remain sceptical and press for change.

Asian values

A brief examination of the much-debated question of Asian values will illustrate the point.[7] Leaders of almost all East Asian countries insist that some of the rights included in the United Nations and other western-inspired declarations of human rights are incompatible with their values, traditions and self-understanding, and that western governments should be more tolerant of their attempts to define and prioritize them differently. While agreeing that these rights are universally valid, the Bangkok Declaration of 1993 insisted that they should be defined and applied in the light of local 'history, culture and religious backgrounds'. The Singapore delegation to the 1995 Vienna conference challenged the very universality of some of these rights. Urging the West not to be 'so blinded by arrogance and certainties as to lose the capacity for imagination and sympathy', the delegation asked it to take a 'more modest approach' lest it should 'fracture the international consensus on human rights'. The widespread western response is to dismiss these appeals to Asian values as self-serving attempts to justify arbitrary power, and to argue that the values are neither unique nor common to all Asian countries and cannot in any case be allowed to subvert or limit human rights.

The western response is too indiscriminate and sweeping to be convincing. The appeal to national or continental values is not unique to East Asians. Many Americans reject the European welfare state or the ban on capital punishment on the ground that they are incompatible with, and cannot be accommodated within, their way of life. And neither they nor the Europeans are prepared to follow the Singaporean or Chinese ban on hard pornography on the ground that it violates liberal values. If these societies are right to cherish their values, there is no reason why East Asians should not uphold theirs.

The other western objections to the East Asian view are no better. It would not do to say that Asian values are not unique to Asian countries, for their leaders not only make no such claim but in fact insist that the West, too, should, and indeed once did, share them and is wrong to allow them to be overridden by the liberal individualist ethos. Nor would it do to say that all East Asians do not share these values. Although East Asian countries differ in important respects, most of their citizens do cherish such 'Asian' values as social harmony, respect for authority, orderly society, a united and extended family and a sense of filial piety. The fact that some of their citizens do not share these is immaterial. After all, the racists, sexists and many conservative members of western societies do not share the value of equality, yet these societies rightly consider it central to their self-understanding and impose it on them without the slightest hesitation. In short, we should not ask the abstract and misleading question whether East Asians have a right to live by or are all agreed on their values, but what these values are and if and how they offend against universal values.

East Asian spokesmen are not a homogeneous group. They raise different kinds of objections to the universalist discourse on human rights and deserve nuanced responses. First, some find the language of rights individualist, legalistic, statist and aggressive, ideally suited in their view to the atomized western society but not to one as cohesive as theirs. They have no objection to many of the basic values underlying the discourse on human rights, but think that these are best realized within a communitarian moral framework based on mutual concern, solidarity, loyalty to the wider society, and socially responsible individualism. They prefer to rely on social and cultural institutions rather than the state, on moral and religious pressure rather than the fear of the law, and aim to foster the consciousness of individual responsibilities and duties rather than of rights. Although this is a very different way of defining and creating the good society to the liberal, it has its virtues and should be welcomed. It is vulnerable to the collectivist danger and unlikely to create a culture conducive to the development of individuality and choice. However, the liberal stress on rights, too, has its limitations, including its well-known inability to nurture the spirit of community and social responsibility vital for regulating the excesses of the culture of rights. No society so far has succeeded in striking the right balance between the individual and the community, and none can be held up as a universal model. East Asian societies should, therefore, not only be left free but encouraged to experiment with new forms of social and political organization consistent with full respect for the minimum universal values.

Second, some East Asian leaders are unhappy not so much with the language of rights as with parts of their content, which they find narrow and heavily biased towards the western liberal democratic form of government. They are better disposed to democracy than to liberalism, and take a more or less organic rather than an individualist view of the former. In their view a good polity should be just, accountable to its citizens, promote economic growth, maintain social harmony, hold society together and reflect the basic values of its people. It does not have to be liberal in the sense of a contractual association between its members pursuing no other collective goals than protecting their rights and maintaining neutrality between different conceptions of the good.

Unlike their western counterparts, East Asian societies share a broad consensus on the nature of the good life, and think that they have a right and even a duty to enforce it out of respect for both the integrity of their way of life and the wishes of the majority. Hence they wish to ban pornography, protect some of their deeply held moral and religious beliefs and practices against irresponsible attacks, and censure films and literary works that incite intercommunal hatred or mock and demean minority or majority communities. They also wish to promote the virtues of filial piety, good neighbourliness and respect for nature by such measures as giving elderly parents the right to sue their children for maintenance and imposing fines on individuals for failing to report a theft or a fire in their neighbour's house or vandalizing the environment. East Asian leaders also point to the problems involved in holding multi-ethnic societies together. Since some of their ethnic groups have no experience of living and working together, racial hostilities are easily aroused and require greater restrictions on free speech and movement than is usual in more stable societies. In many cases of racial unrest the process of trial itself inflames passions and increases tensions, making it unwise to conduct it in the normal western manner. Evidence, too, may sometimes have to be gathered by covert operations, and cannot be submitted to open courts or expected to meet the normal standards of criminal law.

This second East Asian claim respects universal values and human rights but defines, relates and prioritizes them differently. It does not justify tortures, arbitrary arrests, genocide, tyranny, racial and other forms of discrimination, and denial of free elections and basic liberties. All it maintains is that East Asian societies wish to pursue such collective goals as social harmony and cohesion, moral consensus, integrity of the family and economic development, and that these involve different kinds of rights and greater restrictions on individual freedoms than is common in liberal societies. Although some of these goals and the restrictions they entail do not find much favour among liberals, that is not an argument against them. All one can require is that the goals should promote a worthwhile, morally defensible and popularly endorsed vision of the good life, and that the measures used should be proportionate to them and represent a morally justifiable trade-off between human rights.

The third East Asian claim is quite different from the other two. Its advocates, drawn mainly from the ranks of Chinese and Vietnamese leaders, reject the very concern with human rights as bourgeois, western and incompatible with their traditional values and vision of the good life. For them, society is more important than the individual. Social solidarity, a prosperous economy and a strong and powerful state are the highest national goals. And the individual has meaning and value only to the extent that he or she serves society. Since human rights presuppose and reinforce an individualist culture and restrict the state's freedom of action, they are deemed to be inherently reactionary and part of the western design to destabilize and weaken these societies. Following the logic of this argument, the Chinese and other governments reject parts of the democratic system of free elections, multiple political parties, popular participation, peaceful protests, free speech, individual and organized dissent, and the rule of law.

Although this third claim is understandable in the context of Chinese history and is far more complex and nuanced than my brief account suggests, it violates some of the basic values mentioned earlier. It often permits terror, arbitrary arrests, gross violations of personal autonomy, destruction of the family, some of the worst forms of personal humiliation, disregard for human dignity, and the use of individuals as a mere means to collective goals. There might be some justification for some of these practices if the Chinese could show that they are the only way to promote worthwhile goals. This is not the case. Economic development does not require, and is even hampered by, repressive measures. The Great Leap forward, which killed over 20 million people and had to be reversed three years later, could have been avoided or reversed earlier if China had had a free press. The importance of economic development lies in creating the conditions of the good life, and it defeats its purpose if it violates human dignity and self-respect and renders citizens incapable of leading the good life. The same is true of national unity and social solidarity, both of which are worthwhile goals but which are bound to be subverted by the methods the Chinese propose.

The Chinese claim that human rights are incompatible with their traditional values is equally unconvincing. It is true that the traditional Chinese view of the individual requires rights to be defined in less exclusivist, proprietary and absolutist terms than is common in liberal societies. Although there is something to be said for such a view of rights, it can be easily accommodated within a suitably redefined conception of human rights. Furthermore, as their own human rights activists have pointed out, Chinese leaders misrepresent traditional values. There is no evidence that the latter justify arbitrary exercise of power or any of the other practices mentioned above. And if some of them do, they need to be changed, for no values are sacrosanct simply because they are traditional. After all, neither the communist nor even the nationalist values which the Chinese have warmly embraced are part of their tradition. Like their premodern European counterparts, the traditional Chinese society relied on intricate social and moral mechanisms to check the abuse of political power and did not stress individual rights. Their society today is quite different. The emergence of the centralized and bureaucratic state, urbanization, increased mobility of labour and capital, social differentiation, industrialization and increasing liberalization have undermined the traditional mechanisms of social self-discipline and call for effective alternatives. The only ones that have worked reasonably well so far in most societies are the institutions of human rights, constitutionally limited power, a free press, and so on. Since Chinese leaders do not propose a viable alternative, their rejection of human rights is self-serving and suspect.

Given the differences in their history, traditions and moral culture, it is both inevitable and desirable that different societies should differently interpret, prioritize and realize great moral values and integrate them with their own suitably revised thick and complex moral structures. This is the only way we can deepen our insights into the complexity and grandeur of human life and attain increasingly higher levels of moral universality. There is, however, the obvious and sadly all too familiar danger that ill-motivated governments and dominant political groups might misuse their legitimate interpretative freedom to undermine these values. This happens even in mature liberal democratic societies with regard to their constitutionally enshrined fundamental rights, a domestic political analogue of universal moral values. We rely on the courts to protect, interpret and balance these rights, and even they get things wrong from time to time and we turn to the democratic political process with all its limitations. In the international context we need, over time, to develop such judicial and political institutions, but until that happens we have nothing else to rely upon save the kind of cross-cultural interrogation referred to earlier, the moral weight of enlightened world opinion backed up by global economic and political pressure, and in rare cases humanitarian intervention.

5

Understanding Culture

The nature and structure of culture

Human beings seek to make sense of themselves and the world and ask questions about the meaning and significance of human life, activities and relationships. To ask what is the meaning of an activity is to ask questions about its nature and point or purpose; and to ask what is its significance is to ask questions about its worth or value, the kind and degree of importance to be assigned to it, and its place in human life in general. Meaning and significance are closely related, for the significance of an activity depends on how we understand its nature and purpose. To inquire into the meaning of sexuality, for example, is to ask what kind of activity it is, whether it is a purely physical activity or has a wider social and spiritual significance, whether it implies moral commitment on the part of those involved and of what kind, and how its pleasurable, reproductive and other dimensions are related. To inquire into its significance is to ask if and why it is important, its role and place in human life, its comparative importance in relation to other activities and desires, and so forth. The questions about meaning and significance can be asked about every human activity such as writing a book, making money, following a career, voting and protesting against an injustice; about every human relationship such as being a father or a son, a husband or a wife, a neighbour, a colleague, a citizen and a stranger; and also about human life in general.

The beliefs or views human beings form about the meaning and significance of human life and its activities and relationships shape the practices in terms of which they structure and regulate their individual and collective lives. I shall use the term culture to refer to such a system of beliefs and practices. Culture is a historically created system of meaning and significance or, what comes to the same thing, a system of beliefs and practices in terms of which a group of human beings understand, regulate and structure their individual and collective lives. It is a way of both understanding and organizing human life. The understanding it seeks has a practical thrust and is not purely theoretical in nature like that offered by a philosophical or a scientific theory, and the way it organizes human life is not *ad hoc* and instrumental but grounded in a particular manner of conceptualizing and understanding it.

When used *sans phrase* culture encompasses more or less the whole of human life. When adjectivized, it refers to the area or aspect of human life highlighted by the adjective. The terms business culture, drug culture, and moral, political, academic or sexual culture refer to the body of beliefs and practices regulating the relevant areas of human life including the ways in which these are conceptualized, demarcated, structured and regulated. Such terms as gay, youth, mass and working-class culture refer to the ways in which these groups understand their place in society and regulate their internal and external relations. Folk or popular culture refers to the beliefs and practices of ordinary men and women or to culture as it is actually lived, and high culture to the great creative achievements of the talented minds of society. Although high culture aims to go beyond the general culture of the wider society in its concern to explore the universal features of human existence, it invariably retains traces of its local provenance. This is so because even the most creative minds are shaped by their society from their childhood onwards, take their bearings from their experiences within it, use its language, share some of its unconscious assumptions, and expect to be appreciated or at least understood by their fellow-members.

Culture is articulated at several levels. At the most basic level it is reflected in the language, including the ways in which its syntax, grammar and vocabulary divide up and describe the world. Societies sharing a common language share at least some cultural features in common. And when a group of individuals acquires a wholly new language as many colonial subjects did, they also learn new ways of understanding the world. Culture of a society is also embodied in its proverbs, maxims, myths, rituals, symbols, collective memories, jokes, body language, modes of non-linguistic communication, customs, traditions, institutions and manners of greeting. At a slightly different level it is embodied in its arts, music, oral and written literature, moral life, ideals of excellence, exemplary individuals and the vision of the good life. Being concerned to structure and order human life, culture is also articulated in the rules and norms that govern such basic activities and social relations as how, where, when and with whom one eats, associates and makes love, how one mourns and disposes of the dead, and treats one's parents, children, wife, neighbours and strangers.

Every culture develops over time and, since it has no coordinating authority, it remains a complex and unsystematized whole. It has what Raymond Williams (1980) calls residual strands of thought; that is, those that were once dominant and now survive either as historical memories or as undigested elements in the dominant culture. A culture also tends to throw up what Williams calls emergent strands; that is, those semi-articulated bodies of thought that arise out of dissatisfaction with the dominant culture and are currently confined to a small group (Williams, 1980, pp. 10f, 41f). Since both bodies of thought are sources of potential challenge, the dominant culture often seeks to suppress or neutralize them. Every culture is internally varied, speaks in several voices, and its range of interpretive possibility is often indeterminate.

As we have seen, many writers, especially but not only the monists, mistakenly dissociate morality from culture and argue that while culture is local and varies from society to society, morality is inherently universal and only contingently related to culture. Morality is concerned with what kind of life is worth living, what activities are worth pursuing, and what forms of human relations worth cultivating. It presupposes criteria of worth or significance, which in turn presuppose a system of meaning or culture. Every system of morality is embedded in and nurtured by the wider culture and can only be changed by changing the latter. Culture shapes and structures moral life including its scope, content, authority and the kinds of emotions associated with it. Many traditional cultures see nature as a spiritual whole and consider human attitude to it a matter of moral concern; most moderns take a 'disenchanted' view of nature and place human relations with it outside the ambit of morality. In some cultures food is seen as God's gift or a means of sustaining the God-given body, and what one eats, how and with whom are moral matters; in others they have no moral significance. Many Protestant cultures stress the internal dimension of morality and treat it as a separate and autonomous aspect of life; others such as the Chinese, the Hindus and several African societies embed it in a system of rituals and social conventions, and some of them do not even have a separate word for it.

The cultural embeddedness of morality is evident in the way in which the customs, ceremonies and rituals of a culture embody and give meaning to its moral values. Respect for human life, for example, does not remain an abstract moral principle but gets embodied in such things as the customs and rituals surrounding how we dispose of the dead, what we wear and how we conduct ourselves at funerals, how we treat strangers, help the old and the poor, and celebrate the birth of a child. These practices give the relevant moral principle concrete content and deep emotional roots, build up a body of appropriate taboos and inhibitions, and domesticate and relieve the harshness and impersonality of moral demands by integrating them into everyday life. As we have seen, the fact that morality is closely bound up with culture does not mean that it may not be criticized or that there are no universal moral principles.

Although the beliefs and practices of a culture are closely related, they are also autonomous and subject to their own distinct logics. The two differ in at least four important respects. Beliefs are necessarily general, even vague and amenable to different interpretations, whereas practices which are meant to regulate human conduct and social relations are fairly determinate and concrete. Secondly, while beliefs are not easy to discover and enforce, conformity to practices is easily ascertainable and enforceable. Thirdly, beliefs primarily pertain to the realm of thought and practices to that of conduct. Beliefs are therefore more likely to be influenced by new ideas and knowledge, practices by new social situations and experiences. Fourthly, coherence among beliefs is a matter of intellectual consistency and is different in nature from that among practices where it is basically a matter of practical compatibility. Thanks to these and other differences, beliefs and practices, although internally related and subject to mutual influences, are also subject to their own characteristic constraints and patterns of change. A society's beliefs might change but its practices might not keep pace, and vice versa. And when either change at an unusually rapid pace, it might become unduly conservative about the other to retain its sense of continuity or stability. Since ties between beliefs and practices are loose and volatile and there is often a hiatus between the two, no culture is ever a fully consistent and coherent whole.

Although culture and society are inseparable in the sense that there is neither a society without a culture nor a culture which is not associated with some society, the two have different focus and orientation (Carrithers, 1992, pp. 25f). Broadly speaking, society refers to a group of human beings and the structure of their relations, culture to the content and the organizing and legitimizing principles of these relations. Society is primarily concerned with the structure of practices and, while relying on their legitimizing cultural beliefs, it also has its own system of sanctions in the form of ostracism, withdrawal of social status and adverse criticism on which it relies to enforce practices. Members of a society might follow its practices either because they share their cultural meaning and legitimizing beliefs, or because they fear the social consequences of nonconformity, or both.

Our practice of monogamy, for example, is embedded in the meaning and significance our culture assigns to marriage and intergender relations. One might follow it because one shares and respects these beliefs, or because one does not want to appear odd, invite hostile attention, or face the disapproval of one's parents and friends. In the former case one follows it for cultural reasons; in the latter one denudes it of its cultural meaning, views it as a social rather than a cultural practice, and follows it for social reasons. This is a fairly common phenomenon in all societies. Some Hindus follow the norms of their caste system because they accept its cultural authority and meaning, others because of the likely social and economic sanctions. The fact that one observes the practices of one's culture does not mean that one does so for reasons internal to it. This is why a culture can be eroded and hollowed out from within without anyone noticing it, and might even be replaced by another in what the superficial observer takes to be a revolutionary change.

Since culture is concerned with the meaning and significance of human activities and relations, and since this is also a matter of central concern to religion, the two tend to be closely connected.[1] Indeed, there is hardly a culture in whose creation, constitution and continuation religion has not played an important part, so much so that we have few if any examples of a wholly secular or humanist culture. Although modernity might seem to qualify as one, it is in fact an heir to, and is deeply shaped by, the values, ideals, beliefs, and myths of Christianity. This is not to say that we cannot defend modern ideals of human dignity, equality, personal autonomy and individual choice on secular grounds, but rather that this is not why they became an integral part of modern consciousness and enjoy their current popular appeal. Part of the reason why there is a sense of moral crisis today has to do with the fact that we cherish these ideals but neither share their religious rationale nor know how to defend them adequately on wholly secular grounds.

In different cultures religion plays different roles. No culture can be wholly derived from religion for, however detailed it might be, a religion can never cover all areas of human life and anticipate all situations. Hardly any religion tells its adherents how to eat, dress, talk, sit, sleep, brush their teeth or make love. And although it might issue such general norms as that they should respect their parents, it does not tell them whether that involves refraining from smoking in their presence or remaining seated when they are standing. These and other areas are largely dealt with by culture. Culture and religion influence each other at various levels. Religion shapes a culture's system of beliefs and practices, which is why when individuals or communities convert to another religion, their ways of thought and life undergo important changes. For its part culture influences how a religion is interpreted, its rituals conducted, the place assigned to it in the life of society, and so forth, which is why converts carry their culture into their new religion as seen, for example, in the great differences between the Indonesian, Indian, Iranian and Algerian forms of Islam or the Chinese, Egyptian and American forms of Christianity. No religion can be culture-free and the divine will cannot acquire a determinate human meaning without cultural mediation. Christ might be divine but Christianity is a cultural phenomenon.

Although no culture can be exclusively based on religion, it can be shaped by it in different ways and degrees. Some cultures are primarily derived from and heavily dependent on religion, in others religion is only one source of influence and is constantly challenged by the influences of science, secular morality and critical reason, for example. Each type of culture gives rise to its distinctive mode of discourse and sources of change. In the former religion is a dominant voice, and debates about cultural reforms are conducted in religious idioms and centre on different interpretations of religious texts. In a plural culture with different sources of influence, the public discourse on culture is conducted in both religious and secular idioms and is necessarily multilingual. Although a religiously based culture is more conservative, it is sometimes much easier to change. Since it is primarily derived from a single source, it can rapidly undergo fairly radical changes once the central dogmas of the religion are suitably reinterpreted.

Even when religion and culture are closely connected, they are separable in thought and practice. Just as we can abstract away the cultural basis of a practice and follow it for purely social reasons, we can abstract away its religious basis and follow or respect it for cultural or even exclusively social reasons. One might go to church or even believe in God as part of one's religious commitment, or because it is integral to one's culture and sustains one's cultural community, or because it enhances one's social status. And, again, we might celebrate Christmas because of its profound religious significance, or because it represents an important cultural moment in our history, or because it is a good way to affirm our membership of our society or not to attract critical attention.

Belonging to a cultural community, then, admits of much variation and is not homogeneous in nature. Some members might share all its beliefs and others only a few, and the former might differ in their interpretations of or degrees of allegiance to these. Again, some might scrupulously follow all its practices and others only a few, and they might do so for social, cultural or religious reasons or be overdetermined by all three. Since reasons for following practices are inscrutable to others and sometimes even to the agents themselves, we have no means of knowing how committed others or even we are to our culture. Membership of a cultural community thus varies in kind and degree and is sometimes a subject of deep disagreement. Every community lives with this ambiguity and uncertainty. And since its members are rarely agreed on how much ambiguity to tolerate and when some of them could be said to have given up their culture or to constitute borderline cases, no culture is free of the tensions that all this generates.

Since a culture's system of beliefs and practices, the locus of its identity, is constantly contested, subject to change, and does not form a coherent whole, its identity is never settled, static and free of ambiguity.[2] This does not mean, as it is sometimes argued, that it has no identity. It is rare, even impossible, for the entire system of meaning to become a subject of contestation and dispute. The contestation is limited to some areas, and is only possible because of a broad consensus on others. Again, although a culture is never static, not all aspects of it change at the same time. Some change but others do not, and the former change at different rates. Like the identity of an individual, that of a culture changes slowly and in parts, allowing its members time to absorb and adjust to changes and reconstitute its identity on a new basis. It is only when the changes are extensive, rapid, or introduced by factors over which the community has no control that its members are unable to rely on their cultural resources to navigate their way through life and experience a sense of moral panic.

Individuals experience cultural conflict when they subscribe to or live by two different systems of meaning and significance either wholly or partially. In the former case the conflict encompasses all the significant areas of their lives, as in the case of an individual who feels deeply drawn both to the traditional Muslim or Catholic and the modern secular and liberal views of life and is unable to reconcile or make up his mind between them. In the latter case the conflict is limited to particular areas of life, as is the case with an individual who is torn between, say, the traditional Hindu and the modern western views of sexuality, relations with parents, or attitudes to strangers, children and siblings. While such limited conflicts are part of life in almost every modern society and its members generally know how to cope with them, comprehensive and deep conflicts are not easily resolved and can lead to moral confusion and schizophrenia and even self-destruction.

Since cultures are created against the background of the shared features of human existence, it is impossible for them not to share at least some beliefs and practices in common. This does not mean, as is sometimes argued, that they form a continuum and cannot be distinguished or individuated. After all, languages too share much in common, but that does not prevent us from recognizing and distinguishing them and appreciating their uniqueness. Although some cultural beliefs and practices overlap, others do not, and the former are assigned different meanings and significance by different cultures. Cultures are distinguished from each other both by the content of their beliefs and practices and the manner in which these are internally related and form a reasonably recognizable whole. They do not have a single overarching Herderian spirit or Montesquieuean principle which an outsider can uncover and use to individuate and define them. Their identity is complex and diffused, cannot be summed up in a neat set of propositions, and can only be grasped by a deep and intimate familiarity with them.

Individuals relate to their culture in several different ways, of which three are most common. Some individuals deeply cherish its system of meaning and significance and seek to lead culturally authentic lives by scrupulously living up to its ideals of a good father, son, husband, wife, neighbour, colleague, and a good human being. Since a culture often contains different strands of thought and since its system of meaning is stretchable, a culturally authentic life necessarily involves selectivity and can be led in several different ways. As long as we take a plural and nonessentialist view of authenticity, such a life has its own appeal. Although it is narrow and inward-looking, it keeps alive the central values of the culture, deepens its moral, spiritual and other resources, and sets an example of a whole and integrated life. Some individuals are more innovative. While remaining rooted in their culture, they judiciously borrow such beliefs and practices as they find valuable in others and enrich and broaden it. Like a culturally authentic life, such a culturally innovative life can take different forms depending on what one borrows and how. It has experimental vitality, brings different cultures into a fruitful dialogue without uprooting the individual from her own, and has much to be said for it.

Some other individuals are culturally footloose, owing loyalty to no single culture, floating freely between several of them, picking up beliefs, practices and lifestyles that engage their sympathies, and creating an eclectic way of life of their own. Although in judicious hands such a way of life can be highly original and creative, it also runs the risk of becoming shallow and fragile. Lacking historical depth and traditions, it cannot inspire and guide choices, fails to provide a moral compass and stability, and encourages the habit of hopping from culture to culture to avoid the rigour and discipline of any one of them. It is a culture of quotations, a babble of discordant voices, and not a culture in any meaningful sense of the term. In some but by no means all of postmodernist literature, there is a tendency to romanticize this approach to culture, based on the mistaken belief that all boundaries are reactionary and crippling and their transgressions a symbol of creativity and freedom. Boundaries structure our lives, give us a sense of rootedness and identity, and provide a point of reference. Even when we rebel against them, we know what we are rebelling against and why. Since they tend to become restrictive, we need to challenge and stretch them; but we cannot reject them altogether for we then have no fixed points of reference with which to define ourselves and decide what differences to cultivate and why.[3] A nomadic cultural voyager, driven by a morbid fear of anything that is coherent, stable, has history and involves discipline and delighting in difference for its own sake, has no basis on which to decide which boundaries to transgress, why, what new world to build out of such acts of transgression, and which differences do really make a difference As Hegel showed in his analysis of the French Revolution, culturally unbounded and unguided freedom, the culture of the pure will, destroys both itself and the world around it.

The dynamics of culture

A society's culture is closely tied up with its economic, political and other institutions. No society first develops culture and then these institutions, or vice versa. They are all equally vital to its survival, emerge and develop together, and are influenced by each other. While acknowledging this fact, many writers have wondered if one of these institutions exercises a determining or at least a decisive influence on the rest. Marx, for example, gave pride of place to the mode of material production, rightly arguing that culture did not exist in a social vacuum, that it often performed the ideological role of legitimizing the prevailing system of economic and political power, that it could not be understood independently of the latter, and that it was subject to constant reintepretation and manipulation. He was, however, wrong to think that material production occurred in a cultural vacuum, that it was logically and temporally prior to culture, and that the latter lacked the power to exercise an independent influence on it. Herder saw this more clearly than Marx, but made the opposite mistake of ignoring the enormous power of the economic system. Montesquieu rightly stressed the influence of climate and geography, Hegel that of ideas, and Weber that of religion, but each again went wrong in neglecting the influence of other factors. All, alike, made the further mistake of ignoring the differences between societies and historical periods, and thinking that the same factor exercised more or less the same influence in all of them.

We need not here enter into the debate on the relative importance of cultural and other factors, and simply note the obvious fact that none of them is wholly powerless or devoid of independent agency. As for culture, our main concern, it influences major social institutions in several ways. The manner in which a society organizes its economic and political life depends on how it defines, legitimizes and regulates, and what meaning and significance it assigns to, the pursuit of wealth and the exercise of power, respectively. Although the classical Athenians had the capacity to develop much of the technology of the Romans, they did not do so because of their aesthetic sensibilities and their views on man's relation to nature and the good life. In India the dominant Brahmanic culture discouraged economic and technological development because it took a low view of these activities and denied them royal patronage, moral legitimacy and social respectability. In premodern societies economic activity was subject to all manner of constraints derived from the prevailing views on the nature and purpose of human life and the scope and content of justice, with the result that it lacked the dignity and independence needed to come into its own and develop capitalism.

Even as culture shapes the economic, political and other institutions, it is in turn shaped by them. In their own different ways they structure the lived world, delimit the range of possible human activities and relations, give shape to fundamental human experiences, and profoundly influence the context and content of culture. Furthermore, since no system of economic and political power can rely on physical force alone, it needs to legitimize itself in the eyes of its members especially the oppressed and the marginalized, and that involves suitably shaping their cultural and moral beliefs. Not surprisingly, no dominant class ever leaves culture alone. For their part the oppressed and the marginalized cannot rely on protests and force alone to secure justice, and need to reinterpret or challenge the relevant aspects of the prevailing culture. Since culture is a source of legitimacy and power, all political and economic battles are fought out at the cultural level as well, and all cultural struggles have an inescapable political and economic dimension.

No culture is ever free of contestation and change. Class, gender, generational and other conflicts are endemic in all societies and seek suitable cultural expressions. Even when such conflicts are absent or muted, members of a cultural community are likely to disagree on their interpretations of their cultural beliefs and practices. And even in the absence of such disagreements, a culture can never remain stable and static because of the very nature of its constituent beliefs and practices. All beliefs are necessarily general and articulated in terms of inherently indeterminate concepts, and need to be reinterpreted in the light of new situations and knowledge. Although practices are more specific, they too need to be adapted to new and unexpected circumstances. Their adherents cannot therefore avoid stretching the boundaries of the prevailing system of beliefs and practices and opening up new interpretive possibilities, sometimes with consequences they neither intend nor approve of. Culture thus is not a passive inheritance but an active pro-

cess of creating meaning, not given but constantly redefined and reconstituted. It does have a structure which directs and delimits the range of
new meanings, but the structure is relatively loose and alterable. Even
as a culture shapes its adherents' forms of consciousness, they in turn
redefine and reconstitute it and expand its cognitive and evaluative
resources. In this respect as in many others, it is like a language, a precondition and a context as well as a product of human choices, a source
of constraint which is also a medium of creativity.

A society's culture also changes in response to several other factors,
such as technology, conquest, wars and even natural calamities, often
in a manner it neither understands nor even recognizes. The Ika tribe in
Africa was long known for its optimistic view of the world, familial
loyalty and hospitality to strangers. Thanks to a most tragic and protracted famine, which caused enormous human suffering and threw up
most vicious forms of human behaviour, their social structure disintegrated, traditional moral restraints gave way, their respect for human
life weakened considerably, and their system of beliefs and practices
underwent radical and unexpected changes. Wars, especially modern
ones, are momentous events in the life of any society. They involve collective mobilization, great material and human sacrifices, intense passions and a simplified definition of national identity to inspire the country and distinguish it sharply from its enemy, all of which leads to a
profound economic, moral and cultural upheaval in national life. Linda
Colley (1992) has perceptively analysed how British cultural self-
understanding was profoundly altered by the Napoleonic wars.

Technology is a source of great cultural changes as Marx articulated
with unparalleled acuity. Every major technological change affects
both the processes and the relations of production, and hence the economic, political and cultural organization of society. It requires new
forms of discipline, new habits and traits of temperament, new modes
of structuring and exercising power, and new forms of co-operation. It
might also increase leisure, foster new interests and hobbies, and throw
up new forms of social relations and regulations. The vast changes in
the meaning and significance of sexuality and the relations of reproduction brought about by new reproductive technology are too obvious
to need elaboration. Even something as simple as the introduction of
television can inaugurate significant changes in a culture. In India as in
many other developing countries night-time activities are centred
around television. Men and women sit together to view it and build up
common subjects of conversation, quarrels and sources of pleasure, all

leading to the gradual weakening of the traditional distance between the two sexes. For similar reasons, status differences between the young and the old have also begun to diminish. Since food is prepared early or brought in from outside, the rest of the day is now planned differently. And since large families often live in small rooms which now include the television, the symbol of public space *par excellence*, the nature of the domestic and public spaces and their traditional relations are being increasingly reconceptualized and reconstructed.

Cultural community

Just as a body of people sharing a common language, religion and structure of civil authority constitute respectively a linguistic, religious and political community, a body of people united in terms of a shared culture constitute a cultural community. Cultural communities are of several kinds. Some share nothing in common save their culture. Some also share a religion, especially when their culture is religiously derived. Some share common ethnicity. Indeed, since every culture is the culture of a particular group of people, its creator and historical bearer, all cultures tend to have an ethnic basis. However, the two can part company. An ethnic community might lose its traditional culture, as when it migrates or abandons that culture in favour of another. And a culture might lose its ethnic rootedness, as when it is freely adopted by or imposed on outsiders. When we talk of a cultural community, we abstract away these and other differences and refer to a community based on a shared culture irrespective of how the latter is derived and what else it shares in common.

A cultural community has two dimensions, cultural and communal. It has a content in the form of a particular culture, and a communal basis in the form of a group of men and women who share that culture. Although the two are closely related, they are distinct enough to be separated in thought and practice. One might retain one's culture but lose or sever ties with one's cultural community; for example, immigrants or those who cherish their culture but leave their community because they find it oppressive or otherwise uncongenial. The opposite happens when one retains one's ties with one's cultural community but not one's culture; for example, those who for some reason reject their culture but remain deeply attached to their community and might even remain its members if it was open-minded enough to tolerate dissenters. When a community's culture changes or is abandoned in favour of another, it remains the same community, now united in terms of another shared culture. Its cultural identity is different, but since its membership, historical continuity and so on are unaltered, its communal or ethnic identity remains the same.

The term 'our' culture refers not to one in which we are born, for we might emigrate or be given up for adoption and raised in another culture, but one in terms of which we understand and organize our individual and collective lives. 'Our' culture is one we live, which has shaped us, and with which we identify. And we recognize those as members of our cultural community who share its beliefs and participate in its practices. Like all communities cultural communities are not, and cannot be, just imagined communities, for imagination needs content, an experental basis, constant reinforcement and social relevance. Rather they are participatory communities, nurtured daily by the knowledge or the belief that their members share a common moral and social vocabulary and know how to converse with and behave towards each other in different situations. Members of a lively community read the literature of other cultures, watch their films, listen to their music and enjoy their cuisine. Although these might influence some of them, give them enormous pleasure, and hover over their cultural horizon, they do not form part of their collective culture, partly because culture is shared with other members of their community who might not be influenced by them, and partly because their influence might not extend to reshaping the system of beliefs and practices of those who are. Though not part of their culture, these influences remain part of their intellectual environment and constitute an unincorporated alien resource they may one day activate to reshape their culture.

To be born and raised into a cultural community is to be deeply influenced by both its cultural content and communal basis. Human beings are born with a cluster of species-derived capacities and tendencies and are gradually transformed by their culture into rational and moral persons. Culture catches them at a highly impressionable and pliant stage and structures their personality. They learn to see the world in a particular way, to individuate and assign certain meanings and significance to human activities and relationships, and to conduct the latter according to certain norms. They also acquire particular habits of thought and feeling, traits of temperament, inhibitions, taboos, prejudices, and musical, culinary, sartorial, artistic and other tastes. They build up a body of sentiments and memories, acquire love of certain kinds of sounds, smells and sights, heroes, role models, bodily gestures, values, ideals, and ways of holding and carrying themselves. Since all these are often acquired unconsciously and in the course of living within a more or less integrated way of life, they strike deep roots and become an inseparable part of their personality. Sometimes even a most searching self-examination cannot uncover their presence and, when it does, one is too close to them to take even a moderately detached view.

Growing up within a cultural community also means building up common bonds and developing a sense of solidarity with its other members. The bonds grow out of shared beliefs, common objects of love, shared historical memories and so on, though they can also sometimes transcend these and persist in their absence. One acquires a network of close relations and a system of support, and becomes bound to other members by the ties of mutual expectations and common interests. One also develops the necessary psychological and moral skills to find one's way around within the community, to know almost instinctively what to say and how to behave in different situations, to pick up and responds to non-verbal signals and allusions, and relate to others in an unselfconscious manner. A sense of rootedness, effortless communication, a structured moral life and ease of mutual understanding, all of which are important parts of human well-being, are the spontaneous products of the membership of a stable cultural community.

Membership of a cultural community, then, has two major consequences. It structures and shapes the individual's personality in a certain way and gives it a content or identity. It also embeds him or her within, and identified with, a particular group of people. Identity and identification are closely related. One identifies with a body of men and women because one shares a common identity with them, and one's identification with them gives that identity a social basis, emotional energy and a measure of stability and objectivity.

Every culture is also a system of regulation.[4] It approves or disapproves of certain forms of behaviour and ways of life, prescribes rules and norms governing human relations and activities, and enforces these by means of reward and punishment. While it facilitates choices as Raz and Kymlicka argue, it also disciplines them as Foucault argues. It both opens up and closes options, both stabilizes and circumscribes the moral and social world, creates the conditions of choice but also demands conformity. The two functions are inseparable and dialectically related. Every moral order is a particular kind of order and both protects and confines those who are part of it. While valuing the indispensable place of culture in human life, we should also be mindful of its regulative and coercive role and the way it institutionalizes, exercises and distributes power. Its system of meaning and norms are not and cannot be neutral between conflicting interests and aspirations. They create and legitimize a particular kind of social order, and advantage some groups more than others. While appreciating that culture means much to its members and deserves respect, we should remain critically watchful of the damage it causes to some or even all of them.

Although human beings are shaped by their culture, they are not constituted or determined by it in the sense of being unable to take a critical view of it or rise above its constitutive beliefs and practices and reach out to other cultures. Cultural determinism makes sense only if we assume that culture is a cohesive and tightly structured whole that is not itself influenced by anything external to it, and that individuals are a passive and pliant material devoid of independent thought. Neither assumption is valid. Culture does not exist by itself. It is integrally bound up with, and influenced by, the economic and political arrangements, level of technological development and so on of the society concerned. Being one of the several factors shaping the individual, and being itself subject to the influence of others, culture lacks the autonomy and power to exercise the determining role. Furthermore, since every culture includes several, sometimes conflicting, strands of thought and is subject to contestation and conflicting interpretations, it never confronts its members as a homogeneous and cohesive whole. Its different elements point in different directions, leaving its members enough critical space to resist being overwhelmed by it.

As for human beings, they are never pliant, passive and devoid of independent resources. Culture is possible because individuals have certain species-derived capacities and dispositions which may be structured and modified but which cannot be eliminated. Since the causal efficacy of culture is subject to these constraints, it can never exercise a determining influence. Furthermore, no society can function without cultivating its members' powers of thought, and it cannot wholly predict or control the direction these might take. It also encourages individuals to think critically about the beliefs and practices of outsiders as part of its self-reproductive mechanism, and has no way of preventing their critical faculty from being turned towards their own culture. Human beings are also capable of dreaming dreams of better conditions, comparing themselves with other members of society, demanding justification for their differential treatment, and seeing through specious and self-serving arguments. It is hardly surprising that even after centuries of conditioning, Hindu untouchables and black slaves in the West Indies and elsewhere remained deeply sceptical of the dominant legitimizing ideology. Again, members of a cultural community come into contact with other cultures or at least hear or read about them. This gives them a comparative point of reference, and alerts them to the fact that human life can be understood and organized in several different ways and that their own is contingent and changeable.

In the light of our discussion, we can reject two extreme views. Human beings are neither determined by their culture, nor are they transcendental beings whose inner core or basic nature remains wholly unaffected by it. Their culture shapes them deeply, but they are able to take a critical view of it and rise above it in varying degrees. The extent to which they do so cannot be generalized, for that depends on the nature of the culture and the critical resources available to its members. Other things being equal, a culture that is isolated from others, derived from a single source as in the case of a religiously-based culture, or has no traditions of dissent, tends to exercise a more decisive influence on its members than one that differs from it in these respects. This is so because, unlike the latter, it confronts its members as a relatively homogeneous and cohesive whole and offers them limited critical resources with which to resist being overwhelmed by it. Even within a culture different individuals and groups are differently influenced by it. Other things being equal, those who are familiar with other cultures, or had the opportunity to develop their powers of critical self-reflection, or have reasons to be sceptical of their culture because of the unjust treatment it metes out to them, are likely to be less deeply shaped by it than others.

Loyalty to culture

Membership of any community entails obligations, and *prima facie* cultural community cannot be an exception. This raises the question whether one has obligations to it, how they are derived, and what their content is. The question has been raised with particular poignancy by a number of writers in recent years. In the aftermath of the publication of *The Satanic Verses*, Edward Said criticized Salman Rushdie for using his intimate knowledge of his community to feed the anti-Muslim prejudices of the West and showing a 'lack of loyalty' to it, and Ali Mazrui accused Rushdie of 'cultural treason'. Many African Americans level charges of 'betrayal' and 'disloyalty' against those of their members who fail to stand up for their community, turn their backs on it, or go over 'to the other side' and feed the cultural and racist prejudices of the white majority. They have even built up a disdainful vocabulary of criticism consisting of such terms as 'cultural scabs', 'Uncle Toms' and 'coconuts'.

As we have seen, a cultural community has two dimensions, cultural and communal. When we speak of obligations and loyalty to one's cultural community, we might mean to one's culture or to one's community. We shall take each in turn.

Prima facie the idea of loyalty or obligation to one's culture appears strange, for it is not clear how one can have a moral relationship with such an impersonal entity as culture. In fact it is not as strange as it seems. We often talk of the scientist's or the artist's duty to be true to science or art. This is an elliptical way of saying that they should be true to the central values and ideals of science such as the disinterested pursuit of truth and a scrupulous regard for evidence, or to those of art such as the fearless exercise of imagination and pursuit of artistic truth. In a similar vein religious people speak about being true to their religion, and liberals about being loyal to the principles and values of the liberal tradition. Loyalty to a culture is no different, and refers to loyalty to a way of life including its values, ideals, system of meaning and significance, and moral and spiritual sensibilities.

The idea of loyalty to a culture then makes sense, the only question being what its basis and content are. As we saw earlier, our culture gives coherence to our lives, gives us the resources to make sense of the world, stabilizes our personality, and so on. Its values and ideals inspire us, act as our moral compass, and guide us through life; its arts, rituals, songs, stories and literature fill us with joy and add colour and beauty to our lives; and its moral and spiritual wisdom comforts and helps us cope with the inevitable tragedies of life. While all this refers to what our culture has done for and to us, we might also think that its ideals, system of meaning and aesthetic, spiritual and other achievements represent a worthwhile vision of human life and make a unique contribution to the cultural and moral capital of mankind. During the Second World War the British rightly thought that their way of life was worth dying for, not only because it was theirs but also because it represented a great human achievement of universal and permanent value.

We then feel and should feel a sense of loyalty to our culture because of its profound contribution to our lives and also perhaps because of its universal value (Tamir 1993, pp. 130f). If we think that it has no worthwhile ideals, is highly oppressive, has poorly equipped us for leading the good life or distorted our intellectual and moral development, our obligation or loyalty to it is considerably weakened. No culture, however, is wholly worthless, for then it is unlikely to command the allegiance of its members and last long. And even a culture with exiguous resources stabilizes human life, orders human relations, creates some measure of trust between its members, and is a source of at least some good. While our culture has therefore at least some claim on our loyalty, it may be overridden if on balance our judgment of it is negative.

Assuming that our culture is reasonably rich, our loyalty to it generates several duties. We have a duty to cherish the memories of those who creatively contributed to it and sustained it during trying times, and to exemplify its noblest ideals, both as an expression of our gratitude and as an earnest of our continuing commitment to our cultural inheritance. We also have a duty to preserve and pass on to succeeding generations what we think valuable in it, to defend it against its perverse misrepresentations, a point made by Edward Said in his criticism of Rushdie, and to protect it against wanton attempts to destroy or discard it, a point made by many a leader of the developing world against those compatriots of theirs who blindly throw away their precious cultural heritage in favour of cheap cultural imports of dubious value. Loyalty to a culture also involves a duty to explore, deepen and enrich its resources and remove its defects. No culture is perfect, and it is bound to include beliefs and practices that are perverse and sit ill at ease with its values and ideals. To love one's culture is to wish it well, and that involves criticizing and removing its blemishes.

The idea of loyalty to one's cultural community is not as unfamiliar as that to one's culture. It implies loyalty not to the ideals, values and so forth of a culture, but to the community of men and women built around these. Just as we owe and generally feel a sense of loyalty to our families, schools and political and religious communities, we also owe

it to our cultural community. One is grateful to it for providing a network of support, solidarity, moral and emotional resources, and a sense
of rootedness. Since a culture can only be preserved by a community,
one is also indebted to the latter for keeping the culture alive, sometimes against formidable challenges and at a considerable cost. The
obligation of loyalty is stronger if the community is in danger of disintegration from external threats as is the case with many a native people,
or if it has been traumatized by the most horrendous experiences as in
the case of Jews in the aftermath of the Holocaust. In the latter case an
additional dimension is introduced by the duty to cherish the memories
of, and express continuing solidarity with, the millions who died pointless deaths.

Loyalty to one's cultural community generates duties, some of which
are similar to those entailed by loyalty to one's culture. These duties are
owed to the members of one's community and not to the ideals of one's
culture. And since they arise from the kinds of considerations mentioned earlier, they often persist even if one decides to reject one's culture. The structure of norms, conventions, values and practices which
underpins and maintains a cultural community is built up over a long
period of time. We inherit it, benefit from it and, as Dworkin puts it,
'have some duty, out of simple justice, to leave the structure as we
found it' (1985, pp. 232f). Since cultural freeriding, nihilism, circum-
venting cultural and moral constraints in pursuit of narrow self-interest
or gratification of fleeting impulses, and so forth are the surest way to
destroy a cultural community, its members have a duty to resist these
temptations. They also have a duty to defend it against mischievous
misrepresentations and not to allow themselves to be used by others for
such purposes, a point made by many African Americans against those
of them who readily endorse anti-black prejudices in the hope of material and other rewards. Obligations to one's community also include the
duty to expose and fight against its injustices and repressions. Mahatma
Gandhi expressed this well when he said that he so deeply loved his
community that he could not bear to see it disfigured by such practices
as untouchability, child marriages and caste oppression.

Cultural communities are not voluntary associations like clubs, political parties and pressure groups, and are wholly misunderstood if conceptualized as such. They are not instrumental in nature in the sense of
being designed to promote, and to be discarded if they fail to promote,
extrinsic interests. Unlike voluntary associations, again, they are not

deliberate human creations but historical communities with long collective memories of struggles and achievements and well-established traditions of behaviour. We do not join but are born into them, and are not so much their members as part of them. Our associational identity is elective whereas our cultural identity is an inheritance which we may either accept or reject. Unlike voluntary associations we are deeply shaped by our cultural communities and derive our values and ideals from them. Although we might leave them, we cannot do so in the same way as we leave voluntary associations. Once we resign our membership of the latter, we generally have nothing to do with them. This is not possible in relation to the cultural community. We might, of course, avoid participating in its collective life, discourage its members from entertaining certain expectations of us, and marry outside it, but none of these can sever all our ties with its culture or other members. We continue to retain some of its culture including its language, collective memories, ways of carrying ourselves, and at least some attachment to its rituals, music, food and so forth. And even when we leave our cultural community, our relations, close friends and other might not, and then we remain associated with it in varying degrees. And if *per impossible* we can manage to discard both its culture and all our communal ties with it, outsiders might continue to identify us with it, making it extremely difficult and unwise for us to dissociate ourselves from it altogether. If others continue to see and despise me as a Jew or a black man even when I no longer define myself in this way, both my sanity and self-interest require me to find a way of strategically aligning myself with the community while retaining a critical distance from it.

A cultural community performs a role in human life that a voluntary association cannot. It gives its members a sense of rootedness, existential stability, the feeling of belonging to an ongoing community of ancient and misty origins, and ease of communication. And it does all this *only because* it is not a conscious human creation and one's membership of it is neither a matter of choice nor can be easily terminated by oneself or others. Just as a voluntary association becomes oppressive and defeats its purpose when it begins to behave like a cultural community, the latter becomes fragile, contingent, subject to volatile human preferences and interests, and defeats its very point when it behaves like or becomes a voluntary association. Both cultural communities and voluntary associations have their proper places in life, and the recurrent liberal tendency to reduce the former to the latter must be resisted.

Cultural interaction

Every cultural community exists in the midst of others and is inescapably influenced by them. It might borrow their technology, and the latter is never culturally neutral. It might also be consciously and unconsciously influenced by their beliefs and practices. Even when it is not, their very presence leads it to distinguish itself from them by stressing some beliefs and practices more than others, particularly when it is involved in a conflictual relationship with them. Other cultures are not a mute external fact but shape its self-definition, and constitute a silent and unacknowledged presence within it.

It is difficult to think of any culture save perhaps the most primitive and isolated that is not influenced by others. The culture of classical Athens was profoundly influenced by the earlier Athenian culture, those of other Mediterranean countries, Egypt and countries further east, as well as by its constant attempt to distinguish itself from Sparta and Persia. Christianity was a product of Judaism, Oriental cultures, Roman religious and political beliefs and practices and Greek philosophy, as well as its concern to separate itself first from Judaism and then from Islam. Islam was deeply shaped by Judaism, Christianity, pre-Islamic religious beliefs and practices and the Aristotelian philosophy, as well as by its concern to establish a separate identity from the other two Semitic religions. The modern West has drawn heavily on the intellectual and technological achievements of Greek, Roman, Indian, Chinese and other civilizations, and is deeply shaped by its persistent tendency, especially during the colonial period, to contrast itself with and establish its superiority to the rest of mankind. In short, cultures are not the achievements of the relevant communities alone but also of others, who provide their context, shape some of their beliefs and practices, and remain their points of reference. In this sense almost all cultures are multiculturally constituted.

The trend towards intercultural interaction has gained considerable momentum in recent years. Thanks to globalization, technology travels freely across the globe and carries its cultural inscriptions. The successful ways of organizing the economy and running industrial organizations developed in one country are borrowed by others who cannot make good use of them without reproducing their cultural preconditions. Transnational communications giants such as the CNN, Sony, Warner Brothers and News International transmit a standardized western culture, and to a lesser extent some non-western cultural beliefs, practices and products as well, to different parts of the world. Increased migrations of people bring cultures into closer contact, and transnational diasporas act as both intercultural transmitters and synthesizers. Thanks to the concentration of advanced educational institutions in the West and the failure of the rest of the world to throw up comparable counterparts of their own, the future elite of the latter travels west, taking its sometimes half-understood culture back home and leaving behind small deposits of their own.

Globalization, of course, primarily originates in and is propelled by the West, and involves westernizing the rest of the world. However, matters are not so simple (Appadurai, 1990, pp. 295–310). Non-western ideas also travel on its back, as is evident in the New Age movement and the spread of non-western religions, medicine, goods, arts and literature to the West. Furthermore, western ideas cannot easily graft outside their cultural home unless they are suitably modified in the light of what in their producers' views the non-western world appreciates or customarily associates with the West. Western cultural exports thus are often not authentically western but a product of double abstraction, involving the West's abridgment of its culture based on its analogous abstraction of the rest of the world. Such abstract western caricatures travel back home and distort the West's own self-understanding and ways of life. Western exports do not make local sense unless they are adjusted to local cultures as defined paradoxically by westernized local elites. Globalization, therefore, involves localization and at least some appreciation of and respect for cultural differences.

While all this is true, the fact remains that western culture today enjoys enormous economic and political power, prestige and respectability. Its interactions with other cultures occur under grossly unequal conditions, and those at the receiving end often find it difficult to make autonomous choices. Unable to arrest the disintegration of their traditional cultures which have hitherto given meaning to their lives and held them together as communities, they experience a veritable moral panic and become vulnerable to pedlars of a fundamentalist return to an allegedly pristine past. Uncritical and wholesale assimilation of western culture is not the answer for them, because inherited cultures cannot be discarded like clothes or new one assimilated without appropriate indigenization. A return to the certainties of the past is not the answer either, for these are largely products of nostalgic myth-making and are neither related to contemporary reality nor carry conviction with many of their members. The only course of action open to such societies is to undertake the momentous task of creatively reinterpreting their culture and judiciously incorporating those elements of western culture that they approve of and can assimilate. This is a task for their cultural leaders, and the government's job is largely limited to creating the conditions of a national dialogue, encouraging cultural experimentation, ensuring that external agencies do not manipulate and distort the internal debate, and giving the indigenous cultural activities and 'industries' judicious encouragement and assistance.

Cultural diversity

Cultural diversity or the presence of a variety of cultures and cultural perspectives within a society has much to be said for it. The first systematic case for it was made by J. S. Mill, Humboldt, Herder and others and has been recently restated with important modifications by Berlin, Raz and Kymlicka in particular. Briefly they advance one or more of the following four arguments in support of it. First, cultural diversity increases the available range of options and expands freedom of choice. This argument makes an important point but is exceedingly restrictive. Since it values other cultures only as options or potential objects of choice, it gives no good reason to value such cultures as those of indigenous peoples, religious communities, the Amish or the Gypsies which are not realistic options for us. Indeed, the argument implies that the more different other cultures are from our own, the less reason we have to cherish them. As we shall see, the opposite is often the case. It does not make out a convincing case for mainstream cultures either. Since we are deeply shaped by our culture and find it too much of a moral and emotional wrench to give it up or radically revise it or even introduce into it the beliefs and practices of another, other mainstream cultures are rarely options for us. Furthermore, the argument gives no good reason to cherish cultural diversity to those who are perfectly happy with their culture and have no wish to add to the options provided by it.

Second, some writers argue that since human beings are culturally embedded, they have a right to their culture, and that cultural diversity is an inescapable and legitimate outcome of the exercise of that right. This argument shows the inescapability but not the desirability of cultural diversity. It establishes why membership of one's culture is important but not why cultural diversity is; why one should enjoy access to one's own culture, not why one should also have access to others. Furthermore, giving individuals a right to their culture does not by itself ensure cultural diversity. If the wider society has an assimilationist thrust, or if the dominant culture is overpowering and respects and rewards only those who conform to it, members of other cultures would lack the capacity, the confidence and the incentive to retain their cultures, leading over time to the withering away of cultural diversity. It is therefore not enough to grant them the formal right to their culture. Society should also create conditions conducive to the exercise of that right, such as respect for differences, nurturing minority self-confidence, and provision of additional resources to those in need of them. The wider society would not wish to incur the cost involved, welcome the required changes in its institutions and way of life, and restrain its assimilationist impulse unless it can be persuaded that cultural diversity is in its interest or a value worth cherishing.

Third, Herder, Schiller and other romantic liberals advance an aesthetic case for cultural diversity, arguing that it creates a rich, varied and aesthetically pleasing and stimulating world. They make a valid point, but it is too weak and vague to carry the moral burden placed on it. Aesthetic considerations are a matter of taste, and it is not easy to convince those who prefer a uniform moral and social world. Cultures, furthermore, are not merely objects of aesthetic contemplation. They are moral systems and we need to show that their diversity is not only aesthetically but also morally justified. If we cannot, as the monist insists, then either the moral case for uniformity overrides the aesthetic one for diversity or we need to find some way of resolving their conflict.

Finally, Mill, Humboldt and others link cultural diversity to individuality and progress, arguing that it encourages a healthy competition between different systems of ideas and ways of life, and both prevents the dominance of any one of them and facilitates the emergence of new truths. As we saw earlier, although Mill weakened the force of this argument by tying it too closely to a particular view of human excellence, it contains important insights. However, it suffers from several limitations. It takes a largely instrumental view of cultural diversity and does not appreciate its intrinsic value. Since it stresses progress, it also needs to provide criteria of it; these are not only difficult to agree upon but predetermine the outcome of cultural diversity and delimit its permissible range, hardly the way to encourage the unexpected and the new. Finally, since cultural diversity is linked to competition, it cannot defend the rights of indigenous peoples, the Amish, orthodox religious groups and others who have no wish either to compete or to discover new truths.

Although a convincing case for cultural diversity must include these and other arguments, I suggest that it can best be made by approaching the subject from a different perspective. Since human capacities and values conflict, every culture realizes a limited range of them and neglects, marginalizes and suppresses others. However rich it might be, no culture embodies all that is valuable in human life and develops the full range of human possibilities. Different cultures thus correct and complement each other, expand each other's horizon of thought and alert each other to new forms of human fulfillment. The value of other cultures is independent of whether or not they are options for us. Indeed they are often valuable precisely because they are not. Although a native people's way of life is not an option for us, it serves important cultural purposes. By cherishing such commendable values and sensibilities as harmony with nature, a sense of ecological balance, contentment, innocence and simplicity, which our way of life has to sacrifice in order to attain its characteristic form of excellence, it both reminds us of our limitations and reassures us that the values are not lost altogether. Its unassimilable otherness challenges us intellectually and morally, stretches our imagination, and compels us to recognize the limits of our categories of thought.

Cultural diversity is also an important constituent and condition of human freedom. Unless human beings are able to step out of their culture, they remain imprisoned within it and tend to absolutize it, imagining it to be the only natural or self-evident way to understand and organize human life. And they cannot step out of their culture unless they have access to others. Although human beings lack an Archimidean standpoint or a 'view from nowhere', they do have mini-Archimidean standpoints in the form of other cultures that enable them to view their own from the outside, tease out its strengths and weaknesses, and deepen their self consciousness. They are able to see the contingency of their culture and relate to it freely rather than as a fate or a predicament. Since cultural diversity fosters such vital preconditions of human freedom as self-knowledge, self-transcedence and self-criticism, it is an objective good, a good whose value is not derived from individual choices but from its being an essential condition of human freedom and well-being (Weinstock, 1994).

The diversity of cultures also alerts us to that within our own. Used to seeing differences between cultures, we tend to look for them within our own and learn to do them justice. We appreciate that our culture is a product of different influences, contains different strands of thought, and is open to different interpretations. This makes us suspicious of all attempts to homogenize it and impose on it a simplified and singular identity. It also encourages an internal dialogue within the culture, creates a space for critical and independent thought, and nurtures its experimental vitality. As we saw in our discussion of Christianity, tolerance of external and internal differences complement and reinforce each other. A culture or a religion that considers itself the best and suppresses others or fears and avoids contacts with them tends to take a unified and homogeneous view of itself and suppress its internal differences and ambiguities as well.

Cultural diversity creates a climate in which different cultures can engage in a mutually beneficial dialogue. Different artistic, literary, musical, moral and other traditions interrogate, challenge and probe each other, borrow and experiment with each other's ideas, and often throw up wholly new ideas and sensibilities that none of them could have generated on their own. What creative writers do at a sophisticated level, ordinary men and women do unselfconsciously in their daily encounters. A British Indian taking invasive pictures at a religious ceremony was gently asked by an English friend if that was a common practice in India and did not offend the feelings of the gathering. The Indian and his friends got the message and behaved better on future occasions. When their white colleague died, an Afro-Caribbean asked their common white friend to join him in calling on the widow. His friend reluctantly agreed, was pleasantly surprised by her welcome, and came to appreciate that the largely unquestioned English practice of leaving the bereaved alone could do with a change. In these and other ways communities educate and even 'civilize' each other provided, of course, that none is too overbearing and self-righteous to welcome criticism. They also represent different talents, skills, forms of imagination, ways of looking at things, forms of social organization, different senses of humour, and psychological and moral energies, all of which constitute a most valuable resource which can be fruitfully harnessed in such different areas of life as scholarship, sports, business, management, creative arts, industry and government.

To say that cultural diversity is desirable for these and other reasons is not to say that the prevailing forms of it should be preserved. A culture has no authority other than that derived from the willing allegiance of its members, and it dies if they no longer subscribe to its system of beliefs and practices. Practices may be compelled but not beliefs, and once the latter are lost, practices become largely social and lose their cultural meaning. No culture can therefore be preserved by force or artificial means. Those keen to preserve the existing forms of cultural diversity sometimes argue that although such new cultures as we might create could be better or just as good, they are bound to suffer from a grave disadvantage. Being products of conscious human choices and individualist in their orientation, they can be constantly unscrambled and replaced by others, and cannot by their very nature form the basis of stable communities. Cultural conservatives also argue that unlike the long established existing cultures with the accumulated weight of tradition behind them, new cultures have no history, traditions, evocative collective memories, intergenerational continuity, a coherent narrative and so on, and that encouraging them would destroy the great historical achievements of the past without putting anything worthwhile in their place. They point to the case of long-established religions which no new ones have been able to replace, and contend that it is better to reform and cherish those we have rather than seek to create new ones.

The conservative argument is not without its merits. Cultures are easy to undermine but exceedingly difficult to create. It is therefore unwise to destroy what has stood us in a reasonably good stead for centuries. Furthermore, although the new cultures we might create could be better or just as good, they might also be worse, and in matters so central to human existence, one needs to be cautious and resist the spirit of postmodernist adventurism. While all this is true, it misses out many important dimensions of culture. If the existing culture does not command the allegiance of its members, there is simply no way to keep it alive. Furthermore, all existing cultures need radical changes because of their deep-seated sexist, racist and other biases which cause considerable suffering to large sections of their members. Every age also has its distinct needs, experiences and aspirations, and cultures must be adapted to these if they are to conduce to human flourishing. Indeed, since every historical epoch gives rise to different conceptions of time, tradition, self, space and so on, the kind of culture that suited earlier ages might not be relevant or feasible in ours. In short, although a cultural community may legitimately stand up for its moral values and vision, it should also allow for experimentation and innovation and ensure a judicious balance between continuity and change.

Some of the arguments I made above for cultural diversity are open to an obvious objection. A critic might argue that he is perfectly happy with his culture and that, as long as it enables him to lead a reasonably good life, he sees no point in acquiring access to others. While conceding that they have rich resources, he might argue that one cannot have all the cultural wealth in the world and that one should, or that he personally prefers to, concentrate on fully exploiting the resources of his own admittedly imperfect way of life. He might also argue that since self-consciousness, critical self-knowledge and so forth plant doubts about the value of one's way of life and deny one the minimum certainties necessary for a stable life, they are not desirable virtues, at any rate not for him and others like him who would rather live by their simple faith than risk losing it in search of higher truths. For these and other reasons he might prefer a culturally homogeneous society or, if he were already living in a plural one, prefer to live within his own cultural tradition. This raises the question whether and how we can convince him that a culturally homogeneous society, or a way of life confined to one cultural tradition, has less to be said for it than a culturally plural society or a culturally open way of life respectively. We shall take each in turn.

A culturally homogeneous society has its strengths. It facilitates a sense of community and solidarity, makes interpersonal communication easier, sustains a thick culture, is held together with relative ease, is psychologically and politically economical, and can count on and easily mobilize its members' loyalties.[5] It also, however, has a tendency to become closed, intolerant, averse to change, claustrophobic and oppressive, and to discourage differences, dissent and what J. S. Mill (1964) called experiments in living. Since it has limited resources for internal resistance, it can be as easily mobilized for evil as for good purposes. It is narrowly based and lacks the conditions necessary for the development of such great intellectual and moral virtues as intellectual openness, humility, tolerance of differences, critical self-consciousness, powers of intellectual and moral imagination, and extensive sympathy. Our hypothetical critic is wrong to underestimate these virtues and to believe that he can do without them. He wishes to explore and exploit the resources of his own culture, but these are often more exiguous than he imagines and could benefit from a sympathetic dialogue with others. Even when his culture is reasonably rich, such a dialogue deepens his insight into it and helps him identify, nurture and exploit its resources better. He wants moral certainty, which is better secured by uncovering and reflecting on the grounds of his beliefs than by forcibly suppressing the inevitable doubts with all the attendant insecurity and anxiety.

We can also argue that, other things being equal, a culturally diverse society can reproduce most of the desirable qualities of the homogeneous society, but the reverse is not the case. There is no obvious reason why a culturally plural society should not develop a sense of community, solidarity, common loyalties and a broad moral and political consensus; I later show how it can do so. By contrast, a culturally homogeneous society cannot provide the creative tensions of an intercultural dialogue, expand imagination and moral and intellectual sympathy, and so forth. Although a culturally diverse society is not better in all respects, it is likely to achieve a better balance of the qualities desirable in a good society.

We must also consider the contemporary historical reality. Thanks to globalization and the changing nature of modern technology, no society today can insulate itself against external influences. Capital, technology, people, ideas and so on move freely across territorial boundaries and introduce new forms of thought and life. Thanks to the liberal and democratic spirit of our age, hitherto marginalized groups demand recognition, and the resulting internal dissent undermines old certainties. Since cultural diversity characterizes almost all societies albeit in different degrees, they must either find ways of coming to terms with and even profiting from it, or suppress or marginalize it by somehow homogenizing themselves. The latter is impossible because it involves an unacceptable degree of internal repression, limited contacts with the outside world, forcible assimilation of cultural minorities, restrictions on foreign travel, control of the media, total bans on foreign literature and technology, and so forth, and even then it has no chance of success as the examples of Iran, Saudi Arabia and many other developing countries demonstrate. The only choice open to any society today is to manage and build on the creative potential of its diversity.

A society must suit the temperament, traditions, needs and psychological and moral resources of the people involved. And a culturally homogeneous society has its obvious strengths. Although we cannot, therefore, conclude that a culturally plural society is necessarily and universally better, we may legitimately say that it has more to be said for it both in principle and in the current historical context. The same conclusion can be extended to groups wanting to lead culturally self-contained lives within a multicultural society, such as the Amish, orthodox Muslims, Catholics and Jews, the indigenous peoples and gypsies. Culturally open and self-contained ways of life have their strengths and weaknesses. The former can be shallow, eclectic, bland, thin and devoid of coherence and historical depth, just as the latter can be repressive, intolerant, narrow, inward-looking and authoritarian. A way of life must also suit the needs, circumstances and the temperament of the people involved, and cannot be prescribed in the abstract. No group today, however, can lead a self-contained and isolated life. Unless it is territorially concentrated and isolated, and often not even then, it cannot altogether avoid the influence of the wider society and remain as homogeneous as hitherto. It must therefore find ways of accommodating the demands of its inescapable internal diversity and reconstituting the traditional culture on a new basis.

If some individuals or groups freely choose to live within their traditional culture, we should respect their decision. Multiculturalism is not committed to the view that only the culturally open way of life is the best; indeed if it were, it would reproduce the monist mistake and betray its inspiring principle. It recognizes that the good life can be led in several different ways *including* the culturally self-contained, and finds space for the latter. It does, of course, hold that, other things being equal, there is more to be said for a culturally open and diverse than for a culturally self-contained way of life. However, since it appreciates that the latter has its virtues, adds to the richness of the wider society, suits some communities better and represents their autonomous choices, it respects it and does not require all its members to conform to a single model of human excellence.

Evaluating cultures

It is sometimes argued that cultures are incommensurable and should be judged in their own terms. Both propositions are half-truths. Cultures have aesthetic, moral, literary, social, spiritual and other dimensions. Since the standards required to judge these are too disparate to be reducible to a single general standard, the idea of judging, comparing and grading whole cultures is logically incoherent. Even so far as their moral lives are concerned, cultures represent unique and highly complex visions of the good life, and cannot be measured on a single scale. Insofar as the incommensurability thesis asserts this, it makes a valid point.

Although we cannot compare whole cultures, we can do so in specific aspects. We can show that one culture's literature is richer and explores with greater sensitivity a wider range of human emotions and experiences than another's, or that its spirituality is deeper and its view of God nobler, more inspiring and less terrifying than that of another. The moral and political aspects of cultures are also amenable to such a comparison. It is a demonstrable fact about human beings that they are corruptible, fallible, prone to misjudgment, partiality and bias. We can evaluate cultures in terms of the ways in which they guard against these limitations, and argue that those that check, regulate and distribute power and allow for open expressions of disagreement and debate are less prone to hypocrisy and misuse of authority, more stable and more conducive to human flourishing, and in that respect better than those that do not. Again, it is a demonstrable fact of human life that human beings grow into sane adults only under certain conditions; that they suffer when subjected to a climate of terror or when systematically humiliated, or when their loved ones are killed or tortured or raped at will; that their capacities for love, sympathy and disinterestedness are limited; and so forth. We can compare cultures on the basis of the extent to which they respect the constraints of these and other universally shared human features. Since the latter are culturally mediated, we need to be extremely careful as to how we use them. Children do need a loving environment but that need not take the form of a nuclear family, and power needs to be checked but the checks need not take the form of liberal constitutionalism. Once we take cultural differences into account, we have the required resources to make cross-cultural comparative judgments.

As for the view that cultures should be judged internally or in their own terms, it is, again, only partly valid. It is valid in the sense that we should understand cultures from within before passing judgments on them, should not expect them to conform to our standards of right and wrong, and that no external judgment is likely to make much sense to their members, let alone have any impact on them, unless it resonates with their moral self-understanding. Once we go beyond these and other generalities, the idea of judging a culture in its own terms becomes deeply problematic. It rests on a positivist view of culture and assumes that the latter has a fixed body of values carrying a fixed set of meanings. As we have seen, no culture is like that. Its beliefs and values are of different levels of generality, and need to be interpreted to suit new and unexpected situations. Its systems of meaning, too, are constantly stretched to allow for different interpretative possibilities. A culture is not static and contains both the residues of its largely dormant past beliefs and prefigurations of the newly-emergent ones. In short, every culture is too multistranded, fluid and open-ended to have 'fixed terms' in which to evaluate it. A couple of examples will illustrate the point.

Orthodox Hindus defend the caste system on the ground that it is sanctioned by the scriptures. Its critics appeal to the higher principle of the unity of life and oneness of all beings that lies at the heart of many of these scriptures, and argue that the caste system is incompatible with it. Both, alike, judge the system in terms of the resources of the Hindu culture itself and reach opposite conclusions. To take an example from a very differently constituted culture, liberal society considers equality to be one of its central values, and for decades defined it to mean equality of respect and rights. Socialists challenged this on the ground that formally equal rights were empty unless their bearers had the resources to exercise them equally effectively, and that an adequate definition of equality should include a broad equality of these resources. Liberals argued that socialists were overextending the meaning and even subverting the idea of equality by smuggling in the very different idea of social justice; socialists rejoined that they were only giving it a coherent and realistic meaning and accused liberals of disingenuously restricting the term within the narrow confines of the capitalist society. For liberals, equality of rights was the central value of their society, and socialists were importing an external value. For socialists, liberal society was committed to a wider sense of equality and they were appealing to its own internal value. Even if the two had agreed that equality of rights was the central value of liberal society, they would have disagreed about its meaning and implications. For liberals it involved formal equality of rights, for socialists equality of power and resources. Each claimed to judge liberal society in its own terms and reached very different conclusions.

Every culture is exposed to others and cannot avoid comparing itself with them. A section of its members might be attracted to some of the latter's beliefs and practices, and either genuinely read them back into their tradition or reinterpret it to legitimize the foreign import. In a culture with a long history it is almost always possible to find elements which can be suitably interpreted to yield critical resources. The women's campaign for equality is a good example of this. Attracted by the modern idea of equality, advocates of women's equality in Muslim societies reinterpreted their tradition and claimed to find support for their demand. They pointed to the fact that the Prophet's wives were powerful women with careers of their own, that his first wife ran a flourishing business, that his young and favourite wife Ayesha had views of her own and sometimes disagreed with him, that one of the *hadiths* reports him as saying that women should be accorded equal respect, and that the long history of Islam has witnessed many a powerful woman ruler and soldier. Similar reinterpretations have also occurred in the Judaic, Christian and other traditions. Reformers' criticisms in each case were both internal and external in nature, the latter in their original inspiration, the former in their grounding and mode of articulation, thus cutting across and rendering untenable the internal–external distinction presupposed by the internalist critique of culture (cf. Walzer, 1994, pp. 10f).

It might be argued that in all these cases the conservative view is more faithful to the tradition than the reformist, and that reformers are somewhat disingenuous. Although the criticism of the reformers is sometimes justified, it misunderstands the nature of culture and the point of the hermeneutic struggle. A culture has no essence. It includes different strands of thought, and reformers are right to highlight those that have been marginalized, suppressed or misconstrued by the dominant interpretation of their tradition. Furthermore, every tradition can be read in different ways, none of them definitive and final. Although the reformist interpretation might not be wholly accurate, it is plausible and based on at least some evidence, and it is up to the cultural community to decide whether or not to accept it. A culture cannot survive unless it addresses the issues and aspirations of the age. While conservatives might be more faithful to its texts or history, they risk losing their alienated followers' allegiance and undermining the viability of their culture. Reformers might be wrong or even disingenuous in their interpretations, but they at least keep their culture alive and vibrant.

When loyalty to its past tragically comes into conflict with its future, the reformer makes the right choice.[6]

Respecting cultures

It is sometimes suggested that we have a duty to respect other cultures and even that all cultures deserve equal respect. This is a misleading way of conveying an important insight. It would help greatly to approach the subject by taking the more familiar case of respect for persons. We can take it for granted that we have a duty to respect other persons. This involves, among other things, respecting their autonomy including their right to run their lives as they please. However, it does not prevent us from judging and criticizing their choices and ways of life. Obviously our judgement should be based on a sympathetic understanding of their world of thought from within, as otherwise we both misjudge their choices and do them injustice. However, if after careful consideration and listening to their defence we find their choices perverse, outrageous or unacceptable, we have no duty to respect and even a duty not to respect these choices. We separate the right and its exercise, and do not allow our attitude to one to influence that to the other. Their right does not forfeit our respect because it is exercised badly, and our respect for it does not entail respect for its manner of exercise. The separation is not absolute, and situations might arise when the exercise of the right is so systematically perverse that we might wonder if the individual should continue to enjoy it at all.

We might fruitfully approach the question of the proper attitude to other cultures along similar lines. A culture has two dimensions, a community whose culture it is and the content and character of that culture. Respect for a culture therefore means respect for a community's right to its culture and for the content and character of that culture. The two forms of respect have different bases. We should respect a community's right to its culture for a variety of reasons, such as that human beings should be free to decide how to live, that their culture is bound up with their history and identity, that it means much to them, and so forth. Every community has as good a right to its culture as any other, and there is no basis for inequality.

As for culture itself, our respect for it is based on our assessment of its content or the kind of life it makes possible for its members. Since every culture gives stability and meaning to human life, holds its members together as a community, displays creative energy, and so on, it deserves respect. However, after a sensitive and sympathetic study of it from within, we might conclude that the overall quality of life it offers its members leaves much to be desired. We might then think that we are unable to accord it as much respect as another which is better in these respects. Although all cultures have worth and deserve basic respect, they are not equally worthy and do not merit equal respect. When judging other cultures we should be careful, as argued earlier, not to seek to mould them in our image. Although we are right to insist on the kinds of basic values discussed earlier, we should neither inflate the list nor disallow their cultural mediation. Respect for human dignity, for example, should be insisted upon, but it should not be confused with liberal individualism, and similarly the area of personal choice is crucial to human well-being, but should not be equated with full-scale autonomy as defined by Raz, Dworkin and even Kymlicka. Broadly speaking, if a cultural community respects human worth and dignity, safeguards basic human interests within the limits of its resources, poses no threat to outsiders and enjoys the allegiance of most of its members, and thus provides the basic conditions of the good life, it deserves to be respected and left alone.

When confronted with another culture, we should then respect the relevant community's equal right to cherish and live by it as well as judge its content and base our overall response on both. This is where monists and culturalists go wrong. The former argue that since some cultures are superior, they have a right to impose themselves on others, making the mistake of concentrating on the content of the culture and ignoring both the community's right to it and the basic respect owed to each culture. Culturalists make the opposite mistake of assuming that since every community has a right to its culture, we are not entitled to judge, criticize or press for changes in it. We should respect the community's right to its culture but should also feel free to criticize its beliefs and practices. In exceptional cases when these are outrageous and it seems incapable of changing them, we might wonder if we should continue to respect its right to autonomy. However, no cultural community is devoid of reformist resources, its constitutive beliefs and practices are best changed from within, and the outsider is unlikely fully to understand its complexity. While we may rightly press for change, and urge that the community should practise internal democracy and allow public debate, we should generally respect its autonomy. How much pressure to put on it and of what kind depend on our relation to it. If it is outside our territorial boundaries we have no direct responsibility for it, do not share a common life with it, lack intimate knowledge of it and so on, and hence our right and duty are limited. If it is within our territorial boundaries the situation is different, though again much depends on whether the community concerned wishes to lead a self-contained life as the Amish and ultra-orthodox religious groups do, or to maintain limited contacts with the wider society as indigenous peoples do, or to become an integral part of it as is the case with immigrants. The greater its involvement with the wider society, the greater is the latter's right and duty to be concerned about its way of life.

In all these cases one general point needs to be borne in mind. There is a persistent tendency in some sections of western society to act as global missionaries and assume that other societies are all devoid of reformist resources and need western guidance and 'moral leadership'. I have argued above that the assumption is unfounded and a source of much colonial, neocolonial and other forms of violence. The West has taken nearly 2000 years and the murder of millions of Jews to face up to and deal with its anti-Semitism, over half as many and enormous human suffering to challenge its racism and so on, and can do with a large measure of humility and self-criticism. If western societies can reform themselves without external assistance, there is no reason to assume that the rest of humankind cannot, unless it is supposed to consist of a less gifted species. There is a profound difference between respectful moral concern for the well-being of other societies and insensitive hectoring in a spirit of moral superiority. The former is most welcome, the latter to be avoided at all cost.

6

Reconstituting the Modern State

Although the modern state as we know it today shares some of its constitutive features with its historical predecessors such as the Greek *polis*, the Roman *civitas*, and the medieval kingdom and empire, it defines them differently, possesses additional features of its own, and represents a novel political formation. It is not a culturally neutral instrument of order and stability as it is often assumed to be, but is embedded in a particular vision of political order. When it began to emerge in the late-fifteenth and early-sixteenth centuries, different social groups with different interests and expectations sought to shape it in different ways, giving rise to much political struggle and philosophical discussion concerning its nature, structure, functions and place in social life. Over time, one model or theory of the state gained political and philosophical ascendancy and decisively shaped its structure. It had a strong liberal orientation and was championed by the rising bourgeoisie and the professional classes. For convenience and in order not to identify it with a particular political and philosophical doctrine, I shall call it the dominant theory or model of the state. Since states have to survive in the real world and make messy adjustments and compromises, few of them conform to the model, but the latter remains the ideal they seek to approximate and by which they measure their success.[1]

In premodern western and non-western polities territory played a largely instrumental role. A polity was distinguished by its way of life, and the latter not the territory was its locus of identity and primary object of loyalty. Many African tribes defined their collective identities in terms of their traditional ways of life, moving to new places with their gods and totems to ensure their sense of continuity. Traditional Muslim societies defined themselves in terms of their shared body of personal laws and practices, and when their members migrated individually or collectively they carried these laws with them. That is why Muslim kingdoms and Ottoman rulers left Jews and Christians free to lead their traditional ways of life, and believed that their authority did not extend over the latter. This was also broadly the case in traditional Hindu societies, and, with some variations, under the Roman empire and in medieval Europe. The Greek *polis* defined and distinguished itself as a people sharing a common way of life, and the territory it occupied had only a limited political, moral and legal significance. In all these polities territorial boundaries, although reasonably clear, were relatively porous whereas social boundaries were rigid and zealously guarded.

In the modern state territory enjoys unprecedented importance. It is the material basis or the body of the state and is unambiguously marked off from others, lest there should be any doubt in the minds of its members and outsiders where it begins and ends. Its territorial boundary encloses its members and gives them a distinct geographical and political identity including a collective name. To enter the territory of the state is to enter its jurisdiction and be subject to its authority. Unlike almost all earlier polities, the modern state offers protection to everyone who happens to be within its territorial boundaries, irrespective of whether or not they are its full members. In Athens such protection was a political privilege available only to its citizens, and the outsider required a citizen patron to qualify for it. In the feudal polity, protection and the right to claim indemnity against attack or harm were limited to those owing fealty to the lord. It is hardly surprising that the inhabitants went with the territory and were subject to the laws of whoever acquired it. Unlike most premodern polities, which were socially exclusive and denied citizenship to those who did not share their ways of life, the modern state can accommodate total strangers and might even be composed of them.

The importance of territory to the modern state was officially confirmed by the Treaty of Westphalia of 1648 (Spruyt, 1994). For a long time non-territorial agencies were independent and autonomous agents able to enter into binding relations with governments. The Hanseatic League, founded in the middle ages and made of self-governing merchant cities, was an important European power and made treaties with sovereign governments. Like the papacy it was excluded from being a party to the negotiations that led to the Peace of Westphalia and was eventually dissolved. Within a territorial unit the state was regarded as its sole collective spokesman. The morally dubious notion that the state's primary concern is to safeguard its territorial integrity rather than its way of life or its citizens' interests, and that it must defend 'every inch' of even its uninhabited and remote territory at a considerable cost in human lives, is distinctly modern.

In many earlier polities individuals had multiple identities, for example ethnic, religious, social and territorial. Since some of these identities cut across territorial boundaries, individuals remained relatively free to cross these for social, religious and other purposes. The identities and the concomitant loyalties were accepted as an inescapable feature of social life and regarded as independent sources of rights and duties that limited the government's authority. The modern state is almost unique in privileging territorial identity. Its members do, of course, have multiple identities, affiliations and allegiances, but territorial identity is overarching and dominant, a point securely established by the Treaty of Westphalia and all subsequent international agreements. Unlike its earlier counterparts the modern state territorializes and totalizes human relations and sets up a legally and morally self-contained unit only contingently related to others. This was why classical natural law theorists such as Vitoria, Suarez and Grotius were deeply worried lest it should stand between the individual and the 'great human society' or the 'universal human community', break up the latter into closed communities and deny either the fundamental moral obligations human beings 'naturally' owed one another[2] or the religious obligations Christians owed their fellow-religionists irrespective of territorial boundaries.

The modern state also represents a historically unique mode of defining and relating its members. Unlike premodern polities which were embedded in and composed of such communities as castes, clans, tribes and ethnic groups, it has increasingly come to be defined as an association of individuals. It abstracts away their class, ethnicity, religion, social status, and so forth, and unites them in terms of their subscription to a common system of authority, which is similarly abstracted from the wider structure of social relations. To be a citizen is to transcend one's ethnic, religious and other particularities, and to think and act as a member of the political community. Because their socially generated differences are abstracted away, citizens are homogenized and related to the state in an identical manner, enjoying equal status and possessing identical rights and obligations. The state and the citizen represent two interdependent polarities of the political relationship, each defined in formal and abstract terms. Since the two are directly related, the modern state is suspicious of, and feels threatened by, well-organized ethnic, religious and other communities lest they should mediate the relations between it and the citizen and set up rival foci of loyalty. Unlike premodern polities, the modern state does not generally grant them legal recognition and political status, invest them with rights or allow citizens' loyalty to them to be on a par with it. Its individualist basis shows the extent to which it institutionalizes liberalism in its very structure and self-understanding.

The authority of the modern state is not a collection of discrete rights and prerogatives; these are all aspects or attributes of a unitary, basic and overarching power called sovereignty. Almost all earlier polities were characterized by plural systems of authority, each with its own distinct source and manner of functioning. And often they all had to agree before the ruler's decision became binding. As for the specifically legal authority, it too was plural, consisting of different and mutually irreducible powers, each valid within a specific area. In the modern state different systems of authority are replaced by sovereignty, the unitary, supreme and legally unlimited power from which all other powers are deemed to be derived. Sovereignty is deemed to be inherent in the state in the sense that the latter possesses it by virtue of being what it is. It is the state's constitutive, corporate and historically continuous attribute and belongs to it alone. Unlike pre-statal politics, the ruler or the government does not possess sovereignty. It only possesses the right to exercise sovereignty when that right is acquired according to clearly stated procedures. This distinction between authority and sovereignty is unique to the modern state.

The modern state then is constituted in terms of, and expected to meet, the following six requirements:

- First, it should be territorially distinct, possess a single source of sovereignty and enjoy legally unlimited authority within its boundaries.
- Second, it should rest on a single set of constitutional principles and exhibit a singular and unambiguous identity. A state whose constitution enshrines a mixed body of principles, or applies them differently to different parts of the country or different sections of citizens, is deemed to possess a hybrid or confused identity and to form

what Pufendorf called *corpus irregulare monseto simile* (an irregular body, like that of a monster).

- Third, citizens of the state should enjoy equal rights. And since their social, cultural and other differences are abstracted away, equal rights generally mean identical or uniform rights. The state represents a homogeneous legal space within which its members move about freely, carrying a more or less identical basket of rights and obligations.
- Fourth, citizenship is a unitary, unmediated and homogeneous relationship between the individual and the state. Since it involves abstracting away cultural, ethnic and other identities and seeing oneself solely as a member of the state, all citizens are directly and identically related to the state, not differentially and through their membership of intermediate communities.
- Fifth, members of the state constitute a single and united people. They may be divided along ethnic, cultural and other lines, but these are politically irrelevant and do not detract from the fact that they are one people and that the majority of them is entitled to speak and act in the name of all of them.
- Finally, if the state is federally constituted, its component units should enjoy broadly the same rights and powers, as otherwise citizens in different parts of the country would posses different rights, thereby detracting from the principles of equal citizenship and homogeneous legal space.

The modern state is a remarkable and truly original European achievement. It raises the individual above religious, ethnic and other forms of communal consciousness and creates an unprecedented regime of personal liberties and rights. It eliminates personalized rule and replaces it with an impersonal system of government in which the citizen is subject only to the authority of the law. It establishes equality between its members, bypasses the social hierarchies of status, caste and class, and nurtures their sense of dignity. It also provides them with an impersonal and enduring object of allegiance and loyalty, widens their moral sympathies, creates shared citizenship and a space for collective action, and represents the triumph of human will over natural and social circumstances. Not being based on the unity of race, ethnicity, religion or substantive moral beliefs, it is able to provide space for personal autonomy and cultural and religious freedom. It fosters a sense of community among its otherwise unrelated members, institutionalizes their sense of mutual concern, and gives their collective life both a public focus and a historical continuity. By interposing itself between society and government, it protects each from the unrestrained domination of the other, and creates conditions for a relatively inviolate private realm, an autonomous civil society, and an autonomous public realm governed by publicly articulated and debated norms of rationality.

The modern state, however, has several limitations, the one central to our discussion being its preoccupation with political and cultural homogeneity. This is not a contingent failing or an aberration, but is inherent in the way it has been defined and constituted for past three centuries. All its citizens are expected to privilege their territorial over their other identities; to consider what they share in common as citizens far more important than what they share with other members of their religious, cultural and other communities; to define themselves and relate to each other as individuals; to abstract away their religious, cultural and other views when conducting themselves as citizens; to relate to the state in an identical manner, and to enjoy an identical basket of rights and obligations. In short, the state expects all its citizens to subscribe to an identical way of defining themselves and relating to each other and the state. This shared political self-understanding is its constitutive principle and necessary presupposition. It can tolerate differences on all other matters but not this one, and uses educational, cultural, coercive and other means to ensure that all its citizens share it. In this important sense it is a deeply homogenizing institution.

Since the state presupposes and seeks to secure homogeneity, it has a tendency to become a nation. It is often argued that nation and state are different kinds of political organization, and that the nation-state was a result of the unfortunate nationalist hijacking of the state. This does not explain why nationalists were able to do so, why states after states proved willing accomplices, and why this did not happen to premodern polities. Although liberal states are hostile to ethnic nationalism, they are keen on its so-called civic variety, which is really only another way of articulating the homogeneity lying at the basis of the modern state. It is striking that almost all the major theories of the state such as the liberal, the communitarian and the nationalist take it for granted that it should be uniformly and homogeneously constituted, and differ only in the kind and degree of homogeneity they prefer. Liberals insist that all citizens should define themselves in individualist terms; communitarians that they should subscribe to common substantive goals; and nationalists want them to share a common national identity and culture.

The modern state makes good sense in a society that is culturally homogeneous or willing to become so. In multi-ethnic and multinational societies whose constituent communities entertain different views on its nature, powers and goals, have different histories and needs, and cannot therefore be treated in an identical manner, the modern state can easily become an instrument of injustice and oppression and even precipitate the very instability and secession it seeks to prevent. This will become clear as we examine the case of Canada whose current predicament well highlights the difficulties created by the dominant theory of the state in most multicultural societies.

The Canadian debate

For over a quarter of a century the French-speaking majority in Quebec have insisted that they constitute a distinct cultural community with their own history, language, legal system, values, conception of their place in the world, collective consciousness of being a distinct people, and so forth. In their view their cultural identity is being increasingly eroded by the combined pressure of the federal government and the economically and linguistically dominant Anglophones in Quebec, and the only way to preserve it is to secure greater political autonomy by suitably restructuring the Canadian state. For the Quebecois, Quebec is not just a province of Canada like any other, but a co-founder of the Canadian federation and entitled to full equality with the rest of English-speaking Canada, as guaranteed by the Quebec Act of 1774, the Constitution Act of 1791, and the British North America Act of 1867. Indeed, it had entered the Canadian federation 'on the faith of a promise of equality and of respect for our authority in certain matters that to us are vital', and in the expectation that Canada would be a binational state. The Quebecois consider it an act of betrayal that with the exception of Ontario and New Brunswick, the French-speaking people in the rest of Canada were pressurized to abandon their language and culture, and are themselves determined to avoid that fate at all cost.

With that objective in mind, Quebec made two sets of demands. It wants the Canadian state to recognize it as a 'distinct society', enshrine this in its Charter, and define itself as a binational country committed to nurturing its dual identity.[3] This would confirm Quebec's status as a Francophone homeland, mark it out from other provinces and ethnic groups, and require the Supreme Court of Canada to take its cultural needs into account when adjudicating on the constitutionality of its laws. Quebec's other demands are more specific and relate to the powers it thinks it needs to preserve its identity. It wants the right to control immigration into Quebec and to require immigrant children to go to French schools. It also wants the right to do all that is necessary to make French its dominant *lingua commune* and give Quebec a 'French visage', including the right to require that all commercial signs should be in French, that all products sold in Quebec have French labels, that all workplaces of a certain size should conduct their business in French, and so on. Quebec also demands that the Canadian Charter and all future constitutional amendments should apply to it only with its consent, and that at least three justices of the Supreme Court should be Quebeckers.

After considerable resistance and protracted negotiations, the rest of Canada has met many of Quebec's demands. Quebec now has considerable control over immigration, most though not all the powers it needs to promote the French language, its own pension plan, and a right to diplomatic representation abroad. Economically and politically it has not done badly either. It annually receives over Canadian $3.1 billion more from the federal government than it pays in taxes, and during most of the past 30 years Canadian prime ministers have come from Quebec. But this falls short of Quebec's demands in two important respects. The Meech Lake Accord of 1987, which recognized it as a 'distinct' society and the Francophone presence as a 'fundamental characteristic' of Canada, was not ratified by all the provincial legislatures in time, and enjoyed the support of just over 20 per cent of Canadians outside Quebec. Quebec is also bound by the Canadian Charter, some of whose provisions prevent it from pursuing the cultural and language policies it wishes to pursue and would be able to do if it were an independent country. Since most of the Quebecois remain dissatisfied, the threat of Quebec's secession is real as confirmed by a referendum three years ago.

As in all such cases the reasons for the rest of Canada's reluctance to meet Quebec's basic demands are mixed. Some think that it is determined to secede anyway and that no amount of accommodation will stop that. For some others, Canada would be a more cohesive society without Quebec and should let it go. Some would like to accommodate

Quebec but fear that that would provoke similar demands in other provinces and render Canada so messy, weak and asymmetrical that it would not last long or be a country to which they would be proud to belong. Yet others simply cannot make sense of Quebec's conceptualization of the Canadian political reality. For them Canada is not a binational country, for such a description takes no account of the Aboriginal peoples, homogenizes English-speaking Canada, and ignores Quebec's own minorities. It is not a bicultural country either but multicultural, composed of several old and new cultural communities of which the Quebecois are only one. While agreeing that Quebec is a distinct society, they insist that its distinctness has declined after the 'silent revolution' of the 1960s and that other provinces are just as distinct.

It is not my concern to analyse the politics of Canada or arbitrate between the competing conceptualizations of its history and origins. I intend instead to explore the reasons why a large number of Canadians, who otherwise sympathize with Quebec's aspirations and delight in their country's bicultural ethos, feel that its demand for an asymmetrical federation goes against their deeply held beliefs about how a state should be constituted.[4]

1. Every state should be based on a single set of legal and political principles to which all its citizens owe their allegiance and which form the basis of their patriotism and collective identity. The Canadian Charter of Rights and Freedoms lays down such principles. Quebec's demand to reinterpret and limit its application makes Canada an incoherent and ill-shaped polity.
2. Quebec's demand for a privileged status and the asymmetrical federation that this creates violates the principle of the equality of the provinces that should characterize a well-constituted federal state.
3. All Canadians are 'above all' Canadians and only secondarily and derivatively Quebecois, Ontarians or anything else. Quebec's view that its citizens are Quebecois first and only secondarily Canadians privileges the Quebec identity, dilutes the significance of Canadian citizenship, and weakens the unity of the Canadian state. Quebec is a part of Canada and cannot be allowed to claim moral and political equality with it.
4. As its Charter shows, Canada is a liberal state committed to upholding the fundamental rights of its citizens. Quebec's wish to restrict them in order to preserve its French identity has a collectivist thrust and cannot be allowed. When it is pointed out that Quebec's respect

for fundamental rights is just as great as that of the rest of Canada, that it has its own *Charter des Droits* which in some respects is more liberal than its national counterpart, and that it generally seeks to restrict only the relatively unimportant rights, critics rejoin that all parts of Canada should subscribe to the same basic rights, define and prioritize them in the same way, and should be liberal in a more or less identical manner. Quebec's proposal to create a different system of rights amounts to creating a state within a state and undermines the singularity of the Canadian state.

5. Citizens of a state should enjoy equal rights and freedoms regardless of where they live. The restrictions Quebec intends to impose on individual rights do not obtain in other parts of the country, and offend against the principle of equal citizenship.

6. The Canadian state represents a single and united people, and majority decision binds them all. Since the Quebecois are a minority within Canada, they are wrong to dictate its constitutional arrangements and should have the democratic grace to accept the system of rights agreed upon by the majority of their countrymen.

All six arguments spring from the dominant theory of the state sketched earlier and highlight its inability to cope with deep diversity. As for point 1, although it is not always necessary for a country to have a constitutionally enshrined bill of rights, a good case can be made out for it in a multicultural society provided that the rights enjoy broad support among its constituent communities, do not enshrine the domination of one culture, and, subject to certain constraints, allow the communities to interpret and prioritize them to suit their culture, traditions and aspirations. The Canadian Charter fails all three tests. It was adopted in the teeth of Quebec's opposition. It enshrines the liberal-individualist view of human rights and frustrates and, according to some commentators, was designed to frustrate Quebec's cultural aspirations. And it does not give Quebec sufficient power to reinterpret its provisions. Some of these difficulties could be overcome by recognizing it as a distinct society with all that it entails, which is why Quebec is right to press for it.

The second argument is mistaken because it fails to appreciate that when provinces have different histories, backgrounds and needs, to treat them as if they were the same is to treat them unequally. Indeed, to call them all provinces is to impose a uniform identity on what are otherwise very different collectivities. Quebec is not so much a province as a national society or a territorially concentrated cultural community, and is qualitatively different from most of the rest of the country. Furthermore, like any other federal state the Canadian state acknowledges that since different provinces are unequally endowed in their natural and human resources, the poorer ones should be given additional resources to equalize them with the rest. This is why it follows the policy of equalization of payments; the Canadian Constitution Act of 1982 allows provinces with higher than average unemployment to prefer their own residents to migrants from others; and unlike English-speaking Canada which is governed by the common law, Quebec is governed by the Napoleonic code. Since the Canadian state rightly takes account of the economic and legal differences between its provinces, there is no obvious reason why it should not take account of their cultural differences as well.

The third argument makes an important point but exaggerates and misunderstands it. Citizenship is an important status and no political community can last long unless its citizens identify with it. Since some Quebecois see Canada as a necessary nuisance or no more than a source of financial benefits, they need to be reminded that they are political freeriders and cannot claim rights and benefits without acknowledging the corresponding obligations and loyalties. As we have seen earlier, they also need to define their Quebecois identity in such a manner that it does not exclude or undermine their Canadian identity. However, this is very different from saying that the two are inherently incompatible, that one cannot be equally loyal to both Quebec and Canada, or that one might not relate to the latter through one's mediating membership of the former. For centuries European states insisted that their members should share a common religion and doubted the loyalty of those who did not. Over time and after much bloodshed they realized that this was counterproductive, and that the best way to win over their members' loyalty was to respect their religious differences within a suitably broadened theory of citizenship. A similar lesson needs to be learnt in relation to ethnic and especially national differences. The lesson is harder to learn because, unlike religious groups, territorially concentrated national minorities compete with the state on its own terrain and demand a more or less equal share in the exercise of its jurisdictional authority over their territories. Unless we find ways of accommodating the demand, and that involves redefining the traditional view of the state's relation to its territory, we run the risk of provoking a cycle of secessionist violence and undermining the very unity and stability for whose sake the demand is resisted.

Arguments 4 and 5 rest on a common fallacy. Whether or not Canada should be a liberal state must be decided by all its major communities and not by one of them alone. Even when they all agree that it should be one, there is no reason why they should all subscribe to a uniform version of liberalism. There is no single and universally valid way to be a liberal any more than there is to be a Christian or a Hindu. The American Bill of Rights does not include rights to culture and language whereas their Indian and Canadian counterparts do, the United States gives far greater importance to freedom of speech than do France and Britain, and so on, but it would be misleading to say that only one of these countries is 'truly' liberal. There is no reason why Quebec should not be free to define and apply liberal principles in a manner that best suits its cultural goals and develop its own distinct form of liberalism, or even evolve a kind of good society which, while incorporating essential liberal values, rests on different foundations. There is also nothing wrong or even unusual about having somewhat different rights in different parts of the country. After all, in most federal polities laws, and therefore citizens' rights and obligations, vary from state to state. In the United States some states ban hard pornography but others do not, and some give greater welfare rights to their citizens than do others.

Argument 6 is valid but fails to appreciate its limits. The principle of majority rule presupposes a single and homogeneous people who see themselves and behave as one. Just because a group of men and women share a common state, they do not constitute a single people. They might over time become one but they might not, and until they do they are clearly not one. Quebec is obviously not a foreign country in Canada and is bound to the latter by close political, economic, historical, emotional and other ties. However, since the Quebecois also have a distinct history, culture, traditions and so forth, and constitute a more or less distinct people, they both are and are not a part of the Canadian people. Peoplehood is not a closed and exclusive category such that one cannot belong to more than one people. Since Quebec is a distinct society, it cannot be bound without its consent by the majority of the rest of Canada in matters that are central to its identity and in which it is not a part of the Canadian people.

In the light of our discussion the arguments against Quebec's demand for recognition as a distinct society and an asymmetrical federation are unjustified. This is not to say that all of Quebec's demands are justified or that it has pursued them with requisite sensitivity to the deepest fears and anxieties of the rest of Canada.[5] Some of its nationalist spokesmen have so heavily privileged their *Quebecois* identity over the Canadian, and taken such pleasure in mocking Canada or reducing it to a weak, amorphous and largely instrumental federation, that the rest of the country has sometimes rightly wondered if it should reconstitute the state to accommodate Quebec. Our concern, however, is not to judge the political wisdom of the parties involved, but to highlight the ways in which the dominant theory of the state has muddied the debate and rendered the problem intractable.

The Indian debate

The kind of debate taking place in Canada is to be found in many other countries as well; in some of which it involves not only the territorially concentrated but also other minorities. Take the case of India. Recognizing that the state of Kashmir is culturally distinct and anxious to preserve its identity, Article 370 of the Indian Constitution gave it powers and protections not available to other Indian states, and subsequent legislation barred citizens of the rest of the country from settling and buying land in Kashmir. A few years ago the Constitution extended many of these provisions to the newly created states in the North Eastern region, where the culturally distinct and economically backward tribal communities were anxious to preserve their ways of life including control over their lands.

Partly out of respect for their religious and cultural identities and partly to assuage their fears of Hindu rule, the Constitution of India allowed its religious minorities to retain their personal laws and undertook not to change these without their consent. India has a common criminal but not civil law, and the Constitution hoped that the latter would be developed over time. It remained vague on whether the minority personal laws were subject to the constitutionally enshrined set of fundamental rights, and the Supreme Court subsequently ruled that they were not. The Constitution also exempted minority educational institutions from the policy of affirmative action who, unlike their majority counterparts, do not have to set aside a proportion of seats for the ex-untouchables and economically backward tribal communities. It did so partly to preserve the distinct cultural character of minority institutions and partly because the beneficiaries of affirmative action are all Hindu and their current predicament is largely a result of

Hindu oppression or neglect. The Indian parliament or state legislatures have passed laws banning bigamy among Hindus but not among some minority communities, they exercise greater administrative control over Hindu religious institutions than over the non-Hindu, and regulate the activities of criminals masquerading as Hindu holy men but not their counterparts in other communities. Reasons for such a differential treatment are complex. Most Hindus trust the state and are prepared to allow it to act as their reformist arm. Since Hindus form a majority, the scale of religious corruption in absolute terms is also greater. The state hopes that by starting with them, it will set an appropriate example to minority communities.

All this has aroused considerable opposition among many militant Hindus and some liberals, broadly on the same grounds as those invoked in relation to Quebec. It is argued that the state should be based on a single and uniform set of fundamental principles, that it should have a uniform legal system, that the principle of equal citizenship requires all citizens throughout the country to have exactly the same body of basic rights and obligations, that allowing minority personal laws and giving the communities concerned a veto over changes in them compromises the sovereignty of the state, that the state should take no cognisance of religious, ethnic and other identities, and so on. Since the Indian state 'deviates' from the model of a 'properly consti-tuted' state, and has both liberal and nonliberal elements which give it what Pufendorf called an 'irregular shape, like that of a monster', crit-ics argue it should be radically rationalized. The implications of this are clear. Kashmir should lose its special status, minority religious, educa-tional and other institutions should be subjected to the same require-ments as their Hindu counterparts, minority personal laws should not be recognized, India should enact a single civil code, and the state should in general stop 'privileging' and 'pampering' its minorities.[6]

The Indian case illustrates once again the difficulties of applying the dominant theory of the state to societies characterized by deep diversi-ties. Its minorities have reacted most strongly against the proposed rationalization of the state, and forced the predominantly Hindu Bharatiya Janata Party which is currently in power to tone down or shelve its proposals. The proposals are not only politically unworkable but have no basis in justice. When different communities have different needs and are not alike in relevant respects, it is unjust to insist on treat-ing them alike. Like Quebec, Kashmir has a distinct history, identity, traditions and so on, and needs powers not demanded by or necessary for other Indian states. This is equally true of the Punjab with its distinct Sikh identity, and the North Eastern states with their tribal identities. Muslims, Christians, Parsis and other national minorities have their distinct ways of life, and a common civil code either cannot be easily evolved out of their different systems of personal laws or runs the risk of enshrining the views of the powerful Hindu majority. Since the state cannot remain indifferent to the iniquities of some of these laws and needs to insist on certain basic principles of justice, the only just and practicable course of action is to aim at what the Catholic Bishops' conference in 1998 called a unified rather than a uniform civil code. Such a code lays down common principles of gender equality, individual liberty and social justice and leaves the minorities free to follow their suitably revised personal laws. Since most Indians define themselves as both individuals and members of particular communities and demand both individual and collective rights, there is no reason either why the Indian state should not have both liberal and nonliberal features and reflect its citizens' dual political identity.

The search for new political formations

Broadly speaking, the modern state represents the institutional integration of several different functions within a single territorial and political unit. It is the sole defender of its territorial integrity, provides the only legitimate system of authority within its boundary, regulates the economy, safeguards and transmits the national culture, and is a symbol of the collective identity of its citizens. Thanks to new military technology, globalization, interlocked economies, dominance of multinational corporations, emergence of regional and continental consciousness, and assertions of cultural, ethnic and other identities, the state's traditional military, political, economic, cultural and symbolic functions today have very different logics. They do not all coincide or vertically converge on the state, and they call for different sorts of subnational, national and international institutions.

This does not mean that the state is withering away or becoming obsolete. It continues to perform an important historical role, as it alone is currently able to provide a stable and democratic structure of authority, to establish the rule of law, to maintain order, to ensure social justice, to manage conflict and to give its citizens a collective sense of agency. Many of its other traditional functions, however, have either lost their relevance and value, or require a different structure of authority, or can no longer be discharged by it on its own. Since it is constantly exposed to external influences and its citizens do not, and cannot be made to, share a moral and cultural consensus, it is no longer a cohesive cultural unit and cannot base its unity on the cultural homogeneity of its citizens. It also cannot claim to embody and legitimate itself in terms of their sense of collective identity, both because many of them no longer place much emphasis on their political identity or privilege it over all others and because some have strong transnational ties and identities. The state cannot discharge its economic and military functions on its own and is not a cohesive economic and military unit. The state is not fully sovereign over its territory and shares it with local and supranational agencies; conversely its sovereignty is not limited to its territory and frequently extends beyond its boundaries. In an age of globalization, migration and footloose capital, territory does not enjoy the degree of inviolability and the moral, emotional and political importance it did earlier. In short the old unity of territory, sovereignty and culture (or identity) that has hitherto propelled the development and consolidation of the modern state and provided its historical rationale is fast disintegrating.

Since we can then neither write off the modern state nor continue with it in its current form, we need to reconceptualize its nature and role. This involves loosening the traditionally close ties between territory, sovereignty and culture and re-examining the assumptions lying at the basis of the dominant theory of the state mentioned earlier. The state need not consist of a single people and could be a community of communities, each enjoying different degrees of autonomy but all held together by shared legal and political bonds.[7] Just as we have a territorially based federal structure to accommodate self-governing regional entities, we could have a culturally based federal structure with its inescapably 'ill-shaped' legal and political arrangements. The sovereignty of the state need not consist of a single and unitary system of authority as most political theorists since Hobbes have insisted, and might involve several centres of authority exercising overlapping jurisdictions and reaching decisions through negotiations and compromise. It might not even extend to all areas of life as most theorists of the state have argued, for the constituent communities might never have alienated their customary rights of self-determination to the state as the individuals in the state of nature are deemed to have done in the traditional contractualist accounts of the sovereignty of the state. The state's sovereignty need not be internally or externally unlimited either, especially if its major communities cut across state boundaries. It might then be more realistic for the states involved to share their sovereignty in certain areas and exercise it through cross-border political institutions, as is currently being done in the case of Northern Ireland, or to create a wider political framework with the power to lay down and enforce rules concerning how they should treat their minorities as in the case of the European Union.

There is also no reason to believe that the state should represent a homogeneous legal space, for territorially concentrated communities with different histories and needs might justly ask for different powers within an asymmetrical political structure; or that every state should have a uniform system of laws, for its different communities might either not be able to agree on them or might legitimately demand the right to adapt them to their circumstances and needs. The state should obviously treat all its communities equally but that need not entail identical treatment. Some communities might trust and authorize it to play an active reformist role in their internal affairs, whereas others might take the opposite view, making state neutrality desirable in one case but not in another.[8]

The task of exploring new modes of constituting the modern state and even perhaps altogether new types of political foundation is particularly acute in multicultural societies. They need to find ways of pluralizing the state without undermining its unity and the ability to act decisively in the collective interest. Every multicultural society needs to devise its own appropriate political structure to suit its history, cultural traditions, and range and depth of diversity. It cannot even begin to do so without liberating its political imagination from the spell of the dominant theory and its assumption of a single and universally valid model of a properly constituted state.

7

The Political Structure of Multicultural Society

A multicultural society faces two conflicting demands and needs to devise a political structure that enables it to reconcile them in a just and collectively acceptable manner. It should foster a strong sense of unity and common belonging among its citizens, as otherwise it cannot act as a united community able to take and enforce collectively-binding decisions and regulate and resolve conflicts. Paradoxical as it may seem, the greater and deeper the diversity in a society, the greater the unity and cohesion it requires to hold itself together and nurture its diversity. A weakly held society feels threatened by differences and lacks the confidence and the willingness to welcome and live with them.

A multicultural society cannot ignore the demands of diversity either. By definition diversity is an inescapable fact of its collective life and can neither be wished out of existence nor suppressed without an unacceptable degree of coercion and often not even then. Furthermore, since human beings are attached to and shaped by their culture, and their self-respect is closely bound up with respect for it, the basic respect we owe our fellow-humans extends to their culture and cultural community as well. Respect for their culture also earns their loyalty, gives them the confidence and courage to interact with other cultures, and facilitates their integration into wider society. As we have seen, cultural diversity is also desirable for society as a whole and represents a valuable collective asset.

Since no multicultural society can or should ignore the demands of diversity, the assimilationist mode of political integration advocated by Conservatives, nationalists, some communitarians and proponents of comprehensive liberalism is inherently unsuited to it. The assimilationist takes the nation state as his ideal and believes that no polity can be stable and cohesive unless its members share a common national culture, including common values, ideals of excellence, moral beliefs and social practices. As a custodian of society's way of life, the state is assumed to have the right and the duty to ensure that its cultural minorities assimilate into the prevailing national culture and shed all vestiges of their separate cultures. In the assimilationist view the choice before minorities is simple. If they wish to become part of society and be treated like the rest of their fellow-citizens, they should assimilate. If they insist on retaining their separate cultures, they should not complain if they are viewed as outsiders and subjected to discriminatory treatment.

There is nothing wrong with assimilation. If minorities freely decide to assimilate into the dominant culture, their decisions should be respected and they should be given every opportunity and help to do so. The question, however, is whether this degree of assimilation is necessary to ensure political unity and should be made a precondition of equal citizenship. The answer to that is in the negative. For reasons discussed earlier, minorities have a right to maintain and transmit their ways of life, and denying it to them is both indefensible and likely to provoke resistance. Furthermore, it is not clear what they are to be assimilated into. The assimilationist assumes that society has a coherent and unified cultural and moral structure, and that is rarely the case. Although the moral and cultural structure of a society has some internal coherence, it is not a homogeneous and unified whole. It varies with class, religion and region, is made up of diverse and even conflicting strands, and consists of values and practices that can be interpreted and related in several different ways. The assimilationist ignores all this, and either offers a highly abridged and distorted view of national culture or equates it with that of the dominant group.

If minorities are left free to negotiate their relations with the wider society and have an incentive to do so, they might decide to assimilate, but they are less likely to do so if assimilation is imposed, rushed or brings no benefits. The Jews have survived two millennia of a strong assimilationist pressure from Christians, the ethnic and cultural minorities in the Soviet Union have survived the most brutal repression, the formidable economic and cultural pressures of the United States have not succeeded in creating a melting pot, and the most determined attempts by the Algerian and Sudanese governments have failed to assimilate the Berbers and the southern Sudanese Christians respectively.

There are several reasons why the pressure to assimilate does not always succeed. Cultures are too deeply woven into the lives of their members to be jettisoned at will. Most of them, further, are embedded in or at least intertwined with religion, and outsiders cannot assimilate into them without changing their religion, which they are often reluctant to do. Cultures are also extremely complex structures of beliefs and practices, and their nuances, unspoken assumptions and deepest sensibilities cannot be easily acquired unless one is born into them. Total cultural assimilation therefore requires biological assimilation, and many outsiders are unwilling to pay that price. Assimilation is also generally unable to redeem its promise of full and unqualified acceptance. Even when one assimilates into the dominant culture after a strenuous effort, there is always the danger that one's slightest difference or past background might be made the basis of discrimination by the whole or a section of the wider society. The demand for total assimilation springs from intolerance of differences, and for the intolerant even the smallest differences are sources of deep unease.

The assimilationist pressure sometimes has the opposite consequences to those intended by its champions. When a society refuses to accommodate the legitimate demands of its cultural minorities, the latter seek to exploit such spaces as society itself provides to legitimize their demands. For reasons too complex to discuss here, modern western society is extremely sensitive to religion and does not wish to appear intolerant of deeply held religious beliefs and practices. Minorities are naturally tempted to take advantage of this, and demand recognition of their differences on the grounds that these are an integral part of their religion. The Sikh's turban no longer remains a cultural symbol, which is what it largely is, and becomes a badge of religious identity. The Hindu refusal to eat beef, the Muslim use of loudspeakers to call the faithful to prayer, and the Rastafarian dreadlock are all turned into mandatory religious requirements. The unfortunate consequences of the religionization of culture are obvious. Religion acquires a considerable influence over the development of the culture concerned, religious leaders assume undue authority, critical voices are silenced, and the easily negotiable cultural demands take on a strident and uncompromising religious character. Frightened by the spectre of religious militancy, liberal society throws up its own brand of secular militancy, and the consequent polarization of society takes its toll on the normal political process of deliberation and compromise.

When the religionization of their demands does not yield the desired results, minorities are sometimes tempted to legitimize them in ethnic terms, accusing wider society of undermining their ethnic identity and even of ethnocide. Cultural practices are then ethnicized, given a pseudo-natural grounding, and assigned a spurious identity-sustaining role. The same process that occurs in the religionization of culture is reproduced here with similar results. If cultural differences were accepted as a normal part of life, those involved would not need to ground them in something as intractable and non-negotiable as religion and ethnicity. Religious and ethnic differences would, no doubt, remain, but they would not become politicized, turned into the last bastions of cultural defence, and given more importance than they deserve.

Modes of political integration

In much of the literature on the subject three modes of political integration are canvassed as most likely to reconcile the demands of unity and diversity. For convenience I shall call them proceduralist, civic assimilationist, and millet models. Since they are well-known, the barest outlines should suffice.[1]

In the proceduralist view the deep moral and cultural differences to be found in multicultural societies cannot be rationally resolved, and our sole concern should be to ensure peace and stability. This requires a largely formal and neutral state laying down the minimally necessary general rules of conduct, subject to which citizens remain free to lead their self-chosen lives. If the state were to pursue substantive goals of its own, it would violate the moral autonomy of, and discriminate against, those taking different views of the good life. According to the preceduralist the formal and minimal state combines maximum political unity with maximum diversity; the former because it stays clear of its citizens' moral and cultural disagreements and makes no controversial demands on them, the latter because it imposes the fewest constraints on their choices. This view, whose origins go back to Hobbes, has been recently restated with some modifications by Michael Oakeshott (1972), Robert Nozick (1974) and Chandran Kukathas (1992a).

The civic assimilationist view occupies a halfway house between the proceduralist and the assimilationist.[2] Unlike the proceduralist, it argues that the political community requires agreement not only on its structure of authority but also on a shared culture; but unlike the assimilationist, it insists that the latter should not be comprehensive and encompass all areas of life. For it the unity of the political community lies in its shared *political* culture, which includes its public or political values, ideals, practices, institutions, mode of political discourse, and self-understanding. Unless its citizens share such a culture, they cannot engage in a meaningful dialogue, formulate and resolve their differences and pursue common goals. Subject to the constraints of the shared political culture, citizens should be free to lead their self-chosen lives in the private realm. For the civic assimilationist the public realm represents uniformity; and the private realm, which includes the family and the civil society, represents diversity. The former ensures unity, provides principles to determine the permissible range of diversity, and gives society the confidence to tolerate and even welcome deep differences in the private realm. The origins of this view go back to Locke and the founding fathers of the American republic, and it has been restated with suitable modifications by the later Rawls (1993a) and Habermas (1993).

For the advocates of the millet model, human beings are above all cultural beings embedded in their communities. All that deeply matters to them – their customs, practices, values, system of meaning, sense of identity, historical continuity, norms of behaviour and patterns of family life – are derived from their culture. As an essentially legal and administrative institution, the state has no moral status, and its sole *raison d'être* is to uphold and nurture its constituent cultural communities. It is not a community of communities, for that implies that it has an independent moral basis and its own distinct goals, but a union or a loose federation of communities, a bare framework within which those communities should be free to pursue their traditional ways of life and engage in necessary social, political and economic interactions. The state is expected not only to refrain from interfering with their internal affairs, but also to recognize and institutionalize their autonomy, enforce their customs and practices, and so on. Individuals are assumed to owe their primary loyalty to their respective communities, and derivatively and secondarily to the state.

*   *   *

Judged by their ability to reconcile the demands of unity and diversity, the three theories outlined above are all unsatisfactory in varying degrees. The proceduralist assumes that however different their conceptions of the good life might be, all citizens can readily agree on what structure of public authority is most likely to achieve peace. The assumption is unwarranted. The structure of authority can rest on a secular or a religious foundation. If the former, it can be based on universal franchise or one limited by race, class or gender. The universal franchise in turn can be equal or weighted towards the intellectual elite, as J. S. Mill (1964) had argued, or university graduates as was the case in Britain until 1948. The system of elections might be direct or indirect and take individuals as its basic units as the liberals advocate, or corporate groups as Hegel, some pluralists and others have urged. The authority of the state might be absolute or limited by a constitutionally prescribed system of separation of powers. The choice between these alternatives is moral in nature, and based on our views on such questions as the grounds and limits of civil authority, the functions of government, how it should treat its citizens, the nature of the individual, and the importance of political participation. Since individuals deeply disagree on these matters, the proceduralist is wrong to assume that decisions on the structure of political authority are purely instrumental or pragmatic in nature and easily arrived at.

Even if a state scrupulously avoided substantive goals, it would need to decide whether or not to allow slavery, polygamy, polyandry, incest, public hangings, euthanasia, suicide, capital punishment, abortion, violent sports involving animals, coerced marriages, divorce on demand, gay and lesbian marriages, unconventional sexual practices, rights of illegitimate children to inherit 'parental' property, racial discrimination, and so on. If it does not legislate on these matters, it indicates that it does not consider them sufficiently important to the moral well-being of the community to require a uniform and compulsory mode of behaviour. If it legislates, it takes a moral stand and coerces those taking a different view. Whatever it does, its actions have an inescapable moral dimension. This is also true of such policy matters as the system of taxation, allocation of public resources, and the importance to be attached to different rights and the kinds of limitations placed on their exercise. The proceduralist cannot explain how citizens are to debate let alone resolve these questions.

A morally and culturally neutral state which makes no moral demands on its citizens and is equally hospitable to all cultures and conceptions of the good is logically impossible. And since every law coerces those not sharing its underlying values, a morally and culturally non-coercive state is a fantasy. Some states might, of course, be less coercive than others, but no state can be wholly free of moral and cultural biases and the concomitant coercion on those who disapprove of its structure or actions. Even a state that institutionalizes such values as liberty and equality coerces those who are opposed to them. Since the structure and exercise of political authority are never morally neutral, the unity of a political community cannot rest on procedural foundations alone. It requires at least some agreement on what the political community is about and how it should be governed. Since the proceduralist does not explain how such agreement can be secured in a multicultural society, his account of the unity of the state is incoherent.

The proceduralist is on stronger grounds when he claims that his state provides a considerable space for cultural diversity. Since it is not committed to a substantive vision of the good life, its laws and policies make minimum demands on its citizens and leave them free to pursue their self-chosen goals. However, as we saw, the state cannot be morally as neutral as the proceduralist imagines, and hence the space for diversity is not as great as he claims. Furthermore, in most multicultural societies a particular culture is generally dominant and enjoys considerable economic and political power. By contrast others suffer from obvious structural and other disadvantages and cannot flourish or even survive for long without public moral and material support. The same dynamics of the competitive economy that creates vast economic inequalities and a disadvantaged underclass operates in the cultural sphere as well. Indigenous communities, for example, have no hope of maintaining their ways of life unless the state restricts the movement of people and capital into their territories and grants them powers of autonomy and cultural self-regulation, all of which are ruled out by the proceduralist. When cultures enjoy unequal power, as they generally do, the procedural state works to the disadvantage of minority cultures.

Although the civic assimilationist view avoids the mistakes of the proceduralist and has much to be said for it, it is open to three objections. First, since it separates private and public realms too neatly, it is unable to give a coherent account of those institutions that straddle both. For example, the school educates future citizens, and has a political dimension. However, since children are not just citizens but also human beings and members of the relevant cultural communities, their parents and cultural community have a vital interest in their education, which makes the school a cultural institution that belongs to the 'private' or civic realm. If we stressed the former, we would have to treat the school as a public institution subject to the control of the state and ignore parental cultures and choices; if the latter, we would reach the opposite conclusion. If, however, we stressed both as we should do and as many societies are increasingly doing, the civic assimilationist theory offers no guidance on the structure and functions of the school.

Religion also defies the private–public distinction. Religious persons see life as a whole and seek to live out their deeply held beliefs in their personal and collective lives. This confronts the civic assimilationist with a dilemma. If he confined religion to the private realm as he generally does, he would discriminate against religious people, alienate them from public life, provoke their resistance, and endanger the very unity for whose sake he excludes religion from the public realm. If he admitted it into the public realm, he would jettison or at least blur the private–public distinction and face the acute problem of how to deal with what would now be a multicultural public realm.

Secondly, the civic assimilationist view insists that while cultural communities are free to lead their self-chosen lives within the private realm, they should accept the political culture of the wider society. This ignores the fact that the latter is a product of history and reflects and registers the political consensus prevailing at a given point in time. As the demographic composition of society changes, or the latter throws up new ideas and movements, or when its dominant values and practices are shown to bear unduly heavily on those who are new to it or whose historical experiences are different, the established political culture needs to be suitably revised. Women's groups, not all of them feminists, have highlighted the patriarchal bias of the dominant liberal culture and pressed for its radical reassessment. There is no reason why cultural minorities should be denied that right.

What is true of society's values is also true of its political symbols, images, ceremonies, collective self-understanding and view of national identity. They, too, reflect and reproduce a particular historical consensus and need to be suitably revised when shown to misrepresent or ignore the presence, experiences and contributions of marginalized groups or to be out of step with the changes in the demographic composition of society. These groups may rightly ask that the wider society should grant them suitable public recognition in the collective expression of its identity. Such recognition confers public legitimacy on their presence, recognizes them as valued members of the community, and facilitates their integration. 'We' cannot integrate 'them' so long as 'we' remain 'we'; 'we' must be loosened up to create a new common space in which 'they' can be accommodated and become part of a newly reconstituted 'we'.

Thirdly, the civic assimilationist attempt to combine a monocultural public realm with a multicultual private realm has a tendency to work against the latter. The public realm in every society generally enjoys far greater dignity and prestige than the private realm. The culture it institutionalizes enjoys state patronage, power, access to valuable resources, and political respectability, and sets the tone of the rest of society. Although other cultures are free to flourish in the private realm, they exist in its overpowering shadow, and are largely seen as marginal and worth practising only in the relative privacy of the family and communal associations. Subjected to the relentless assimilationist pressure of the dominant culture, their members, especially youth, internalize their inferior status and opt for uncritical assimilation, lead confused lives or retreat into their communal ghettos.

The older generation of Jewish immigrants to Europe and the USA have frequently remarked that when young they used to feel deeply embarrassed if their parents spoke Yiddish in public, wore traditional dress or performed their religious and other ceremonies in public, and that over time they lost their language, cultural pride and in some cases even the culture itself. This sad phenomenon has not disappeared even in more relaxed times such as ours. A couple of years ago when I was travelling by train in Britain, I was sitting opposite an elderly Pakistani couple and next to their adolescent daughter. When the crowded train pulled out of the station, the parents began to talk in Urdu. The girl felt restless and nervous and started making strange signals to them. As they carried on their conversation for a few more minutes, she angrily leaned over the table and asked them to shut up. When the confused mother asked why, the girl shot back, 'just as you do not expose your private parts in public, you do not speak in *that language* in public'. One wonders if she would have felt so distressed if her parents had been speaking French. Though no one presumably had told her so, she knew that the public realm belonged to whites, that only their language, customs, values, bodily gestures and ways of talking were legitimate in it, and that minority ethnic and cultural identities must remain confined to the private realm. In a society dominated by one culture tolerance is not enough to sustain diversity in the private realm as the civic assimilationist assumes. Public institutions including the state need to play an active and supportive role. We shall later see what this involves.

The millet model has its merits, and hence its long historical pedigree. Ancient Greece and Rome allowed the communities of traders, travellers and others settled in their midst to be governed by their own customs and practices. In medieval England the Lombards and the Baltic merchants of the Hanseatic League lived in separate enclaves, ran their affairs according to their own customs, and paid the crown a tribute in return for its protection. This was also the practice in ancient and medieval China, where Ibn Batuta, a fourteenth-century Muslim traveller, found a congenial home in the self-governing Muslim quarters away from the 'skilled and civilized' but 'strange' majority community. Contemporary India and Israel have incorporated some elements of the millet model into their political structures and respect the personal laws of their minority and majority communities.

Respecting the autonomy of a cultural community is sometimes the only way to bring or keep the community within the wider political community as is the case in Israel, or to give it the confidence to interact with and evolve its own pattern of relationship with wider society as is the case in India, Nigeria, Sudan and many other multicultural societies with histories of intercommunal conflict. In some cases it is also just, as when there is a danger of the majority community imposing its own vision of the good life on its minorities as in India and other developing countries, or when the minority community's way of life is distinct and self-contained as with the Amish in the United States, Australian aborigines and tribal peoples in India. Cultural autonomy also adds to the cultural diversity of society with all the advantages mentioned earlier.

The millet model, however, goes far beyond cultural autonomy and self-government and claims to provide the organizing principle of the entire society. It is open to several objections. By breaking up society into self-contained communities and disallowing all but minimally necessary interaction, it militates against the development of common social and political bonds without which no political community can act effectively and maintain its unity and cohesion. The Ottoman millet system worked for centuries only because the imperial form of government ruled out a shared public life and treated non-Muslims as second-class citizens. It had great virtues including a remarkable record of religious toleration that puts Europe to shame, but it also froze religious communities, arrested the growth of common bonds, and could not cope with the demands of democracy and common citizenship. Besides, individuals belong to several communities such as the ethnic, the religious and the cultural, which do not necessarily coincide, thereby making it difficult to decide which community's autonomy to protect. Furthermore, since members of a community rarely take an identical view of their culture, institutionalizing its autonomy risks perpetuating the role of the dominant elite and threatening basic individual liberties to which the wider society cannot remain wholly indifferent, especially when disaffected individuals create disorder or ask for its help. Again, the millet model might make some sense in an undeveloped agricultural economy, but none in an industrialized society in which constant social and economic mobility and close interactions between groups break through the communal barriers and require a shared economic and political life with a common body of rules, norms and practices.

In the above I have examined four views on the political structure of multicultural societies and found them defective in different degrees. The assimilationist theory more or less ignores the claims of diversity, and the millet theory those of unity. The proceduralist and civic assimilationist theories respect both, but fail to appreciate their dialectical interplay and strike a right balance between them. They confine unity and diversity to separate realms and draw too neat a distinction between the private and public spheres with all the difficulties that these create. Since they view diversity as a fact to be accommodated rather than a value to be cherished and leave it to the precarious mercy of the cultural and political marketplace, they also work to the disadvantage of minority cultures and do not create a climate conducive to cultural diversity. If we are to develop a coherent political structure for a multicultural society, we need to appreciate the importance of both unity and diversity and establish a satisfactory relationship between them. Since different multicultural societies have different histories and traditions and include different kinds of cultural diversity, each needs to develop its own appropriate political structure. Since, however, they all face the common problem of reconciling the demands of unity and diversity, certain general principles apply to them all. These principles, which I discuss below, are not intended to prescribe a model but to act as navigational devices.

Structure of authority

Peace is the first desideratum in every society, particularly the multicultural whose tendency to provoke acute conflicts is further compounded by its inability to rely on a shared body of values to moderate and regulate them. At all costs a multicultural society must find ways of holding itself together long enough to enable its different communities to become used to each other and build up common interests and mutual trust. It needs a collectively agreed structure of authority entitled to speak and act in the name of the community, and hence a constitution that lays down the manner of constituting such an authority, its manner of exercise and area of jurisdiction. The constitution is not an ideological document laying down once and for all a body of political principles, for it would then foreclose new developments and restrict the community's political imagination, but a body of procedures and norms that is acceptable to all under its authority.[3] The procedures and norms cannot be deduced from abstract standards of fairness, for if the latter are unacceptable to those involved, they neither carry political authority nor are likely to be observed in practice. The constitution is a political document hammered out in difficult negotiations and embodying such consensus as is thrown up by the parties involved. It shapes, structures and stabilizes the wider political process, and is in turn embedded in and sustained by the latter. Although it is the source of all legal authority within the community, its own authority is political in nature and derived from the continuing popular acceptance of it.

It is not always easy to agree on the basic principles of the constitution in a multicultural society. The more substantive they are, the greater the likelihood of disagreement. It should therefore do no more than prescribe the basic structure of civil authority, its area of jurisdiction and mode of exercise. There are bound to be people who are, for various reasons, unable to agree upon even such a minimal constitution. Wherever possible and when it is not likely to store up future trouble or provoke widespread resentment, they need to be won over by appropriate concessions and placed under a weak moral or at least a prudential obligation to respect the constitution. Some groups of ultra-orthodox Jews in Israel deny the very legitimacy of the state of Israel, which in their view is expected to be created by a messianic intervention rather than by human efforts.[4] The founding fathers of the state of Israel wisely won them over by agreeing to leave them alone in certain areas, exempting them from many of the ordinary obligations of citizenship and giving them financial and other support. They are obviously a privileged group, but most of their fellow citizens thought the price worth paying, partly to bring them under the authority of the new state, partly out of the belief that they represent a valuable strand within the Jewish culture, and partly in the hope that the sense of security and the common experience of living together with secular Jews would bring about appropriate changes in their ways of thought and life (Beilin, 1992, ch. 3). The Constitution of India showed similar political prudence when it won over its religious and cultural minorities by granting them the kinds of collective rights and exemptions discussed earlier (Mahajan, 1998, chs 3 and 4).

There is a strong case for a constitutionally enshrined system of fundamental rights in a multicultural society. They affirm the equal dignity and status of all citizens, give pride of place to rights considered essential to the good life, and build them into the very structure and self-understanding of the state. They check the excesses of populism and reassure minorities that their claims to equality and justice are not dependent on the vagaries of normal politics. They also provide the minimum basis of national unity, prescribe the limits of cultural diversity, and structure the political debate on minority practices. By giving minorities the necessary self-confidence and requiring the state to respect certain norms, a statement of fundamental rights helps create a climate in which different communities can interact in a relatively relaxed manner and build up mutual trust and goodwill. It is hardly surprising that every multicultural society has increasingly felt compelled by its experiences to move in the direction of enshrining such a statement in its constitution.

Although the case for fundamental rights is overwhelming, the dangers highlighted by their critics are real and need to be guarded against. A deeply divided society might be unable to agree upon their content, and the attempt by the majority to impose them is likely to exacerbate the situation, as is the case with the otherwise excellent Canadian Charter of rights and freedoms. In such situations the society concerned should either wait until there is a consensus or settle on a fairly thin statement of rights, leaving it to the courts to give them a substantive content and the normal political process to build a consensus around it, as Israel has done with the widely accepted concept of human dignity. There is also the danger that fundamental rights might be used to silence unconventional voices, prevent public expressions of deep differences, or impose a premature closure on the outcome of intercultural dialogue. Although there is no infallible way of avoiding this, the risk can be minimized by limiting fundamental rights to matters essential to all defensible forms of good life and on which a broad cross-cultural consensus can be obtained. They should obviously be substantive enough to serve their intended purpose, but should not impose a specific vision of the good life and subtly subvert the prevailing forms of cultural diversity.

Thanks to the enormous influence of the American experience, it is commonly believed that the constitutionally guaranteed system of fundamental rights necessarily requires a Supreme Court, that the latter alone has the power to interpret and enforce them, that its decision is final and cannot be challenged, and that it extends to striking down offensive legislation. All four assumptions, especially the last three, need to be reconsidered if the judiciary is not to undermine or emasculate the democratic political process and usurp a political role. Fundamental rights do not occupy a separate realm of their own, but are embedded in and nurtured by democratic politics. Since they have both a legal and a political dimension, we need to find ways of integrating the judicial and the political process. We might give Parliament or its equivalent the right to ask the Supreme Court to reconsider its decisions in highly controversial cases, or give the Court the power to make a declaration of incompatibility and ask the Parliament to reconsider the offending legislation but not to strike it down itself, and so forth. New Zealand, Britain and several other countries are experimenting with some of these ideas, and they deserve careful attention.

Justice

In every society the state plays a vital role in fostering a sense of justice and common belonging. Its role is even greater in a multicultural society in which it is one of the few sources of unity, provides a focus to the shared life, and is expected to set an example of how to rise above narrow communal prejudices and points of view. It is therefore of the utmost importance that the institutions of the state should be, and be seen to be, impartial in their treatment of the members of different communities. This is particularly important in the case of the police.

They enforce the law and maintain order, and discharge two of the state's crucial functions. They are the first and most important link in the long chain of justice and determine what is fed into and is likely to come out of the judicial system. They come into daily contact with citizens, who judge the otherwise remote and impersonal state in terms of their experiences of the police. And as the only institution of the state that is constantly exposed to the unsavoury side of society, the police are also likely to be the most deeply corrupted by it. It is hardly surprising that in all multicultural societies their behaviour is often the focus of much minority discontent and protest. It is essential to ensure that their exercise of authority is regulated by clearly defined procedures, above all suspicion of partiality, and its misuse subjected to severest censure and punishment. It is also crucial that they should be as representative of the wider society as possible consistent with the demands of professional competence and integrity. This gives different communities the opportunity to work together, counter each other's biases, and learn to look at themselves from a wider perspective. It also prevents the identification of the state with one particular community and ensures that different communities become used to exercising authority over each other.

As the sole source of legally secured justice in society, the state needs to ensure that its citizens enjoy equality of treatment in all significant areas of life such as employment, criminal justice, education and public services. Negatively equal treatment involves absence of direct and deliberate or indirect and institutionalized, discrimination. The former occurs when those in charge of decision-making are guided by prejudices against certain groups of people, the latter when the rules and procedures they follow contain unnoticed discriminatory biases and work to the systematic disadvantage of particular communities or groups. The rule that policemen should be six feet tall, or that a candidate for an academic post must have acquired his first degree within the country, discriminates against Asians and immigrants respectively. The law should require all public institutions periodically to examine the hidden biases of their rules and procedures, and should set up appropriate bodies such as the Commission for Racial Equality in the UK and the Equal Employment Opportunity Agency in the USA to ensure that they do so. In the absence of such provisions, highly prized areas of life run the risk of becoming the unmerited preserves of a particular community, with the consequent alienation and exclusion of the rest.

Positive equality requires equality of rights and opportunities. All citizens should enjoy equal rights, and these should include not only the usual repertoire of civil, political, economic and other rights but also cultural rights. The latter refer to the rights an individual or a community requires to express, maintain and transmit their cultural identity. Since culture is an integral part of an individual's sense of identity and well-being, cultural rights are part of human rights, and a good society should guarantee them to all its citizens. Besides in every society the majority community generally sets its cultural tone and is effortlessly able to affirm and express its cultural identity. Justice requires that, subject to the limits to be discussed later, the same opportunity should be extended to the minority communities as well. By giving them the sense of security they need to express their identity and interact with the wider society, cultural rights also earn their loyalty and good will and facilitate their integration. Principles of justice regulate matters essential to the good life and relate to what Rawls calls the basic structure of society. The basic structure is not economic and political only, as Rawls maintains, but also cultural, and hence principles of justice should deal not only with liberties and material resources but also with cultural rights and opportunities. The politics of recognition is therefore part of a wider and nuanced theory of justice, with the crucial difference that unlike liberties and resources, recognition cannot be individually enjoyed or centrally distributed and calls for a more complex conception of justice. We shall return to this later (Chapters 10 and 11).

All citizens should enjoy equal opportunities to acquire the capacities and skills needed to function in society and to pursue their self-chosen goals equally effectively. This may involve giving additional help to those who need it to overcome disadvantages derived from cultural differences or past acts of injustice. Such help does not constitute what is tendentiously called compensatory discrimination, for its purpose is not to compensate for past injustices but to help these groups overcome their historically inherited disadvantages and to equalize them with the rest. Such equalizing measures are justified on grounds of justice as well as social integration and harmony. If a cultural community were to feel powerless, or be disproportionately disadvantaged, or excluded from mainstream society, it would not be able to realize its potential, would feel unjustly treated and remain a source of constant tension. As I discuss later (Chapter 8) the concept of equal opportunity requires great sensitivity when applied across cultures.

Decentralization of power has a particularly important role to play in ensuring justice in multicultural societies. Since different communities regularly encounter each other in the normal course of life at local or regional levels, respect for their differences at these levels matters to them greatly and shapes their perceptions of each other and the state. It is also easier for the local and regional bodies to accommodate differences than it is for the central government, because the adjustment required is more readily identified, limited in scale, not too costly and is generally free from the glare of publicity. There is also greater room for experimentation, mistakes are more easily corrected, and different areas can learn from each other's good practices. It is therefore crucial to build up strong local and regional units of government and use them to foster a vibrant civic culture. As recent research has demonstrated, intercommunal tensions are less frequent and more easily managed when there is an extensive local network of formal and informal cross-communal linkages nurturing the vital social capital of mutual trust and cooperation (Varshney, 2001).

Intercommunal conflicts thrive on memories of real or imagined past acts of injustice. The more bitter the memories, the more intractable the conflicts and the more difficult it becomes to restore normal relations between the communities involved. It is therefore vitally important in a multicultural society to resolve conflicts promptly in a just and humane manner and to prevent accumulation of painful memories. As for the inherited memories of the past, society needs to find ways of both pacifying the tormented consciousness of its erstwhile victims and paving the way for intercommunal reconciliation on the basis of a carefully worked out system of 'transitional' and restorative justice. A public apology for a grave past injustice is one way, provided that it is genuine, based on full knowledge and acceptance of the nature of the injustice involved and accompanied by a willingness to make at least some amends for it. This was the case in Australia when its Prime Minister, Paul Keating, backed up his apology in 1992 for the violence to the Aborigines and the theft of their land by white colonisers with appropriate legislation and financial help. As a rule, perpetrators of injustice do not want to remember the past and their victims do not wish to forget it, and their divided attitudes to it render a shared future impossible. It is vital to avoid both obsessive brooding over the past and a willed amnesia and to confront, understand and accept the past as well as break with it by rectifying its injustices and agreeing to conduct future relations on a just basis. The pain of past humiliations is best assuaged not by melodramatic demands for forgiveness from the erstwhile victims whose agony they sometimes aggravate by the implicit attempt at moral blackmail, but by a genuine and firm promise of a just future made in a spirit of collective responsibility.[5]

Collective rights

In a multicultural society, cultural communities generally demand various kinds of rights they think they need to maintain their collective identity. Some of these rights, usually called group, collective or communal rights, are not easy to accommodate within liberal jurisprudence, and raise difficult questions such as whether the concept of collective rights is logically coherent and what kinds of collectivities may legitimately claim what kinds of rights (Bauböck, 1994a, ch. 11; Kymlicka, 1995, ch. 3; Jones, 1999).

Just as individual rights are those of which the individuals are the bearers, collective rights are those of which human collectivities are the bearers. Human collectivities are of several kinds, ranging from groups united by transient or long-term common interests to historical communities based on a shared way of life. The term 'collective rights' is generic, and group, communal and other rights are its species. Like human collectivities, rights also cover a wide spectrum and encompass rights to non-interference, exemption from normal requirements, self-government, claims on society's resources, and so on. When we talk of collective rights, we need to be clear about the kind of collectivity we have in mind, the sense in which we use the term 'right', and the content of the right.[6]

Collective rights can be acquired in one of two ways. Individuals might pool their rights together or alienate them to the collectivity; we might call these *derivative collective rights*. The rights of trade unions, clubs, and so on are of this kind. Secondly, collectivities might acquire their rights *sui generis*, by virtue of being what they are and not derivatively from their members. We might call them *primary collective rights*. The rights of medieval towns to self-government including the levy of taxes, exclusion of outsiders and the right to make representations to the king, the rights of Christians and Jews to self-government under the Ottoman empire, and a tribe's right to its sacred sites and traditional esoteric knowledge fall under this category. These rights belong to the relevant collectivities *qua* collectivities and cannot be drived from their individual members for the simple reason that the latter *qua* individuals have no such right. Collectivities are human beings related to each other in certain ways and, although they are made up of individuals, they sometimes form new and independent entities making autonomous claims of their own. The distinction between derivative and primary collective rights relates to their nature or mode of acquisition, not to their rationale or mode of justification. All rights derive their justification from their contribution to human well-being, and in this respect there is no difference between the two kinds of collective rights. To say that primary collective rights are not derived from or reducible to individual rights is therefore not to say that the collectivities involved have interests independently of those of their members.

While derivative collective rights are readily conceded, primary collective rights are not, on the grounds that only the individuals can be primary bearers of rights and that all collective rights are reducible to them. The objection is based on one or more of the following four grounds:

- Rights presuppose the capacities for agency and reciprocity which only individuals possess.
- Secondly, they are ways of recognizing the moral status of and showing respect for their bearers, and only individuals, being ends in themselves, have such a status.
- Thirdly, rights are means of protecting and promoting fundamental interests, and only the individuals can have interests.
- Finally, rights can only be given to those who exist or are 'real'. Individuals satisfy the condition whereas collectivities are either wholly fictitious or elliptical ways of referring to individuals.

None of these arguments is persuasive. Animals and children can have rights though neither possess the capacities for agency and reciprocity. We grant them rights if we think it desirable, and appoint or authorize adults to exercise them on their behalf. It is not true either that collectivities lack the capacity for agency or reciprocity, for they generally have their decision-making procedures and act through their accredited representatives.

As for the second argument, it is not true that only human beings have dignity and moral status. God has both in the eyes of the believer. For Australian Aborigines the spirits of the dead and the sacred mountains and forests have a moral status. For Hindus and Buddhists all sentient beings have a moral status, and deserve respect and compassion. Human communities too can have a moral status, for they give meaning and a sense of rootedness and belonging to their members, which is why the latter are often prepared to give up their lives for them. Furthermore, it is a mistake to think that rights are ways of recognizing and respecting a preexisting moral status. They are also ways of conferring it, and hence the question is not whether human collectivities have a moral status but whether they should have it.

The third argument makes the crucial point that only human beings have interests, can suffer or prosper, feel miserable or happy, and so on, but goes wrong in defining human interests in narrowly individualist terms. Some of our interests are individual in nature; for example, I want to live, write a good book, or have a happy marriage. Some others are shared with and pertain to us as members of the community and can only be pursued together; for example, we want our political community to continue to exist, be peaceful and not torn by conflicts, culturally rich and vibrant, characterized by civility and mutual trust, or be respected and admired in the world. These are either our interests as a community and in that sense our collective interests, or form the shared background or precondition of our individual interests, and hence our common interests. In either case they may rightly be called the interests of the community.

Finally, it is not true to say that only the individuals exist and the collectivities do not. Individuals can certainly be seen, felt, touched, and so on, but there is no good reason to accept such a crude and narrow criterion of existence or reality. Britain, the United States, the Catholic Church, the United Nations, the western tradition of philosophy and the University of Hull exist, although they cannot be seen or touched. Human collectivities exist through the forms of consciousness, beliefs, practices, rituals and so on of their members and persist over time when these are institutionalized, intergenerationally transmitted and imaginatively appropriated by their members. They are made up of individuals, but equally the latter are shaped by them. Neither can be reduced to the other and declared either self-subsistent or fictitious.

Collective rights, then, are possible and can be derivative or primary in their origins. The former are created by pooling together individual rights, the latter are *sui generis*. Primary collective rights are of two kinds. First, although they belong to human collectivities, they are or can only be enjoyed and exercised by individuals. Israel's Law of Return gives diasporic Jews the right to settle in Israel. The right is possessed by the diasporic Jewish community as a whole but exercised by its members individually. This is also the case with a Sikh's right to wear a turban and a Muslim employee's right to time off for prayer. For covenenience I shall call these *individually exercised collective rights*. Second, some collective rights belong to collectivities and are, or can be, exercised by them collectively. The right to national self-determination (assuming that it is a right), the right of a community to make representations to the government or be consulted by it on issues of vital interest to it, a university's right to self-government, and so on, are of this kind. At a different level the Catholic Church's right to grant or refuse divorce and expel its members, and the Church of England's right to officiate at the coronation ceremony and to representation in the House of Lords also belong to this category. For convenience I shall call them *collectively exercised collective rights*. Some of the rights in both categories are rights to non-interference by the state or other outside bodies, some others involve positive claims on them, yet others fall somewhere in between.

Although collectivities *can* be the bearers of rights, it is sometimes argued that they *should* not be granted rights because they are likely to misuse these and threaten individual rights. The argument is flawed. All rights can be misused including individual rights. If we were to be consistent, we would have to deny the latter as well, and that is absurd. The argument also privileges individual rights over group rights, and there is no good reason to make such an assumption. If collective rights can be used to oppress individuals, individual rights too can be used to damage and destroy communities. Not all individual rights always trump all collective rights, for much depends on the relative importance of the rights in question and their context and consequences. Indeed, the contrast between individual and collective rights is overdrawn and ignores their highly complex relationship. Some collective rights threaten individual rights; for example, the right of a group to enforce moral conformity or expel its members or deny them the right of exit. Some are the very preconditions of individual rights; for example, a political community's right to self-government or independence. And some collective rights protect individual rights and empower their bearers because organized groups and communities are better able to defend the rights of their members than the latter can do individually; for example, a community's right to its culture, language or educational institutions makes it easier for its members to retain their culture or language than if these were solely matters of individual rights.

The case for collective rights, then, cannot be dismissed out of hand. We need to ask which collectivities should have what rights under what conditions. The question can only be answered in terms of considerations of human well-being, the basis and rationale of all rights, individual as well as collective. Human well-being cannot be defined in the abstract. Although we can identify universally common components of it as we did earlier, every political community interprets and prioritizes them in its own way, has its own thick notions of human flourishing, and arrives at its own ideas on the content and conditions of human well-being. While some collective rights can claim universal validity, others vary from society to society. Different societies would therefore reach different decisions on which collectivities should enjoy which rights.

It would seem that a collectivity has a *prima facie* claim to rights if it meets one of the following overlapping conditions:

- First, it means a great deal to its members, enjoys a moral status in their eyes, and they wish to preserve it. The Amish, religious sects and traditional communities, for example, fall under this category.
- Second, its existence is vital to the fundamental interests of its members, and the latter can only or best be promoted by the community enjoying the right of collective action. The indigenous peoples in Canada, Australia, India and elsewhere, and the Basques, the Kurds and other national minorities meet this condition.
- Third, a community is deeply insecure and would not and cannot integrate into mainstream society without certain guaranteed rights. Muslims and other religious minorities in post-independence India, and Christians in Sudan, Egypt and other Muslim countries in which a strong majority is determined to impose its vision of the good life on them fall under this description.
- Fourth, a community has long been subjected to systematic oppression, lacks the confidence and the ability to compete with the rest of society, and needs to be equalized with the latter by appropriate remedial or supportive group-specific measures. The ex-untouchables in India and African Americans in the United States meet this condition.

- Fifth, a community has the potential to make a valuable and unique contribution to the wider society, and can only do so if it is given the rights required to preserve its identity and attain its characteristic form of excellence. Deeply religious groups and monastic orders belong to the category.
- Sixth, some communities are based on shared doctrines of which they see themselves as custodians, and can only function and contribute to their members' and wider society's well-being when endowed with appropriate rights. This is why, although it can cause much suffering and restrict individual liberties, most states respect, say, the Catholic Church's right to excommunicate its members or deny them divorce, and exempt it from the provisions of their anti-sex discrimination legislation.

This is all rather sketchy and each of these conditions, which entitle a collectivity to claim rights, needs to be argued and articulated at greater length. However, it is only intended to indicate how we might go about assessing the claims for collective rights. In each case the nature and content of rights would vary, depending on what is required to achieve their intended purposes. Some collectivities might merit only the right to non-interference, some might merit exemption from certain general requirements, yet others might rightly claim positive support of the state and other public institutions. In some cases we might think it better not to grant rights with all their legal and other complications, and settle the matter by accommodation or by imposing duties on others. This is a decision about how best to meet the legitimate claims of the collectivities involved, and does not affect the validity of the claims themselves.

While a collectivity merits rights under certain conditions, the rights have no meaning unless it is able to act as a collective agent and possesses the requisite institutional structure to take and enforce its decisions. Furthermore, since individual rights are just as, or even more, important and deserve to be safeguarded, its decision-making procedure should be broadly acceptable to its members, provide them with a collectively acceptable mode of redress and allow them the right to exit without excessive cost. Although it is not necessary that the collectivity should allow elections, representative institutions, and so on, for that is a matter for its members to decide, it is crucial that its internal functioning should enjoy their broad-based support. Exit from a community can never be cost-free, for no community worth belonging to treats its members' departure with indifference or which they can leave without a sense of loss. However, the cost should not involve depriving them of their legitimate claims on its resources or what is widely accepted as theirs.

When confronted with the claims of cultural communities to different kinds of rights, we should then ask such questions as whether these promote their members' or wider society's well-being, whether granting rights is the best way to do so, whether communities have the institutional resources to exercise these rights and provide an acceptable mechanism for a trade-off between these and individual rights in cases of conflict, and what the overall social, financial and other costs are. Answers to these questions do not always coincide. Although a community's claim might be legitimate, it might lack the requisite institutional resources, or be internally oppressive and refuse to change. We need to weight up these and other considerations. And since there is no infallible or incontrovertible method of doing so, we should reach a decision by means of a democratic dialogue between the parties conducted in a spirit of goodwill and compromise.[7]

Common culture

Like any other society, a multicultural society needs a broadly shared culture to sustain it. Since it involves several cultures, the shared culture can only grow out of their interaction and should both respect and nurture their diversity and unite them around a common way of life. For those accustomed to thinking of culture as a more or less homogeneous and coherent whole, the idea of a multiculturally constituted culture might appear incoherent or bizarre. In fact such a culture is a fairly common phenomenon in every culturally diverse society (Appiah, 1994, 1996).

Take something as mundane as cuisine. Chinese cuisine was initially an exotic import in the West, but over time many of its members acquired a fondness for it and made it an integral part of their dietary culture. Those who enjoyed their traditional food at home visited Chinese restaurants from time to time, and moved with ease between the two. In recent years a further development has taken place. The Chinese and western cuisines are no longer wholly separate. Each has borrowed the other's ingredients, method of cooking, and so on, and transformed and been in turn transformed by the other. This has meant two things. Each cuisine has suitably incorporated some elements of the other and acquired a multicultural dimension. Secondly, a distinctly multicultural cuisine has begun to emerge, borrowing elements from both and integrating them into something wholly new. While resembling both cuisines in several aspects, it has an unmistakable identity and vitality of its own. Since there are several ways of integrating the elements borrowed from the two cuisines, the new cuisine in turn has taken different forms, all sharing a common spirit of multicultural experimentation but producing different results.

A similar twofold process occurs in other areas of life as well, such as music, dance, the arts, literature and lifestyles, and to a lesser extent even in such highly traditional and culturally resistant areas as religion, moral values and ways of thought. In each case different cultural traditions influence each other and acquire a multicultural dimension. And new multiculturally constituted musical, literary and other traditions also emerge, imaginatively transforming the elements borrowed from different traditions into something wholly different. One only has to consider how the current American culture has drawn heavily on and creatively transformed the great contributions of the Irish, Jewish, African American and other minority cultures into a distinct and unmistakable collective culture. The two processes, the multiculturalization of the existing traditions and the emergence of multiculturally constituted new ones, are closely related and reinforce each other. When a tradition is multiculturalized, it sees the new multicultural tradition as continuous with and carrying further its own internal multiculturalization. Conversely, the new tradition is embedded in and constantly nurtured by the spirit of multicultural experimentation at work in each of the separate traditions.

In a multicultural society cultures constantly encounter one another both formally and informally and in private and public spaces.[8] Guided by curiosity, incomprehension or admiration, they interrogate each other, challenge each other's assumptions, consciously or unconsciously borrow from each other, widen their horizons and undergo small and large changes. Even when their interaction is limited, the very awareness of other traditions alerts each to its own contingency and specificity, and subtly alters the manner in which its members define and relate to it. Over time they tend to throw up a new composite culture based on their respective contributions and insights and possessing a somewhat fuzzy but recognizable identity of its own. It is neither their lowest common denominator nor a mere collection of their arbitrarily selected beliefs and practices, but a more or less distinct culture in which these are all redefined, brought into a new relationship, and compose a loosely-knit whole. Once developed, it forms the basis of their interaction, helps create a common ethical life, and throws up a body of common principles that inform public policies and structure political discourse.

Like all cultures the interculturally created and multiculturally constituted culture is an unplanned growth. Its contents are broadly but not universally agreed, and remain subject to dispute. It is relatively open-ended, multistranded, pulls in different directions, and is constantly in the making. It has enough coherence and stability to make intercultural communication possible but not enough to escape periodic contestation. Since it grows out of the interaction between different cultures, it is internally plural and both unites them and respects their diversity. Not all members of society approve of all its aspects equally, but they all find enough in it to own it as theirs and give it different degrees of allegiance.

Just as a truly representative public opinion can only emerge from a dialogue between equal citizens, a multiculturally constituted common culture can emerge and enjoy legitimacy only if all the constituent cultures are able to participate in its creation in a climate of equality (Young, 1990, chs 4, 8). They should enjoy more or less equal respect, equal opportunities for self-expression, equal access to private and especially public spaces, equal ability to interrogate each other, and more or less equal power and resources. Once these and other equalities necessary for a fair and effective interaction are ensured, the dialogue follows its own logic and its outcome cannot be predetermined. Since cultures are not all equal in their vitality and richness, their respective contributions might not carry equal conviction with others and find an equal space in the common culture that eventually emerges from their dialogue. Furthermore, no society is a clean slate and intercultural interaction does not occur in a historical vacuum. Since the long-established culture of a society is deeply inscribed in its beliefs, institutions and practices, it has certain inbuilt advantages. The multiculturally constituted common culture is therefore bound to contain a bias towards it.

In order to facilitate the emergence of a multiculturally constituted common culture, both private and public realms need to encourage intercultural interaction. The two realms are part of a common way of life and deeply influence each other. If the public realm were to be monoculturally constituted it would discourage diversity in the private realm, and unless the spirit of multiculturalism flourished in the latter the multiculturally constituted public realm would lack vitality and support.

The development of a common culture cannot be officially engineered both because cultures do not develop in that way and because no state can be trusted with such power. However, since a common culture is vital to the unity and stability of a multicultural society and the good relations between its members, the state cannot remain uninterested in it either. Furthermore, cultural neutrality or *laissez faire* privileges the dominant culture and does not ensure the equality of power, resources and so on that are required for a genuine intercultural interaction. While the government should not directly intervene in intercultural interaction and seek to influence its outcome, it should ensure that the interaction takes place under conditions of equality. It should not be culturally neutral or indifferent but even-handed, empowering all cultural voices to participate in a common dialogue (Carens, 2000).

So far as the private realm is concerned, the development of a multiculturally constituted common culture requires a flourishing civil society providing ample opportunities for different cultural communities to meet and pursue common cultural, economic and other interests on a regular and relaxed basis. Such common pursuits get them used to each other, increase cross-cultural understanding and trust, and build up the skills required to negotiate and live with their unresolved differences. They also forge bonds of cross-cultural friendships and common material interests, and make it easier to bear the burden of occasional incomprehension and irritation inherent in most intercultural encounters.

Although intercultural associations and activities tend to spring up in every lively society, they might not do so on a sufficiently large scale, or lack vitality and vigour, or become too paternalistic to serve their purpose, or function under unequal conditions. Well-conceived public policies playing a largely facilitating role then have an important role to play. Official and unofficial spokesmen of the wider society should publicly welcome the presence and contributions of different cultures, patronize their social and other events, and so forth, and help build up their self-confidence. Museums and art galleries, which define and celebrate the national heritage, should include and suitably integrate minority contributions which are also an integral part of a multicultural society's common heritage. Local and regional consultative committees composed of the representative of different communities, multifaith networks and so on, facilitate intercultural dialogue and provide valuable institutional spaces for cross-cultural cooperation. Multicultural arts exhibitions, literary, musical and other events, and film festivals build up shared sources of pleasure and foster a multicultural ethos in society at large.

As far as the public realm is concerned, the development of a multiculturally constituted common culture requires a different pattern of intercultural interaction. If the public realm were to require citizens to speak the established political language in a standard accent and appeal only to the prevailing political values as Rawls, Bruce Ackerman and Joshua Cohen insist, it would discourage the participation of those unused or unsympathetic to either. It should welcome new conceptual languages, modes of deliberation, forms of speech and political sensibilities, and create conditions in which their creative interplay could over time lead to a plural public realm and a broadbased political culture. Even established political values should not be treated as nonnegotiable. If they can be shown to be unfairly biased against certain cultures or to exclude other equally worthwhile political values, a critical dialogue on them should be welcomed as a step towards a richer moral culture enjoying a broad cross-cultural consensus.

Since the public realm sets the tone of the rest of society and wields considerable power and prestige, it should ensure adequate representation to cultural communities. Ideally their members should be able to find their way into it through normal competitive channels. However, this may not always be possible because of the prejudices of wider society or major political parties, the structural biases of established institutions, or the low self-esteem of minority communities. There is then a strong case for some form of affirmative action in favour of the excluded communities. It gives them public visibility, access to political power and the opportunity to speak for themselves rather than be spoken for by others and to do so in their characteristic modes of thought. It also integrates them into the wider society, sensitizes the latter to the issues it is otherwise unlikely to encounter, and fosters habits of cross-cultural deliberation. This is amply demonstrated by the experiences of the USA and, especially, India where, despite its obvious practical difficulties, occasional misuse and injustices to isolated individuals, the policy of affirmative action for the ex-untouchables and tribal communities has done much to redress past injustices, integrate them into mainstream society and foster a shared public culture (Parekh, 1992).

When both private and public realms create propitious conditions for equal intercultural interaction with such judicious government help and intervention as might be appropriate in different societies, a multiculturally constituted common culture is likely to develop. It forms the basis of a shared way of life and underpins and gives the state moral and emotional roots. The spirit of multiculturality flows freely through all areas of life and becomes such an integral part of citizens' self-understanding that they accept differences as an important and valuable feature of their society. The multiculturally constituted common culture fosters a common sense of belonging among citizens and provides a shared language and body of overlapping values growing out of, and sustained by, a dialogue between them. Like any other culture, it cherishes and cultivates, through educational and other institutions an appropriate body of intellectual and moral virtues necessary to sustain a multicultural society, such as the ability to uncover common grounds behind differences, the willingness to accept and delight in differences, the spirit of moderation, cultural curiosity, and the capacity to live with unresolved disagreements. In such a society unity and diversity are not confined to public and private realms respectively, but interpenetrate and permeate all areas of life. Its unity therefore is not formal and abstract but embedded in and nurtured by its diversity; and the latter, being grounded in and regulated by the shared interactive framework, does not lead to fragmentation and ghettoisation (Spinner, 1997, ch. 8).

Multicultural education

The kind of multiculturally constituted culture sketched earlier is best sustained by a multiculturally oriented system of education. Multicultural education has become a subject of much heated controversy, especially in the United States. The dominant opinion there is that one of the main tasks of education is to initiate pupils into the American 'national culture' or 'creed', to cultivate in them a strong sense of 'national identity' and create a 'cohesive nation. Some groups of African Americans and others have argued that the such an education marginalizes them, takes a demeaning view of them and so on, and that the main aim of education is to sustain pupils' ethnic or cultural identity, cultivate a sense of pride in their history and achievements and help create cohesive ethnic communities. Despite their differences both views share a common and misguided philosophy of education. For both, the aim of education is to sustain community, be it the wider political community or the narrower ethnic community, and to present it in a favourable light. Both see education in political and instrumental terms, take homogeneous views of the relevant communities and advocate monocultural education.[9]

Basically, multicultural education is a critique of the Eurocentric and in that sense monocultural content and ethos of much of the prevailing system of education. Eurocentrism asserts the following two theses. First, modern, that is post-seventeenth century, European civilization represents the highest form of life reached by humankind so far and provides the standards by which to judge all others. Second, it attained its glory unaided by, and owes little if anything to, non-European civilizations. Its formative influences are taken to be three, all European. Its intellectual and political foundations were laid by classical Athens and Rome, both presumed to be European. Its moral and religious foundations were laid by Christianity which, although non-European in origin, was radically reshaped in the light of the Greco-Roman heritage and became a progressive force only after it had undergone much cultural filtering at European hands. Its third major source was the rise of individualism, secularism, science, technology and so on, all assumed to be the unique achievements of modern Europe and based on its premodern heritage. The aims of education are to cultivate those capacities, attitudes, values and sentiments that created, currently underpin and are cherished by European civilization, including the capacities for critical and independent thought, individualism, the scientific and secular spirit, and pride in European history and culture. The content of education, too, is provided by European civilization, and its literature, history, geography and so on form the substance of these subjects. The general ethos pervading the educational system highlights the glory and uniqueness of European civilization and underplays or ignores the achievements and contributions of others.

The limitations of such an educational system are obvious. It is unlikely to awaken students' intellectual curiosity about other cultures, either because they are not exposed to them or because they are presented in uncomplimentary terms, or both. It is also unlikely to develop the faculty of imagination. Imagination, the capacity to conceive alternatives, does not develop in a vacuum. It is only when one is exposed to different societies and cultures that one's imagination is stimulated and consciousness of alternatives becomes an inseparable part of one's manner of thinking. Since monocultural education cannot avoid encouraging the illusion that the limits of one's world are the limits of the world itself, that the conventional ways of thought are the only valid ones, it blots out the awareness of alternatives and stifles imagination.

Monocultural education also stunts the growth of the critical faculty. Students taught to look at the world from the narrow perspectives of their own cultures are bound to reject all that cannot be accommodated within its categories. They are likely to judge other cultures and societies by the norms and standards of their own, and find them odd and even worthless. And in judging their own society in terms of its own norms, they are not likely to take a genuinely critical attitude to it. Since monocultural education blunts the imagination which alone gives a cutting edge to the critical faculty, they can hardly resist celebrating the 'glory' and 'genius' of their own civilization or society and remain vulnerable to the deadly vice of narcissism.

Monocultural education also tends to breed arrogance, insensitivity and racism. Imprisoned within the framework of his own culture, the student cannot accept the diversity of values, beliefs, ways of life and views of the world as an integral part of the human condition. Nor surprisingly he tends to feel threatened by them, not knowing how to cope with them and resenting others for being different. Since he has little knowledge of other societies and cultures, he is likely to understand them in terms of superficial generalizations and stereotypes and do them grave injustice. This is indeed how the Victorians built up a hierarchy of human societies. They placed African societies at the bottom, Asians a little higher, the Mediterranean still higher, and so on up to the English whom they regarded as representing the highest stage of human development. When asked why other societies had remained backward, the usual tendency was, and is, to give a racist explanation. The 'genius' of the white 'race' has enabled it to achieve great heights, and misfortunes of other societies are due to the inferiority of their 'race'. Such an attitude, albeit in an attenuated form, is still discernible in many of our textbooks and teachers.

Monocultural education, then, is simply not good education. If the aim of education, as all the great educationists have rightly argued, is to develop such worthwhile human capacities as intellectual curiosity, self-criticism, the ability to weigh-up arguments and evidence and form an independent judgment, to cultivate such attitudes as intellectual and moral humility, respect for others and sensitivity to different ways of thought and life, and to open students' minds to the great achievements of humankind, the educational system should be as free of Eurocentrism and all other varieties of ethnocentrisim as is humanly possible. A good education should expose pupils to different conceptions of the good life, systems of belief and modes of conceptualizing familiar experiences, and get them to enter into the spirit of other cultures, see the world the way they do and appreciate their strengths and limitations. While rightly developing the powers of independent thought, analysis, criticism and so on, it should also cultivate 'softer' and less aggressive capacities such as sympathetic imagination, the ability to get under the skin of others and feel with and for them, the willingness to look at oneself from the standpoint of others, and the capacity to listen to them with sensitivity and sympathy. Students are members of their ethnic and cultural communities, citizens of their political community, and also human beings. A good educational system needs to attend to all three. It should help pupils understand the history, social structure, culture, languages, and so on of their cultural and political communities in order to enable them to understand themselves better and find their way around in these communities. However, to limit education to this is to take a highly impoverished and narrow view of it. Education is concerned with humanization not just socialization, with helping students become not just good citizens but also integrated human beings with well-developed intellectual, moral and other capacities and sensibilities, and able to feel at home in the rich and diverse human world.

The area where the principle of multicultural education is most relevant is obviously that of the curriculum. A multicultural curriculum should satisfy two conditions. First, it should not be unduly narrow. No curriculum can cover everything in the world. If it became a conducted tour of the world, it would be exceedingly superficial, trivialize great events, serve no educational purpose, and do more harm than good. Ideally it should familiarize students with the major representative forms of the subject in question, concentrate on some of them, and so stimulate them that they follow up the rest on their own.

The report on the teaching of history by the federal education panel in the United States published in 1992 gives some idea of how the history curriculum could be organized. While rightly insisting that western history must remain an important part of the curriculum in western schools and that such non-western history as is included should be digestible, it emphasizes that students should have a sense of the way the larger world has developed and the position of western civilization within it. Accordingly, it divides human history into eight eras and focuses on developments that affected large numbers of people and had broad significance for later generations. It includes the Greek city-states, the Roman Empire and modern European history, but also China's Sung dynasty, the Mauryan Empire in India and the Olmea civilization which influenced the Zapotec and Mayan civilizations in Mesoamerica. As the report explains, the immediate purpose behind such a broadbased study of history is to give the student a firm understanding of their community's past, a reasonably intelligent and sensitive understanding of the major periods in the history of most of the rest of the world, and the capacity to explore the similarities, differences and interconnections between them. And the deeper purpose behind it is to stimulate students' curiosity and imagination, broaden their sympathies, and help them appreciate both the unity and the diversity of the human species.

The field of literature has become a subject of much unnecessary debate in recent years. Defenders of the traditional curriculum argue that we should continue to concentrate on the classics or canons and resist the pressure to include the fashionable and largely minority-based literature whose literary worth has not yet been proven by the critical judgment of history. Although this is an understandable reaction to the misguided lobby that wants to 'fire the canon', the debate is misconceived. As their advocates rightly argue, the classics explore the basic features of the human condition with great insight and subtlety, and are of universal value and appeal. They have a technical virtuosity, exploit the language and its resources with considerable courage, and provide the best medium to acquire the necessary literary skills. They also articulate the ways of thought, structures of consciousness and forms of sensibility of their age, and constitute irreplaceable records of vital nodal points in the growth of the civilization of the community concerned.

While these and related arguments make out a strong case *for* classics, they do not amount to a case *against* non-classics. Even assuming that we can give a coherent meaning to the term 'classics' and agree on the criteria for identifying them, the fact remains that they are human creations and have their own biases and limitations. They articulate some forms of experience and not others, do so from specific perspectives, and are products of their age which they never wholly succeed in transcending. They therefore need to be supplemented by works that explore the structures and forms of experiences of historically marginalized groups such as women, slaves, the poor, the oppressed, migrants and colonial subjects. These works might lack the technical virtuosity of the classics, but they have compensating advantages. They explore new experiences or familiar ones from neglected and unusual angles, reflect a spirit of defiance and playfulness, explore the sensibilities, moods and types of pain and pleasure falling outside the experiences or the literary genres of classical writers, and so on. What is more, it is only by including them in the curriculum and subjecting them to stringent literary criticism that we can create a climate in which such literature can throw up its own classics over time. The classics do have a vital place in education, but there is no obvious reason why one should be forced into choosing between them and the rest.

The second condition that a well-conceived curriculum should satisfy has to do with the way it is taught. It is not enough to broaden the curriculum and include different religions, cultures, texts and systems of belief; one should also bring them into a fruitful dialogue. Whether it is slavery, colonialism, the position of women, the family, the industrial revolution, the rise of the trade unions or civil and external wars, the individuals involved experienced them differently and reached different judgments on them. Each event has not one but several overlapping histories and is amenable to different narratives, all of them partial and biased though some more so than others. Since events and institutions are multifaceted, so is the truth about them, and a balanced judgment on them can only be formed in a conversation between different perspectives. One of the central aims of education should be to equip the student to participate in such a conversation and, thereby, to broaden her sympathies and get her to appreciate the complexity of truth and the irreducible diversity of interpretations without nervously seeking for a final answer. Ideally, histories and experiences of minority communities should not be taught separately but integrated into the general history of the community. This ensures that their particular experiences and historical memories do not become ghettoized and obsessive and find their proper place in the collective memory and self-understanding of the society as a whole.

When defined in this way, multicultural education is not open to the criticisms generally made of it. It is argued that it fosters the cult of ethnicity, undermines common culture, leads to the Tower of Babel, distorts history and undermines social unity. Far from ethnicizing education, it deethnicizes cultures and makes them a shared human capital. It is committed to the basic values of liberal society, broadens them to include others and helps create a plural and richer common culture. It encourages a dialogue between cultures, equips students to converse in multiple cultural idioms, and avoids the cacophonous incomprehension of the Tower of Babel. It challenges the falsehoods of Eurocentric history, brings out its complexity and plural narratives, and it also fosters social cohesion by enabling students to accept, enjoy and cope with diversity. Properly understood and freed from the polemical exaggerations of its advocates and detractors, multicultural education is an education in freedom, both in the sense of freedom *from* ethnocentric prejudices and biases and freedom *to* explore and learn from other cultures and perspectives. The two freedoms are inseparable, for one cannot be free from an ethnocentric perspective unless one has access to others, and one lacks such an access if one remains trapped within the confines of one's own perspective.

National identity

Like any other community, a political community needs to, and as a rule tends to, develop some idea of the kind of community it is, what it stands for, how it differs from others, how it has come to be what it is, and so forth; in short a view of its collective or national identity (Miller, 1995; Walzer, 1992b; Gilbert, 1998). Its shared conception of its identity serves several purposes. It satisfies the intellectual curiosity of its members as to what makes it the kind of community it is, why it is this and not some other community, and what belonging to it involves. The political community includes millions of people whom one has never seen and might never see but for whose sake one is expected to pay taxes, make sacrifices, and even give up one's life. It also spans countless past and future generations to whom again one is bound by common ties of affection, interests and obligations. Its sense of national identity bonds these individuals and generations, and articulates and explains why they all form part of a single community. It unites its members around a common self-understanding and gives focus and energy to their sense of common belonging. It also inspires them to live up to a certain collective self-image and cultivate the relevant virtues, facilitates the community's self-reproduction and intergenerational continuity, fosters common loyalties, and orders their moral and political life. It does not remain purely cerebral but becomes embodied in national rituals, symbols and ceremonies, and engages their emotions. The shared view of national identity has a particularly important role in a multicultural society because of its greater need to cultivate a common sense of belonging among its diverse communities.

Although every political community needs a view of its national identity, the latter also has a dark underside and can easily become a source of conflict and division. Every long-established political community includes several different strands of thought and visions of the good life. Since every definition of national identity is necessarily selective and must be relatively simple to achieve its intended purposes, it stresses one of these strands and visions and delegitimizes or marginalizes others. The history of a community, too, is necessarily complex and can be read in several different ways, and a definition of national identity runs the risk of oversimplifying it and glorifying the role of some groups and denigrating that of others. A definition of national identity can also become a vehicle of silencing dissident voices and moulding the entire society in a particular image with all its authoritarian and repressive implications. The danger is particularly acute in a multicultural society with its inevitable diversity of values, visions of the good life and interpretations of history.

We are thus confronted with a paradox. A shared sense of national identity is necessary but also potentially dangerous, a force for both unity and division, a condition for the community's cohesion and reproduction which can also alienate large sections of its citizens and become a cause of its fragmentation. If it is to serve valuable purposes and avoid obvious dangers, it needs to meet certain conditions:

- First, the identity of a political community should be located in its political structure and not the widely shared personal characteristics of its individual members, in what they share publicly and collectively as a community not in what is common to them as individuals. It should therefore be defined in politico-institutional rather than ethno-cultural terms, in terms of the institutions, values, mode of public discourse and so on that all citizens can be expected to share as members of a community rather than their habits, temperament, attitude to life, sexual practices, customs, family structure, body language and hobbies. The ethno-cultural characteristics are too vague to specify and agree upon, are rarely shared by all or even a majority, pertain to their private lives, at best define a people and not a political community (Germans and French but not Germany or France), and can easily become an instrument of suppressing unconventional lifestyles and forms of behaviour.

- Second, members of a multicultural society belong to different ethnic, religious and cultural groups, and these identities deeply matter to them. The prevailing view of national identity should allow for such multiple identities without subjecting those involved to charges of divided loyalties. There is no reason why one cannot be both Scottish and British, Quebecois and Canadian, Basque and Spanish, Breton and French, and Hindu or Sikh and American. Although there is no conflict in principle between ethnic, religious and other identities on the one hand and national identity on the other, it can arise in practice if either of them were to be so defined as to exclude or undermine the other. If being American means being Protestant and Anglo-Saxon then clearly Christians of other denominations, non-Christians, Asians and others cannot be or feel fully American. And if being Scottish involves being anti-English, or if being Muslim involves political loyalties and commitments incompatible with those to Britain and its political way of life, then they cannot be accommodated within even the most capacious definition of British national identity. If national identity is to leave sufficient space for other identities, both need to be defined in an open and inclusive manner and brought into at least some degree of harmony.

- Third, the national identity of a community should be so defined that it includes all its citizens and makes it possible for them to identify with it. National identity is about who belongs to the community and is entitled to make claims on it. Minorities cannot feel part of the community if its very self-definition excludes them and treats them as outsiders. When some leaders of the Malay community insist their country is Malay and not Malaysian Malaysia, they make Malays the sole owners of the community and treat the Indians, the Chinese and others as outsiders who should be tolerated but not given equal rights and citizenship. When leaders of the Baltic Republics, Fiji, Trinidad, Guyana and other countries define their national identity in terms of the indigenous or the numerically dominant community, their definition excludes minorities, such as the Russians, Indians, Chinese and erstwhile colonizers.

In all these cases it is argued that since some groups of people are recent arrivals, bought by the colonial powers or planted by a dominant neighbour, they do not have as much claim on the country as the rest. The argument is flawed. Many so-called indigenous people often turn out to be outsiders if one goes further back in history, and differ from the rest in having arrived or been brought only a few decades earlier. Again, although it is true that some minorities once came as colonizers or were recruited by colonial powers, it is an irreversible legacy of history and cannot be held against their present descendants who have known no other home, struck their roots in the country, identify with it, and whose moral and political claims are therefore just as strong as those of the rest. The term 'second or third-generation immigrant' is deeply misleading, for the sons and daughters of immigrants are not themselves immigrants.

• Finally, the definition of national identity should not only include all citizens, but also accept them as equally valued and legitimate members of the community. Although in many multicultural societies the majority community is willing to grant its citizens equal rights, it feels possessive about the country for democratic, historical and other reasons and insists that the definition of national identity should reflect its privileged status.[10] While granting equal rights to all its citizens, including its Serbian and other minorities, the 1990 constitution of Croatia maintains that it is the 'national state of the Croatian people' and realizes their 'thousand-year dream' of an independent state of their own. The Constitution of Macedonia makes it the 'national state of the Macedonian people', defined not in political but ethnic terms. The Romanian Constitution goes further. While giving equal rights to all its minorities, it makes the unity of ethnic Romanians the foundation of the state, Romanian the official language of the country, 'Awake Romanians' the national anthem, and so on. In Malaysia, three 'pillars' are considered central to its national identity, *bahsa* (language or Malay), *agama* (religion or Islam) and *dan raja* (monarchy), all three closely connected with the majority. In Thailand, the three 'central elements' of national identity include *sasana* (religion or Buddhism), *mahakasat* (monarchy) and *chat* (nation), the first being the religion and the second the royal dynasty of the majority community. Israel is officially the state of its Jewish majority, its name and all its national symbols are Jewish, its Law of Return privileges Jews, and so forth. Although its Arab minority of just under 20 per cent enjoys broadly equal civil and political rights with the rest and a reasonably secure cultural space of its own, it is 'exempted' from joining the armed forces and denied employment in enterprises associated with the military.

In all these cases minorities feel aggrieved and alienated, and have often protested against their inferior or 'second-class' status. The Macedonian Constitution was strongly opposed by, and passed without the consent of, its 30 per cent Albanian minority. The Croatian Constitution was criticized by its Serb, Slovene, Slovak, Hungarian and Muslim minorities. And the Israeli, Malaysian and Thai definitions of national identity have provoked similar objections from their respective minorities. Minorities contend that since the state is officially appropriated and declared to be the national home of the majority community, they are seen as less authentic 'sons of the soil', less reliable and patriotic than the rest, less entitled to demand respect for their culture and religion, and passed over in politically sensitive appointments. These fears are not ill-founded. In Malaysia, for example, making Islam one of the three pillars of its national identity has encouraged a general distrust of non-Muslims and led to widespread demand that the country be declared an Islamic state. Minority spokesmen also argue that they enjoy equal rights as individuals but not as communities for, unlike the majority community, they do not enjoy collective rights to cultural self-expression, access to public resources, and recognition of their presence in the symbols of the state and the definition of national identity.

Many of these and related minority criticisms are justified, and there is a strong case for defining national identity in a broad and collectively acceptable manner. By including minorities in the community's self-definition and giving them official recognition, such a definition legitimizes and values their presence and makes it possible for them to accept it with enthusiasm. It also protects the state against nativist or majoritarian pressures, and it does not undermine the inescapably dominant status of the majority which is bound to assert itself in the normal political process anyway. Indeed, precisely because of this, it is in its own interest not to rub it in by explicitly enshrining its dominance in the definition of national identity. When a majority community defines itself as a nation and seeks to monopolize the state, it provokes its minorities to define themselves as nations or ethnic groups. Minority ethnicity is often a defensive reaction against majority nationalism. Both justice and political wisdom dictate that the majority community should resist the temptation to claim the cultural ownership of the political community.

Although this is the ideal to aim at, it is not always practical. The history of most countries is tied up with that of particular ethnic or cultural groups who have played a decisive role in their development, shaped their current character, and whose values and experiences are deeply inscribed in their major institutions; for example, the English in the UK and the Anglo-Saxons in the USA. Furthermore, some countries such as Israel have come into existence to realize the nationalist aspirations of the dominant community, and cannot be expected to undergo radical changes including give themselves different names, anthems and self-definition without alienating their majorities and suffering a profound crisis of identity. Even when countries define their identity in non-communal terms, the influence of the majority community seeps through its institutions, practices and symbols in subtle ways. Although the founding fathers of the Indian republic scrupulously sought to avoid defining its national identity in Hindu terms, its name ('India that is Bharat' as the very first article of its Constitution defines the country), national anthem (written in Sanskritised Bengali), national motto (drawn from the Hindu epic *Mahābhārata*), and so on are all drawn from the majority Hindu tradition.

All this means that defining the national identity of a multicultural society is an exceedingly difficult enterprise involving reconciliation of conflicting demands (Mason, 1999, pp. 271f). The definition cannot and should not be culturally neutral as it then satisfies nobody and lacks the power to evoke deep historical memories, nor biased towards a particular community as it then delegitimizes and alienates others, nor culturally so eclectic as to lack coherence and focus. There is no easy way to reconcile these and other requirements, and each political community has to strike its own balance. There are, however, several general considerations that could guide its choice (Tamir, 1993, pp. 162f).

Although a political community cannot deny or reject its historically inherited identity, it can officially declare itself multicultural as Canada, Australia and other countries have done. This affirms its cultural plurality, legitimizes its minorities, and counters such cultural biases as its self-definition, symbols and institutions inevitably contain. While retaining the current self-definition, it can also give it a broader meaning as Prince Charles did when he remarked that, as a monarch, he would like to be the 'Defender of Faith' including both Christian and non-Christian religions rather than of 'the Faith' as is currently the case. Even when it is unable to avoid altogether the majority-based view of national identity, the political community can counter its symbolic and practical impact by providing ample autonomous cultural spaces to its minorities and making them a *de facto* part of its national identity. Although Buddhism is part of Thai national identity and figures prominently in its national rituals, the state there has agreed to respect the rights of the Muslims of southern Thailand to maintain their religious schools, and of the *khadi* courts to adjudicate matters relating to marriage and the family. Israel's commitment to respect Arab cultural identity, uphold their personal laws, fund their schools and so on represents another, albeit limited way to make its national identity effectively plural. In the ultimate analysis the definition of national identity matters to minorities because it risks delegitimizing them, damaging their material and other interests, and making it difficult for them to identify with the political community. Once these are fully taken care of, it should not much matter if the definition retains some bias towards the dominant majority community.

Conditions of success

I have argued that a multicultural society is likely to be stable, cohesive, vibrant and at ease with itself if it meets certain conditions. These include a consensually grounded structure of authority, a collectively acceptable set of constitutional rights, a just and impartial state, a multiculturally constituted common culture and multicultural education, and a plural and inclusive view of national identity. None of them by itself is enough. However legitimate its basis, no structure of authority can hold a society together and count on its continuing allegiance unless it acts justly and ensures its citizens the basic conditions of the good life. Justice, however, is not enough because it is what I might call a cold and impersonal virtue. It prevents accumulation of resentment, frustration and anger and generates a basic sense of satisfaction with the political community, but does not by itself foster an enthusiastic commitment to and a sense of moral and emotional identification with it, without which the community cannot sustain itself in times of crisis or even evoke willing sacrifices of personal interest during normal times. One might enjoy all the rights of citizenship and be a formally equal member of the community, and yet feel that one is an outsider and does not quite belong to it if its cultural ethos and self-definition have no place for one. This is how, for example, many African Americans in the United States, Asians and Afro-Caribbeans in Britain, Arabs in Israel, and Muslims and until recently Sikhs in India feel about their respective communities. Belonging is about full acceptance and feeling at home, and justice, which is about rights and interests, satisfies only one of its preconditions.

Justice is also inherently contentious and, *contra* Rawls, there is no uniquely rational and conclusive way to resolve deep disagreements about its criteria, limits and relative importance in the political life of the community, especially in multicultural societies. It is also only one of several political values, and needs to be balanced against the requirements of social harmony, integration of the excluded groups into the mainstream society, a rich and vibrant cultural life, and a sense of social solidarity. This is why, although unjust to some individuals, a wisely applied policy of affirmative action is sometimes justified to achieve these and other worthwhile values. For these and related reasons, justice cannot be the sole basis of the political community or even its highest or 'first' virtue. We should do justice to justice itself and keep it in its proper place, neither underestimating nor exaggerating its importance.

While ensuring justice to all its citizens and communities, a multicultural society needs a plural collective culture of the kind described earlier and a shared sense of national identity. The former, which grows out of a constant conversation between different cultures, both respects them and provides a shared vocabulary of daily intercourse and common interests and sources of enjoyment. The latter enables different individuals and communities to identify with the political community, recognize it as theirs, and build up a sense of loyalty to it. Although both are important, they remain relatively ineffective unless accompanied by justice secured by a legitimate and consensually grounded structure of authority.

When these and related conditions obtain in a multicultural society, it is likely to develop a common sense of belonging among its diverse communities. Since they are subject to the civil authority they accept as legitimate, have their basic rights guaranteed, are justly treated and enjoy respect for their cultural identities, they have no grounds for discontent. And since the collective culture values and reflects their contribution and provides a common bond with others, and since the shared sense of national identity cherishes their presence, they have every incentive to give the community their willing allegiance and even to feel proud of belonging to it. While cherishing their respective cultural identities, members of different communities also share a common identity not only as citizens but as full and relaxed members of wider society, and form part of a freely negotiated and constantly evolving collective 'we'. This does not mean that members of such a society will not deeply disagree about important issues or find each other occasionally exasperating and incomprehensible, but rather that they are likely to feel sufficiently committed to it to live with their differences and not to want to harm its well-being. Political communities are exceedingly difficult to hold together and, as history shows, there is no means of knowing what might precipitate their break up. A multicultural society that creates the conditions discussed earlier has done all that can be expected of it. If that proves inadequate, it should avoid repressive violence and accept its misfortune as part of the inescapable frailty of all human institutions. As Machiavelli wisely observed *virtú* minimizes but does not altogether eliminate the power of *fortuna*.

8

Equality in a Multicultural Society

Much of the traditional discussion of equality suffers from a weakness derived from the mistaken theory of human nature in which it is grounded. As we saw earlier, many philosophers understand human beings in terms of a substantive theory of human nature and treat culture as of no or only marginal importance. Broadly speaking they maintain that human beings are characterized by two sets of features, some common to them all such as that they are made in the image of God, have souls, are noumenal beings, have common capacities and needs or a similar natural constitution; and others varying from culture to culture and individual to individual. The former are taken to constitute their humanity and are ontologically privileged. Human beings are deemed to be equal because of their shared features or similarity, and equality is taken to consist in treating them in more or less the same way and giving them more or less the same body of rights.

I have argued that this view of human beings is deeply mistaken. Human beings are at once both natural and cultural beings, sharing a common human identity but in a culturally mediated manner. They are similar and different, their similarities and differences do not passively coexist but interpenetrate, and neither is ontologically prior or morally more important. We cannot ground equality in human uniformity because the latter is inseparable from and ontologically no more important than human differences. Grounding equality in uniformity also has unfortunate consequences. It requires us to treat human beings equally in those respects in which they are similar and not those in which they are different. While granting them equality at the level of their shared human nature, we deny it at the equally important cultural level. In our discussions of the Greek, Christian and liberal philosophers we have seen that it is also easy to move from uniformity to monism. Since human beings are supposed to be basically the same, only a particular way of life is deemed to be worthy of them, and those failing to live up to it either do not merit equality or do so only after they are suitably civilized. The idea of equality thus becomes an ideological device to mould humankind in a certain direction. A theory of equality grounded in human uniformity is both philosophically incoherent and morally problematic.

Human beings do share several capacities and needs in common, but different cultures define and structure these differently and develop new ones of their own. Since human beings are at once both similar and different, they should be treated equally because of both. Such a view, which grounds equality not in human uniformity but in the interplay of uniformity and difference, builds difference into the very concept of equality, breaks the traditional equation of equality with similarity, and is immune to monist distortion. Once the basis of equality changes so does its content. Equality involves equal freedom or opportunity to be different, and treating human beings equally requires us to take into account both their similarities and differences. When the latter are not relevant, equality entails uniform or identical treatment; when they are, it requires differential treatment. Equal rights do not mean identical rights, for individuals with different cultural backgrounds and needs might require different rights to enjoy equality in respect of whatever happens to be the content of their rights. Equality involves not just rejection of irrelevant differences as is commonly argued, but also full recognition of legitimate and relevant ones.

Equality is articulated at several interrelated levels. At the most basic level it involves equality of respect and rights, at a slightly higher level that of opportunity, self-esteem, self-worth and so on, and at a yet higher level, equality of power, well-being and the basic capacities required for human flourishing. Sensitivity to differences is relevant at each of these levels. We can hardly be said to respect a person if we treat with contempt or abstract away all that gives meaning to his life and makes him the kind of person he is. Respect for a person therefore involves locating him against his cultural background, sympathetically entering into his world of thought, and interpreting his conduct in terms of its system of meaning. A simple example illustrates the point. It was recently discovered that Asian candidates for jobs in Britain were systematically underscored because their habit of showing respect for their interviewers by not looking them in the eye led the latter to conclude that they were shifty and devious and likely to prove unreliable. By failing to appreciate the candidates' system of meaning and cultural practices, interviewers ended up treating them unequally with their white counterparts. Understandably but wrongly, they assumed that all human beings shared and even perhaps ought to share an identical system of meaning which predictably turned out to be their own. This relatively trivial example illustrates the havoc we can easily cause when we uncritically universalize the categories and norms of our culture.

Like the concept of equal respect, that of equal opportunity, too, needs to be interpreted in a culturally sensitive manner. Opportunity is a subject-dependent concept in the sense that a facility, a resource, or a course of action is only a mute and passive possibility and not an opportunity for an individual if she lacks the capacity, the cultural disposition or the necessary cultural knowledge to take advantage of it. A Sikh is in principle free to send his son to a school that bans turbans, but for all practical purposes it is closed to him. The same is true when an orthodox Jew is required to give up his yarmulke, or the Muslim woman to wear a skirt, or a vegetarian Hindu to eat beef as a precondition for certain kinds of jobs. Although the inability involved is cultural not physical in nature and hence subject to human control, the degree of control varies greatly. In some cases a cultural inability can be overcome with relative ease by suitably reinterpreting the relevant cultural norm or practice; in others it is constitutive of the individual's sense of identity and even self-respect and cannot be overcome without a deep sense of moral loss. Other things being equal, when a culturally derived incapacity is of the former kind, the individuals involved may rightly be asked to overcome it or at least bear the financial cost of accommodating it. When it is of the latter kind and comes closer to a natural inability, society should bear at least most of the cost of accommodating it. Which cultural incapacity falls within which category is often a matter of dispute and can only be resolved by a dialogue between the parties involved.

Equality before the law and equal protection of the law, too, need to be defined in a culturally sensitive manner. Formally a law banning the use of drugs treats all equally, but in fact it discriminates against those for whom some drugs are religious or cultural requirements as is the case with Peyote and Marijuana respectively for the American Indians and Rastafarians. This does not mean that we might not ban their use, but rather that we need to appreciate the unequal impact of the ban and should have strong additional reasons for denying exemption to these two groups. The United States government showed the requisite cultural sensitivity when it exempted the ceremonial use of wine by Jews and Catholics during Prohibition.

Equal protection of the law, too, may require different treatment. Given the horrible reality of the Holocaust and the persistent streak of anti-semitism in German cultural life, it makes good sense for that country to single out physical attacks on Jews for harsher punishment or ban utterances denying the Holocaust. In other societies, other groups such as blacks, Muslims and gypsies might have long been demonized and subjected to hostility and hatred, and then they too might need to be treated differently. Although the differential treatment of these groups might seem to violate the principle of equality, in fact it only equalizes them with the rest of their fellow-citizens.

In a culturally homogenous society, individuals share broadly similar needs, norms, motivations, social customs and patterns of behaviour. Equal rights here mean more or less the same rights, and equal treatment involves more or less identical treatment. The principle of equality is therefore relatively easy to define and apply, and discriminatory deviations from it can be identified without much disagreement. This is not the case in a culturally diverse society. Broadly speaking equality consists in equal treatment of those judged to be equal in relevant respects. In a culturally diverse society citizens are likely to disagree on what respects are relevant in a given context, what response is appropriate to them, and what counts as their equal treatment. Furthermore, once we take cultural differences into account, equal treatment would mean not identical but differential treatment, raising the question as to how we can ensure that it is really equal across cultures and does not serve as a cloak for discrimination or privilege.

In this chapter I shall discuss the kinds of difficulties raised by the principle of equality in a multicultural society. Rather than discuss them in abstract theoretical terms or by means of hypothetical examples which rarely capture their complexity, I shall analyse the real dilemmas multicultural societies have faced and the ways in which they have sought to deal with them, and end by briefly drawing out their important theoretical implications.

Equality of difference

In multicultural societies dress often becomes a site of the most heated and intransigent struggles. As a condensed and visible symbol of cultural identity it matters much to the individuals involved, but also for that very reason it arouses all manner of conscious and unconscious fears and resentments within wider society. It would not be too rash to suggest that acceptance of the diversity of dress in a multicultural society is a good indicator of whether or not the latter is at ease with itself.

In 1972, British Parliament passed a law empowering the Minister of Transport to require motor-cyclists to wear crash-helmets. When the Minister did so, Sikhs campaigned against it. One of them kept breaking the law and was fined twenty times between 1973 and 1976 for refusing to wear a crash-helmet. Sikh spokesmen argued that the turban was just as safe, and that if they could fight for the British in two world wars without anyone considering their turbans unsafe, they could surely ride motor-cycles. The law was amended in 1976 and exempted them from wearing crash-helmets. Although this was not universally welcomed, Parliament was right to amend the law. Its primary concern was to ensure that people did not die or suffer serious injuries riding dangerous vehicles, and it hit upon the helmet meeting certain standards as the best safety measure. Since the Sikh turban met these standards, it was accepted as an adequate substitute for the helmet.[1]

This became evident in the subsequent development of the law as it related to Sikhs. Although the Construction (Head Protection) Regulation 1989 requires all those working on construction sites to wear safety helmets, the Employment Act 1989 exempts turban-wearing Sikhs. The latter does so because it is persuaded by its own scientific tests that the turban offers adequate though not exactly the same protection as the helmet, and is thus an acceptable substitute for it. One important implication of this argument is that if a turbaned Sikh were to be injured on a construction site as a result of another person's negligence, he would be entitled to claim damages for only such injuries as he would have suffered if he had been wearing a safety helmet. The law does not allow anyone to work on a construction site without an acceptable head-gear. However, it is willing to compromise on the helmet if two conditions are satisfied. First, the alternative head-gear should offer an equivalent or at least acceptable level of protection. And second, those opting for it should themselves bear the responsibility for such *additional* injury as it may cause. The law lays down a minimally required level of protection and uses it to regulate the permissible range of cultural diversity. So far as the minimum requirement is concerned, it places the burden of injury on those causing it. The burden of additional injury is borne by those who for cultural reasons choose to meet the minimum requirement in their own different ways. Such an arrangement respects differences without violating the principle of equality, and accommodates individual choice without imposing unfair financial and other burdens on the rest of their fellow-citizens.

In Britain, Sikhs in the police and armed forces are entitled to wear turbans. In Canada it has led to a heated debate. Although most major police forces across the country allowed Sikhs to wear turbans, the Royal Canadian Mounted Police did not. When it finally decided to allow them, a group of retired officers organized a campaign involving 9000 letters and a petition signed by 210 000 people. They argued that the RCMP should be, and seen to be, free from political and religious bias and that the Sikh's turban, being a religious symbol, 'undermined the non-religious nature of the force' and violated other Canadians' 'constitutional right to a secular state free of religious symbols'. They also contended that since the Sikhs insisted on wearing the turban, they gave the impression of valuing their religion more than their police duties and would not be able to inspire public trust in their impartiality and loyalty to the state. In the eyes of the critics, Canada had taken its multiculturalism too far and should insist on the traditional Stetson. The matter went to the Trial Division of the Federal Court of Canada, which ruled that the objection to the turban was 'quite speculative and vague', and that the turban did not compromise the non-religious character of the RCMP. Three retired officers of the RCMP appealed to the Supreme Court, which dismissed the appeal and upheld the right of Sikhs to wear the turban.

Although the objection against the turban smacks of cultural intolerance and treats Sikhs unequally, it is not devoid of merit. The RCMP is a powerful and much-cherished national institution and, since Canada has few national symbols, there is something to be said for retaining the

Stetson. However, one could argue that precisely because the RCMP is a national institution, it should permit the turban and become a representative symbol of the country's officially endorsed multicultural identity. Furthermore, several provincial forces as well as the Canadian Courts and House of Commons allow Sikhs to wear turbans with no suggestion that this compromises the discharge of their official duties, diminishes their loyalty to the state, or detracts from the country's secular character. There is no reason why the RCMP should be different. Besides, wearing a turban does not signify that the wearer values his religion more than his professional integrity, nor does his replacing it with a Stetson indicate the opposite. Pushed to its logical conclusion, the criticism of the turban would imply that those wearing the traditional Stetson are likely to be partial to whites and hostile to others. One would therefore have to replace the Stetson with a culturally neutral headgear, which would have the double disadvantage of satisfying neither Sikhs nor whites and leaving the basic problem unsolved. Again, it is not at all true that Canada is committed to a narrow and bland form of secularism. If it were, it would have to change its coat-of-arms, disallow prayer in the Federal Parliament, expunge reference to God in the swearing-in ceremony of Cabinet ministers, and so on. Since opponents of the turban are unsympathetic to these changes, their objection is specious and discriminatory.

The diversity of headdress has raised problems in other societies as well, especially in relation to the armed forces and the police, the official symbols and guardians of national identity. Samcha Goldman, an orthodox Jew serving in the secular capacity of a clinical psychologist in the United States Air Force, was asked to resign when he insisted on wearing his yarmulke, which the Air Force thought was against its standard dress requirement. When the matter reached the Supreme Court, it upheld the decision of the Air Force by a majority of one, arguing that the 'essence of the military service is the subordination of the desire and interests of the individual to the needs of the service'. It is striking that the Court saw the yarmulke as a matter of personal desire or preference rather than a religious requirement which Goldman was not at liberty to disregard (Sandel, 1996, pp. 69f). Justifying the Court's decision, the Secretary of State argued that the uniforms of the armed forces were the 'cherished symbols of service, pride, history and traditions', and that allowing variations in them was bound to 'operate to the detriment of order and discipline', foster 'resentment and divisiveness', 'degrade unit cohesion', and reduce combat effectiveness. The Supreme Court decision rightly outraged many members of Congress, which by a sizeable majority passed a law permitting religious apparel provided that it did not interfere with military duties and was 'neat and conservative'.

There is much to be said for uniforms in the armed forces. Since they are closely identified with the state and symbolize its unity, their uniforms reinforce the consciousness of their national role and create an appropriate corporate ethos. And it goes without saying that they should be suitable for combat. However, this has to be balanced against other equally important considerations. If the yarmulke, turban and other religious apparels were to be disallowed, Jews, Sikhs and others would be denied both an avenue of employment and an opportunity to serve their country. Furthermore, the United States is a culturally diverse society made up of people of different religious faiths. There is no obvious reason why its national symbols including military uniforms should not reflect that fact. Besides, if differences of mere headdress are likely to detract from collective solidarity and unit cohesion, the differences of colour, accent and facial features are likely to do so even more, and we would have to exclude blacks, Asians and others from joining the armed forces. In short, while the uniform should not be discarded, it should be open to appropriate modification to accommodate genuine religious, cultural and other requirements, provided of course that they do not compromise military effectiveness.

The controversy concerning uniforms occurs in civilian areas of life as well, where it raises issues that are at once both similar and different. Since no question of national unity or symbolism is involved, the controversy has no political significance. However, it involves far more people, usually women, and has a great economic significance.

Many Asian women's refusal to wear uniforms in hospitals, stores and schools has led to much litigation and contradictory judgements in Britain. A Sikh woman who, on qualifying as a nurse, intended to wear her traditional dress of a long shirt (*quemiz*) over baggy trousers (*shalwar*) rather than the required uniform, was refused admission on a nursing course by her Health Authority. The Industrial Tribunal upheld her complaint on the ground that since her traditional dress was a cultural requirement and did not impede the discharge of her duties, asking her to replace it with a uniform was unjustified. The Tribunal was overruled by the Employment Appeal Tribunal, which took the opposite and much criticized view. Since rules about nurses' uniforms are laid down by the General Nursing Council, the latter promptly intervened under government pressure and made more flexible rules. This enabled the Health Authority to offer the Sikh woman a place on the course on the understanding that as a qualified nurse her trousers should be grey and the shirt white.

This was one of many cases in which lower courts took one view and the higher courts another, or the same court took different views in similar cases. The discrepancy arose because courts used two different criteria in deciding such cases. Sometimes they asked if the job requirements were *plausible* or understandable; that is, if 'good reasons' could be given for them. On other occasions they thought that such a criterion justified almost every demand, and insisted that job requirements should be *objectively necessary*; that is, indispensable for discharging the duties of the jobs concerned. It sounds plausible to say that since loose hairs could cause infection or pose a risk to public health, surgeons or those working in chocolate factories should not be allowed to sport beards. However, the requirement turns out to be objectively unnecessary, for beards do not mean loose hair and, if necessary, they can always be covered by a suitable clothing. After all, we do not ask people in these jobs to shave hair off their heads and arms.

Although the test of objective necessity is reasonable, it runs the risk of taking a purely instrumental view of job requirements and stripping the organizations concerned of their cultural identity. Take the case of nurses' uniforms. One could argue that since these are not objectively necessary for carrying out the required medical tasks, anyone may wear anything. This is to miss the crucial point that they symbolize and reinforce the collective spirit of the nursing profession and structure the expectations and behaviour of their patients. The instrumental view of rationality implicit in the test of objective necessity is also likely to provoke resentment against minorities whose cultural demands might be seen to undermine a much-cherished tradition. It is also unjust because, while it respects the cultural identity of the minority, it ignores that of the wider society. The concept of objective necessity should therefore be defined in a culturally sensitive manner and do justice to both the minority and majority ways of life. This means that uniforms should be kept in hospitals, schools and wherever else they are part of the tradition and perform valuable symbolic, inspirational, aesthetic and other functions, but be open to appropriate modifications when necessary. Such an arrangement neither deculturalizes the organizations concerned and renders them bland, nor eclectically multiculturalizes them and renders them comical, but preserves and adapts the tradition to changing circumstances and facilitates minority integration into the suitably opened-up mainstream society.

Equal treatment

In the cases discussed so far, it has been relatively easy to identify what aspects were relevant and what equal treatment consisted in. Situations sometimes arise when such judgements are not at all easy.

In most societies the law declares that a marriage is void if contracted under duress, a concept not easy to define in a culturally neutral manner. A British Asian girl, who had married her parentally-chosen husband because of the threat of ostracism by her family, asked the court to annul her marriage on grounds of duress. The court declined, arguing that duress only occurred when there was a 'threat of imminent danger to life and liberty'. This culturally insensitive interpretation of duress was rightly criticized. Not surprisingly the court did a complete *volte face* a few years later and declared void the marriage of another Asian girl under similar circumstances. It took the view that although acute social pressure did not amount to duress for a white British girl, it did so for her Asian counterpart.

The Asian girl is clearly treated differently, raising the question whether the difference amounts to privileging her. *Prima facie* it would seem that she is offered an *additional* ground for dissolution of marriage, and is thus being privileged. However, this is not the case. The law lays down that absence of duress is the basis of a valid marriage. Since ostracism by the family virtually amounts to social death and hence to duress in Asian society but not in white British society, the differential treatment of the Asian and white girls does not offend against the principle of equality. It does not give the Asian girl an additional ground for divorce, only interprets the existing one in a culturally sensitive manner.

The recognition of cultural differences might sometimes entitle a person to do things others cannot do without necessarily implying unequal rights. Many countries allow Sikhs to carry a suitably covered *kirpan* (a small dagger) in public places on the ground that it is a mandatory symbol of their religion. If other citizens asked to do that, their request would be turned down. This raises the question whether non-Sikhs can legitimately complain of discrimination or unequal treatment. There is no discrimination because their religious requirements are just as respected as those of the Sikhs. As for the complaint of inequality, there is a *prima facie* inequality of rights in the sense that the Sikhs can do things others cannot. However, the inequality arises out of the different demands of the same basic right to religion and does not confer a new right on the Sikhs. Some religions might require more of their adherents than do others, and then the same right would encompass a wider range of activities. Their adherents have the same right as the rest and its scope too is the same, only its content is wider.

Contextualizing equality

Sometimes we know what is relevant in a given context, but find it difficult to decide if two individuals are equal in relation to it. Take *l'affaire du foulard* which first surfaced in France in September 1989 and has haunted it ever since.[2] Three Muslim girls from North Africa, two of them sisters, wore *hijab* (head scarf) to their ethnically mixed school in Creil, some 60 kms north of Paris. In the previous year 20 Jewish students had refused to attend classes on Saturday mornings and autumn Friday afternoons when the Sabbath arrived before the close of the school, and the headmaster, a black Frenchman from the Caribbean, had to give in after initially resisting them. Worried about the trend of events, he objected to the Muslim girls wearing the *hijab* in the classroom on the grounds that it went against the *laicitée* of French state schools. Since the girls refused to comply, he barred them from attending the school. As a gesture of solidarity many Muslim girls throughout France began to wear *hijabs* to school and the matter acquired national importance. To calm the situation the Education Minister, Lionel Jospin, sought an opinion (*avis*) from the *Conseil d'Etat*. The *Conseil* ruled in November 1989 that pupils had a right to express and manifest their religious beliefs within state schools and that the *hijab* did not violate the principle of *laicitée*, provided that such religious insignia did not 'by their character, by their circumstances in which they were worn... or by their ostentatious or campaigning nature constitute an act of pressure, provocation, proselytism or propaganda', the decision on which was to be made by the local education authority on a case-by-case basis.

The vagueness of the ruling not only failed to give the headmaster clear guidance but publicly revealed the ambiguities of the official policy. Soon there were more incidents of *hijab*-wearing and protests by Muslims, provoking counter protests by secular Frenchmen. The standoff was finally resolved when one of the girls voluntarily, and the other two under pressure from King Hassan of Morocco, agreed to drop the scarves to the shoulders in the classroom. The issue flared up again in November 1993 when the principal of a middle school in another city barred two girls from the school for wearing the *hijab*. In response, hundreds of Muslim girls, their number at one stage reaching 2000, started wearing *hijab* to the school. On 10 September 1994 the Education Minister, Francois Bayrou, ruled that while wearing 'discreet' religious symbols was acceptable, 'ostentatious symbols which in themselves constitute elements of proselytism or discrimination' were unacceptable and that the *hijab* fell under that category. Headscarves were now banned as a matter of public policy, and school decisions to the contrary were declared void.[3]

The national debate on the *hijab* went to the heart of the French conceptions of citizenship and national identity and divided the country. Some advocated *laicitée ouverte*, which largely amounted to a search for a negotiated solution with the Muslims. Some others, including Madame Mitterrand, saw no reason for banning the *hijab* and advocated the right to difference and the concomitant celebration of plurality. Yet others questioned the rigid application of the principle of *laicitée* and argued for the teaching of religion in schools, both because of its cultural importance and because pupils would not be able to make sense of contemporary global conflicts without some knowledge of it.

These views, however, were confined to a minority. The dominant view was firmly committed to the practice of *laicitée* and hostile to any kind of compromise with the Muslim girls. It was eloquently stated in a letter to *Le Nouvel Observateur* of 2 November 1989, signed by several eminent intellectuals and urging the government not to perpetrate the 'Munich of Republican Education'. As the 'only institution consecrated to the universal', the school must be a 'place of emancipation' and resist 'communal, religious and economic pressures' with 'discipline' and 'courage'. For the signatories to the letter, as for a large body of Frenchmen, France was a single and indivisible nation based on a single culture. The school was the central tool of assimilation into French culture and could not tolerate ethnic self-expression. The *hijab* was particularly objectionable because it symbolized both a wholly alien culture and the subordinate status of women. Wearing it implied a refusal to become French, to integrate, to be like the rest. Since *laicitée* was a hard-won principle of long historical standing, the French state could not compromise with it without damaging its identity. As Serge July, the editor of *Liberation*, put it, '...behind the scarf is the question of immigration, behind immigration is the debate over integration, and behind integration the question of *laicitée*'.

The principal argument against allowing Muslim girls to wear the *hijab* then, was that it violated the principle of *laicitée* and went against the secular and assimilationist function of state schools. If Muslim spokesmen were to argue their case persuasively, they needed to counter this view. While some tried to do so, most realized that it raised many large and complex questions that did not admit of easy and conclusive answers, and that such a debate would take years to settle and did not help them in the short run. As it happened, French state schools did not strictly adhere to the principle of *laicitée*, and allowed Catholic girls to wear the cross and other insignia of religious identity and the Jews to wear the *kipa*. Muslims decided to articulate their demand in the language of equality and argued that, since they were denied the right enjoyed by the other religious groups, they were being treated unequally.

Defenders of the ban, including the Minister of Education, rejected the Muslim charge of discrimination on the ground that the *hijab* was not equivalent to the cross, and that the two groups of girls were *not* equal in relevant respects. First, unlike the 'discreetly' worn cross, the 'ostentatious' *hijab* was intended to put pressure on other Muslim girls and entailed 'proselytization'. Second, unlike the freely-worn cross, the *hijab* symbolized and reinforced women's oppression. Third, unlike the unself-consciously worn cross, the *hijab* was an ideologically motivated assertion of religious identity inspired by a wider fundamentalist movement which the schools had a duty to combat.[4]

Although there is a good deal of humbug, misplaced anxiety and false alarm in these arguments, they are not totally devoid of substance. Both the cross and the *hijab* are religious symbols, and hence bases of equal claims. However, religious symbols cannot be defined and compared in the abstract, both because they rarely have exactly equivalent significance and because they acquire different meanings in different contexts and historical periods and might sometimes even cease to be religious in nature. We need to contextualize them and compare them not abstractly or 'in themselves' but in terms of the character and significance they might have acquired at a particular point in time. The question is not whether the *hijab* is the Islamic equivalent of the Christian cross, but whether in contemporary France wearing the *hijab* has broadly the same religious significance for Muslims as wearing the cross has for Christians. Since we cannot therefore dismiss the ban in the name of an abstract right to equal religious freedom, we need to take seriously the three arguments made in support of it and assess their validity.

As for the first argument, the *hijab* is certainly visible but there is no obvious reason why religious symbols should be invisible or be of the same type. Besides, there is no evidence to support the view that the *hijab* was intended to proselytize among non-Muslims or to put religious pressure on other Muslim girls beyond the minimum inherent in the wearing of religious symbols. Conversely, the cross is not necessarily discreet for Catholic girls do sometimes display, flaunt and talk about it, it is clearly visible when they engage in sports, swimming and such other activities, and it is visible even otherwise except that we do not see it because of its familiarity. Once the *hijab* is allowed, it too would become invisible.

The second argument which contrasts the freely-worn cross with the coerced *hijab* is no more persuasive. It assumes that parental pressure is necessarily wrong, a strange and untenable view, and that choices by adolescent girls are always to be preferred over parental preferences, which is no more tenable. Furthermore, we have no means of knowing that wearing the cross was a free choice by Catholic girls and that Muslim girls wore the *hijab* only under parental or communal pressure. It is true that the latter had hitherto avoided it. However, nothing follows from this for it is quite possible that they now defined their identity differently or felt more confident about expressing it. Indeed, the father of the two Creil girls said that the decision to wear the *hijab* was theirs and that he had been trying to convince them out of it. Since he might be saying this under pressure or to avoid embarrassment, we might refer to the remark of a young girl who was inspired by the three Criel girls to start wearing the headscarf in 1994:

> I feel completely liberated by the veil. As soon as I put it on, I felt as if I'd blossomed. The veil allows a woman no longer to be a slave to her body. It is the belief that a woman can go far through means other than using her body.

The third argument for the ban is equally unconvincing, for wearing the *hijab* need not be a form of ideological self-assertion any more than wearing the cross is. As for the fears about the rise of fundamentalism, a term that was never clearly defined, they were speculative and irrelevant to the argument. Only three out of scores of Muslim girls had worn the *hijab*, and the father of two of them had not only no history of religious activism but was positively embarrassed by the publicity. There was not much evidence either that most of the French Muslim community was becoming religiously militant. Some of them did show considerable sympathy for traditional values but that was not against the law, represented a kind of cultural conservatism shared by many a Frenchman, and hardly amounted to fundamentalist militancy.

Allowing the cross and other Christian symbols but not the *hijab* then clearly amounted to treating Muslim girls unequally. Some French leaders conceded this, but insisted that the inequality was justified in order to liberate the girls from their traditional patriarchal system and to prepare them for an autonomous life. There is something to this argument, as equality is one value among many and needs to be balanced against others. However, it is open to several objections. It assumes without evidence that the girls' decision to wear the *hijab* was not autonomous. Furthermore, autonomy is difficult to define and impossible to measure or demonstrate, and any attempt to violate equality in its name opens the door to all manner of specious reasoning and arbitrary interference with pupils' ways of life. What is more, if the school started aggressively promoting autonomy, it would create a threatening and alienating environment in which girls would not feel relaxed enough to pursue their education. Parents, too, would lose confidence in it and deny it their support and cooperation.

The widely shared belief that the *hijab* symbolizes and reinforces female subordination ignores its complex cultural dialectic. Muslim immigrants in France, Britain and elsewhere are deeply fearful of their girls entering the public world including the school. By wearing the *hijab* their daughters seek to reassure them that they can be culturally trusted and will not be 'corrupted' by the norms and values of the school. At the same time they also reshape the semi-public world of the school and protect themselves against its pressures and temptations by subtly getting white and Muslim boys to see them differently to the way they eye white girls. The *hijab* puts the girls 'out of bounds' and enables them to dictate how they wish to be treated. Traditional at one level, the *hijab* is transgressive at another, and enables Muslim girls to transform both their parental and public cultures. To see it merely as a sign of subjection, as most secular Frenchmen and feminists did, was to be trapped into crude cultural stereotypes and fail to appreciate the complex processes of social change and intercultural negotiation it symbolized and triggered. This is not at all to say that all Muslim girls saw the *hijab* in this way, but rather that at least some did. Since the school and local authorities had no reliable means of ascertaining who wore it for what reasons, and since female subordination is too large an issue to be tackled by banning the *hijab*, they should have restrained their republican zeal and left the girls alone subject to the requirement of non-proselytization.

The issues raised by the *hijab* are not confined to France. In Britain the state funds thousands of Anglican, Catholic and Jewish religious schools, but it has until recently rejected Muslim requests for similar schools. Its real reasons, often stated in private and sometimes hinted at in public, are mainly two. First, the state funds religious schools because it expects that in addition to grounding their pupils into the basic principles of their religion, they will also develop their analytical and critical faculties, provide secular knowledge, and prepare them for life in a democratic and secular society. This is a difficult balance to strike, which non-Muslim religious schools have been able to achieve after a long struggle. Since Muslim schools are likely to become nurseries of reactionary ideas in the current fundamentalist phase of Islam, they are unlikely to achieve the basic objectives of education. Second, state funding of religious schools in Britain is the result of particular historical circumstances. British society now realizes that such schools lead to ghettoization and are in general undesirable. Since it cannot renege on its past commitments to existing schools, it can at least stop perpetuating the problem by refusing to fund new ones.

Opponents of Muslim schools therefore argue that no inequality is involved in denying state funding to Muslim schools while continuing to provide it to other religious schools. Equality requires equal treatment of those who are equal in relevant respects. The relevant respect here is the capacity to provide a balanced religious and secular education. Since Muslim schools lack that capacity, they cannot be treated on a par with other religious schools. The second argument has a different thrust. It does not say anything about whether or not the two kinds of schools are equal in relevant respects, but it asserts that the state has decided to change its policy on funding religious schools. Since it cannot abrogate its past commitments, it must continue to fund Christian and Jewish schools. Although this involves treating Muslims unequally, such inequalities are inherent in social life and cannot be avoided. Long-established groups often enjoy rights based on past commitments and policies. When the policies are changed, they retain rights that are no longer available to newcomers.

Opponents of state funding for Muslim schools make the important theoretical point that equality should not be understood in purely formal and abstract terms. Just because some religious communities enjoy state-funded schools, it does not *necessarily* follow that denying them to Muslims amounts to inequality, for they might not be able to fulfil the socially prescribed objectives of education or the state might sincerely wish to discontinue such schools. Rather than accuse their opponents of being anti-Muslim, racists, and so forth on the basis of an abstract and untenable view of equality, we need to ask if their arguments have any merit.

The first argument is suspect. To say that Islam is currently going through a fundamentalist phase is a gross exaggeration, true at best of some but not of all Muslim countries. More to the point, it is not at all true of British Islam. Since the British government allows privately-funded Muslim schools, it evidently shares this view and is wrong to raise the bogey of fundamentalism only when state funding is involved. There is also a rise in Christian and Jewish fundamentalism, but the British government has shown no interest in acquiring greater control over or issuing suitable warnings to state-funded Christian and Jewish schools. It is, of course, possible that Muslim schools could become nurseries of fundamentalism and fail to achieve their objectives. However, there are ways of guarding against this. The government has the right to inspect and regulate schools including their curriculum, pedagogy and general ethos, and has enough power to counter such forms of fundamentalism as might arise in Muslim schools. The power is bound to be greater, and its exercise more acceptable, if the state also funds them.

The second argument is no better. The British state certainly has the right to change its policy on funding religious schools. This involves not only denying state funding to new schools, but also phasing out the existing ones over a mutually agreed period of time, something which the British state shows not the slightest sign of doing. There is no evidence either that it is putting pressure on them to become secular or even to reduce the religious content of their curriculum. Since neither of the two arguments advanced by the government is valid, the denial of state funding to Muslim schools is unjustified.

In the light of our discussions of the *hijab* controversy in France and the state funding of Muslim schools in Britain, it should be clear that equal treatment of cultural communities is logically different from that of individuals. Unlike the latter, it is deeply embedded in and inseparable from the wider cultural and political relations between the communities involved. Besides, cultural communities often contain a wide variety of views on a subject and cannot be homogenized and reified. The case for intercultural equality should not therefore be made in such abstract and ahistorical terms that it ignores genuine differences between and within the communities involved or fails to address the deepest anxieties of the wider society. We should take a contexualized view of equality, identify what respects are relevant, and demand equal treatment of those shown to be equal in these respects. *If* the *hijab* really is different from the cross (which it is not), then Muslim girls may legitimately be denied the right to wear it without incurring the charge of discriminating against them. And *if* Muslim schools do really run the risk that their critics fear (which they do not), or if the British state does really wish to discontinue religious schools (which it does not), then they may legitimately be denied state funding without offending against the principle of equality.

Taking such a contextualized and politically and historically sensitive view of equality, no doubt, creates its own problems. We leave too much space for specious reasoning and alarmist fears, and run the risk of not knowing how to compare differences, how to separate relevant from irrelevant differences, how to determine and assess the context, and so on. It is therefore tempting to take the more dependable route of insisting on the general right to equality, and argue that since Christians and Jews have a right to their schools, Muslims too must have a right to state-funded schools. In the light of what I have said, the temptation should be resisted. If we ask the law to take such a mechanical and simplistic view of equality, then we cannot consistently ask it to take cultural differences into account in the case of the Sikhs and the marriage of the Asian girl discussed earlier. The question therefore is not whether Muslims have a right to religious freedom but what, if anything, that right entails in a specific context, and that involves deciding *what* features of the context are relevant and whether Muslims are equal in respect to *them*. The movement from a general right to equality to the right to a specific treatment in a specific context, that is, from a general right to religion to the right to wear the *hijab* in the school, is not direct and deductive but contexually mediated.

The danger that such a contextualized view of equality might encourage discrimination and disingenuous reasoning is real. The French ban on the *hijab* and the British government's denial of publicly funded Muslim schools were at least in part motivated by anti-Muslim sentiments, and we need to guard against this. We can do so in two ways. We should insist that equality requires identical treatment and place the onus of justification on those seeking to depart from it. Thus British Muslims should be assumed to be entitled to state-funded schools, and it is up to the government to show to the satisfaction of all concerned why such schools might legitimately be denied to them. Secondly, it should be possible for the unconvinced minorities to appeal against government decisions to such public bodies as the courts or the Commission on Human Rights. The reason why the controversy dragged on for years in France and Britain and still remains unresolved in France has to do with the fact that Muslims had no recourse to such a body. Neither country has a Commission on Human Rights although Britain is now moving in that direction, and allows appeal against such 'administrative matters'.

Limits of equality

It is sometimes difficult to decide what constitutes equal treatment because several different forms of treatment fit that description. England has long had an established church which enjoys rights not available to other religions. Two archbishops and 24 bishops sit in the House of Lords, the Church of England alone has the right to officiate at such state ceremonies as coronations and royal weddings and to perform pastoral duties in the armed forces, the reigning monarch is the 'Defender of the Faith' (a title conferred by the Pope on Henry VIII), their children can marry only Protestants, and so on. England also has a law proscribing blasphemy against Christianity. In return for these privileges the monarch, or more accurately, the government of the day exercises several powers over the church. It appoints senior bishops and has a right to intervene in the internal affairs of the church, bishops take an oath of loyalty to the monarch, changes in the constitution of the church have to be ratified by Parliament, and so forth. The Anglican clergy are also barred from becoming members of Westminster Parliament.[5]

In the aftermath of the Rushdie affair in 1989, leaders of non-Christian religions, especially Islam, began to complain that the established church and the anti-blasphemy law privileged Christianity and treated them unequally. Their complaint received two different responses. Some, mainly conservatives, rejected it on the ground that since Britain was a Christian *society* in the sense that Christianity meant much to most of its members and was a source of many of their moral values, and also a Christian *state* in the sense that a historical settlement between the state and the Church of England had made Christianity an integral part of the former's corporate identity, Christianity rightly enjoyed a special political status. It was woven into the very structure of British national identity, and could not and should not be treated as just one religion amongst many. Others, mainly but not only the liberals, conceded the Muslim charges of discrimination, and mostly agreed that the principle of equality required disestablishment of the Anglican church, but disagreed about the anti-blasphemy law, some advocating its abolition and others its extension to all religions.

Most Muslim spokesmen rejected the conservative response. First, no historical settlement could claim permanence as it was a product of its time and subject to revision in the light of new circumstances, Second, such a positivist argument justified existing privileges and denied justice to newcomers. Third, the principle of equality, which Britain claimed to uphold, required that all religions should be treated equally irrespective of their age and historical role. So far as the liberal view was concerned, Muslim response was, again, generally hostile. While some endorsed the disestablishment of the Anglican church, most were opposed to it. In their view the established church gave religion a valued public status and should be extended to other religions as well. As for the anti-blasphemy law, almost all Muslim spokesmen endorsed its extension and strongly disapproved of its abolition. The latter gave them only a negative and formal not a positive and real equality. Indeed, since there was a vast inequality of power and status between the two religious communities, the abolition was likely to make no difference to the securely established Christianity but bound to have disproportionately adverse effects on minority religions. Some Muslim spokesmen also argued that their religion was under particular threat in the current climate, and that it was consistent with the principle of equality to grant special protection to the weak.

We are confronted with a wide variety of views concerning what the principle of religious equality requires in relation to both the established church and the anti-blasphemy law, and need to decide which of them is more persuasive. Religious equality could be understood in two senses. It could mean equal respect for religions taken as collective wholes or for the religious beliefs and practices of individuals; that is, it could mean equality *of* religions or equal right *to* religion. The latter is beyond dispute in a liberal and indeed any decent society. The former is not so simple. Like all other societies Britain has a distinct history, traditions and way of life, and hence a particular cultural character which makes it the kind of society it is and distinguishes it from others. Among other things it is profoundly shaped by Christianity, as is evident in its moral life, myths, political and moral discourse, literature, art and self-understanding. Since Britain cannot leap out of its cultural skin, to deny the Christian component of its identity a privileged status is wrong (because it denies the bulk of its citizens their history) and likely to provoke widespread resentment. It is also dangerous because when sentiments and sensibilities that are deeply inscribed in a way of life are denied legitimate public expressions, they often tend to reappear at other levels in ugly forms. Besides, once the religious beliefs of all citizens are equally respected, no apparent injustice is done to minorities if the religion of the overwhelming majority is given some precedence over theirs, especially when it is a long-established part of the structure of the state and doing so has no adverse effects on their rights and interests.

While all this is true, it is also the case that Britain has undergone marked demographic changes in recent decades. It now has a sizeable number of religious minorities with their own distinct histories and traditions, about which they feel just as strongly as the rest of the British citizens do about theirs. The minorities are an integral part of British society, and deserve not only equal religious and other rights but also an official acknowledgement of their presence in both the symbols of the state and the dominant definition of national identity. The acknowledgement cannot be equal because they have not shaped the British identity as decisively as Christianity has, are not an equally deep and pervasive presence in British political culture, and do not form as integral and central a part of British society as Christianity does. Since they are not equal in *this* respect, they cannot demand *equal* recognition in its self-definition. They are, however, an integral part of British society and can rightly demand at least *some* public recognition by the state.

Any reasonable interpretation of religious equality, understood as equality of religions, must take account of both these facts. The only way to do so is both to accept the privileged status of Christianity and give some public recognition to other religions. Christianity may rightly remain the central component of British collective identity, provided that other religions receive adequate, though not necessarily equal, recognition and representation in the institutions, rituals and ceremonies of the state. For example, representatives of other religions could be appointed to the House of Lords along with Anglican bishops; state ceremonies such as the coronation and Remembrance Day could be broadened to include a non-Christian component; and the ruling monarch could patronize non-Christian festivals and events. In so doing, British society both retains its historically acquired religious identity and publicly acknowledges its current multireligious composition. Britain might, of course, decide to disestablish the Anglican church as many within and outside the church think it should, but that is an altogether different matter and is not required by the principle of religious equality. *So long as* it retains the established church, it may legitimately privilege Christianity provided that other religions receive their due.

As for the anti-blasphemy law, it is only contingently related to the established church. In an earlier era the two went together; in today's liberal climate they need not. There are four possible ways of dealing with the law; namely, to keep it as it is, to abolish it, to extend it to all religions, or to protect only the religion(s) under threat. The anti-blasphemy law relates to people's religious beliefs and practices and seeks to protect them against scurrilous, abusive or offensive attacks. Since the religious beliefs and practices of all citizens deserve equal respect, the first alternative which privileges Christianity is discriminatory and deserves to be rejected. The fact that Christianity is the religion of the majority is relevant in other contexts but not in this one, for here we are concerned with civil rights and not with the political expression of national identity. Since every religion can claim to be under threat and there is no way to adjudicate their claims in a collectively acceptable manner, the fourth alternative too is ruled out. This leaves us with the second and third interpretations. Since Christianity enjoys cultural and political preeminence and minority religions are relatively powerless, abolition of the anti-blasphemy law would have a disproportionately adverse effect on them. Unless there are other reasons for abolishing the law, the third interpretation that it should be extended to all religions has most to be said in favour of it *so far as* the principle of equality is concerned. Equality, however, is not the only value. We also need to take into account the importance of free speech, the claims of secular citizens, the difficulties of defining religion and blasphemy, the merits and demerits of the state's endorsement of religion, and so on. When we do that, we might perhaps conclude that the law deserves to be abolished.

Implications

In the light of our discussion of the problems involved in applying the principle of equality in a multicultural society, several important conclusions follow. When we take legitimate cultural differences into account, as we should, equal treatment is likely to involve different or differential treatment, raising the question as to how we can ensure that the latter does not amount to discrimination or privilege. There is no easy answer to this. As a general rule it would seem that different treatments of individuals or groups are equal if they represent different ways of realizing the same right, opportunity or in whatever other respect they are intended to be treated equally, and if as a result none of the parties involved is better-off or worse-off. The Sikh who is allowed to carry a *kirpan* and a Christian who is not are treated differently but equally because they are both exercising the same right in different ways and because the former does not secure an advantage over or at the expense of the latter. And an Asian girl whose marriage is declared void when contracted under threat of parental ostracism, and a white girl whose marriage under similar circumstances is not, are both treated equally though differently because they are subject to the same general rule that duress voids a marriage. In all such cases we need to consider the nature and the purpose of the right or the rule involved, and show that the differential treatment is justified in terms of it. Disagreements are bound to arise at both levels, especially the former. Since there is no way to resolve them conclusively, cross-cultural application of equality will always remain vulnerable to the opposite charges of privileging or discriminating against a particular group.

In a multicultural society one might sometimes need to go further and grant not only different but also additional rights to some groups or individuals. This may be necessary either to equalize them with the rest or to achieve such worthwhile collective goals as political integration, social harmony and encouragement of cultural diversity. If some groups have long been marginalized or suppressed, lack the confidence and the opportunity to participate as equals in mainstream society, or are subjected to vigorous assimilation, we might need to give them rights not available to others, such as special or disproportionate representation in parliament, the cabinet and other government bodies and the right to consultation and even perhaps a veto over laws relating to them. The purpose of such additional rights is to draw the groups involved into the mainstream of society and give substance to the principle of equal citizenship.

There may also be groups in society who have been traumatized by their recent history, or feel culturally insecure, or are under particular threat. We may then need to give them rights not available to the majority in order to reassure them, promote social harmony, give them a stake in the country's political stability and foster a common sense of belonging. Born in the trauma of the partition of the country and the enormous intercommunal violence that accompanied it, the Constitution of India wisely decided to grant its minorities several additional rights. In Canada and the USA, indigenous peoples enjoy negative and positive rights required to protect their ways of life that are not available to others. Some countries such as Australia, Canada and India place a high value on cultural diversity and give extra resources and rights to their cultural minorities to help them flourish and contribute towards the creation of a rich and plural society. In these and other cases minorities are clearly favoured and in some respects even privileged, but that is justified if it is in the larger interest of society. Such additional rights and resources can easily arouse a sense of injustice and resentment among the majority, and even become a cloak to buy minority electoral support. They must therefore be granted only when justified, and their purpose should be clearly stated and explained.

Liberals, who insist that all citizens should enjoy equal rights, feel troubled by such additional rights to minorities, and either disapprove of them or justify them on the ground that they are intended to equalize these groups with the rest of their fellow-citizens. Their first response represents the triumph of dogma over prudence and is sometimes a recipe for disharmony and disorder in a multicultural society. Their second response makes moral and political sense but misrepresents the basis of the rights. While some additional rights of minorities are meant to equalize them with the rest, others are designed to promote such worthwhile collective goals as social harmony, cultural diversity and a common sense of belonging. Like equality, they too are important values and we need to balance their competing demands.

Although society has a duty to treat all its citizens equally, its ability to do so is necessarily limited. It has a dominant language, and no language is culturally neutral. While it should cherish its minority languages and help their speakers acquire competence in the dominant language, it cannot always give these an equal public status. Every society also has a historically inherited cultural structure which informs its conduct of public life. While it has a duty to modify it to accommodate the legitimate demands of its minorities, it cannot do so beyond a certain point without losing its coherence and causing widespread disorientation, anxiety and even resistance. This is likely to lead to unequal treatment of its cultural minorities in certain areas, about which in spite of all its good intentions it might be able to do little. In all western societies Sunday is a day of rest for obvious cultural and religious reasons. This puts Muslims at a disadvantage who, unlike Christians, cannot join communal prayer on Friday, their holy day. Although provisions should be made to accommodate Muslim employees and reduce the inequality, it is difficult to see how it can be eliminated altogether without unscrambling the prevailing cultural structure and incurring an enormous social and financial cost. Such inescapable inequalities occur in even more acute forms in other areas of life as well. Which inequalities are eliminable, at what cost, and who should bear it are bound to be a matter of dispute. Since often there is no one just or rational way to resolve the disputes, they are best settled by discussion, negotiation and compromise.

9

Logic of Intercultural Evaluation

A multicultural society is likely to include communities some of whose practices offend against the values of the majority. It cannot tolerate them indiscriminately because it has a duty both to raise its voice against morally outrageous practices and to safeguard the integrity of its own moral culture. However, if it disallowed all it disapproved of, it would be guilty of moral dogmatism and extreme intolerance and would miss the opportunity to take a critical look at its own values and practices. This raises the question as to how a multicultural society should decide which minority values and practices to tolerate within what limits.

Consider the following practices which have aroused different degrees of public concern in recent years:

1. Female circumcision.
2. Polygamy.
3. Muslim and Jewish methods of slaughtering animals.
4. Arranged marriages, practised mainly but not only by Asians. The practice ranges from a largely formal parental approval of their offsprings' choices of spouses to foisting ones on them.
5. Marriages within prohibited degrees of relationship; for example, Muslims can marry their first cousins, and Jews their nieces, both of which are viewed with disfavour in some western societies.

6. The practice, common among some African communities, of scarring their children's cheeks or other parts of the body as part of the initiation ceremony.
7. The Muslim practice of withdrawing their school-going girls from such activities as sports, athletics and swimming lessons that involve wearing shorts and exposing parts of their body.
8. Muslim girls wearing the *hijab* or headscarf in schools. Although it is allowed in most western countries, it continues to arouse varying degrees of opposition in some of them.
9. Sikh refusal to wear helmets rather than their traditional turbans when driving motor cycles or doing dangerous work on building sites, to take off their turbans when taking oaths in court or bowing before the speaker in the House of Commons, and to shave off their beards when working in places that involve handling of food.
10. Refusal by gypsies and the Amish community to send their children to schools either altogether or after reaching a certain age on the grounds that modern education is useless for them and alienates them from their community.
11. Requests by Hindus to be allowed to cremate their deceased on a funeral pyre, scatter the ashes in rivers and, in rare cases, to drown rather than cremate their corpses.
12. Subordinate status of women and all it entails including denial of opportunities for their personal development in some minority communities.

In order to decide whether or not to tolerate these and other practices, we need guiding principles. In much of the popular and philosophical discourse four principles are generally canvassed. Since they are well-known and I am only concerned to draw attention to them rather than examine them closely, I shall not elaborate on them. Some writers appeal to universal human rights or more generally to universal moral values, and argue that since these represent the moral minimum and are culturally neutral, they provide the universally valid standards of evaluation.[1] For some others every society has a historically acquired character or identity embodied in its core or shared values. Since the latter form the basis of its way of life, it has both a right and a duty to disallow practices that offend against them. I shall call this the principle of core or common values.[2] Some writers maintain that since moral values are culturally embedded, society should disallow only those practices that cause harm to others, for to go further would amount to cultural 'imperialism'. I shall call this the no-harm principle.[3] Finally, some argue that since universally valid values are not available, since the concept of core values is problematic, and since harm cannot always be defined in a culturally neutral manner, the most desirable and indeed the only possible course of action is to engage in an open-minded and morally serious dialogue with minority spokesmen and act on the resulting consensus. Although such a consensus might involve making concessions and compromises that many of its members might feel uneasy about, it is all that they have to go on in a deeply divided society. I shall call this the principle of dialogical consensus.[4]

Although each of these views contains important insights, and hence their appeal, they are all defective in different degrees. As we saw earlier it is possible to arrive at a body of universally valid values, and we may rightly insist that practices that offend against them are inherently suspect. However, such values are too thin and few to cover all important areas of life. They deal with the most basic aspects of human life about which there is generally little serious disagreement, and fail to guide us once we go beyond these. Not surprisingly, with the exception of a couple of practices on our list, they are largely irrelevant to the discussion of the rest. Furthermore, universal values and human rights need to be interpreted, adjusted to the unique circumstances and cultural traditions of each society, and prioritized in cases of conflict. Since disagreements on these and related issues cannot be resolved by appealing to the values themselves, moral universalism is of limited help.

Although, as we shall see later, the appeal to society's shared or core values has much to be said for it, it too runs into difficulties. As they are generally defined, these values are supposed to be shared by all or at least the vast majority of the members of society and to form the basis of their personal and collective lives. It is doubtful if any but the most traditional society has core values in this sense. Take liberal society. Is equality of the sexes its core value? Not for fascists, sexists, and many conservative and religious persons. It is certainly an important liberal value, but not all members of liberal society are liberals. Is respect for persons its shared value? Racists, fascists, anti-Semites and others either do not agree or do so only because the value is defined so vaguely as to be meaningless. Even if a society can be shown to have common values, they might be morally unacceptable. Inequality is a shared value in slave-owning, racist and caste-based societies, but we would not wish to argue that it should therefore be cherished let alone enforced on their egalitarian minorities. Besides, the core values of a society might include respect for minority values, as they do in liberal and most other societies, and then they cannot be used as a non-negotiable moral standard. Furthermore, the core values of a society can be defined, prioritized, related and traded off in several different ways. Since its members are likely to disagree about these, the appeal to these values does not take us very far. They do, of course, structure debates on disputed issues but do not resolve them.

As for the no-harm principle, it is largely unproblematic when physical harm is involved, though even here the sixth practice mentioned above raises interesting issues. But it offers no guidance as to whether or not to ban such practices as incest, polygamy, arranged marriages, euthanasia and any of the others listed earlier. They either involve highly complex notions of emotional, moral and other types of harm to others and to the agents themselves about which consensus is difficult to obtain, or raise issues that cannot be adequately conceptualized and discussed in the simplistic language of harm.

As for the principle of dialogical consensus, a dialogue is certainly necessary to resolve deep moral and cultural disagreements, and we shall later see how it should proceed. However, it is unlikely to take us far in the abstract and contextless form proposed by its advocates. Unlike philosophical deliberation about politics, a political dialogue occurs within a particular society with a particular moral structure, history and traditions, and its participants are not abstract moral beings but constituted in a certain way. Their disagreement is not about whether the disputed practice is desirable 'in general' or 'in principle', but whether it is desirable in their society, for men and women like them, and fits in with their values and self-understanding. The dialogue cannot therefore be open-ended and free-floating and must start with and centre on the prevailing values, which provide its vocabulary, structure its context, and impose limits on its direction and likely outcome.

I suggest that there is no single principle in terms of which disputed practices can be evaluated. We start and cannot but start with what I shall call society's operative public values, which provide the context and point of orientation for all such discussions. These values, however, are not sacrosanct and non-negotiable, and may themselves be questioned. The resulting dialogue, in which different values are brought into a creative interplay and balanced and traded-off, yields an inherently tentative consensus that helps us decide on a generally acceptable response to disputed practices.

Intercultural dialogue

With the exception of a deeply divided society, and perhaps not even that, every society requires for its survival and smooth functioning at least some agreement on what values and practices should regulate the conduct of their collective affairs. These values and practices often acquire their dominant position through a prolonged process of indoctrination and coercion, and continue to be actively or passively contested by marginalized groups. However, whatever their origins, history and mode of reproduction, over time they become part of society's moral structure and are embodied in its major social, economic, political and other institutions. Its members may personally hold and live by different values, but in their interpersonal relations they are expected to abide by those the society collectively cherishes. Unlike the core or shared values referred to earlier, these values are limited in their scope and largely confined to the publicly relevant and regulated areas of individual life.

The common life is lived at three levels, and hence a society's public values are suitably articulated at each of them. First, they are enshrined in its constitution which lays down the basic legal and moral design of the polity including the fundamental rights and sometimes the obligations of its citizens. Second, the values are also embodied in laws which flesh out the constitutionally enshrined values and relate them to the daily lives of citizens. Although constitutional and legal values are closely related, they are different in nature. The former are general and regulative; the latter are specific and substantive and subject to the constraints of but not derived from constitutional values. For example, the constitution may require that all citizens should be treated equally. That by itself does not entail monogamy, for equality of the sexes only implies that men and women should enjoy equal rights to choose their marriage partners, not that they should marry only one person. When the law prescribes monogamy, it both respects and goes beyond the constitutional value of the equality of the sexes.

A society's public values are also embodied in the norms governing the civic relations between its members. These relations occupy an intermediate realm between the structured relations of organized public life and the intimate relations of personal and private life. Although some aspects of civic relations are governed by laws, most are not and cannot be. Relations between neighbours, people queuing for or travelling by public transport, car drivers, fellow-students, colleagues and strangers belong to this category. They are regulated by a body of civic values and practices and constitute society's civic culture. When the newly arrived North African immigrants to Israel allegedly haggled over the fare with the bus driver or asked him to make an unscheduled stop nearer their homes, they were told that this was not how things were done in Israel; that is, that the Israeli civic culture was quite different to the one they were used to. And when a visiting Pakistani professor in a British university was told not to ask his students to do his weekly shopping for him, he was in effect told that such relations were governed in Britain by different civic values to those prevailing in his country.

The constitutional, legal and civic values represent society's public culture, give shape and substance to its inevitably vague conception of the good life, and constitute what I have called its operative public values.[5] They are values because society cherishes, endeavours to live by, and judges its members' behaviour in terms of them. They are public because they are embodied in its constitutional, legal and civic institutions and practices and regulate the public conduct of its citizens. And the values are operative because they are not abstract ideals but are generally observed and constitute a lived social and moral reality. The operative public values of a society constitute the primary moral structure of its public life. Although they inescapably influence and are influenced by the personal values of its members, the two are distinct in their nature, authority and mode of legitimation.

Although the operative public values of a society are interrelated, they do not form a coherent whole and sometimes pull in different directions. And although they can be stated in general and abstract terms, they lose much of their meaning when dissociated from the procedures and practices in which they are embodied. They are not static, and change in response to changes in the society's circumstances and self-understanding. The are not beyond criticism, and are often contested and only provisionally or pragmatically accepted by some of its members. They are not rigid either and are amenable to different and sometimes opposite interpretations. They are also interlocked in the sense that each limits and partly defines the content of others, and they cannot be neatly catalogued or summarized. They are of varying degrees of generality, interpenetrate each other, and cannot be easily individuated. By and large they form a complex and loosely-knit whole and provide a structured but malleable vocabulary of public discourse.

Since society is collectively and publicly committed to its operative public values, their authority remains unaffected even if some of its members do not personally subscribe to them. Some members of a liberal society might not believe in the equality of the sexes or 'races', but that does not excuse them from adhering to it in their public behaviour. In so far as that is the case, they are subjected to moral coercion. In every society characterized by moral disagreement, and that includes not only the liberal but most human societies, such coercion is inescapable and can be reduced but never eliminated. Those subjected to it either eventually internalize or at least come to see the point of the values or remain untransformed and retain a hiatus between their personal and public beliefs. Both are familiar phenomena, and every society copes with them as best it can.

Since the operative public values represent the shared moral structure of society's public life, they provide the only widely acceptable starting point for a debate on minority practices. We may respond to the practices in several different ways, such as ban them, discourage them, tolerate them, encourage them, or celebrate and hold them up as examples to the rest of society. In each case our initial judgement is based on society's operative public values. When a minority practice offends against them, it invites disapproval. However, that is not a reason to disallow it. The practice forms part of the minority way of life, and society owes it to its minority to explore what the practice means to it, what place it occupies in its way of life, and why it considers it valuable. Furthermore, the operative public values are not themselves beyond criticism and change. Since they generally represent a particular conception of the good life, and since every conception of the good life is partial, they are likely to discriminate against or bear unduly heavily on those whose historical experiences and conceptions of the good are different. Every society therefore needs to periodically reassess its operative public values, and the fact that a minority practice offends against some of them provides it with a welcome opportunity to do so.

Rather than use the operative public values as a crude and non-negotiable standard for evaluating minority practices, society should engage in a dialogue with the minority. Since it disapproves of the minority practice, it needs to give reasons, and that involves showing why it holds these values and how the minority practice offends against them. For its part the minority needs to show why it follows the practice and offer a defence of it. By its very nature the dialogue cannot centre on the merits and demerits of the minority practice alone, for the practice would not have been a subject of dispute if the wider society had not disapproved of it on the basis of its operative public values. The dialogue is therefore bifocal, centring both on the minority practice and the society's operative public values, both on the minority's and the wider society's way of life.

The dialogue need not be and is generally not polarized. The public debate on the merits and demerits of a disputed practice tends to trigger off a debate within the minority community itself. Since the society at large questions the practice and asks the minority community to abandon or defend it, some members of that community would wish to take advantage of the occasion to inquire if it is really central to their way of life and whether it is on balance worth continuing. It is likely that outsiders, too, will join in its internal debate, some defending and others criticizing the practice. A similar debate is also likely to occur within the society at large. While some might vigorously defend the relevant operative public values, others might use the occasion to take a critical look at them and ask whether they are really worth preserving or mere historical excrescences surviving out of moral inertia and reflective of an earlier and now superseded moral consensus. It is more than likely that minority spokesmen might themselves wish to participate in the wider social debate and seek to influence it in a particular manner.

The debate on a minority practice then takes place at several levels and has a profoundly transformative effect on all involved. It triggers off debates within the minority community, within the wider society, and between the two. And in each case the participants are unlikely to be confined to the communities concerned. Furthermore, although the debate begins with a specific practice, it broadens out to cover both the majority and minority ways of life and sometimes opens up large and unexpected sets of issues. It also forces each party to become conscious of its values and reasons for holding them, and contributes to their critical self-knowledge. Although the context of the public debate sometimes encourages them to close ranks and feel unduly defensive about their ways of life, the stronger compulsions of the shared life often tend to prevail and persuade them to explore common interests and values.

The debate on a morally controversial minority practice generally proceeds in three stages. The stages are neither successive nor all necessary; they overlap and any one of them might be skipped. Since the controversial practice offends against one or more of the wider society's values, the minority community is required to defend it. Its initial response is to appeal to the cultural authority of the practice and argue that it is therefore binding on it. If the practice does not violate society's operative public values, it should be allowed. If not, the wider society would wish to rejoin that no culture is self-authenticating and that even a culturally authoritative practice cannot be tolerated if it is morally unacceptable. It might also take a different approach and argue that the practice is a mere custom, a historical excrescence, and not a part of minority culture.

At this stage minority spokesmen would wish to argue that although unacceptable in itself, the practice is interlocked with other valuable practices and central to their way of life, which would be undermined if it were to be disallowed. The wider society might be persuaded by the argument and decide to tolerate the practice. But if it considers the practice too offensive to be tolerated, it would rejoin that no way of life is sacrosanct and that it should be changed if it has to depend for its survival on such practices.

Since the minority is no longer able to defend the practice either in terms of its cultural authority or its community-sustaining role, its spokesmen need to step outside their culture and appeal to values the wider society itself subscribes to or can be persuaded to share. They could argue that, properly understood, the practice is no different from some of the practices of the wider society itself, or that although it realizes different values they enrich the society and should be respected. If their case is persuasive, the practice should be allowed. If the majority remains unconvinced and cannot see the point of the values the practice claims to realize, a difficult situation arises. Since moral values cannot be debated and defended in an objective and conclusive manner, and since it is difficult to be wholly detached and open-minded about one's moral values, the dialogue involves passages of incomprehension, intransigence, irreconcilable differences. It might then be better to postpone the decision on the disputed practice in the hope that the passage of time and the fusion of ideas brought about by formal and informal public discussions will create enough common ground and willingness to facilitate a consensus or at least a negotiated compromise in future. If the matter is urgent and the practice in question morally unacceptable, the operative public values of the wider society should prevail for at least three important reasons. First, they are woven into its institutions and practices and cannot be radically revised without causing considerable moral and social disorientation. Second, while a society has an obligation to accommodate the minority way of life, it has no obligation to do so at the cost of its own, especially if it remains genuinely unconvinced by the minority's defence of the practice. Third, when the minority consists of immigrants they need to appreciate that since they are unfamiliar with the wider society's way of life, they should defer to its judgement in contentious matters. They also need its support to counter the resentment their presence generally provokes among some sections of society, and are more likely to secure it if, after making their point, they gracefully accept its decision.

Female circumcision and other practices

Since our discussion so far has been abstract, it would be useful to take a few minority practices, ranging from the least to the most controversial, to show how our analysis applies to them.[6]

It is a Hindu practice to scatter the ashes of the dead in rivers, and in rare cases to submerge the corpses in deep waters rather than cremate them. Both practices, especially the latter, aroused unease and met with some initial resistance in Britain. However, it was widely appreciated that they were central to the Hindu way of life, meant much to the Hindus, and did not offend against any of the operative public values of British society, the only relevant public interest being that they should not put public health at risk. Quite sensibly the Water Act 1989 allowed both, provided that the persons concerned obtained a license. The license is given if the ashes are disposed of in tidal or estuary waters or in the sea within 12 miles of the coastline. The suitably weighted down corpses can also be disposed of in this manner, and local boatmen are available for making the necessary arrangements.

Many Hindus prefer to cremate their dead on a funeral pyre rather than by electric means. This is disallowed in almost all western societies largely on aesthetic and hygienic grounds. The objections are ill-conceived. Aesthetic considerations are matters of taste and should not be imposed by law, and the Hindu practice poses no risk to public hygiene. Since no operative public values of liberal society are offended by it, the practice should be allowed in closed and officially designated places, as is the cases in such countries as India, Guyana, Trinidad and the Netherlands.

The Jewish and Muslim method of slaughtering animals has been a subject of continuing debate in many western societies. For a variety of religious reasons having to do with the nature of slaughter and the symbolic significance of food, the two communities believe that the animal should be conscious and not stunned before being slaughtered. Some animal rights activists and even others have argued that although this method of killing is quick and effective, the animal is conscious of being killed and suffers pain both before and during the slaughter and that the practice should be banned. This is not as easy a question as the Hindu practice of scattering the ashes of their dead, but there are good reasons to allow the practice. Although it is not integral to the Jewish and Muslim ways of life in the sense that they would suffer profound disorientation if it were to be disallowed, it is religiously sanctioned, means much to the two communities, and is closely tied up with their other beliefs and practices. Spokesmen of the two communities are also able to offer a reasonable defence of it, arguing that pain to the animal is nil or at best minimal and that, if animals were allowed to be killed at all, the pain lasting barely a few seconds should not be given greater moral weight than the cultural sentiments of the two communities. Furthermore, the practice does not violate any of the operative public values of the wider society, and the popular sensitivity to animal pain is not yet so intense and widespread as to make the practice deeply offensive or morally unacceptable. If things were to change radically, the practice might need to be reconsidered as was recently done in Norway which, following much public discussion and after making appropriate provisions for *kosher* or *halal* food, decided to ban it with the willing consent of its Jewish and Muslim communities.

The Asian practice of arranged marriages has aroused some unease in many liberal societies. It covers a wide spectrum ranging from the almost automatic parental endorsement of spouses freely chosen by their offspring to parental imposition of them. Although the practice has no religious basis, it is interlocked with other practices, plays an important part in sustaining the Asian way of life, and means a great deal to its adherents. They are also able to offer a reasonable defence of it. They argue that marriages are likely to be happier and last longer if parents consent to them and feel morally and emotionally committed to their success. In the Asian view individuals are an integral part of their family, and their lives belong not just to them but also to their families. It therefore makes sense for parents to have a say in who their sons and daughters marry and how they lead their lives. Asian spokesmen also point to the fact that many of their youths themselves welcome both the parental advice and the wider network of social support that arranged marriages provide.

Many liberals would like to ban or at least discourage the practice on the grounds that it offends against the values of personal autonomy and choice. As we saw earlier, there is no justification for holding up personal autonomy and choice as universal values, especially in such culturally crucial matters as marriage. If young Asians are happy for their parents to choose or help them choose their spouses, they have chosen to be chosen or co-chosen for, and their choices should be respected. Even if they have made no such conscious choices and are content as a matter of social routine to leave such decisions to their parents, they should have the same right as others to run their personal lives. It is, of course, crucial that they should not be coerced into marriages against their explicitly stated personal wishes. The wider society is therefore right to ban imposed marriages or those contracted under duress as defined in a culturally sensitive manner, but to go further is to be guilty of moral dogmatism and unjustified cultural interference.

The origins of female circumcision are unknown, but in one form or another it seems to have existed for centuries. In ancient Rome metal rings were passed through the labia minora of slaves to prevent procreation; in medieval England women in certain sections of society were made to wear metal chastity belts to prevent promiscuity during their husbands' long absences; evidence from mummified bodies in ancient Egypt suggests that both excision and infibulation were performed; in Tsarist Russia as well as in nineteenth-century England, France and the United States, clitoridectomy was practised as a 'cure' for epilepsy, hysteria and insanity.

Female circumcision takes three forms: *sunna* or 'traditional' circumcision involving the removal of the prepuce and the tip of the clitoris; excision or clitoridectomy involving removal of the clitoris and often part or all of the labia minora; and infibulation or Pharaonic circumcision, including removal of the clitoris, the labia minora and part of the labia majora, and stitching up of the two sides of the vulva leaving a smooth surface and a small opening for urine and menstrual blood. Of the three, the first involves minimum physical harm and does not seem to be very different from male circumcision. Although the latter has sometimes been criticized on medical and more recently on psychological grounds and involves some degree of physical mutilation, it is widely allowed. Unless female circumcision is shown to cause graver harm, there is no obvious reason to treat it differently. All that society is entitled to insist upon is that it should be done by qualified people under public supervision and medically acceptable conditions. The other two forms of circumcision are quite different in nature and I shall concentrate on them.

In either of these two forms, it is practised in at least 25 countries in Africa, the Middle East and parts of Southeast Asia. It is common in some Muslim countries but not others, and in the former it predates Islam and is to be found among some non-Muslims as well. There are as many as two million female circumcisions a year, and over 80 million women living today have undergone it. It is banned in all western countries, and this has caused considerable unease among a section of Muslim immigrants. The practice deeply offends against some of the basic human or universal values as well as the operative public values of liberal society. It inflicts irreversible physical harm, is sexist in nature, violates the integrity of the child, makes irreversible decisions for her, endangers her life, and removes an important source of pleasure. It therefore deserves to be banned unless its advocates offer compelling reasons that measure up to its enormity.

The defence mounted by its advocates proceeds along the three stages mentioned earlier. First, it is required by their religion or culture, and hence is binding on them. Second, it is tied up with their other moral and social beliefs and practices and is integral to their way of life. It guarantees the girl's virginity by ruling out sexual intercourse in the case of Pharaonic circumcision and saves her from social suspicion, makes it easier for her to find a suitable husband, protects her family against ignominy resulting from her likely indiscretions, and in these and other ways plays a crucial role in sustaining the traditional way of life. Third, according to its advocates, the practice promotes important values which all societies should share or at least respect. It regulates the girl's sexuality, facilitates sexual self-discipline and self-control, protects her against obsession with sex during her adolescence, and leads to a psychologically healthy life. Sometimes female circumcision is also defended on aesthetic grounds. Female genitals are deemed to be ugly and ill-shaped and circumcision is seen as a way of making them more symmetrical and attractive. Notions of cleanliness and strange myths about the nature and significance of the clitoris are also invoked.[7] Since these are not moral arguments, are rarely advanced in public and marginal to the main defence of the practice, I shall ignore them.

None of these defences measures up to the gravity of the harm caused by the practice and provides reasons to override the objections to it. The fact that it is sanctioned by religion or a culture is *a* reason but never a *conclusive* one for allowing it. As it happens, it has no religious or cultural sanction. There is no mention of it in the *Koran* and only a passing and ambiguous reference in one of the *hadiths*. It is not practised in many Muslim countries and has provoked strong opposition among some sections of the very communities in which it is common.

As for the second defence, it grossly exaggerates the social value of the practice. The latter neither guarantees virginity, as the premarital practice of hymenorrhappy shows, nor protects the girl against social suspicions and indiscretions. It also causes a deep psychological trauma, renders her incapable of a normal sex life, and leads to postmarital frigidity, irritability, moodiness, depression and anxiety. Since other communities which also cherish virginity manage to achieve it without harmful means, there is no reason why Muslims cannot. The largely critical views of women who have themselves undergone the practice and the indefensible beliefs about the female sexuality from which it derives its legitimacy also count against it. It is, of course, true that there is a considerable social pressure to conform to it and that dissenting families sometimes pay a heavy price. However, the answer lies not in continuing the practice but in judiciously reforming the way of life that makes it necessary. Social pressures form a vicious cycle forcing individuals to do things they would rather not, and can only be removed by legally banning the unacceptable practice.

The third defence fares no better. Sexual discipline and self-control are certainly important values, but so are mental and physical health and sexual fulfilment. And if the former are secured in a brutal manner and at the expense of the latter, their value is considerably reduced. What is more, blocking the physical possibility of a vice hardly amounts to cultivating the relevant virtue. Again, there is strong evidence to show that far from eliminating or even reducing the adolescent obsession with sexuality, circumcision tends to intensify it. And since it bars normal modes of sexuality, it is known to encourage perverse and harmful forms.

We can then challenge the defence of female circumcision by questioning its assumptions, underlying values, allegedly beneficial consequences, and cultural importance, and show that it is too weak to override the strong moral and other objections listed earlier. Our discussion is obviously somewhat sketchy and hurried and is only designed to show how the debate on the subject could proceed and be resolved. Since the practice is fairly widespread among the immigrant communities and their societies of origin, the ban on it should be enforced with compassion and sensitivity and accompanied by a reformist campaign by their leaders.[8]

We have so far discussed female circumcision in relation to children. What if it were to be demanded by an adult member of a minority community in full possession of her senses?[9] This is not a purely hypothetical situation. A 30-year old Nigerian academic who heard me attack it at a conference pointed out privately that it was common among some groups of women in her community to undergo clitoridectomy after the birth of their first child, and that she had herself had it done when she was 26. Her reasons, as well as theirs, had to do with the regulation of sexuality, a rite of passage, a symbolic break with the past, and a way of reminding themselves that from now onwards they were primarily mothers rather than wives whose maternal duties took precedence over personal pleasure.

How should we respond to such a demand? Surely an adult and sane woman should be free to do what she likes with her body. Naturally such a right is not absolute. If someone wanted her arms amputated or eyes gouged out as a form of penance, or out of a sense of guilt, or to avoid doing or being tempted by evil, we would not allow it on such grounds as that it would render her incapable of discharging her normal social obligations, lead her to make excessive demands on society's resources, and that her proposed action violates our ideas of how human beings should treat their bodies. None of these grounds except perhaps the last applies in the case of adult circumcision.

The woman involved could also argue that western society allows the transplant, enlargement or reduction of breasts, reconstruction of the nose and the lips and almost the entire face, tattooing and body piercing. While western women feel strongly about their facial parts, she feels equally strongly about her genitals and wonders what the difference is. She might go further and argue that, since society allows males to engage in surgical enlargements of their genitals, denying her the right to circumcision is discriminatory. Indeed, if she is an uncompromising feminist, she might even contend that male-dominated society disapproves of clitoridectomy because males define female sexuality in a certain way, prefer women to offer them or to experience themselves a particular kind of sexual pleasure, and that denying her the right to circumcision is sexist in its assumptions and implications and takes away her basic right to define her sexual identity.

While all this suggests that an adult woman should be free to undergo clitoridectomy and even infibulation, other factors point in the opposite direction. Although it might be her free choice, it could also be a response to acute social pressure, not perhaps in every case but certainly in many. And even if it is her free choice, we might wonder if people should be free to do with their bodies whatever they like. Given the history of the communities concerned, it is also likely that if she were to be allowed, the practice would be used for purposes we strongly disapprove of and even extended to younger women and children. There is also the danger that other adult women might be put under pressure to engage in it.

Our decision as to whether or not to allow adult female circumcision needs to be based on a careful weighing up of these and other considerations. We have four choices. First, we might allow it without restriction. Second, we might allow it subject to clearly specified conditions, such as that it should be voluntary and undertaken in response to deeply held beliefs. Third, we might ban it altogether. And fourth, we might ban it but make exceptions when the demand for it is genuinely voluntary and based on deeply held moral beliefs. The first course of action does not signify society's collective disapproval of it, and should be ruled out. Since the third shows no respect for the woman's freedom of choice and culture, it too should be ruled out. This leaves us with the second and fourth courses of action. In practice they amount to more or less the same thing, but send out very different messages. The second course of action implies that society sees nothing wrong with the practice and only objects to its misuse; the fourth implies the opposite. Since the practice is objectionable for reasons discussed earlier, the fourth course of action seems the most defensible.

I have so far discussed adult female circumcision in the context of minority communities among whom it is a standard practice. What if it were to be demanded by a member of the majority community on moral or aesthetic grounds? Here culture does not enter the picture and the woman's decision stands on its own. The question then is how much weight to give to individual choices and whether and what limits society should impose on them. The decision is not easy. On the one hand uncoerced individual choices should be respected and, since society allows breast transplants and so forth, it should also perhaps allow adult female circumcision. On the other hand we rightly restrict people's choices even in relation to their own bodies; we do not, for example, allow them to sell their body parts. Besides, it could plausibly be argued that circumcision is not quite like breast transplant or liposuction for it involves physical mutilation in a way that the latter does not. We might also feel that we should discourage certain ways of treating one's body, that circumcision blunts the medical and moral sensibilities of those required to perform it, and so forth. We have the same four choices as in the case of women from minority communities, and need to decide on the basis of a careful weighing-up of all the relevant considerations. We might arrive at the same decision as in their case, as I think we should, but our reasons would be somewhat different.

The fact that our decision as to whether to allow a cultural practice cannot and should not be based on abstract moral principles or the right to autonomy alone but also on its cultural and historical context, likely consequences and so on becomes clear if we took the case of *sati*, the largely defunct Hindu practice of a widow immolating herself on her husband's funeral pyre.[10] The practice is of unknown origin, and in one form or another goes back a long time. During the early days of British rule when it became fairly widespread in some parts of the country, Hindu leaders themselves began to campaign against it and created a climate which made it easier for the British to outlaw it in 1829. Incidents of *sati*, however, continued to occur, including in post-independence India, but they were relatively rare and aroused no public concern. The situation changed in 1987 when Roop Kanwar, a well-educated 18-year-old Rajput girl and married for eight months to a well-educated young man, mounted her husband's funeral pyre watched by thousands of enthusiastic admirers. Although accounts of the incident vary, the circumstantial evidence suggests that she was drugged. In any case the incident aroused considerable passion all over India, some strongly supporting and others vehemently condemning it. It would seem that a large number of Hindus approved of the woman's action as judged by the size of public demonstrations in support of it.

Although the practice was already banned, the pressure on the government to do something was considerable. Within a few months of the incident the Indian Parliament passed a law outlawing its 'glorification'. Indians remained free to argue in favour of it, but not to idealize and celebrate it in public.

The government ban aroused opposition among influential sections of public opinion including the liberal. In their view it restricted the woman's right to do what she liked with her life, denied her the freedom to live by her deeply held religious beliefs, and interfered with the Hindu way of life. Although these objections raise important questions concerning the freedom of religion, individual autonomy and so on, and cannot be lightly dismissed as was done by the secularists and the feminists, they are deeply flawed. An individual's life is not exclusively his or hers; others including those closely related to them also have a claim on it, which is why suicide is subject to moral constraints. Furthermore, like other kinds of freedom, religious freedom can never be absolute and may be restricted when used for unacceptable purposes. One cannot kill an infidel or an idolater because one's religion requires it. Since the practice of *sati* has the limited authority of the tradition behind it, it puts intense pressure on a distraught, confused and socially vulnerable woman to take her life. The fact that her death is of considerable financial benefit to her in-laws provides an additional motive for the pressure. It removes a claimant to the dead man's property and the rest of the family's resources, and enables her in-laws to turn their house into a commercially profitable shrine. The practice also reinforces woman's inferiority, devalues human life, generates fear bordering on psychological terror among newly-wedded women and even men, and deprives children of parental love and support.

For these and related reasons, the practice deserves to be banned. This would, of course, cause deep distress to a widow who sincerely believed that it was her duty to die with her husband or that she would go to hell if she did not. However, such women are rare, and their religious freedom can be restricted in the wider interest of women as a whole and society's own operative public values. It might be argued that while banning the practice, the law could grant a kind of 'conscientious exemption' to those women who undertake it voluntarily and out of deeply held religious beliefs suitably ascertained by government officials, the position I suggested in relation to adult female circumcision. Although there is something to be said for such a compromise, there are several complicating factors. Unlike circumcision, the adult woman's self-immolation is a source of financial and other benefits to her in-laws and even her parents, and hence open to much abuse. It also occurs at the most stressful and vulnerable time of her life, and is therefore unlikely to be free and rational. Furthermore, the proposed compromise neither challenges the sexist bias of the practice, nor counters the influence of unscrupulous religious leaders eager to manipulate the religious sensibilities of illiterate and gullible people. On balance banning the practice altogether is therefore the best course of action. If Hindu society were to ensure full equality to women in all areas of life, if they were able to think independently and decide for themselves between alternative ways of understanding their cultural traditions, and if they could be counted upon to act freely, there would be a case for conscientious exemption. None of these preconditions obtains in contemporary India. This is not so much paternalism as a way of contextualizing rights and liberties and creating proper conditions for their intelligent exercise. And even paternalism, understood as restricting individual choices in their own collectively articulated best interests, has a legitimate place in all societies that have not yet attained perfection, and that include all present and foreseeable ones.

Polygamy

Polygamy, including both polygyny (more than one wife) and polyandry (more than one husband), is banned in all western societies. Since polygyny is practised by some Muslim communities they feel unjustly treated and have campaigned for the ban to be lifted on two grounds, one positive the other negative; the former offering a reasoned defence of it, the latter attacking the ban as incoherent, hypocritical, even racist (Cligent, 1970; Gbadegesin, 1993).

Muslim defence of polygyny is fivefold and corresponds to the three stages mentioned earlier. The first argument invokes the cultural authority of the practice, the rest appeal to its importance to their way of life and the worthwhile values it allegedly realizes:

● First, polygyny is both a cultural and a religious practice sanctioned respectively by tradition and the *Koran*.

- Second, in most societies it is common to divorce a woman if she is infertile or sexually incapacitated or if the married partners are emotionally or sexually incompatible. Since divorce causes considerable suffering to all involved, it is more humane to allow the husband to take a second wife without having to divorce the first.
- Third, all males are tempted to stray from the path of matrimonial fidelity and sometimes strike up extramarital liaisons with all the deception, insecurity and tensions that these entail. It would help all concerned and is also more honest if the man were allowed to marry the woman involved rather than break up the existing marriage or lead a life of deceit.
- Fourth, extramarital relations sometimes result in children who carry the stigma of illegitimacy all their lives, and the males involved have no social or even financial obligations to them or to their mother. In such cases it is more sensible not only to allow but to require the man concerned to marry the woman and accept full responsibility for their children.
- Fifth, in some societies the gender ratio is skewed and women outnumber men. This results in compulsory spinsterhood for many of them, undesirable pressure on monogamous marriages, and even prostitution. In such situations polygyny has much to be said for it. After the Nigerian civil war when the town of Calabar was swarming with unmarried women and widows, even the Christian tribal elders preferred to allow polygyny to their members rather than risk the obvious dangers.

Muslim spokesmen argue that even if their defence of polygyny were to be found unconvincing, western society would be wrong to ban it. First, the law and even much of public opinion allow individuals to cohabit with more than one woman (or man) so long as they do not marry. Since cohabitation is little different from marriage, western societies endorse polygamy in practice. Second, a married man is at liberty to take a mistress (or mistresses). Although there are important differences between wife and mistress, they should not be exaggerated. The relationship in both cases is long-term and non-casual, free from monetary transactions characteristic of prostitutes and call-girls, involves emotional commitments and mutual obligations, and is not easily terminated. Muslims argue that for all practical purposes a man with a mistress is engaged in polygyny and neither the law nor social opinion in the West is much exercised about it.

Third, unlike most past and present societies, the law in liberal society imposes no hardship on either the married man or his mistress. He is at liberty to bequeath her his property; she is at liberty to take his name; neither is deprived of their civil and other rights, viewed as 'devoid of character', or their testimony in the courts discounted or given less weight. Fourth, the law allows easy divorce. Given the prevailing rate of matrimonial breakdowns, on average nearly a third of men (and women) enter into at least two marriages over a lifetime. Muslims ask why this is not considered polygyny. Polygyny means more than one wife irrespective of whether they are simultaneous or consecutive. To restrict it to simultaneous partners is to offer a biased definition of it. And even if one accepts it, there is no obvious reason why having consecutive partners should be considered morally superior to having them simultaneously. Muslims also argue that divorce often occurs against the background of a new relationship, and for a while the two relationships are run in tandem. This is virtual polygamy, and shows that the dividing line between it and monogamy is difficult to draw.

I have so far sketched both the Muslim defence of polygyny and critique of western society's ban on it. Although both make interesting points, neither is convincing. The Muslim defence is open to the fundamental objection that it violates the principle of the equality of the sexes, which is an operative public value in liberal society, and that is a good enough reason to insist on it. One can go further and argue, as I did earlier, that equality is not just a western or liberal but a rationally defensible universal moral value. Men and women share distinctly human capacities and needs in common, have a broadly equal potential, are equally capable of choice and self-determination and so on, and are therefore entitled to equal dignity and rights. What is no less important, the opposite assertion is extremely difficult to substantiate. No Muslim has been able to make out a defensible case for women's inequality except on the basis of such discredited arguments as that they have poorly developed powers of rational thought, that their physiology renders their judgements unreliable, and that granting them equality would undermine the institution of the family and subvert the social order (Goodwin, 1995). Since we can rightly insist on the equality of the sexes, we can ban polygyny on that ground alone without having to justify monogamy. If Muslims were to rejoin that they do not accept the principle of equality of the sexes, and that imposing it on them amounts to cultural imperialism, we could reply that we have offered a reasonably persuasive defence of it, that they have advanced no convincing arguments against it, and that we are therefore entitled to insist on it. It might offend against the Muslim's deeply held beliefs, but no belief is incorrigible and self-authenticating. If it is ill-founded and has patently harmful consequences, we have no obligation to respect it.

In addition to rejecting the Muslim defence of polygyny on the grounds of its sexism, we can also show that each of their five arguments is flawed in different degrees. As for the first argument, the *Koran* does not require but only permits polygyny, and that too is subject to two conditions. It should be motivated not by passion but compassion for widows and orphans. And the husband should be able to treat his wives with *equal* respect and love, a condition the vast majority of men cannot meet and which, as we shall see, is rendered exceedingly difficult by the very dynamics of polygynous relationship. Indeed, as the *Koran* itself says; 'You are never able to be fair and just as between women even if it is your ardent desire'. This is one of the reasons given by the Tunisian religious authorities for banning polygyny. Furthermore, the fact that the *Koran* permits it is at best a reason but not a conclusive reason for allowing it. The *Koran* rules out a number of things such as interest on savings, lust, consumption of alcohol, accumulation of wealth, and even the nation-state and nationalism. Since most Muslims disregard most of these injunctions, their selective adherence to polygyny is disingenuous.

As for the next four arguments, the fifth can be readily conceded. When the gender ratio is extremely skewed in favour of men, polygyny makes sense as a way of establishing some form of moral order in inter-gender relations. It is, however, not the only alternative for many societies cope with such situations in quite different ways. And the fact that it is morally expedient does not make it morally commendable. In any case, since no existing society faces such a problem, the argument has no practical relevance.

Although the remaining three arguments make some sense in societies that strongly disapprove of divorce, infidelity and illegitimacy and confine the women involved to degrading conditions, they are flawed. Polygyny keeps women subordinate and dependent on the precarious mercy of their husbands. And it also involves their emotional and sexual exploitation and leads to an unhealthy climate of jealousy, intrigue and insecurity. It is not obvious that these and related consequences are less damaging than those that polygyny seeks to prevent, or that women themselves might not prefer the hardship of divorce or the stigma of illegitimate children to such advantages as polygyny brings. Even if polygyny could be shown to be a lesser evil in certain societies, that is so only because they frown upon divorce, illegitimacy and so on and treat the women involved as social pariahs. The better thing to do is to change these attitudes by attacking the structure of patriarchal authority that generates and nurtures them.

I have so far concentrated on criticizing the Muslim case for polygyny. What if Muslims conceded the principle of equality of the sexes and extended to women the right to marry polygamously? Should polygamy then be allowed? The demand for it could just as easily come from non-Muslims as well, and the right to it would have to be granted to all. Polygamy is not easy to dismiss for it does not violate any of the great universal or even the operative public values of liberal society. It is based on free choices of the parties involved, and liberal society is committed to respecting these. Liberal society claims to encourage experiments in living, and polygamy is one of them. It claims to be non-paternalist, and should not tell people how to lead their personal lives. It acknowledges diversity of tastes, temperaments and emotional needs, and should allow polygamy to those so inclined. It respects unconventional sexual orientation, and should consistently extend it to polygamy. It welcomes healthy competition between different ways of life as a means of discovering the truth about them, and cannot insist on monogamy as the only valid form of marriage, at least until all others have been tried out. In the light of all this, can we make out a reasonably strong case for monogamy?

In constructing a case for monogamy we should be careful not to equate it with one of its many possible forms. Marriage may be arranged or self-determined, romantic or non-romantic, love-based, duty-based or a matter of convenience, and our defence of monogamy should be as neutral as possible between its these and other forms. Again, monogamy is a common practice in many cultures, which defend it on different grounds. In a multicultural society we should defend it in a manner intelligible and hopefully acceptable to different communities including Muslims. The standard Christian or romantic defence of it is relatively easy, but does not serve the purpose. I sketch below the outlines of such a defence.

Whatever its form, marriage involves at least two individuals who wish to live together, hopefully but not necessarily forever. Although their relations with each other are not and need not be closer or morally more important than those with their parents, brothers, friends and so on, they are significantly different from the latter. Marriage involves sexual intimacy, and all that goes with it. Married partners know each other in a way that others do not, wittingly or unwittingly reveal aspects of themselves to each other that they cannot reveal to others, are emotionally bonded to each other in a way that they are not to others, and their relationship has an intensity that is unique to it. They share their deepest feelings, make common plans for themselves and their children, and relate to others as a single unit. All this remains true whether their marriage is arranged or self-chosen, romantic or non-romantic, occurs within a nuclear or a joint family.

Given the nature of their relationship, married partners need to build up at least some degree of mutual trust, commitment, affection, and an instinctive understanding of each other's desires, needs and moods. Even if they have known each other before marriage, their relationship acquires a different character after marriage, and they now need to get to know each other at a different level. In the case of some forms of arranged marriages, this task begins after the marriage and is even more demanding. Getting to know another person well enough to live with him or her is a difficult and prolonged process, and requires time, energy, leisure, a relative absence of outside interference, and an emotionally relaxed environment. The monogamous relationship provides these conditions better than the polygamous. Not that the latter cannot, but rather that it is unlikely to do so under normal circumstances.

To develop a relationship of trust, commitment and understanding with even one person is taxing enough; to introduce a third party let alone several more is likely to kill it. Time, energy, patience, the capacity for deep emotional commitment and good will are limited, and the more they are shared the less of them are available for each person. Besides, as we know from the accounts of polygamous marriages in other societies and triangular relationships in our own, they breed jealousy, rivalry, anxiety, insecurity, invidious comparisons and mutual manipulation. Since each wife (or husband) knows that she (or he) is substitutable and hence dispensable, they lack a sense of special bonding and their relationship is likely to remain superficial and insecure.

Marriage involves children, and the latter need ideal conditions in which to grow up into sane and responsible adults. They require a secure, stable and loving environment, constant personal attention, opportunities to build up close relations with their parents and with each other, and identifiable figures of authority to discipline them and build up their will power and capacity for self-determination. Children also need to feel valued and acquire a sense of their own worth, and that requires that they are and know themselves to be unique and irreplaceable in the eyes of their parents. A monogamously-based family is best equipped to create these conditions.

Since monogamous marriage is highly demanding, it sometimes fails. However, it is striking that when that happens, the parties involved do not reject the practice of monogamy but only change partners. When people go through more than one marriage, each marriage is self-contained, lived in its own terms, and involves exclusive mutual commitment. To have two consecutive wives is therefore qualitatively different from having them simultaneously. Since the nature of the relationship in each case is wholly different, to call the former serial polygamy is as perverse as calling polygamy plural monogamy.

Since monogamy involves sexual discipline which some find trying, they seek from time to time to escape its constraints. However, such lapses are associated with a sense of guilt or at least unease, and incur at least some measure of social disapproval. This is why such lapses occur secretly, provoke charges of deception and betrayal, and require an explanation. None of these would happen if monogamy were not a deeply valued liberal practice. Since lapses occur, society has to decide how to deal with them. It could either take a harsh view of them and impose social and legal punishment of the kind familiar in premodern and some contemporary Muslim societies, or tolerate them with varying degrees of disapproval. Muslims are right to argue that, strictly speaking, the former is the only course of action open to a society deeply committed to monogamy.

Such a punitive approach, however, has its dangers. It has not worked in the traditional, including Muslim, societies where lapses are not at all uncommon. And since they attract severe punishment, they often lead to hypocrisy, social blackmail and witchhunts. Besides, although liberal society values monogamy, it also values freedom of self-exploration, tolerance, learning from one's mistakes, self-fulfilment and so on, and needs to strike a balance between them. It prefers its members to observe the constraints of monogamy voluntarily rather than under threat of death or loss of basic rights, and encourages married partners to be honest with each other rather than practise sexual fidelity against the background of dishonest feelings and adulterous thoughts. Again, we need to appreciate the complex social logic of institutions and practices. They stabilize social life by laying down the socially necessary moral minimum, affirming society's values, providing a moral compass, imposing at least some discipline on human behaviour, and influencing motives. However, they must also accommodate themselves to human failings and can easily lose their credibility and authority if they become excessively rigid and intolerant of deviations. This is why we chafe against the discipline of monogamy and yet insist on retaining it. The Muslim critic rightly exposes the lapses and hypocrisy of liberal society, but misreads their nature and rationale.

How would a Muslim critic respond to the kind of case we have made out for monogamy? The case is twofold. First, monogamy establishes a non-manipulative, trustful, affectionate and mutually supportive relationship between married persons. Second, it provides a propitious environment for bringing up children. The Muslim critic might reject one or both of these arguments.

As against the first argument, he might rejoin that it uncritically privileges the western individualist view of marriage. Marriage is conceptualized differently in different cultures, some of which view it as a familial or communal rather than an individual act. In these cultures married partners are embedded in a wider network of relationships, and their marriage is expected not to replace or disturb but to subserve and fit into these relationships. In addition to being a good wife, the spouse should also be a good daughter-in-law or sister-in-law and help look after the husband's parents, younger brothers and sisters. Unlike the western romantic view of marriage, the marital relationship here is not morally privileged or emotionally more intense than other relationships. As such there is nothing special about it, and it does not call for friendship, romance or exclusive mutual commitment. A romantic marriage may perhaps need to be monogamous, but there is no obvious reason why all marriages should be romantic. A society might view marriage as a way of sustaining the community rather than a form of personal fulfilment or deep emotional bonding. When such a view of marriage is widely accepted in it, its members are suitably socialized into accepting the necessary discipline and developing the required mental attitudes. As a result their polygamous relationship is free from the possessiveness, jealousy and so on that characterize the triangular or quadrangular relationships in the individualist West.

As for the second argument that monogamy provides ideal conditions for the moral and emotional development of children, a Muslim might rejoin that polygamous marriage can provide it just as well as and even better than the monogamous. It has more role models, more adults of diverse talents and temperaments to identify with, and more children to play with. Unlike a monogamous marriage, children in a polygamous marriage are not so intensely bonded with their parents that they seek exclusive attention or are haunted by fear of rejection or devastated by their death, and are therefore likely to develop a greater sense of security, self-confidence and autonomy.

Although the Muslim rejoinder makes interesting points and highlights the difficulties of intercultural comparison, it is unconvincing. Contrary to Muslim assertion, there is no necessary connection between monogamy and individualism. Historically the former preceded the latter by centuries, and there is no reason why monogamous marriage could not be embedded in a communal network. Furthermore, although human beings can be socialized into marrying and living with multiple partners, all the available evidence from such societies indicates that the relationship is never easy and nothing like the Muslim idealisation of it, which is in any case based on polygynous marriages and not tested against the background of the full equality of the sexes. Besides, as societies become industrialized and urbanized, communal networks tend to disintegrate and married couples set up separate units. If they are to make a success of their marriage, they need to build up a relationship of mutual trust, understanding and friendship talked about earlier. Again, once traditional communities break up, rendering most forms of human relationship impersonal and devoid of warmth and intimacy, marital relationship acquires unusual importance. Married partners now look to each other for such things as a sense of security, intimacy, intuitive understanding, deep emotional reassurances and the feeling of being valued that the wider community had hitherto provided. The monogamous relationship is far more likely to provide these than the polygamous.

Since the polygamous marriage is likely to be marked by jealousy, unhealthy competition for affection, insecurity, intrigue and mutual manipulation, it is also unlikely to create an environment conducive to the balanced growth of children. It is true that the child in a polygamous family has more role models and is not intensely identified with one of them. However, such a family at best includes a couple more adults than its monogamous counterpart, and hardly amounts to the kind of community the Muslim critic has in mind. And although the plurality of role models has its advantages, it also has its disadvantages. The opportunity to play off adults against each other, the rivalry among them for the child's affection, the relative lack of a clear structure of authority and so on, mean that children lack a moral and emotional focus, are subjected to conflicting moral and emotional demands, and are less likely to develop their powers of self-direction and self-discipline.

Although the principle of the equality of the sexes is formally neutral between monogamy and polygamy, monogamy is more conducive to its realization, a further argument in its favour. Muslim and for that matter Hindu, Christian and most other cultures contain a deep-seated sexist bias, and have for centuries subjected women to social, economic and other inequalities. If polygamy were to be permitted, men would be more likely to take advantage of it than women, thereby reinforcing and even increasing the inequality between the two and further devaluing the status of women. Besides, monogamy has a strong equalizing influence. It gives the woman a sense of dignity, self-esteem and security, a relatively inviolable private space of her own, and more or less equal rights over her husband's property and their children. As against this, some have argued that polygyny in fact increases the status and power of women because they now have the security and strength of solidarity, are able to share the domestic responsibility, and even to release each other for a career.[11] There is little hard evidence to support this view. Since wives can be played off against each other and easily dispensed with, they have neither a sense of security nor enough common interests to build up bonds of solidarity. Polygyny does reduce the demands on each of the wives, but such advantages as this brings are outweighed by the psychological tensions and anxieties mentioned earlier and can in any case be secured in more acceptable ways.

Although these and similar responses to the Muslim critic will not fully convince him, they ought to go at least some way towards getting him to appreciate the value of monogamy. They involve appeals to certain values, empirical generalizations about the conditions under which they are most likely to be realized, and judgements based on them. The values involved in stressing a trustful, affectionate and non-manipulative relationship are fairly general and likely to be shared by most Muslims. There may be some disagreements about empirical generalizations, but these can be minimized by appealing to psychological and sociological researches, anthropological accounts of polygamous marriages, and above all the experiences of Muslim societies themselves as described by their own writers. Once the disagreements over values and empirical generalizations are reduced, the ground is prepared for at least some measure of agreement on the desirability of monogamy. To counter the charge of cultural bias we might point to the fact that many Muslim societies themselves have begun to move away from polygyny. Although only Tunisia has actually banned it, several others positively discourage it.[12] Since they can be assumed to have a deep regard for their religion and culture as well as considerable experience of the social effects of polygyny, their actions further strengthen the case for monogamy.

Liberal society then is right to ban the practice of polygyny. The practice violates the principle of the equality of the sexes and has the unfortunate consequences sketched earlier. So far as polygamy is concerned, the case is not so conclusive. Although monogamy is morally more defensible than polygamy, the latter is not an unmitigated evil, for it does not *by itself* violate human dignity, equality, freedom, or any other great moral value. If it can be shown not to have unacceptable consequences, if the current inequality of economic power, social status and self-esteem between men and women were to end, if women were able to make equally uncoerced choices with men, and if a sizeable section of society were to press for polygamy, we might need to reconsider our view. Since these conditions do not obtain today, we are right to continue to disallow it.

General observations

I have sketched the outlines of a theory of intercultural evaluation and applied it to concrete cases, and it would be useful to highlight some of its important complications. Evaluating minority practices is necessarily contextual in the sense that it occurs within the context of a particular political community whose operative public values provide both its starting point and constant frame of reference. The values help distinguish morally indifferent from morally relevant practices and indicate why some of the latter are *prima facie* unacceptable. Although society's operative public values structure and shape the discourse, they are not non-negotiable. If minority spokesmen can show that the values discriminate against them, or rest on too narrow a conception of the good life, or are incoherent, the wider society needs to provide a persuasive defence of them or be prepared to reconsider them. This is also the case with minority values, whose spokesmen must either defend them adequately or revise and even abandon them. In an intercultural dialogue neither the majority nor the minority way of life can escape the other's scrutiny.

Although intercultural evaluation is contextual, there is no reason why the participants may not appeal to universal values. As we have seen, there are such values and they form the basis of moral claims. If the operative public values of a society violate them as they do in the case of racist, fascist, sexist and tyrannical regimes, they may rightly be challenged. The universal values, however, need to be interpreted, adjusted to local circumstances, and related to the moral and cultural structure of the society concerned; in short, contextualized if they are to carry conviction. Although they can be used to question the operative public values of society, they also depend on the latter for their relevance, meaning and effectiveness. Neither automatically trumps the other, and the two stand in a dialectical and mutually regulative relationship.

While intercultural evaluation has a moral aspect, it is not exclusively moral in nature. A cultural practice is three-dimensional in nature. It carries a normative authority inherent in a cultural practice, is part of and helps maintain the relevant way of life, and has a specific content which enjoins a particular mode of behaviour. An adequate assessment of it must take all three into account and not just its content as moral evaluation tends to do. Although we might find a practice morally problematic or even undesirable, we might decide to allow it because of its binding nature and community-sustaining role. The cultural and moral dimensions of a practice need to be balanced and traded-off, and that depends on how central the practice is to the relevant way of life and its degree of moral unacceptability.

No cultural practice can be judged in isolation from the wider social context and its likely long-term consequences. When judged by themselves we may see nothing wrong in voluntary adult female circumcision, polygamy, sale of body parts, or *sati*. However, we might feel that in the light of a society's history, traditions of inequality of power and cultural ethos, such practices are likely to be misused, fail to realize their intended purpose, or lead to unacceptable long-term consequences, and should be banned. Since consequences play an important part in our assessment of a practice and since they are historically contingent, we might ban it in one society, or at one time in its history, or under one set of circumstances, but not another without incurring the charge of moral inconsistency.

Like all political discourse intercultural dialogue is necessarily multistranded, heterogeneous, and involves arguments of different kinds and levels of generality. In some cases the argument is analogical: since we allow breast transplants or cohabitation with multiple partners, we should also allow female circumcision or polygyny. Sometimes it appeals to universal values: children should not be subjected to irreversible harm and women should be treated equally with men. On other occasions the operative public values are treated as the final court of appeal: we will not allow censorship of creative works or acts of *sati* because they violate our central or constitutive values. On yet other occasions an appeal is made to society's historical or cultural identity: we will not tolerate polygyny because it goes against all that we stand for or negates the results of years of struggle. In short, each party to the dispute deploys the kind of argument that comes easily to it or is likely to yield it the desired outcome. Unless the argument is patently irrelevant or wholly unintelligible to others, it cannot be ruled out. Intercultural evaluation is, therefore, necessarily messy and involves constant shifts of levels, styles and idioms. This sometimes makes it most exasperating and calls for considerable patience and sympathy.

10

Politics, Religion and Free Speech

The Satanic Verses

From time to time a multicultural society is bound to throw up situations in which deep cultural and moral disagreements between its different communities come to the fore and create a crisis. In recent years no other event has illustrated these tensions more than the controversy surrounding Salman Rushdie's *The Satanic Verses* (1988). Unlike *Midnight's Children* (1981) in which Rushdie explored his roots in Bombay and unlike *Shame* (1983), an inferior work in which he wrote about Pakistan, *The Satanic Verses* is almost a meta-novel exploring the nature of the self. Viewing migration as a metaphor for death and resurrection, it examines the ways in which the self, which is inescapably embedded in a particular language, pattern of relationship and natural and social environment, reconstitutes itself in response to changes in them.

Just as a scientific method of inquiry should be adequate to its subject matter, a literary technique should be suited to a sensitive exploration of the relevant area of human experience. Since at least the First World War, magic realism, which combines surrealism with heightened language, has appealed to many writers as the only literary mode in which to depict a reality that continually overtakes the imagination and refuses to conform to conventional canons of rationality or even intelligibility. The interplay between the extraordinary and the mundane that occurs in so much Latin American fiction or in Gunter Grass's (1959) *Tin Drum* is not merely a literary technique, but a reflection of the world in which the fantastic is often part of everyday life. Not surprisingly, Rushdie uses the hallucinatory devices of magic realism to capture the immigrant's experiences of the world, and his novel abounds in strange and impossible events. A girl subsists on a diet of butterflies; two men falling from an aeroplane miraculously survive, one sprouting an angelic halo, the other horns and a tail; they undergo bizarre experiences, and much of the novel is full of dreams occurring within dreams. Such events, described in an appropriately melodramatic and racy prose and taking liberties with the ordinary rules of grammar, spelling and propriety, are intended to give the reader some idea of just how fantastic life has become for a migrant. Anxious to break down the conventional dualism of good and evil and to explore the 'ethic of impurity' as he once called it, Rushdie deliberately mixes up the sacred and the profane, fact and fiction, the holy and the obscene, and frequently uses the four letter word both simply and in different and at times somewhat distasteful combinations.

Magic realism takes different forms depending on the level of abstraction adopted by the author. *The Satanic Verses* operates at a relatively low level of abstraction. Rushdie weaves his narrative around fantasized but recognizable men and women and does not create wholly new characters. His characters are not products of what Kant called 'pure' or 'transcendental' imagination, but real people subjected to the free play of fantasy. *The Satanic Verses* is thus a work of fantasy, not of pure fiction, of an imaginatively reinterpreted but not a radically reconstituted reality. Such a blend of magic realism and fantasized history is well-suited to exploring the birth and spread of momentous historical movements in which great individuals and their followers activate their own and each other's myths and fantasies, generate powerful emotions, and reshape their fantasized present in the light of a fantasized past and future. However, this genre also has its dangers. If the writer is not careful, he or she might end up treating recognizable men and women as mere objects of fantasies, as manipulable material for the free play of his imagination. He might then become not just disrespectful and irreverent but supercilious and dismissive, a shade crude and even perhaps exhibitionist, scoring cheap points off half-real characters. If he seeks to explore religion, he runs the further risk of violating its integrity, even vulgarizing it, and outraging conventional norms of good taste. Religion is the realm of the sacred and the holy *par excellence* and arouses strong feelings of piety and reverence, which can be easily offended if subjected to the indelicate play of an undisciplined fantasy.

In two complex chapters which form part of a dream of one of the central characters of *The Satanic Verses*, Rushdie explores the birth and triumph of Islam. He brilliantly delineates Mahound's (Muhammed's) dilemmas, states of mind, dreams, inevitable compromises with the practices and beliefs of the pre-Islamic world, and his reactions to the reactions of that world to his new regime of moral discipline. However, Rushdie does not always find it easy to remain restrained and sensitive. Anger, irreverence and even thinly-disguised contempt inform his style of exploration and choices of images, metaphors and language.

Muhammed is presented in the book as a 'businessman' constantly doing deals with the archangel and God. He 'laid down the law and the angels would confirm it afterwards'. He had 'no time for scruples – nor qualms about ends and means'. His God, too, 'is really a businessman' who offers him convenient bargains and helps him out of embarrassing situations. The archangel is no less 'obliging' and even reduces the initial quota of 40 prayers a day to five in recognition of Muhammed's and his followers' limitations. Islam is called a 'revelation of convenience' and would have adopted a different moral and spiritual code if that had suited Muhammed better. Muhammed is a 'smart bastard', a debauchee who, after his wife's death, slept with so many women that his beard turned 'half-white' in a year. He is presented as a debauched sensualist lying naked and unconscious in Hind's tent with a nasty hangover. Muslims deeply respect Bilal, the emancipated black slave who was the first to convert to Islam. Here, he is an 'enormous black monster, with a voice to match his size'. Muhammed's three revered colleagues, including Bilal, are 'those goons, those f...ing clowns', the 'trinity of scum'. Like any great religious text, the *Koran* is full of rules and injunctions about forms of worship, helping the poor, concern for the needy, moral purity, self-discipline and surrender to the will of God. *The Satanic Verses* mockingly reduces it to a book spouting rules about how to 'fart', 'f...' and 'clean one's behind', and why only two types of sexual activity are legitimate, one of them being sodomy (that tired anti-Muslim canard yet again).

Another passage relates to Muhammed's 12 wives. When Ayesha, his young and favourite wife, protested against his taking on so many more, the novel goes on:

> Who can blame her? Finally he went into – what else? One of his trances and out he came with a message from the archangel. Gibreel had recited verses giving him full divine support. God's own permission to f... as many women as he liked. So there: What could poor Ayesha say against the verses of God? You know what she did say? This: Your God certainly jumps to it when you need him to fix things up for you.

There is also a vividly depicted brothel scene in which 12 inmates take on the names and act out the part of Muhammed's wives to attract customers, the 15-year-old Ayesha being the most popular. Rushdie has argued that the scene was intended to provide a profane antithesis to and thus to highlight and accentuate the holy. However, since the holy has been treated in a mocking manner throughout the novel, the brothel scene does not serve that purpose; rather it appears as a further attempt to mock the holy by sexually fantasizing about and symbolically violating Muhammed's wives, whom Muslims regard as their role models.

These and similar passages in *The Satanic Verses* occur in a dream of Gibreel Farishta, who then develops the dream into a cheap movie in which he himself plays the role of the archangel. The story is thus doubly relativized, first as a dream of a demented individual and then as a bad dream, and presented as a playful invention. This might seem to suggest that Rushdie in fact disapproved of and even intended to ridicule and disown the ideas expressed in the passages. However, in a work in which fact and fiction, reality and dream, are intentionally mixed up and rendered inseparable, the dream could not be dismissed as a 'mere' dream and the dreamer as 'just' a demented character. The fact that the details of the dream stay close to history and relate to real historical characters reinforces the point. And in any case the fact that the ideas expressed in these passages are part of a dream does not diminish their offensiveness in the eyes of those who believe that such things should not be said at all, whether by a sane or a demented person and knowingly or in a dream.

Responses to Muslim protests

Soon after the publication of *The Satanic Verses* on 26 September 1988, British Muslims began to campaign against it.[1] Their objections were threefold. First, the book gave a totally inaccurate account of Islam and spread 'utter lies' about it. Had the book not stayed so recognizably close to history, its 'gross inaccuracies' would not have mattered. Under the circumstances they did, and Muslims said they had a right to stand up for the honour of their faith and the integrity of their cultural heritage.

Second, Muslims argued that *The Satanic Verses* was 'abusive', 'insulting', 'scurrilous', 'vilifactory' in its treatment of men and women whom they considered holy and of whose sacred memories they were custodians. It discussed their religion in a most 'obscene', 'indecent', 'filthy' and 'abominably foul' language, violated all norms of civilized discussion, and was guilty of *Shatam an-Nabi*, an insult to Muhammed, for Muslims an unforgivable capital crime. Muslim leaders insisted that they were not opposed to a serious critique of their religion, after all libraries were full of them and their authors had come to no harm, but to Rushdie's tone, attitude and language.

The third Muslim complaint was that the book had demeaned and degraded them in their own and especially others' eyes. It reinforced many of the traditional stereotypes and added a few more into the bargain. It presented them as barbarians following a fraudulent religion created by a cunning manipulator and devoid of a sound system of morality. As a Muslim as well as a scholar of Islam, Rushdie owed it to his culturally besieged community to counter the 'myths' and 'lies' spread about them, or at least to refrain from lending them his authority. Instead, he had joined the Orientalist discourse and harmed their moral and material interests.

Initially, Muslim leaders were content to demand that the book should carry a note disclaiming its historical credentials and that its author should apologize. Later they asked that the book should be banned and existing copies withdrawn from public libraries. If it could not be banned, they wanted it to be issued after removing the offending passages. They also demanded that in order to prevent the occurrence of such provocative books in the future, the existing anti-blasphemy law which protected Christianity should be extended to other religions as well especially Islam.

When their noisy but peaceful protests and fairly large but mostly unreported demonstrations got them nowhere, a small group of Muslims publicly burned a copy of the book on 2 December 1988. That, too, aroused no national interest. Evidently a London solicitor advised them that they stood a better chance of attracting attention if they burned a copy *after* alerting the national media. They did that in Bradford on 14 January 1989 and secured instant national publicity, but not of the kind they had expected. Rather than stimulate a reasoned discussion of their grievances, the book-burning incident led to a torrent of denunciation. They were called 'barbarians', 'uncivilized'. 'fanatics', and compared to the Nazis. Many a writer, some of impeccable liberal credentials, openly wondered how Britain could 'civilize' them and protect their progeny from their 'medieval fundamentalism'. Hardly anyone cared to point out that only a few months earlier, several Labour Members of Parliament had burnt a copy of the new racist immigration rules outside the House of Commons without raising so much as a murmur of protest.

Muslim protests in Britain were also beginning to attract attention abroad. Some Muslim leaders unwisely internationalized the issue by seeking the support of heads of Muslim states. In response to these and other events, the late Ayatollah Khomeini pronounced a death sentence on Rushdie on 14 February 1989, and called on Muslims all over the world to execute it. A few days later Rushdie went into hiding. Khomeini's *fatwa* marked a turning point in the development of Muslim consciousness. Tolerant and even a little timid until then, they suddenly experienced a sense of power. They had now managed to extract a statement of regret from Rushdie, commanded media attention, were courted by the British government, and had succeeded in shifting national attention from themselves to *The Satanic Verses.* The sense of power, combined with a mean desire for revenge at having been ignored for so long, generated a new mood of aggressive intolerance among some of them. Those who knew better lacked the courage and good sense to warn their community against the enormity of the contemplated act. The orthodox had the field all to themselves and did everything to whip up anti-Rushdie hysteria. The national press tended to exacerbate the situation. It sent correspondents to interview Muslim leaders and the young and confused Muslim youth with leading questions, and created the overwhelming impression that the *entire* Muslim community was seething with a bloodthirsty spirit of vengeance. Unintentionally the press united the Muslim community, created a new orthodoxy, and made support for the *fatwa* a badge of Muslim identity and solidarity. Many British Muslims disapproved of killing Rushdie, and well knew that it would gravely damage their interests and distract public attention from the real issue, which was what to do with the book. Few, however, had the courage or the wisdom to dissociate themselves from, let alone condemn, the *fatwa*.

Muslim demands received little serious attention. Most of the liberal and conservative press was hostile, accusing Muslims of preferring a theocratic to a liberal secular society and bringing Britain nothing but shame. There was much discussion of whether the country had an obligation to tolerate the intolerant and even whether multiculturalism was not a dangerous doctrine. Several liberal politicians and leader-writers wondered if Britain had not made a 'mistake' in letting in 'too many' Muslims. Even Roy Jenkins, the father of the Race Relations Act 1976 and a politician of immaculate liberal credentials, lamented that 'we might have been more cautious about allowing the creation in the 1950s [sic] of a substantial Muslim community here'. He went further and reached the most bizarre conclusion that the Muslim behaviour had strengthened his reluctance to admit Turkey into the European community.[2]

The rejection of the Muslim case was so fierce that some liberals who dared criticize Rushdie were subjected to much unfair criticism. Rushdie attacked Hugo Young for suggesting that although *The Satanic Verses* should not be banned, it would be unwise to issue it in a paperback. John Le Carre was mocked for making a similar suggestion. In his 'Open Letter to Rushdie', Michael Dummett (1990), a Catholic Professor of Logic and Metaphysics at Oxford University, criticized him for failing to appreciate that people could be deeply insulted and hurt when what they held most dear was mocked and vulgarized. Rushdie lacked 'the concept of something's being holy' and shared the western intellectual's arrogant assumption that religious believers 'may properly be affronted, indeed deserve to be affronted'. Michael Dummett became a subject of much ridicule. In July 1990 *The Sunday Telegraph* did a profile of him under the headline 'The Silly Sage of Race Relations' and called his 'Open Letter' 'the most shameful' document of our age. Indeed, the writer thought that since free speech was a 'sacred faith' for the 'civilized man', the latter was bound to feel affronted by Dummett's letter and could on his own logic be justified in threatening Dummett's life!

It was depressing to note how the legitimate rage against the Ayatollah's murderous impertinence and some mindless Muslim support for it escalated step by even sillier step to a wholly mindless anger first against all *Bradford* Muslims, then against all *British* Muslims, then against *all* Muslims, and ultimately against *Islam* itself. There is quite a pile of disturbing material in this metamorphosis which anyone interested in the phenomenology of secular consciousness might profitably analyse. Some liberal commentators, a few of them with a leftist past such as Fay Weldon, became instant experts on the *Koran*, attacking its alleged inhumanity and 'bloodthirsty' conception of Allah and unfavourably comparing it to the Bible and its 'loving' God.

As for the substantive issues raised by the Muslim spokesmen, they received a short and standard reply forcefully stated by two of the liberal government ministers. The 'fundamental principles' of British society were non-negotiable, 'freedom of speech and expression and toleration of different opinions' being among them. 'The same freedom which has enabled Muslims to meet, march and protest against the book also preserves the author's right to freedom of expression for so long as no law is broken.' The demand for a ban on the book was an attempt to 'chip away at the fundamental freedom on which our democracy is built'. In the conflict between freedom and fundamentalism, the British society's response had to be robust and unambiguous (Parekh, 1990a, pp. 85–7).

No writer cared to point out that even the self-confident Christians had taken a long time coming to terms with films on Jesus. Until the 1960s a strict protocol governed his depiction and it was considered disrespectful to display his face on the screen. *The Last Days of Pompeii* (1935), *Quo Vadis* (1951) and *Ben-Hur* (1959) show him from afar and feature only his hand or foot. In *King of Kings*, Jeffery Hunter who played Jesus had to remove all bodily hair because it detracted from Jesus's divinity! *The Last Temptation of Christ* was irreverent but not at all abusive or mocking. As Scorsese himself said: 'I wanted to show a Christ you could agree with, a real earthy Jesus'. He went on, 'it was never my intention to shake anyone's faith, but rather to ignite faith'. Yet his film provoked a public outcry unprecedented in the history of religious films. Militant Christians launched a media campaign condemning Universal Pictures, the film's distributor, staged a mock flagellation of Christ outside the home of Lee Wasserman, chairman of the parent company of Universal Pictures, and so intimidated cinema owners that several movie chains refused to show the film. After initial resistance, Christians came to accept Jesus as a righteous rocker in *Jesus Christ Superstar* and an innocent clown in *Godspell*, but they took to the barricades when he was portrayed as a charlatan in *The Passover Plot*. The film was picketed out of existence after only a few weeks and never heard of again. It would seem that Muslims were only a few years behind Christians in these matters, and the latter were in no position to claim moral superiority or greater religious maturity over them.

With several notable exceptions, much of the public debate in the national press, then, was disappointing. It largely concentrated on the threat to Rushdie's life, and when it discussed Muslim demands, it conceptualized the issue as one of conflict between freedom and fundamentalism, the former central to and the latter representing a mortal threat to the British way of life. Rushdie was intimately linked with and became a potent symbol of the survival of the British way of life itself. This way of thinking left little conceptual space for a discussion of the kinds of issues Muslims were keen to put on the public agenda.

Once the passions aroused by Muslim protests calmed down, the situation changed somewhat, and triggered off long overdue debates within and between the Muslim community and wider society. Some Muslim writers began to wonder if they had gone too far in their support of the *fatwa*, how they should come to terms with the liberal commitment to free speech, and what their rights and obligations as immigrants were. Although the debate was patchy, it did lead to some intellectual churning within the Muslim community and created a limited space for internal dissent. As one would expect in a mature democracy a similar debate also occurred within wider society. Several religiously minded liberals appreciated the strength of the Muslim case. Although they did not support the ban on *The Satanic Verses*, they insisted that religious issues deserved to be discussed with greater sensitivity, that religion had a valuable public role, that it should not be undermined by mindless attacks, and that the widespread liberal hostility to religion needed to be rethought. Even secular liberals began to express similar views. Thanks to such an internal debate conducted both in print and in informal discussions, British society began to throw up a wider variety of views than before.

Once several individuals within the two communities began to rethink their respective positions, the earlier rigidity was relaxed and a common ground began to appear. Rushdie's own critical reflections on the book and his admission of an error of judgement a year later facilitated the process. This generated a paradox common to political debates on contentious issues. Once the parties involved showed greater mutual understanding and lowered the political temperature, they created one of the necessary preconditions of rational debate.

While this made the debate *possible*, it also removed the sense of urgency and rendered the debate or at least its resolution *unnecessary*.

Logic of political discourse

Although the debate surrounding *The Satanic Verses* had several unusual features largely arising from the fact that it involved religion, a relatively powerless and recently arrived immigrant minority and a death threat, it is not unrepresentative of public debates in general and those involving cultural, religious and ethnic minorities in particular. Since it offers valuable insights into the nature, structure and limits of public debate in a multicultural society, it would be useful to draw out some of its important lessons.[3]

First, a contentious issue can be resolved relatively easily or at least prevented from getting out of control if it is identified, isolated and dealt with at an early stage. Most societies, however, do not possess the required degree of sensitivity or think that the controversy would die down if ignored. By the time the issue dominates the public agenda, the protesting group is likely to have suffered considerable humiliation and frustration and invested its pride and passions in its demands, all of which makes the resolution of the issue that much more difficult. The Rushdie affair would most probably have been resolved peacefully at an early stage if the unproblematic Muslim demand that the book should carry a note disavowing its historicity had been met, or if Rushdie had taken the kind of conciliatory approach he took a year later. However, British society had other priorities, could not be sure about the strength of Muslim feelings, and was deeply worried lest conceding or even seriously debating one Muslim demand should encourage others. Accordingly it ignored or treated their protests with disdain, an understandable but in retrospect perhaps an unwise decision.

Second, the parties involved in public debates on important issues in a multicultural society often tend to talk past each other, both because each tends to define the issue in its own terms that are often not intelligible to others, and because they have only a limited understanding of each other's history, background and way of life. Most conservative and liberal British writers argued that Muslims were opposed to free speech, whereas the latter were only asking why free speech should include untrue and deeply offensive remarks about religions and religious communities. Again many of them insisted that Muslims wanted to protect their religious beliefs from criticism; in fact Muslims had no objection to religious criticism and only wondered why mocking, ridiculing and lampooning religious beliefs, practices and prophets should be confused with genuine and serious criticism. For their part Muslims, too, systematically misunderstood the grounds of the liberal emphasis on free speech, the difficulties involved in restricting it, the depth of British commitment to it, and and so on.

One of the main reasons for this had to do with the fact that the two groups knew little about each other's ways of life and thought. Muslims felt distressed by *The Satanic Verses* for the kind of reasons mentioned earlier. Since these reasons did not form part of the liberal world of thought, liberals had difficulty appreciating their nature, relevance and force. Muslims attempted to articulate their reasons in a liberal language but found it extremely difficult to do so, both because they had few biculturally literate intellectuals and because no such conceptual translation is ever accurate. Furthermore, the reasons they advanced in public were not their real reasons, and hence they felt inauthentic and alienated or confused their followers. Not being well-versed in the liberal discourse on free speech, they also found themselves frequently wrong-footed and were invariably defeated by their liberal opponents who were naturally most at home in that tradition. The debate would have been properly engaged if both parties had been sufficiently bicultural or had made a genuine effort to enter into each other's way of thinking. Since neither condition obtained, Muslims felt bitter and much misunderstood and stopped talking; a large body of liberals agonized about the continuing threat of 'illiberal' and 'fundamentalist' Muslims in their midst and saw no point in continuing discussions with them; and British society as a whole lost the opportunity to develop a self-understanding adequate to its multicultural character.

Third, although dialogue is the only morally acceptable way of settling controversial issues, it is not always available even in a mature liberal democracy. Every society tends to take certain matters for granted or deliberately places them beyond the reach of volatile public opinion. This is understandable and even necessary. It is, for example, a matter of some doubt if a large majority of Americans today would endorse in a national referendum either the First Amendment or the wall of separation between the state and religion as they have been interpreted in recent years. Although a closure is necessary, it can also be premature or biased towards a particular group or culture. When the marginalized groups challenge the closure, they encounter resistance born out of intellectual incomprehension, moral complacency, political inertia, or fear of damage to vested interests. The discontented groups then have no alternative but to protest, partly to overcome the resistance, partly to demonstrate the intensity of their disaffection, and partly to trigger off the process of self-doubt and self-criticism within the majority community. The point of the protest should not to be to replace but to facilitate and enrich the dialogue. Since it is difficult to imagine a human community whose members have an open mind on all issues, protest has a legitimate place in every society. A well-considered theory of political deliberation cannot rely on the power of reason alone and needs to explore when protest is justified, in what form, and how it can be integrated into a rational dialogue.

Fourth, political debate is rarely between equals. Every society is marred by deep inequalities of economic, political and cultural power, and neither political nor even economic equality by itself guarantees cultural equality. This is particularly the case in a multicultural society in which some groups, such as the new immigrants and those who have long been marginalized and silenced, suffer from structural disadvantages They lack enough political and economic power to be a significant political presence. They are culturally and psychologically insecure and ill-versed in the dominant language of discourse. They lack ready access to the media. And in any case the media have their own agenda, lack both the space and the ability to explore sensitive issues in depth, and are under constant pressure to oversimplify and sensationalize them. As a result, the frustrated minority either withdraws into itself in a mood of deep sulk or turns to violence to attract public attention. The Rushdie affair was a good example of this.

One way to avoid such a situation is to provide a public forum where important issues can be patiently and dispassionately discussed by the representatives of different groups. The national parliament is not such a place for it is divided along party lines, unused to debating large questions, might not include minority representatives, and so forth. The courts too have their limits for they are generally adversarial, extremely expensive, and unused to political debates. We therefore need to find new institutional forums where representatives of different communities can meet regularly to explore contentious issues, acquire a better understanding of each other's ways of thinking and living, and hopefully arrive at a consensus on what issues are at stake and what arguments and considerations are relevant to their resolution which can then be fed into the wider public debate. Theories of political deliberation, such as those of Rawls and Habermas, remain unrealistic even utopian without a carefully worked out structure of institutional public spaces conducive to the kind of rational deliberation they propose.

Like all forms of practical deliberation, political deliberation aims to resolve contentious issues. However, this is not its only purpose, and it is not rendered pointless if it fails to deliver a decision.[4] Indeed, to make an agreed decision the *telos* or even the sole *raison d'être* of a dialogue is to take too narrow and instrumental a view of it. Political deliberation is a multidimensional activity and serves several purposes. It deepens mutual understanding between different groups, sensitizes each to the concerns and anxieties of others, leads to an unconscious fusion of ideas and sensibilities, encourages them to explore common areas of agreement, and plays a vital community-building role. Since it requires participants to defend their views in a manner intelligible to others, it encourages them to appreciate the contingency of and thus to take a critical view of their beliefs. *Contra* Rawls, public reason is not a presupposition or a brute fact of political life but the product of political debate, and is constantly reconstituted and pluralized by it. Political deliberation should therefore be judged not merely in terms of its immediate and tangible results but also its moral, epistemological and community-sustaining role. Even so far as its goal of reaching a collectively acceptable decision is concerned, it might not arrive at one, and yet by clarifying issues and encouraging the fusion of ideas, it might generate a consensus behind the backs of the participants and facilitate future agreements in similar circumstances. Consensus is a subtle, complex and dynamic process, and we should not take a static and positivist view of it.

Fifth, it is generally assumed that political deliberation is about exchange of arguments with the victory going to those advancing the most compelling ones. Although this view is not wholly mistaken, it is partial and misses a crucial dimension of political deliberation, namely rational persuasion. Political deliberation is practically oriented in the sense that our aim is to persuade others, to secure their agreement, to get them to see the issue in a certain way. Arguments are an important part of this process but are rarely enough. In many areas of life they are too nicely balanced and too dependent on judgements of likely consequences to have the power to convince. And even when they do, intellectual conviction does not by itself provide a motive for action.

Persuasion relates to an area of life lying between personal taste and logical demonstration. In the former, persuasion is impossible, in the latter unnecessary. If you like vanilla ice-cream and I strawberry ice-cream, I cannot persuade you out of your preference. And I do not need to persuade you that two plus two makes four as the rules of arithmetic leave you no choice. Persuasion is possible and necessary when an activity is based on interpersonally sharable reasons and leaves room for judgement. It has the following features:

- First, unlike arguments in formal logic and mathematics, it is aimed at a specific audience, be it an individual, a group or a community, whom one is trying to persuade.
- Second, it is articulated in terms of considerations the persuadee shares or can be persuaded to share, as otherwise one cannot reach out to him and get him to see things in a desired manner.
- Third, being practically oriented, persuasion is not concerned to answer all possible objections but only those currently made by the persuadee, nor to cover imaginary or hypothetical situations but one currently confronting the parties involved.
- Fourth, to persuade someone is to win him over, to 'woo his assent' as Kant put it. It is of little help and sometimes counterproductive to bludgeon his intellect into submission or make him look a fool by powerful arguments; one should sensitively enter into his world of thought and reach out to the person lying behind the arguments by appealing to his values, emotions, self-interest, shared bonds and self-understanding.
- Fifth, since arguments are rarely compelling or irresistible, the person to be persuaded remains free to accept or reject them. One should therefore be able to count on him to consider the arguments seriously and open-mindedly and to show why he is unpersuaded by these. The freedom that persuasion grants carries a moral responsibility with it. Persuasion entails not only the 'burden of judgement' but also a sense of accountability to others for the way one receives and responds to their arguments.
- Finally, persuasion is non-adversarial in the sense that one sees the persuadee not as an opponent to be defeated but as a fellow-citizen to be won over by arguments and appeals. In persuasion one explores a shared ground, builds common bonds, and forges a

collective 'we'. It is neither like Plato's dialectic with its concern for truth, nor like his rhetoric with its manipulative thrust, but belongs to a wholly different genre.

In persuasion, arguments are obviously important, but so are appeals to emotions, self-understanding, moral values and sense of identity, and the two invariably go hand in hand. We might, for example, ask our fellow-citizens to choose a particular course of action on the grounds that it alone is worthy of us, would make us an object of respect in the world, would have been approved of by the founding fathers of our country, is in consonance with all that is great in our history, serves our long-term interest, or that a tolerant, free, compassionate and Christian society that ours claims to be cannot act otherwise. We advance arguments but also appeal to emotions, self-understanding, the kind of people we are, and so forth. Arguments are embedded in and derive part of their weight and appeal from the latter, and conversely appeals to emotions, shared values, and so on have an intellectual content that is open to critical examination.

It is a rationalist mistake to equate the related but logically distinct concepts of reason and argument. All arguments involve or rest on reasons, but the reverse is not true. When I urge someone not to do something because it is unworthy of her, or goes against her view of the kind of person she is, I am giving her a reason but not advancing an argument, appealing to her not arguing with her. Reason and emotion are not incompatible or even logically distinct in a way that argument and emotion are. Arguments represent particular kinds of reasons and involve a particular form of reasoning, and should not be equated with reasons or reasoning *per se*.

Persuasion, then, is a highly subtle, complex and culturally suffused activity, and its success depends on who the persuader is and how she goes about her task. Although the social radicals in India had long advanced intellectually powerful arguments against the practice of untouchability, they made little impact on their countrymen, whereas Gandhi, whose arguments were often weak but beautifully blended with his countrymen's self-understanding, pride and political ambitions, shook the moral roots of the practice. Martin Luther King successfully persuaded his fellow-Americans to enact civil rights legislation with the help of arguments that had in other hands proved ineffective. This is so because, in persuasion the character and reputation of the persuader are crucial. As Aristotle put it, one is more likely to be persuaded by a person one trusts, whose judgement one respects, who in one's view is guided by good will, and has a good record of giving sensible advice (Garver, 1994, pp. 108, 119, 150, 184, 280). Since persuasion involves values, arguments, emotions and so on, one is also more likely to succeed at it the more one is able to touch deep moral and emotional nerves, evoke unconscious collective memories, and mobilize the deepest self-understanding of one's audience.

Sixth, contrary to what Popper (1945), Rawls (1971, 1993a) and others have argued, political deliberation is not sedate and cerebral like academic deliberation; indeed even the latter is never wholly disinterested and guided solely by the 'weight' of arguments. Arguments have no weight of their own; we give it to them on the basis of our values, intuitions, commonsense, judgement of the likely consequences of the various courses of action, historical experiences and memories, and so forth. It is these factors that shape our ideas of what constitutes an argument as opposed to a statement of personal preference or predilection and what makes it a relevant or a good argument. Furthermore, arguments involve reasons. Since the latter cannot always be disengaged from moral values some of which are incommensurable, arguments are often mutually irreducible and incapable of being weighed on a single scale. To talk of 'weighing-up' arguments and opting for ones that are 'weightier' or 'stronger' is to take a naively homogenous view of them. All arguments are articulated and conducted in a particular language which, *contra* Habermas and Rawls, cannot be 'purified' or purged of its deep cultural and evocative associations either.

The Rushdie affair was a good example of this. Thanks to the painful historical memories of religious wars during the early modern period, many Britons were deeply suspicious of the political role of religion and the religiously inspired restrictions on free speech. And thanks to the recent events in some Muslim countries, they also deeply feared the militancy of the Muslims settled in their midst. For their part, Muslims brought to the debate their memories of centuries of European Islamophobia, colonialism and racism and their current experiences of demonization and marginalization, and saw in the favourable British reception of *The Satanic Verses* a further proof of this. Some of these attitudes and fears on both sides were exaggerated, and it never helps to view the present through the distorted prism of the past. However, they formed an inescapable background to and even an integral part of the political debate, and could not but shape the participants' judgements and responses.

Since all political debates are embedded in the memories of the past and fears for the future, the question as to how we can conduct them in a rational manner admits of no easy answer. To start with, unlike Popper, Rawls, Joshua Cohen (1989, 1998) and others, we should not take too rationalistic a view of political rationality, for then we expect too much from political deliberation and risk losing faith in it when it fails to meet our expectations. Since political debates are never purely rational, we should aim not so much at refuting our opponent's arguments and convincing them of the validity of our own, though we should certainly do that when possible, as at arriving at a broad and inherently tentative consensus. Furthermore, no dialogue is possible unless each party is prepared to critically examine the fears, judgements and assumptions it brings to the debate and to modify and even abandon them. Take the Rushdie affair. Most British liberals were unwilling to appreciate that their deep historical fears about the public role of religion might be unjustified, that religion might play a useful role in deepening the morally shallow political culture of our age, that Islam in general and British Islam in particular might not be the enemy of liberty that they have taken it to be, and that they might be taking an unjustifiably extreme view of the value of free speech. For their part, most Muslim spokesmen were unwilling to appreciate that the European Islamophobia might have lost some of its earlier intensity, that religion must change with the times, that their traditional reliance on censorship to protect their faith no longer made sense today, and that the refusal to ban a piece of writing did not imply its endorsement.

A radical reexamination of one's fears, anxieties and assumptions is easier when there is sufficient mutual trust and goodwill between the parties involved. If British Muslims had dissociated themselves from Khomeini's *fatwa* and shown some appreciation of the British commitment to free speech, they would have allayed some of the prevailing fears and perhaps encouraged a section of liberal opinion to view their demands with sympathy. Similarly, if the prominent spokesmen of British society had shown some understanding of the reasons for Muslim anger and distress and some sympathy for their cause, and then gone on to show why on balance they considered the ban on *The Satanic Verses* unwise, they would have diffused the Muslim sense of isolation and even perhaps won over some of them to their point of view. With such reciprocal gestures the participants would have lightened the burden of history and altered the political context of the debate. Since they knew relatively little about each other and had only a limited experience of working together, they lacked the mutual trust and commitment required for such gestures.

Finally, the Rushdie affair showed how the political traditions and constitutional structure of a country shape the nature, content and style of political deliberation. Until recently Britain had no Bill of Rights, and hence free speech lacked formal constitutional protection. It also has an anti-blasphemy law, and the legal power to restrict free speech on religious grounds. British Muslims therefore felt that they were not acting improperly in asking for a ban on *The Satanic Verses*. They could not entertain such expectations in the United States, especially with the recent history of the interpretations of the First Amendment. It is hardly surprising that Muslims there did not press or even ask for such a ban. Unlike Britain, again, India has a provision in its Penal Code entitling the government to ban books likely to incite religious hatred or lead to civil disorder. Indian Muslims therefore had to organize only a few demonstrations and threaten disorder to get the book banned. It is also worth noting that British Muslims devoted far greater energy to protesting against *The Satanic Verses* than to other issues such as securing legal recognition of polygyny and other provisions of the *sharia* which mattered more to them. They well knew that while the British political culture allowed a discussion of the ban, it was implacably hostile to the latter.

Political deliberation, then, is contextual and culturally embedded, is never wholly cerebral or based on arguments alone, and no single model of it fits all societies. Rawls's (1971, 1993a) theory of public reason does not seem to appreciate these basic features of it. It has a rationalist bias, homogenizes and takes a one-dimensional view of public reason, assimilates the political to judicial reason, and unwittingly universalizes the American practice, and that too in its highly idealized version. In spite of all its strengths, even Habermas's discourse ethic is vulnerable on all three counts. He sets up a single model of political discourse and fails to appreciate the depth of national diversity. Like Rawls, he too takes a narrowly rationalist view of it, stresses arguments and largely ignores other forms of reasons, takes a homogenous view of political arguments, postulates a culturally unmediated or 'pure intersubjectivity' and a language 'purified'of history, concentrates on 'what' is said and ignores 'who' said it, and often comes close to assimilating political discourse to an idealized model of philosophical discourse.

Communal libel or group defamation

The Rushdie affair, whose impact on British and even European intellectual and political life was considerable, threw up several important questions such as the logic of intercultural dialogue, intercultural equality, demands of common citizenship, rights and obligations of immigrants, communal libel, the nature and limits of free speech, and the place of religion in public life. Since I have discussed all but the last three elsewhere in the book, I shall concentrate on the latter.

In most societies libel is an offence. Broadly speaking it consists in making public, untruthful and damaging remarks about an individual that go beyond fair comment. Libel is an offence not because it causes pain to or offends the feelings of the individual concerned, for the damaging and untruthful remarks made in private do not constitute libel, but because they lower him in the eyes of *others*, damage his *social* standing, and harm his *reputation*. The offence of libel is generally restricted to individuals. Many Muslim, Jewish and other minority spokesmen in Britain, the USA and elsewhere have argued that it should cover racial, religious, ethnic and other communities as well.

Like individuals, communities too can be objects of libel, for one can make public, untruthful and damaging remarks about them which lower them in their own and others' eyes, harm their reputation and social standing, and go beyond fair comment. To say that 'all Jews are secretive, greedy, vindictive and conspiratorial', that 'all blacks are stupid, unruly, licentious and unreliable', or that 'all Indians are devious, cheats, manipulative and undependable' is clearly to libel these communities in the sense defined earlier. This is not to say that isolated individuals within them may not fit the description, but rather that this is equally true of some in other communities. These are not fair comments but malicious and mischievous stereotypes with unfortunate long-term consequences.

Communities are obviously different from individuals. They do not think, feel and suffer in a way that individuals do. And when they are libelled, clearly it is their individual members who are libelled. However, they are libelled not as unique individuals but as members of particular communities, as sharers of a specific cultural, racial or religious background and bearers of traits associated with it. Since individuals are not free-floating atoms but communally embedded, their identity is at once both personal and communal, and their self-respect is tied up with and partly grounded in respect for their community. To say that a community is made up of individuals is to utter a half-truth, for they are themselves in turn at least partially constituted by it. Even as a community does not exist independently of its members, they do not exist independently of it either.

Communal libel is objectionable for several reasons. It is a form of social and political exclusion, a declaration of hostility against a section of one's fellow-citizens, and strikes at the very root of communal life. It adversely affects their job prospects in a manner too subtle to be caught by the law. It lowers the social standing of the individuals involved and demeans them in their own eyes. They also feel ontologically insecure and find it difficult to relate to themselves and to others in a normal and unself-conscious manner when constantly subjected to snide innuendoes and made objects of crude jokes on the basis of their race, colour, gender or nationality. It is sometimes argued that the kinds of remarks about Jews, blacks and others mentioned earlier are light-hearted, meant to get a good laugh, and that their intended victims should not be too prickly or oversensitive. The argument is misconceived. It does not answer the basic question as to why anyone should be at liberty to make such remarks at all and what its moral basis is. Since they show disrespect and cause hurt and harm, there can be no general right to make them unless it can be shown to promote valuable goals. Furthermore, discriminatory treatment of and hostility against sections of our fellow-citizens, which we rightly disapprove of, do not occur in a cultural vacuum. They grow out of and are legitimized by a wider moral climate which is built up and sustained by, among other things, gratuitously disparaging and offensive remarks, each individually perhaps good-humoured and tolerable but all collectively contributing to the dehumanization or demonization of the relevant groups. If everything is speakable then everything becomes doable. A humane society ought to find ways of discouraging such a culture.

Communal libel, then, is morally and politically unacceptable. Not surprisingly several legal systems disallow it in one form or another. Many have laws against incitement to racial hatred, and some against religious and ethnic hatred as well.[5] While some define hatred to include utterances likely to provoke harmful actions against particular groups, others define it broadly to include those that bring the latter into contempt and damage their social standing. The Saskatchewan Human Rights Code (1979) prohibits actions and utterances that 'affront the dignity' of individuals and groups. Basing its judgement on the relevant provisions of the Code, the provincial court there asked the defendants in *Singer* v. *Isawyk and Pennywise Foods Ltd.* to desist from stereotyping blacks as 'incompetent, childish and funny' on the grounds that such remarks diminished their dignity and jeopardized their chances of getting responsible jobs and enjoying equal rights. In 1989 the Government of New South Wales in Australia passed a law declaring unlawful acts that 'incite hatred towards, serious contempt for, or serious ridicule of' persons or groups on grounds of their race. An Illinois statute in 1949 prohibited publications 'exposing the citizens of any race, colour, creed or religion to contempt, derision or obloquy' by attributing 'depravity, criminality, unchastity or lack of virtue' to them. The Supreme Court upheld the statute by a majority of one.[6] Writing for the majority, Justice Frankfurter observed that 'if an utterance directed against the individual may be the object of criminal sanctions, we cannot deny to a state power to punish the same utterance directed at a defined group' or a 'designated collectivity'. The individual's 'job and educational opportunities and the dignity accorded him' depended 'as much on the reputation of the racial and religious group to which he willy-nilly belongs as on his own merits', and the state was right to 'curb false or malicious defamation' of such groups (Sandel, 1996, p. 84).

The proposal to ban communal libel raises three important questions. First, the disinterested search for truth, freedom of speech and the well-being of the community itself require that it should not be insulated against criticism. How can we ensure that fair criticism is not stifled by prohibition of communal libel? Second, since there are several communities and new ones are created through intercommunal marriages and voluntary exit of members, should all of them be protected against communal libel or only a few, and, if the latter, what should be our criteria of selection? Third, is law the best way to protect the social standing and good name of the community? Of the three, the first question need not detain us, for libel laws the world over have found ways of distinguishing between libel and fair critical comment in relation to individuals, and these can be extended with suitable modifications to communities as well.

As to which communities to protect against libel, three criteria seem appropriate. First, communities should be capable of being identified with relative ease. Obviously no community can be defined or demarcated with absolute precision, but such precision is impossible in any area of human life. All that is necessary is that the definition should be clear enough for us to identify the relevant community in most cases. And in borderline or disputed cases it is the job of the courts to adjudicate. Although racial groups, for example, are not easy to define and identify, that has not prevented most societies from enacting laws against racial discrimination and the courts from applying them.

Second, the community should mean much to its members and be at least partially constitutive of their identity, such that an attack on it damages their sense of their self-worth and demeans them in others' eyes. Decisions on these matters, again, are not easy, but in most societies there is a broad consensus that religion, nationality, culture and so forth shape and provide meaning to the lives of individuals in a way that being a Rotarian, a Californian, or a middle-class professional does not.

Third, the community should be shown to be particularly vulnerable to malicious attacks or widespread negative stereotyping and discrimination. The law cannot deal with all evils at once and needs to concentrate on those in need of urgent attention. This means that laws in different countries would need to single out different communities at different points in time. Given the deep streak of anti-Semitism and anti-black racism in western societies, (as indeed in many others), and given the need to counter the malicious stereotypes to which they have both been subjected for centuries with disastrous results, Jews and blacks would seem to qualify for anti-libel laws in most western countries. In the light of the increasing Islamophobia in West European countries, Muslims too might perhaps fall in this category. However, such decisions depend on the political context and judgement and cannot be settled in the abstract.

As for the third question, the law has its obvious limits. It is a blunt instrument and can easily become counterproductive and damage the very communities it seeks to protect if it is too punitive, restrictive or applied insensitively or with excessive zeal. Ideally we should therefore rely on other forms of pressure, such as a powerful press council, organized disapproval by enlightened public opinion, social or economic sanctions against individuals and organizations shown to be guilty of communal libel, and a declarative and non-punitive law. However, when these do not seem enough and the situation requires urgent action, the law might need to intervene. It affirms the community's collective disapproval of certain forms of utterances, lays down norms of public decency, reassures vulnerable and powerless groups, and helps create a climate of civility and mutual respect. It is a little odd for law to prohibit religious, racial or ethnic discrimination but grant more or less absolute immunity to utterances that feed the attitudes and nurture the practices leading to such discrimination.

Free speech

The second important question raised by the Rushdie affair relates to the nature, grounds and limits of free speech. It is widely argued that freedom of speech should be as extensive as possible consistent with the demands of public order. Rushdie put the point well when he said:[7]

> How is freedom gained? It is taken: never given. To be free, you must first assume your rights to freedom. In writing *The Satanic Verses*, I wrote from the assumption that I was, and still am, a free man.
>
> What is freedom of expression? Without the freedom to offend, it ceases to exist. Without the freedom to challenge, even to satirise all orthodoxies, it ceases to exist. Language and the imagination cannot be imprisoned, or art dies, a little of what makes us human.

Rushdie says that *he* is free to offend others and satirize their deeply-held beliefs, but does not explain why *they* should put up with this. His right to free speech imposes a duty on them to refrain from interfering with him even when they are deeply hurt by his remarks; Rushdie does not say why they should accept such an obligation, how it serves their 'human' interests, and what is to be done if they take a different view of these interests. He rightly stresses the importance of art, but respect for one's fellow-humans and what gives meaning to their lives are also part of what makes us human, and he does not explain why art should be privileged over morality and religion. He does not appreciate either that what constitutes art can itself be a subject of dispute, and that his own view need not be accepted as the only one.

That Rushdie's assertion of the writer's more or less unrestrained right to express himself is fraught with difficulties can be illustrated by taking a hypothetical example. Imagine a writer writing about the tragic victims of Auschwitz. He mocks and ridicules them, trivializes their suffering, and presents them as a despicable lot thoroughly deserving the mindless brutality inflicted upon them. He creates scenes of collective debauchery, wife-swapping, incest, cannibalism and Jewish women offering themselves and their young sons and daughters to Nazi guards in return for a few more days of life or a few more crumbs of bread. Not only the Jews but all decent men and women would be deeply outraged by such a 'literary' work, and would feel that it takes unacceptable liberties with Jewish collective memories, insulted the honour and integrity of the dead, and violated the conventions regulating literary freedom. Since the law is a blunt instrument and we are rightly uneasy about giving government the power to censor creative writing, we may not ban such a work, but we would be right to express our sense of outrage and even contempt for the author. This is not at all to say that Rushdie's discussion of Islam is anything like this, but only to show that no literary work can be exempt from moral and social responsibility and norms of decency. As public figures wielding considerable moral, cultural and political power, creative writers are accountable for the exercise of this power not just to each other and the literary establishment but also to society at large.

Suppose the deeply hurt Jews mounted a protest against this hypothetical book and pressed for a ban. On what grounds could we tell them that, although understandable, their demand is wrong and that they should patiently suffer the hurt caused by the book? Many of the traditional arguments for free speech are of little avail. We cannot honestly say that the author was pursuing truth, deepening our understanding of the inmates of concentration camps, or furthering the cause of human progress. We cannot invoke the writer's right of self-expression either, for its very basis and rationale are in dispute. If he or his defenders were to say that we should put up with such isolated aberrations in the larger interest of human freedom, they would have a point. The Jews could then legitimately ask what steps society intends to take to discourage the publication of such works in the future and how it proposes to express its collective disapproval of this one.

This is not to deny that free speech is one of the highest values and can be adequately defended, but rather that it is not as inviolable as is sometimes made out and that the traditional defence of it is unsatisfactory. Its champions tend to consider the question largely from the standpoint of men of ideas, and assume that what is good for them is necessarily good for society as a whole. This is not only philosophically suspect but unlikely to carry conviction in a democratic society whose members might legitimately ask why they should put up with 'iconoclastic attacks' by 'exhibitionist' intellectuals taking 'perverse pride' in knocking established values, as a Catholic bishop put it at the height of the Rushdie controversy. In justifying such rights as those to liberty and property, there is a tendency to concentrate on the beneficiaries, and ignore those who often stand little chance of exercising these rights and for the most part only bear their corresponding burdens. We need to look at the question of free speech from the standpoint of both and show if, how and why it is in the interest of all to allow maximum possible freedom of expression. Many a liberal writer, including J. S. Mill, Constant and de Tocqueville, saw the need for this, but despaired of finding an answer. Free speech, they argued, was and will always remain an elite value constantly under threat from and in need of vigorous political defence against the masses. This is hardly an answer and will not do in an age far more democratic and plural than theirs.[8]

We also need to distinguish between different forms of speech and appreciate that they do not all merit equal and indiscriminate protection. Ordinary social intercourse, communications between professionals and their clients, parliamentary debates, freedom of the press, and creative writings represent different forms of speech with different logics, moral justifications and social consequences. Take freedom of the press. In all liberal societies the press is privately-owned and independent of the government but not of commercial interests. It is often used to promote the political and economic interests of its proprietors, leading in many cases to the biased reporting of events, restricting the range of critical views, manipulation of public opinion and corruption of the deliberative process. Anyone who cares for the political health of a democratic polity would rightly wonder how we can both sustain a robust press and regulate its partisanship and abuses, in just the same way that we have learned to restrict the right to property in the interest of social justice, stable communities, environmental protection, and so on. Since most other forms of speech do not have such fateful consequences and are not embedded in an asymmetrical structure of power, the problems they raise are not so acute, but in so far as they are public acts with small and large public consequences, they too cannot enjoy more or less absolute freedom either.

Free speech is not the only great value, and needs to be balanced against such others as avoidance of needless hurt, social harmony, humane culture, protection of the weak, truthfulness in the public realm, and self-respect and dignity of individuals and groups. There is no 'true' way of reconciling them; it all depends on the history, traditions, political circumstances, and so on of a society. In a country with a long history of inter-ethnic violence, or in which some groups are systematically humiliated or in which religion means a great deal to its members, free speech would be rightly subject to greater constraints than elsewhere. That is why the Indian government was right to ban *The Satanic Verses*, and Rushdie was wrong to lambast it for doing so. And that is also why the Indian government is perhaps right to ban works that glorify self-immolation by widows. To say that such constraints on free speech are a *regrettable* necessity is to presuppose the privileged status of free speech, and there is no warrant for such a belief. No single value trumps all others, and their relative importance can only be decided in the light of the social and cultural context and the likely consequences. Since free speech is an important value and since the government cannot be trusted to regulate it, its excesses are best checked by the press council, publishers' associations, provisions for civil prosecution, public disapproval and so on.

In the light of our discussion, how should we respond to British Muslim protests against *The Satanic Verses*? Our response should be based on a careful weighing up of two sets of factors. First, the book is a serious literary work not a piece of journalistic writing, and hence subject to minimum constraints. It is not a polemical or historical piece of writing either but a novel, and hence entitled to be judged by the criteria relevant to that genre including a considerable freedom of imaginative exploration. The offensive passages occur within the dream of a demented man, and hence not in the same category as unambiguous expressions of abuse and ridicule by the author.

Second, the passages in question reflect bad taste and handle a great theme in a somewhat crude, abusive and offensive language. They also show poor literary judgement, for Rushdie could have easily handled the theme in a manner that did not bear such a close historical resemblance to historical Islam. The Muslim suspicion that he was being deliberately provocative is not easy to dispel. Rushdie also showed a remarkable lack of political judgement as he was well aware of at least half a dozen riots in India and Pakistan triggered off by works containing similar references to the life of Muhammed.

Muslims were therefore right to protest against the book. Their protests had four legitimate objectives: to express their disapproval of it, to urge future writers to show greater sensitivity and self-restraint, to place important questions on the public agenda and, finally, to persuade British society to reconsider its views on the nature and limits of free speech. Muslims were right to do all that was necessary to achieve these objectives, including mounting demonstrations, putting economic pressure on and picketing the publishers, and even perhaps burning a copy of the book. All that went beyond this was unjustified and unwise. They were wholly wrong to threaten violence against Rushdie and his translators and publishers, both because their quarrel was with the book not with them as individuals and because this kind of intolerance can have no place in a democratic society. Since the book was already in the public realm and had attracted considerable attention, their demand for a ban had no meaning. And since their objection was to certain passages, they should have made that clear and defended the rest of the book. Having made their point, they should have left Rushdie alone, declared no interest in harming him, invited him to a public debate on a promise of full security, and patiently mobilized public opinion around the best legal and preferably nonlegal remedies against future works with such lapses.

Religion and public life

Another important question raised by the Rushdie affair has to do with the role of religion in political life. Secularists, who include liberals, conservatives and adherents of many other political persuasions, argue that religion and politics are wholly different activities, pertain to different areas of life, and should be kept separate. In their view, religion is a personal matter, politics a public and communal activity. Religion is concerned with the other-worldly destiny of the human soul, politics with the affairs of this world. Religion is a matter of faith which cannot be coerced; politics involves coercion and deals with matters in which conformity can be demanded on pain of punishment. Religion approaches life in terms of non-negotiable absolutes; politics is concerned with persuasion and aims at an inherently tentative consensus. Since the two are different, religion has little of value to contribute to political life, and such contribution as it might make is outweighed by the havoc it can easily cause. For these and other reasons, argues the secularist, political life should be organized on a secular basis and religion scrupulously kept out of it.

The secularist thesis can take several forms of which two are most common. In its weaker version it separates *state* and *religion* and maintains that the state should not enforce, institutionalize or formally endorse a religion, be guided by religious considerations in its policies and treatment of citizens, and should in general retain an attitude of strict indifference to religion. In its stronger version it also separates *politics* and *religion* and maintains that political debate and deliberation should be conducted in terms of secular reasons alone. Although religion might matter a great deal to individuals, *qua* citizens they should rise above their religious beliefs and be guided by secular reasons alone, partly because political life is only concerned with secular matters and partly because secular reasons are the only ones they all share in common.[9] For some secularists, citizens should arrive at their views on secular grounds alone, others are content to argue that they should at least publicly justify them on these grounds.

Although the two forms of secularism share several common assumptions, they are distinct, which is why many earlier writers such as Montesquieu, Lord Acton, and even Tocqueville advocated its weaker and rejected its stronger version. One might argue that the state should only be concerned with secular *matters*, but not that these should be decided only on secular *grounds*. A law imposing higher taxes on the rich to help the poor might have been passed because many legislators themselves shared or were persuaded by the Christian belief in the brotherhood of all men. The reasons behind the law, and hence its grounds, are religious, but its content is secular; the law passes the weaker secularist test but not the stronger. This might be challenged on the ground that the law indirectly imposes the relevant religious belief on the citizens and thus violates the principle of the separation between state and religion. The argument is flawed. Citizens are not asked or expected to subscribe to the Christian belief but only to obey the law, which they might do for all kinds of reasons including their own religious beliefs or the simple secular duty to respect the authority of the law. After all if the same law has been based on secular grounds such as the Rawlsian theory of justice or the Marxian theory of human solidarity, it would be wrong for religious persons to complain that the state was imposing secular beliefs on them.

The strong secularist thesis that citizens should abstract away their religious beliefs and be guided by secular reasons alone runs into several difficulties. Secular reasons are not politically and culturally neutral. They represent a world view according to which, crudely speaking, the affairs of 'this' world are autonomous and can and should be separated from those of the 'next'. Since the postulation and separation of the two worlds is a secular construct that sits ill at ease with religious consciousness, and which religious persons do not accept, to require them to be guided by secular reasons alone is to discriminate against them. Secular citizens are able to lead whole and integrated lives whereas religious citizens, who are required to bracket out their deepest beliefs, are subjected to moral incoherence and self-alienation. This is not to say that they cannot for political purposes suspend their beliefs, but rather that the self-abstraction involved devalues much of what gives meaning to their lives, deprives them of a moral compass, and involves an invidious form of self-imposed moral censorship. Allowing them to be guided by their religious beliefs but banning them from using these to defend their views in public does not improve the situation. It introduces self-alienation at a different level by requiring them to speak in a language different to the one in which they think. And it also subjects them to the disadvantages arising from the need to switch languages and defend their views in what is for them a second language.

In most societies religious persons constitute a majority. It is difficult to see how they can be asked in a democracy to refrain from acting on their religious beliefs, and any such attempt will only turn them against the political system that denies public expression to what they deeply cherish. The secularist demand makes sense if society is already or on the way to becoming wholly or substantially secular, and if religion either does not matter to people or does so only marginally. As various surveys have shown religion remains an important force in people's lives, and the kind of inexorable and comprehensive secularization predicted and hoped for by secular writers has not occurred even in advanced western societies.[10] Religion is not only very much alive today but refuses to remain confined to the private realm. Ninety per cent of US Congressmen claim to consult their religious beliefs before voting on important issues. Although the figure in other western countries is smaller, it is not negligible. Many activists in the Green movement, anti-racist organizations, campaign for the rights of the native peoples, anti-poverty struggles, peace and disarmament movements, and campaigns for human rights and global justice also claim to derive inspiration from their religious beliefs.

The social and political involvement of religion should not surprise us. Religious people generally seek wholeness in their lives and do not think it possible or desirable to separate their private and political concerns, which is why many of them participated in anti-slavery, anti-colonial, temperance, anti-capitalist, anti-Communist and other movements. Several new factors have emerged to reinforce this trend in our times. Many of the secular ideologies such as communism and even liberalism that have hitherto been the vehicles of radical transformative aspirations have lost much of their appeal and momentum, and there is an increasing demand for new ways of thought. Material satisfaction which has hitherto taken up most of people's energies is today a reality for many in the West, and they now aspire for something different and more fulfilling. They also look for moral discipline in personal and political life and explore new sources of moral motivation and energy. The earlier faith in the ability of science to solve the mystery of the universe or even to provide solutions to social and economic problems has declined, so much so that it is the scientists who are now seeking a rapprochement with religion. The ease with which the Nazi and Communist tyrannies subverted political and civil institutions have made many wonder if religious bodies, whose record of standing up to these regime is no worse and in some cases better than that of secular organizations, might not have a vital role to play in sustaining free societies.

In the light of our discussion, the secularist requirement that citizens should abstract away their religious beliefs and arrive at or even defend their views on secular grounds alone is unacceptable. It discriminates against religious persons and violates the principle of equal citizenship. It is undemocratic and ignores the wishes of a large body of citizens and even perhaps the majority. It is impractical for there is no way of enforcing it. It is counterproductive as it is likely to alienate religiously minded citizens from the political system and create a crisis of legitimacy. It is unwise because it deprives political life of both the valuable insights religion offers and the moral energies it can mobilize for just and worthwhile causes. Since citizenship is not a self-contained area of life with its own distinct values but one of several mediums in and through which human beings express and live out their deepest beliefs, it cannot exclude what matters most to many of them. Rather than abstract away legitimate differences, political life should find ways of recognizing, respecting and within limits accommodating them.

Secularists wonder how any kind of political debate, let alone a sensible one, is possible if different groups of citizens speak in different languages. Their worry is genuine but exaggerated. Political debate in every modern society is multilingual in character and would remain so even if no one spoke in a religious language. Conservatives, liberals, Marxists, fascists and others speak in very different languages. The fact that these languages are all secular does not mean that their differences are shallow or that their speakers understand each other. Many of us have great difficulty understanding the ways of thought of racists, extreme libertarians or even conservatives, and sometimes it is greater than what we face in relation to religious persons whose moral values we often share. If our political life can cope with a variety of secular languages, there is no reason why it cannot accommodate the religious language as well. The fact that it is unfamiliar to some citizens cannot be used as an argument against it.

When some groups of citizens speak in a religious language, we can and do in fact respond to it in various ways. When Martin Luther King pleaded for racial equality on the ground that all human beings are children of God, his demand was readily conceded by most Americans who recognized it as their constitutionally enjoined value. Its religious basis did not become a subject of political debate and was politically relevant only because it indicated why racial equality mattered to King and helped him mobilize like-minded people behind it. A difficult situation arises when the values or practices advocated on religious grounds do not enjoy widespread consensus. The grounds themselves then become subjects of public debate, and the religion concerned exposes itself to public scrutiny. This is what happened when a large body of Christians led by, among others, the Catholic Church demanded a total ban on abortion. The fact that the argument is religious in nature does not mean that it is inaccessible to secular citizens or that they cannot critically engage with it. It can be and was in fact debated at two levels, internal and external.

We could argue, as many did and do, that the Catholic position is internally inconsistent and misrepresents the central doctrines of the Church. The Church is theologically committed to valuing not life *per se* but the human person, and the foetus at least until a certain age is not a person as traditionally defined by Aquinas and several other theologians of the Church itself. We could also argue that since the Church leaves many a contentious economic and political issue to individual conscience, it is wrong to make such a rigid exception in the case of abortion, and that since it allows just wars in which innocent lives are taken, it is wrong not to think in terms of just abortions. We could also show that the Church's view is heavily influenced by the doctrine of the natural right to life and is at odds with the traditional doctrine of the natural law on which it relies in other areas, and that its current stand is of relatively recent origin and out of step with its own earlier approach. Such an internal critique goes a long way towards answering the Catholic argument, and has the additional advantage of triggering off an internal debate and highlighting the diversity of views among the Catholics themselves.

We can criticize the Church's stand on external grounds as well. We could argue that while it is free to ban abortion among its followers and to persuade outsiders, it has no legal or moral right to use the machinery of the state to impose its views on those who disagree with it, and that its attempt to do so violates the central principles of the very constitutional democracy that gives it the freedom to propagate its views. We could also argue that if the Church thinks it right to impose its deepest beliefs on others, liberals are equally justified in imposing on it their own fundamental belief in the equality of the sexes and requiring it to ordain women priests, appoint women cardinals, and periodically elect women Popes. We might follow a different route and contend that since many communities do not welcome children born out of wedlock or have no means to support them, the Church must either provide a nationwide support system or refrain from making irresponsible and impossible demands. We could reinforce the point by showing that unwanted children lack love, carry emotional scars, and so on, and that banning abortion damages human dignity as much as and to an even greater degree than allowing it.

The point of this discussion is not at all to refute the Catholic view of abortion, but to show that religious language in politics creates no more difficulties than the usual variety of secular languages. It might be argued that many secular citizens know little about their own religion let alone others, and cannot and should not be expected to engage in an informed debate with religious persons. The argument is well-taken but overstated. Most citizens have little understanding of highly complex economic and political issues, and yet they are expected to pass judgements on the economic policies of rival political parties. They rightly listen to experts, try to make sense of their arguments, and make up their minds. And when they are completely lost, they trust those experts who inspire their confidence. Religious arguments are no different. In fact since most citizens have a religious background, they are better able to handle religious arguments than the economic. Besides in a society in which a large body of citizens think and argue in religious terms, it is part of the training for common citizenship that future citizens should grow up with some knowledge of their society's major religious traditions. As I argue later, there is a strong academic and political case for teaching religion in schools. Furthermore, multilingual political deliberation is a valuable tool of intercommunal education, enabling each group of citizens to appreciate and learn something from other ways of thinking and evolving a richer and expansive conception of public reason. Reasons are public not because their grounds are or can be shared by all, as the secularist argues, but because they are open to inspection and can be intelligently discussed by anyone with the requisite knowledge or willingness to acquire it.

We have so far discussed the strong secularist thesis that separates politics and religion. As for the weaker secularist thesis that insists on the separation between state and religion, it has much to be said for it. As its proponents rightly argue, identification of state and religion corrupts both, threatens human dignity, restricts liberty of conscience, violates the moral and religious integrity of the individual, denies equal citizenship to those belonging to no religion or to one not officially endorsed by the state, compromises the impartiality of its officials, and so on. The secularist mistake lies in pushing the separation further than is warranted.

Religion is a fact of social life and, so long as it remains so, no state can remain indifferent to it. Given its legitimate secular interest in public order, public morality, public health, social harmony and individual freedom, the state is rightly concerned that religions should not pose a threat to all these by inciting mutual hatred, unduly curtailing their members' liberties, following immoral or unhygenic practices, and so on. More importantly, its citizens make several demands on it on the basis of their deepest religious beliefs, and the state cannot ignore these without violating their moral integrity and inviting resistance. This is why in spite of the 'wall of separation' between the state and religion, the American state allows conscientious objection, respects the religious dietary requirements of its armed forces, appoints and pays for military chaplains, exempts Seventh Day Adventists from working on

Saturdays, allows religious oaths in courts, allows the newly elected president to take the oath on the Bible, and so on. The strict separation of the state and religion would disallow all these, as well as such other practices as beginning Congress sessions with prayers, 'In God we trust' on the dollar bill, and concluding presidential addresses to the nation with 'God bless America'. While some of these practices can be ended if we were so minded others cannot, rendering the radical separation morally unacceptable, politically unwise, and practically impossible.[11]

The secularist is wrong to argue that religion has little of value to contribute to political life. Historically speaking religion has been a source of many an emancipatory movement. Anti-slavery, anti-*laissez faire* capitalist, anti-fascist and other movements were often led by religious leaders or those with deep religious commitments. This is also the case with more recent movements such as India's struggle for independence under Gandhi, the 1960s civil rights campaigns in the United States, the anti-*apartheid* struggle in South Africa, anti-racist movements in Britain, France, Germany, the Netherlands and elsewhere, campaigns for global justice and nuclear disarmament, and protests against the Gulf War especially in the United States. This is not at all to say that secular persons did not or do not play a crucial role in these and other movements, but rather that religious persons also played a part and sometimes displayed a kind of energy, commitment, and the willingness to suffer that were lacking in wholly secular motivations.[12]

Religion also provides a valuable counterweight to the state, nurturing sensibilities and values the latter ignores or suppresses. Just as we need opposition parties to check the government of the day, we need powerful non-statal institutions to check the state. The state has traditionally claimed to monopolize morality, presenting its interests as of the highest importance and deserving of the greatest sacrifices. This attitude needs constant questioning and religion is ideally equipped to do so. It provides an alternative source of morality and allegiance and continues to remind us that a human being is more than a citizen. This is not to deny the obvious fact that religion has often supported aggressive nationalism and horrendous wars, but to say that it also has a universalist and humanitarian dimension which can be used to criticize, embarrass, and contain its nationalist propensities.

Modern social and political life often tends to encourage a quasi-utilitarian attitude to morality. When the main concern is to get on in life and pursue self-interest, rigours of moral life are found burdensome, leading to a tendency to cut moral corners, bend moral principles to personal conveniences, and to legitimize all these by a recourse to moral sophistry. Here, again, religion at its best has much to contribute. It stresses the quality of the inner life and urges human beings to examine the kind of persons they have become. It insists, too, on certain fundamental values and demands that they should not be compromised, at least not without compelling reasons. When the Roman Catholic Church insists on the sanctity of human life and rules out all forms of abortion, it is clearly being absolutist, unworldly, unrealistic and oppressive. However, it also serves the vital function of affirming an important value, nagging our consciences, requiring us to reflect publicly and critically on our moral practices, and forcing us to consider issues we would happily prefer to ignore. We might, and in this and other matters should, challenge and even reject the Church's views, but that does not detract from the fact that its voice deserves to be heard with respect.

As we saw earlier the modern state is abstracted from society and tends to become bureaucratic and remote. While this has enabled it to rise above social, ethnic, religious and other divisions and institutionalize such great values as equality before the law, liberty and common citizenship, it has also been the source of many of its weaknesses. Although the modern state's administrative and moral reach is wider than its earlier counterparts, it is also shallower and more tenuous. The state remains external to society and its interventions are necessarily crude and arouse deep fears. As a result it is incapable of nurturing the moral life of the community and fostering such valuable qualities as moral self-discipline, a sense of personal responsibility, family values, love of the good which alone gives depth and energy to moral life, concern for the weak and the oppressed, and a sense of social obligation. The resulting moral vacuum needs to be filled or else the communal life suffers, and the state itself becomes either hollow or excessively overbearing and authoritarian. Along with the family, schools, voluntary associations and other social institutions, religion plays an important part in sustaining the deeper springs of morality. The fact that a large number of individuals consciously or unconsciously derive their moral values and love of the good from religion reinforces its role in public life.

Religion also performs several other important public functions. It rejects the claims of the state and the economy to be governed by their own narrow values, and subordinates them to wider moral concerns. It stresses the unity of the human species and challenges the tendency to limit morality to the territorial boundaries of the state. It raises issues politicians are often too timid or opportunistic to debate, and broadens the public agenda. As an institution of premodern origin and encompassing several historical epochs, it nurtures a wide range of moral and cultural sensibilities and dispositions. In so doing, it provides a counterpoint to the haughty self-assurance of the rationalist modernity, brings to political life the accumulated insights and wisdom of rich historical traditions, and reminds us of human finitude. It also challenges the privatization and relativization of morality to which liberal societies are particularly prone and insists, even if at times misguidedly, on the objective and universal dimension of morality.

While acknowledging the valuable contribution of religion to political life, we should not ignore its pernicious influences rightly highlighted by the secularists. It is often absolutist, self-righteous, arrogant, dogmatic and impatient of compromise. It arouses powerful and sometimes irrational impulses and can easily destabilize society, cause political havoc, and create a veritable hell on earth. Since it is generally of ancient origin, it is sometimes deeply conservative, hidebound, insensitive to changes in the social climate and people's moral aspirations, and harbours a deep anti-feminine bias. It is often intolerant of other religions and internal dissent, and has a propensity towards violence. It has often struck up most disgraceful alliances with oppressive and inhuman regimes, and used the name of God to justify such evil practices as slavery, crusades, anti-Semitism and untouchability. Sublime when at its best, it can be most vicious and cruel at its worst.

Nothing in human life is an unmixed good and we should not take an unduly rosy or irredeemably bleak view of religion. Rather than keep it out of political life and allow it to sulk and scowl menacingly from outside it, we should find ways of both benefiting from its contribution and minimizing its dangers. This could be done in several ways. The state could give religious institutions a charitable status as it does in all liberal societies, and encourage and give resources to synagogues, churches, mosques and so on to undertake philanthropic and welfare activities such as providing day-care for children, care for the elderly, homes for the homeless, and to help in setting up public conservation projects and neighbourhood associations. It is sometimes argued that public funds should not be used to support sectional interests. If that were so, no public authority would be justified in subsidizing or giving charitable status to museums, art galleries, universities and operas. We rightly want the state to support these activities because they are valuable, shared by sizeable sections of citizens, and add to the richness of collective life. Religion is no different.

We might also explore ways of drawing religious communities into the mainstream of political life. We might set up a national interreligious forum where religious communities can meet on a regular basis, get to know each other and resolve their differences, or an interreligious consultative council with the right to make representations to the government on matters of moral concern to them. There is also something to be said for giving religious bodies access to radio and television for prayer and religious discussion and giving public subsidies to interreligious activities and forums. These and other arrangements serve several purposes. They give the religious communities a moral and emotional stake in the maintenance of free societies by reassuring them that the state values their opinions and that they do not need to sulk or agitate to be heard. They bring religion into the public realm, make it publicly accountable, and subject it to democratic discipline. And they also enrich the quality of public debate by introducing perspectives otherwise likely to be ignored.

There is a strong educational and political case for teaching religion in schools since one of the principal aims of education is to enable pupils to appreciate the great achievements of the human spirit, religion being one of these. Like literature and the arts, religion represents a profound exploration of the human condition, and to deny pupils access to it is both to impoverish them morally and emotionally and to cut them off from the ways of thought and life of a large part of humankind. A society's major religions also generally shape its history, social structure, values and ideals, and to remain ignorant of them is to lack a coherent understanding of the latter. Since many parts of the world are torn by religious conflicts, religious literacy is essential to make sense of the contemporary world.

There are also good political reasons for teaching religion in schools. It brings religion into the public domain where we can collectively decide how it should be taught. If schools do not teach it, children will have to depend on their families and religious organizations, which would only expose them to their own religion and that too from a narrow sectarian standpoint. Besides, once we accept religion as one of the several respectable languages of political life, it is essential that future citizens should understand how a religious person thinks and reasons and should acquire at least some knowledge of their society's major religious traditions. Such shared religious knowledge is as important for intelligent citizenship as knowledge of society's history, geography and constitutional and political arrangements. For these and other reasons even France, which has for decades kept religion out of its schools, decided in the 1980s to bring it back with the full support of the Catholic Church and such secular bodies as the League of Education and the Federation of National Education. Part of the reason why religion arouses strong passions in the United States has perhaps to do with the fact that it is not taught in schools as an academic subject. Religious citizens pick up their religion from sectarian churches, and the non-religious, having never been systematically exposed to it, find it alien and frightening. The dogmatism of one reinforces and is in turn reinforced by the nervous hostility of the other with predictable political consequences.

Although how to teach religion in schools raises different questions, these are not unanswerable. History, civics, literature and social studies, too, were once highly contentious subjects, and there is now a broad consensus on how best to approach them. Once we agree that the reasons for teaching religion are broadly those sketched above, it is clear that it should be taught in more or less the same way as other subjects. The job of the school is not to challenge or subvert its pupils' religious beliefs as the militant secularists argue, nor to reinforce them as the orthodox do, but to discuss them in a comparative, analytical and respectful manner and to provide religious education rather than religious training or indoctrination. It should teach its pupils how the major religions originated, developed, shaped and were shaped by the cultural climate of the wider society, came to be interpreted in a certain manner, threw up doctrinal divisions, and formed alliances with different kinds of political, social, economic and other movements. It should also sensitize them to the similarities and differences between the ways in which different religions come to terms with the contingency of human existence and the tragedies and joys of human life, and encourage them to hold and examine their beliefs in a responsible manner. There are areas such as the teaching of creationism where disputes are likely to arise, but these can be tackled without compromising the school's academic integrity. There is no reason why creationism, for example, should not be taught as long as the school presents it as one view among many, teaches evolutionary and other theories as well, and provides a balanced critical assessment of them all.

Parents who wish to withdraw their children from such a broad-based religious education should be free to do so, as compelling them to act against their deeply held beliefs is both unjust and counterproductive. If some families or religious communities wish to initiate their children into their respective traditions by setting up schools of their own, they should be allowed to do so and even perhaps publicly funded. Such schools instil a distinct set of moral and cultural sensibilities, increase the available range of educational options, add to the variety of collective life by producing citizens with different characters and perspectives on life, respect the wishes of the parents, prevent the state from acquiring the monopoly of education and exercising total control over its content, and so on. Religious schools do have their obvious disadvantages, but these can be avoided by requiring them to conform to certain minimum nationally prescribed curricular, pedagogical, disciplinary and other requirements and subjecting them to periodic inspection. The state's right to do all this is more easily accepted if it also funds the schools involved. A multicultural society needs to provide not only multicultural education but also a multiculturally based educational system accommodating different kinds of schools within an agreed national framework.

While welcoming religion to political life, we need to guard against its dangers. Although there is no foolproof way to do so in a democracy, we are not devoid of resources. A constitutionally enshrined bill of rights guaranteeing liberty of conscience and religious freedom and banning state imposition of religion is vitally important. Religious people must also be required to respect the principles of equal citizenship and democratic decision-making as the necessary preconditions of political participation. Almost every modern society includes citizens belonging to several religions and to none. Just as one of these religions feels strongly about its beliefs, so do others. And since none can claim to be privileged over others, they must accept the need for compromise and accommodation. A religious group that seeks to impose its beliefs on others betrays its inability to accept them as its equals and respect their integrity, and forfeits its claims to their tolerance and goodwill. We welcome religion into the public realm because it represents a distinct and valuable point of view whose participation in the deliberative process enhances the quality of the political debate and the legitimacy of the resulting decisions. An intolerant religion that refuses to engage in an open-minded dialogue with other points of view and respect majority decisions defeats the very grounds for welcoming it. We may under certain circumstances legitimately restrict its freedom and, in exceptional cases, even ban it.

There is a pervasive tendency among religious people to claim to be in possession of divinely vouchsafed infallible truths which they are not at liberty to compromise. This is a wholly false reading of religion. No religion is or can be wholly divine in the sense of being altogether free of human mediation. Its origin and inspiration are divine but human beings determine its meaning and content. The divine will is communicated in a human language with all its obvious limitations. The authorized guardians of the sacred texts too are fallible human beings prone to errors, misjudgments, biases and pressures of dominant interests. There is no religion whose followers are not embarrassed by the misdeeds and misjudgments of their spokesmen in earlier ages.

Since every religion is a human construction based, no doubt, on divine inspiration, its adherents cannot hide behind God's authority and must accept responsibility for what they say and do in His name. It is never enough for them to say that they must do such and such things because God or the Bible or the *Koran* says so. The divine will is a matter of human definition and interpretation, and requires them to show why they interpret their religion in one way rather than another and why they think that their interpretation entails a particular form of behaviour. Religion does involve faith but is not a matter of faith alone, which is why the two should not be equated. It involves judgement, choice and decision, and hence reason and personal responsibility. Religiously minded citizens are therefore never excused from a rational discussion of their politically relevant beliefs and practices. Political life recognizes no infallible truths, only those capable of carrying conviction with the democratic community of citizens.

In the light of our discussion we need to reconsider the standard secularist view of the place of religion in political life. Subject to the qualifications mentioned earlier, state–religion separation makes much sense, that between politics and religion only a little. We need to appreciate that religion matters deeply to people, that they feel alienated from and even despised by a political system that does not allow them to speak in their native idioms, and that religion can contribute much to political life, and should find ways of respecting and welcoming it. In return, we should require religious people to accept the constraints of democratic society, scrupulously respect its basic freedoms and procedures, recognize the intractability and complexity of political life, and appreciate that a religion that becomes too worldly or too close to centres of political power is well on its way to losing its soul and forfeiting our respect. Such an inclusive and religiously sensitive secularism offers the best basis for a creative and mutually beneficial engagement between religion and political life.[13]

11

Conclusion

Almost all societies today are multicultural and likely to remain so for the foreseeable future; this is our historical predicament, and we obviously need to come to terms with it. Since cultural diversity has much to be said for it, our predicament, if approached in the spirit of multiculturalism, can also become a source of great creative opportunities.

Multiculturalism as articulated in earlier chapters is best seen neither as a political doctrine with a programmatic content nor as a philosophical theory of man and the world but as a perspective on human life. Its central insights are three, each of which is sometimes misinterpreted by its advocates and needs to be carefully formulated if it is to carry conviction:

- First, human beings are culturally embedded in the sense that they grow up and live within a culturally structured world, organize their lives and social relations in terms of its system of meaning and significance, and place considerable value on their cultural identity. This does not mean that they are determined by their culture in the sense of being unable to critically evaluate its beliefs and practices and understand and sympathize with others, but rather that they are deeply shaped by it, can overcome some but not all of its influences and necessarily view the world from within a culture, be it the one they have inherited and uncritically accepted or reflectively revised or, in rare cases, consciously adopted.
- Second, different cultures represent different systems of meaning and visions of the good life. Since each realizes a limited range of human capacities and emotions and grasps only a part of the totality of human existence, it needs others to understand itself better, expand its intellectual and moral horizon, stretch its imagination

336

and guard it against the obvious temptation to absolutize itself. This does not mean that one cannot lead a good life within one's culture, but rather that, other things being equal, it is likely to be richer if one enjoys access to others and that a culturally self-contained life is virtually impossible for most human beings in the modern world. Nor does it mean that cultures cannot be compared and judged, that they are equally rich and deserve equal respect, that each of them is good for its members, or that all cultural differences deserve to be valued. All it means is that no culture is wholly worthless, that it deserves at least some respect because of what it means to its members and the creative energy it displays, that no culture is perfect and has a right to impose itself on others, and that cultures are generally best changed from within.

Since each culture is inherently limited, a dialogue between them is mutually beneficial. It both alerts them to their biases, a gain in itself, and enables then to reduce them and expand their horizon of thought. 'To be in a conversation … means to be beyond oneself, to think with the other and to come back to oneself as if to another'.[1] The dialogue is possible only if each culture accepts others as equal conversational partners, who need to be taken seriously as sources of new ideas and to whom it owes the duty of explaining itself. And it realizes its objectives only if the participants enjoy a broad equality of self-confidence, economic and political power and access to public space.

- Third, all but the most primitive cultures are internally plural and represent a continuing conversation between their different traditions and strands of thought. This does not mean that they are devoid of internal coherence and identity but that their identity is plural and fluid. Cultures grow out of conscious and unconscious interaction with each other, partly define their identity in terms of what they take to be their significant other, and are at least partially multicultural in their origins and constitution. Each carries bits of the other within itself and is rarely *sui generis*. This does not mean that it has no powers of self-determination and inner impulses, but rather that it is porous and subject to external influences which it interprets and assimilates in its own autonomous way.

A culture's relation to itself shapes and is in turn shaped by its relation to others, and their internal and external pluralities presuppose and reinforce each other. A culture cannot appreciate the value of others unless it appreciates the plurality within it; the converse is just as true. Since a closed culture defines its identity in terms of its differences from others and jealously guards it against their influences, it feels threatened by and avoids all contacts with them. A culture cannot be at ease with its differences from them unless it is also at ease with its own internal differences. A dialogue between cultures requires that each should open itself up to the influence of and be willing to learn from others, and that in turn requires that it should be self-critical and willing and able to engage in a dialogue with itself.

What I might call a multicultural perspective is composed of the creative interplay of these three complementary insights, namely the cultural embeddedness of human beings, the inescapability and desirability of cultural diversity and intercultural dialogue, and the internal plurality of each culture. When we view the world from its vantage point, our attitudes to ourselves and others undergo profound changes. All claims that a particular way of thinking and living is perfect, the best, or necessitated by human nature itself appear incoherent and even bizarre, for the multicultural perspective sensitizes us to the fact that all ways of life and thought are inherently limited and cannot possibly embody the full range of the richness, complexity and grandeur of human existence. We instinctively suspect attempts to homogenize a culture, return it to its 'fundamentals' and impose a single identity on it, for we are acutely aware that every culture is internally plural and differentiated. And we remain equally sceptical of all attempts to present it as one whose origins lie within itself, for we know that all cultures are born out of interaction with others and shaped by the wider economic, political and other forces. This undercuts the very basis of Afrocentrism, Eurocentrism, Sinocentrism, Westocentrism and so on, all of which isolate the history of the culture concerned from those of others and credit it with achievements it often owes to others.

From a multicultural perspective, no political doctrine or ideology can represent the full truth of human life. Each of them, be it liberalism, conservatism, socialism or nationalism, is embedded in a particular culture, represents a particular vision of the good life, and is necessarily narrow and partial. Liberalism, for example, is an inspiring political doctrine stressing such great values as human dignity, autonomy, liberty, critical thought and equality. However, it has no monopoly of them, and they can be defined in several different ways of which its own definition is only one and not always the most coherent. It also ignores or marginalizes such other great values as human solidarity, equal life chances, selflessness, self-effacing humility, contentment and a measure of scepticism about the pleasures and achievements of human life. And it is insufficiently sensitive to and cannot give coherent accounts of the importance of culture, tradition, community, a sense of rootedness and belonging, and so on. Other political doctrines are just as limited if not more so. Since every political doctrine has a limited grasp of the immense complexity of human existence and the problems involved in holding societies together and creating sensitive, sane and self-critical individuals, none of them including liberalism can be the sole basis of the good society.

What accounts for the relative social stability and cultural richness of most western societies is precisely the fact that they are not based on a single political doctrine or world view. Liberalism, socialism, conservatism and Marxism, and at a different level the secular and religious world views that cut across them, have constantly challenged each other, and each is the richer for the experience. Their continuing contestation and mutually regulating influences have averted the hegemony of any one of them and contained its likely excesses. Each doctrine carries bits of the others within it, and is as a result internally diverse, weakly-centred, and possesses the moral and emotional resources to understand and even respect others. This mutual fusion of ideas and sensibilities has given rise to a broadly shared cultural vocabulary, no doubt varied and messy but for that very reason capable of providing a common framework of discourse. Western societies would not remain open and capable of self-regeneration if they were to be taken over by a single doctrine, including liberalism.

Since multicultural societies represent an interplay of different cultures, they cannot be theorized or managed from within any one of them. They require a multicultural perspective of the kind sketched earlier. It alerts the political theorist to the complex and subtle ways in which his culture shapes his modes of thought and limits his powers of critical reflection, and also offers him a way to minimize these limitations. Although he has no Archimedean standpoint or a God's-eye view available to him, he has several coigns of vantage in the form of other cultures. He can set up a dialogue between them, use each to illuminate the insights and expose the limitations of others, and create for himself a vital in-between space, a kind of immanent transcendentalism, from which to arrive at a less culture-bound vision of human life and a radically critical perspective on his society.

From a multicultural perspective the good society does not commit itself to a particular political doctrine or vision of the good life and ask how much diversity to tolerate within the limits set by it, both because such a doctrine or vision might not be acceptable to some of its communities and because it forecloses its future development. Instead, it begins by accepting the reality and desirability of cultural diversity and structures its political life accordingly. It is dialogically constituted, and its constant concern is to keep the dialogue going and nurture a climate in which it can proceed effectively, stretch the boundaries of the prevailing forms of thought, and generate a body of collectively acceptable principles, institutions and policies. The dialogue requires certain institutional preconditions such as freedom of expression, agreed procedures and basic ethical norms, participatory public spaces, equal rights, a responsive and popularly accountable structure of authority, and empowerment of citizens. And it also calls for such essential political virtues as mutual respect and concern, tolerance, self-restraint, willingness to enter into unfamiliar worlds of thought, love of diversity, a mind open to new ideas and a heart open to others' needs, and the ability to persuade and live with unresolved differences. While nurturing a wide variety of views and fostering the spirit and deepening the morality of dialogue, such a society draws a line against those too dogmatic, self-righteous or impatient to participate in its conversational culture and accept its outcome.

The dialogically constituted multicultural society both retains the truth of liberalism and goes beyond it. It is committed to both liberalism and multiculturalism, privileges neither, and moderates the logic of one by that of the other. It neither confines multiculturalism within the limits set by liberalism and suppresses or marginalizes nonliberal values and cultures, nor confines liberalism within the limits of multiculturalism and emasculates its critical and emancipatory thrust. Apart from its fundamental commitment to the culture and morality of dialogue, the dialogically constituted society privileges no particular cultural perspective, be it liberal or otherwise. It sees itself both as a community of citizens and a community of communities, and hence as a community of communally embedded and attached individuals. It cherishes individuals, their basic rights and liberties and other great liberal moral and political values, all of which are integral to the culture of dialogue. It also, however, appreciates that individuals are culturally-embedded, that their cultural communities are essential to their well-being, that the communities are open and interactive and cannot be frozen, and that public institutions and policies should recognize and cherish their evolving identities and nurture a community of communities based on the kind of plural collective culture described earlier. Unlike the standard liberal approach of the proceduralist, civic assimilationist or comprehensively assimilationist variety, which abstracts away citizens' cultural and other differences and unites them in terms of their uniformly shared economic, political and other interests, it insists that this is neither possible nor desirable and finds ways of publicly recognizing and respecting their cultural and other differences. The common good and the collective will that are vital to any political society are generated not by transcending cultural and other particularities, but through their interplay in the cut and thrust of a dialogue. The dialogically-constituted multicultural society has a strong notion of common good, consisting in respect for a consensually grounded civil authority and basic rights, maintenance of justice, institutional and moral preconditions of deliberative democracy, a vibrant and plural composite culture and an expansive sense of community. And it cherishes not static and ghettoized, but interactive and dynamic, multiculturalism.

A multicultural society cannot be stable and last long without developing a common sense of belonging among its citizens.[2] The sense of belonging cannot be ethnic or based on shared cultural, ethnic and other characteristics, for a multicultural society is too diverse for that, but political in nature and based on a shared commitment to the political community. Its members do not directly belong to each other as in an ethnic group, but through their mediating membership of a shared community, and they are committed to each other because they are all in their own different ways committed to the community and bound by the ties of common interest and affection. Although they might personally loathe some of their fellow-members or find their lifestyles, views and values unacceptable, their mutual commitment and concern as members of a shared community remain unaffected.

The commitment to a political community is highly complex in nature and is easily misunderstood. It does not involve sharing common substantive goals, for its members might deeply disagree about these, nor a common view of its history which they may read differently, nor a particular economic or social system about which they might entertain different views. Decocted to its barest essentials, commitment to the political community involves commitment to its continuing existence and well-being as defined earlier, and implies that one cares enough for it not to harm its interests and undermine its integrity (Mason, 1999; Viroli, 1995, pp. 160–87). It is a matter of degree and could take such diverse forms as a quiet concern for its well-being, deep attachment, affection, and even intense love. While different citizens would develop different emotions towards their community, all that is necessary to sustain it and can legitimately be expected of them all is a basic concern for its integrity and well-being; what one might call patriotism or political loyalty.[3] They might criticize the prevailing form of government, institutions, policies, values, ethos and dominant self-understanding in the strongest possible terms, but these should not arouse unease or provoke charges of disloyalty so long as their basic commitment to dialogue is not in doubt.

Commitment or belonging is reciprocal in nature. Citizens cannot be committed to their political community unless it is also committed to them, and they cannot belong to it unless it accepts them as belonging to it. The political community cannot therefore expect its members to develop a sense of belonging to it unless it equally values and cherishes them in all their diversity and reflects this in its structure, policies, conduct of public affairs, self-understanding and self-definition. Although equal citizenship is essential to fostering a common sense of belonging, it is not enough. Citizenship is about status and rights, belonging is about being accepted and feeling welcome. Some individuals and groups might enjoy the same rights as the rest but feel that they do not quite belong to the community, nor it to them. This feeling of being full citizens and yet outsiders is difficult to analyse and explain, but it can be deep and real and seriously damage the quality of their citizenship and their commitment to the political community. It is caused by, among other things, the narrow and exclusive manner in which wider society defines the common good, the demeaning ways in which it talks about some of its members, and the dismissive or patronizing ways in which it behaves towards them. Although such individuals are free in principle to participate in its collective life, they often stay away or ghettoize themselves for fear of rejection and ridicule or out of a deep sense of alienation.

As Charles Taylor (1994) correctly observes, social recognition is central to the individual's identity and self-worth, and misrecognition can gravely damage both. This raises the question as to how the un- or misrecognized groups can secure recognition, and here Taylor's analysis falters. He seems to think that the dominant group can be rationally persuaded to change its views of them by intellectual argument and moral appeal. This is to misunderstand the dynamics of the process of recognition.

Misrecognition has both a cultural and a material basis.[4] White Americans, for example, take a demeaning view of African Americans partly under the influence of the racist culture, partly because this legitimizes the prevailing system of domination, and partly because the deeply disadvantaged blacks do sometimes exhibit some of the features that confirm white stereotypes. Misrecognition, therefore, can only be countered by both undertaking a rigorous critique of the dominant culture and radically restructuring the prevailing inequalities of economic and political power. Since the dominant group welcomes neither the radical critique nor the corresponding political praxis, the struggle for recognition involves cultural and political contestation and sometimes even violence, as Hegel (1960) highlighted in his analysis of the dialectic of recognition and which Taylor's (1994) sanitized version of it ignores. As we have seen, the politics of culture is integrally tied up with the politics of power because culture is itself institutionalized power and deeply imbricated with other systems of power. Cultural self-esteem cannot be developed and sustained in a vacuum and requires appropriate changes in all the major areas of life. No multicultural society can be stable and vibrant unless it ensures that its constituent communities receive both just recognition and a just share of economic and political power. It requires a robust form of social, economic and political democracy to underpin its commitment to multiculturalism.[5]

Multicultural societies throw up problems that have no parallel in history. They need to find ways of reconciling the legitimate demands of unity and diversity, achieving political unity without cultural uniformity, being inclusive without being assimilationist, cultivating among their citizens a common sense of belonging while respecting their legitimate cultural differences, and cherishing plural cultural identities without weakening the shared and precious identity of shared citizenship. This is a formidable political task and no multicultural society so far has succeeded in tackling it. The erstwhile Soviet Union and Yugoslavia met their violent doom; Canada lives in the shadow of Quebec's secession; India narrowly missed a second partition of the country; Indonesia shows signs of disintegration; Sudan, Nigeria and others are torn by violent conflicts; and the sad story is endlessly repeatedly in many other parts of the world. Even such affluent, stable and politically mature democracies as the United States, Great Britain and France have so far had only limited success, and show signs of moral and emotional disorientation in the face of increasing demands for recognition and equality. Although multicultural societies are difficult to manage, they need not become a political nightmare and might even become exciting if we exuviate our long traditional preoccupation with a culturally homogeneous and tightly structured polity and allow them instead to intimate their own appropriate institutional forms, modes of governance, and moral and political virtues.

Notes

Introduction

1. One might recognize other kinds of differences but not the cultural because one values only self-chosen identities and differences, or because one fears the political power of organized communities, or because one thinks that cultures can be hierarchically graded and the inferior ones denied the right to difference. See Chapters 1 and 2 below. France has long been sympathetic to recognition of differences but not to multiculturalism.
2. Since one might welcome cultural but not moral diversity, and vice versa, cultural and moral pluralism are not necessarily related.
3. Homosexuality might be taken to represent not just a sexual practice or 'orientation' (a fascinating term with both voluntarist and naturalist implications) but a wider perspective on the nature of human beings, the meaning and significance of sexuality, and so on, and then it would constitute not just subcultural but also perspectival diversity.
4. If a cultural community only wishes to be left alone, its demands can be met more easily than if it wants full equality in reshaping the political structure.
5. Cited in Ridge (1981, p. 37). Also Schlesinger (1991, pp. 17f).
6. *One Nation. Many Peoples*, (1991, p. xi).
7. While signing the Covenant on Civil and Political Rights, France declared that Article 27, which talks of 'ethnic, religious and linguistic minorities', did not apply to it, and that its treatment of minority languages was not open to external scrutiny. France claims to follow 'the logic of equality not of minorities'.

    President Mitterrand's period of office marked a significant shift in French self-understanding. Insisting that 'unity' should not be confused with 'uniformity', and 'autonomism' with 'separatism', he argued that 'minority peoples and cultures' should be given 'the right to their difference' and to maintain their 'specificity'. The French Socialist Party thought the only way to counter the 'alienation' and 'homogenization of mentalities' brought about by capitalism was to encourage the 'flowering of regional languages and cultures'. The *Rapport Giordan* (1982) even recommended a *Commission Nationales des Cultures Minoritaires* to encourage the cultures of both territorially concentrated and scattered minorities (such as Jews, gypsies and Armenians), promotion of ethnic theatre, literature, music, and so on. See Safran (1989).

8. A theory of multiculturalism is primarily concerned not with the rights of immigrants or even the minorities in general as is often assumed, but with the place of culture in human life, its political significance, relations between cultures, and so on. One cannot discuss minority rights without asking why minorities *qua* minorities are politically relevant and should have rights, and that in turn requires a well-considered theory of the place of culture in human life in general.

9. I am not happy with the term naturalism but cannot think of another. Basically it refers to a body of thought centred on, and assigning primary explanatory and normative significance to, a conception of human nature. It encompasses both secular and religious views of human nature.

10. Kymlicka (1995, p. 2) makes the valid point that traditional western political philiosophy has not taken full account of cultural diversity.

11. The thought of Charles Taylor, Yael Tamir, Will Kymlicka, Anthony Smith, and others reveals the continuing influence of Herder, just as that of Isaiah Berlin and even Stuart Hampshire shows the influence of Montesquieu, and in the case of Berlin that of Vico as well.

12. Historically speaking liberalism began, at least in the English-speaking world, as a doctrine stressing the contingency of and abstracting away ethnic, religious, cultural and other differences. Not surprisingly it faces acute structural difficulties getting these differences back into its views of man and politics.

13. Gray (1995a, Ch. 9 and 1993, Ch. 18) rightly sees liberal societies as encompassing both liberal and nonliberal cultures and suggests how they should be structured. He sees the two cultures as mute partners rather than as active participants in developing a common culture.

14. Tully (1995, pp. 49ff) stresses the importance of such dialogue and rightly argues that there are several different ways of conducting it. See also Michelfelder and Palmer (1989).

15. Like liberals, conservatives and Marxists, too, have offered theories of multiculturalism. Burke, Figgis, Maitland, *et al.* belong to the first, and Otto Bauer, Karl Renner and others to the second category. For a discussion of the latter, see Nimni (1999).

Chapter 1

1. I draw on Berlin's (1969) influential discussion of monism, but differ from him in defining it more narrowly and distinguishing its various forms.

2. Halbfass (1990) argues that the Greeks were reluctant to learn foreign languages, and even in strictly scholarly works replaced 'barbarian' words with expressions from their own language. This applied to the names of 'barbaric' deities as well, who were all referred to by Greek names, giv-

ing the impression that foreigners were only worshipping Greek gods under different names and in different guises. *Ibid*. p. 14.

3. Connolly (1991, Ch. 5) beautifully captures some of the sources and tensions of Augustine's monism.

4. The writings of many Christian writers were deeply informed by the spirit of universal *caritas*. In criticizing them I am only concerned to show that the ideas of even the noblest minds, when grounded in a monist vision, become sources of intolerance.

5. Diana Eck (1993) puts the point well. 'How do we account theologically for the fact of human religious diversity? ... Theology has come to grips with Aristotle, just as theology has had to come to grips with science and with the fact that the sun does not circle the earth. Coming to grips with the world's religious pluralism is equally challenging to Christian theology today.' Coward (1989) is a valuable exploration of how the dialogue occurs at theoretical and practical levels.

6. The Roman Catholic Church has shown remarkable moral courage and spiritual generosity by its recent willingness to express deep regrets for these and other injustices. This has few if any parallels in other religions.

7. For excellent accounts of the relation between colonialism and race and the way in which racial thinking shaped liberalism, see Pieterse (1990) and Pagden (1991, 1995). The ease with which human beings are racialized and the manner in which such a racially constituted subject informs some areas of current thought are shrewdly exposed in Goldberg (1993).

8. 'In theory as well as in practice, Millian liberalism is a force for cultural homogeneity and against diversity', Gray (1993, p. 260). For a sympathetic critique of my view which appeared too late to be discussed here, see Brown (1999).

9. Although Kant's liberalism was free from the aggressiveness and the glorification of national greatness characteristic of Mill, Tocqueville and others, his thought had even less space for moral and cultural diversity. For him nature represented variety, reason uniformity, and, *qua* rational beings, the good life was the same for all. Mocking Herder's admiration for the 'happy' and easy-going inhabitants of Tahiti, Kant asked 'why they should exist at all' and what the universe would lose if such men who were really like 'sheep and cattle' were to disappear. Kant (1996, pp. 219–20). In wrong hands such a question can have murderous implications.

10. Although moral monism is intolerant of other ways of life, it has at least the great virtue of being concerned about the well-being of the entire humankind. Pluralism might be more tolerant, but it could also imply rejection of or indifference to outsiders. Many Hindu thinkers argue that their religion is 'superior' to Christianity and Islam because it cherishes plural paths to salvation and does not believe in conversion. While some Hindus genuinely accord equal respect to other ways of life, others reject conversion because they consider outsiders impure, are totally unconcerned about them, or are afraid of weakening their caste system. This kind of pluralism is morally no better than aggressive monism.

Chapter 2

1. 'The human mind is impelled to take delight in uniformity', Vico (1984, para 204).
2. It would seem that it was partly because of Montesquieu's sympathetic portrayals of 'strange' practices that his *Spirit of Laws* was condemned by the Theology Faculty of the Sorbonne and placed on the index of prohibited books by the Roman Catholic Church.
3. Attacking the rationalist stress on reason, Herder asked, 'Is the whole body just one big eye?' (1969, p. 199).
4. Glorification of diversity is a recurrent theme in German romanticism. For Schiller every difference is vital to 'the completeness of the universe'. For Friedrich Schlegel the universal reason in which all participated was as important as the differences in which each individual was unlike another. A.W. Schlegel even attacked the 'disposition of good taste' which arbitrarily restricted the emergence of new differences. For Schleiermacher 'pitiable uniformity' was to be avoided by anyone with a feeling for the 'fundamental characteristic of living Nature, which everywhere aims at diversity and individuality (*Mannigfaltigkeit und Eigentümlichkeit*). For all this, see Lovejoy (1961, pp. 299ff).
5. For a defence of Herder against the charge of relativism, see Dallmayr (1998).
6. For Herder (1980, p. 189), every culture is trapped within a given 'mindset' or 'mythology' and has 'no idea' of how other cultures think. We are all like the 'King of Siam' who, when told about ice and snow, declared them impossible.
7. Many of these mistakes mar the otherwise excellent works of Durkheim, Malinowski, Ruth Benedict and other writers. For Malinowski all cultures are functionally integrated. Durkheim shares this view and thinks that weakening integration leads to anomie. Benedict thinks of cultures as if each belonged to a distinct kind.

Chapter 3

1. Isaiah Berlin was one of the first to stress cultural pluralism. Since I have discussed him elsewhere (Parekh, 1982), I ignore him here.
2. Rawls (1993a) largely assumes a shared culture and brackets out not only comprehensive philosophical doctrines but also cultural perspectives. This makes his task much easier.
3. For a discussion of Oakeshott, see Parekh (1995b, pp. 169f).
4. Rawls is right to stress the importance of starting with the public culture of democratic society, but wrong not to appreciate that it varies from one democratic society to another and is contested in each of them. I argue the point in Chapter 9 below.
5. For a further discussion see Chapter 7 below.

6. This is the case with the visions of good society advocated by Marx, socialists, and even such religious thinkers as Gandhi. Justice here is seen as a secondary virtue expressing and transcended in such others as mutual concern, moral solidarity, generosity and love.

7. For a discussion of the persistent tendency to take conflict and deep disagreements out of political life in Rawls, Dworkin and others, see Gray (1995a, pp. 73f) and Bellamy (1999). Honig (1993) shows how the 'displaced' politics appears at different levels and acts as a destabilizing factor. For perceptive critiques of Rawls on this and related points, see Jones (1995) and Sandel (1994).

8. Mulhall and Swift (1996, pp. 228f) highlight the structural biases of Rawls's political liberalism.

9. For an excellent exposition of Raz's thought which reads him differently, see Mulhall and Swift (1996).

10. Margalit and Halbertal (1994) rightly point out that the importance of culture cannot be adequately explained in terms of its autonomy or freedom enhancing role alone. Its most important role is to provide a sense of meaning.

11. For a perceptive critique of liberalism from a pluralist perspective and suggestions as to how it can come to terms with pluralism, see Kekes (1993).

Chapter 4

1. The inquiry into human nature presupposes that humans can and should be clearly distinguished from non-humans, that nature and culture can and should be separated, that we can discover human nature fairly accurately, that things of great significance depend on it, and so on. For reasons too complex to discuss here, these and related assumptions became central to western thought in a way they did not in Hindu, Buddhist, Confucian and Islamic traditions, which have therefore generally taken only limited interest in human nature. In the western tradition itself Sophists devoted little attention to it. Even Plato is primarily concerned with the structure and hierarchy of the human psyche rather than its constitutive tendencies. Aristotle seems to mark a turning point. The concept of human nature acquires enormous importance in Christianity.

2. Berger and Luckman (1966, pp. 67, 69) rightly argue that 'human-ness is socio-culturally variable' because '*Homo Sapiens* is always and in the same measure *homo socius*'. See also Geertz (1973, pp. 43f, 50–1) where he challenges the widely shared assumption that only what is uniformly shared by humans constitutes their humanity.

3. For a brief but fascinating analysis of the distinctive style of Indian thought, see Ramanujan (1990). George Fletcher (1997) offers a fascinating account of the ties between English language and the common law tradition, and the way in which the former structures legal reasoning.

4. For minimum universalism, see Hart (1961), Walzer (1994) and Tuck (1994). Walzer's 'reiterative' universalism cannot easily explain how we can tease out the commonalities between the thick and relatively self-contained moral traditions and translate the categories of one into those of another. For good critiques of Walzer, see Bellamy (1999, Chapter 3) and Carens (2000, Introduction).

5. For a good discussion of human rights across cultures, see An-Na'im (1992), especially the articles by the editor, Richard Falk, William Alford, Virginia Leary, Tom Svensson and Allan McChesney.

6. See Kekes (1993, pp. 210f). We may, of course, make some values absolute by defining them in highly formal and abstract terms, but then they have no normative and critical content. For a balanced discussion of 'Asian values', see Bell (1999), Tang (1995), *Journal of Democracy* (1997), Ames (April 1997) and Mehbubani (1999).

7. The European Court of Human Rights applies the same convention on human rights to 300 million people of very different cultural backgrounds, allowing in one case what it does not in another. Its 'variable geometry' shows one way in which general principles can be adjusted to different traditions and circumstances.

Chapter 5

1. 'No culture has appeared or developed except together with a religion', Eliot, (1948, p. 15). He goes on: the relation between the two is 'so difficult that I am not sure I grasp it myself except in flashes, or that I comprehend its implications' (p. 30).

2. For a brilliant account of the inherent indeterminacy of cultural boundaries and structures, see Bhabha (1993).

3. Hall (1993) provides a sharp critique of the 'trendy nomadic voyaging of the postmodern' thinker pursuing 'difference that does not make a difference'.

4. For a valuable discussion of culture as a regulative system, see Hall (1996).

5. Taylor (1989 p. 127) argues that a morally coherent community with its 'strongly qualified horizons' is 'constitutive of human agency', and its absence a threat to 'human personhood'.

6. I discuss this in *Gandhi* (Parekh, 1997a).

Chapter 6

1. For an excellent account, see Skinner (1989, pp. 90–132, and 1978, vol. 2, especially the conclusion). See also Tully (1995).

2. For further discussion, see Parekh (1997c).

3. Some confusion is created by the use of the word 'distinct'. The Spice Report found that for many Canadians it meant 'superior' or 'superiorly entitled'. If it meant different but equal, they were sympathetic to it provided it did not lead to two different systems of rights and obligations (Webber, 1994).
4. For valuable discussions of these and related points, see Webber (1994, Chs 7 and 8); Taylor (1993, Chs 8 and 9); and Kymlicka (1999).
5. For a good analysis of Quebec's case, see Carens (1994 and 1996–7).
6. For helpful discussions from different perspectives, see Jaffrelot (1996) and Hansen (1999).
7. James Tully (1995) has explored these issues with great insight. He talks about new forms of constitution to suit cultural diversity, more or less takes the modern state for granted. I suggest we need to challenge the relevance of the latter itself to some societies.
8. In many respects earlier polities were more sensitive to cultural differences. From the fourteenth century until 1870, aliens and denizens in England had a right to be tried *de madiatate linguae*, a practice codified in the Statue of the Staple of 1353. Under it they were tried by juries at least half of whose members spoke their language and knew their customs. The point of this was to ensure that they secured justice. The practice was abolished in 1870 partly because it was taken to imply that only the members of one's community could offer a fair trial, and partly because principles of justice were supposed to be the same for all.

Chapter 7

1. For stimulating discussions of the nature and modes of minority integration, see Bauböck (1996), Grillo (1998) and Rex (1996). For an account similar to mine, see Modood (1997). Under the Ottoman millet system, Christians and Jews had their own schools and hospitals. The head of each community was accountable for its good behaviour and payment of taxes. Members of these communities were excluded from military service, and no religious or ideological conformity was expected of them. Isolated individuals within them did rise to important political positions.
2. Civil assimilationism is fairly similar to Rawl's political liberalism.
3. As O'Sullivan (2000) perceptively argues, the authority of the state, as distinct from its power, is a function of the acceptance of its legitimacy, which is best defined in minimalist terms.
4. For a good discussion in relation to Israel, see Paled (1992).
5. Forgiveness is a central category in Christian thought in a way that it is not in almost any other religion. This may partly explain why truth and reconciliation commissions have not formed part of contemporary Hindu, Buddhist and Muslim societies in all of which they are just as badly needed. Gandhi introduced analogous ideas in India but they largely died with him. The philosophy of forgiveness has been most systematically

explored by Christians theologians. The traditional Christian thought stresses its three crucial stages: *confessio oris* (acceptance of truth and guilt), *contrio cordis* (willingness to turn away) and *satisfactio operum* (making amends through good works and acts of justice).

6. For a stimulating discussion of collective rights, see Weinstock (1998).

7. Although the logic of collective rights is different from that of collective pride, shame, guilt, responsibility, obligation and so on, the two share many features in common. Unless we grasp the nature of collective claims, experiences, emotions and so forth we cannot hope to understand the structure of such inherently shared realms of human life as politics, culture and language. To say that 'England needs you' is not to say that all or most Englishmen need you, but rather that a historical community spanning generations, characterized by a particular way of life and occupying a certain territory needs you.

8. 'Paradoxical though it may seem, the United States has a common culture that is multicultural', Ravich (1990, p. 339). Spinner (1997) offers a sensitive analysis of how different cultures influence each other and throw up a composite culture. Although his 'pluralistic integration' has much to commend itself, it is not clear how it justifies his attitudes to the Amish and especially the Hasidim in his Ch. 5. See also Vertovec (1996) and Baubück (1994a).

9. For close ties between education and 'American creed' or 'national identity', see Schlesinger (1991) and Kimball (1990). For a tendentious but lively account, see D'Souza (1992). Schlesinger (1991, pp.127f) shows the powerful hold of Eurocentrism even on a refined and generous mind. For a balanced view, see Galston (1991).

10. Insisting that Serbians 'will not accept' being mere citizens in their 'own' state, some of their leaders argue that 'Serbia shall not be the state of equal citizens but the state of Serbia and loyal citizens'. Cited in Kiss (1998).

Chapter 8

1. For a most thorough discussion of some of these cases, see Poulter (1998).

2. For good discussion of the headscarf controversy, see Galeotti (1993) and Moruzzi (1994). For a similar controversy in Germany, see Mandel (1989).

3. For an interesting summary and interpretation, see 'La saga des foulards', *Le Monde*, 13 October 1994.

4. The *Conseil d'Etat*'s decision on 14 April 1995 permits Jewish students to miss Saturday classes to observe the Sabbath. Since this does not violate the principle of *laicité*, the Conseil's attitude to Muslims is puzzling. See *Le Monde*, 16–17 April 1995, pp. 1 and 9. The French government heavily subsidizes the 'private' Roman Catholic school system, but refuses public funds to Jewish, Muslim and even other Christian schools.

5. See Modood (1997) and Parekh (1990a) for different perspectives on the subject.

Chapter 9

1. This is the standard human-rights approach. It is well-stated in Poulter (1998).
2. For further discussions, see Parekh (1994a, 1995a).
3. This is the standard liberal view whose origins go back to J.S. Mill.
4. Melissa Williams (1995); for a more qualified approach, Gutmann (1993); Young (1990).
5. For a critique of my view, see Tyler (1996) and the reply by Sedgelow (1997). My account in this chapter takes account of Tyler's criticisms.
6. For valuable discussions of these practices, see Poulter (1998).
7. Their reasons also include the naïve beliefs that the clitoris is a residual penis showing lack of 'complete' 'femininity', and that if left alone, it would grow to the size of the male penis. See *Journal of the American Medical Association*, December 1995, vol. 274, no. 21, pp. 1714–16. See also Dorkenoo and Elworthy (1992) and Boddy (1989).
8. In one survey of 3210 females and 1545 males in the Sudan, the ratio of females favouring the practice to those who did not was 5 to 1, and of males 7 to 1. The majority, however, was opposed to the more severe Pharaonic type. El Dareer (1983).
9. In Britain under the 1985 Act, even a sane adult woman cannot undergo circumcision on aesthetic, social or other grounds. In the United States a bill to ban it was introduced in Congress in October 1993, but was not brought to vote and has not been reintroduced. Several American states, however, treat it as a criminal offence.
10. There is no definitive history of it so far.
11. Polygyny is allowed in the Old Testament, and Jesus attacks adultery and divorce but seems silent about polygyny. See J. Cairncross (1974) and Hastings (1974). For a good general discussion of polygamy, see Eugene Hillman (1975). J.S. Mill *On Liberty*, Ch. 4, argues that polygamy is a 'direct infraction' of the principle of liberty because it subordinates women to men. This is only true of polygyny and does not apply to polygamy. Mill allows Mormon polygyny because Mormonism is a voluntary religion which women join out of free will, and condemns 'a civilizade' against it. The Utah branch of the American Civil Liberties Union petitioned its parent body 'to make legal recognition of polygamy a national cause like gay and lesbian rights' on the ground that liberal society should respect 'diversity of life styles'. Mayor Dan Barlow, who has five wives, remarked that 'in the liberal age with all the alternative lifestyles that are condoned, it is a height of folly to censure a man for having more than one family'. A female lawyer, herself one of nine wives, thought that 'it is the ideal way for a woman to have a career and children'. For all this, see *New York Times*, 9 April 1991.
12. Although polygyny is permitted in many Muslim countries, it is subjected to various restrictions. In Syria it is disallowed if the husband is unlikely to have the resources to maintain more than one wife, and in Morocco and Iraq if he is unlikely to treat them with equal justice. In Pakistan and

Bangladesh it is allowed only with the permission of an arbitration council. In Jordan a woman can stipulate at the time of her marriage that her
husband will not take another wife during their marriage.

Chapter 10

1. For detailed references see Parekh (1990b, pp. 59–79) and Appignanesi
   and Maitland (1989, Chs 4 and 5).
2. For the diversity of reactions within the Jewish and other communities,
   see Parekh (1990b).
3. For an excellent discussion of some of the issues raised by the Rushdie
   affair, especially in relation to the claims of identity and belief, see Jones
   (1980, 1990).
4. For a perceptive account, see Gutmann and Thompson (1997).
5. Articles 27 and 28 of the Canadian Charter disallow group defamation of
   women and ethnic, religious and other minorities.
6. For an excellent discussion, see Sandel (1996, ch. 3).
7. 'In good faith', *Independent*, 11 February 1990.
8. For good discussions see articles by Albert Weale, Preston King and
   Susan Mendus in Parekh (1990b).
9. See Audi (1989); Cohen (1998); Greenawalt (1996, pp. 24f and 29f);
   Ackerman (1989, p. 10); Larmore (1987, pp. 53 and 55). Rawls (1993a,
   p. 21) says that citizens may be guided by comprehensive doctrines when
   reflecting on political issues, but not when they 'vote or engage in political advocacy in the public forum'. For a broader view of political discourse that admits religious voices, see Levinson (1992), Carter (1993)
   and Isaac, *et al.* (1999). For a critique from the secularist perspective, see
   Macedo (1998).
10. See Timms (1992); Ingelhart (1990); 'United States Scientists Retain
    Belief in God, Survey Discovers', *Guardian*, 3 April 1993.
11. As Sandel (1996, pp. 55–65) shows, the current interpretation of
    state–religion separation in the United States does not have a long history.
    See also Sandel (1994) for a critique of the restrictive Rawlsian view of
    public reason.
12. For a good discussion, see Casanova (1994).
13. Gandhi insisted that 'religion and state should be separated' and the state
    limited to 'secular welfare', but also that 'those who say that religion has
    nothing to do with politics do not know what religion means'. Iyer (1986,
    vol. 1, pp. 391, 395).

Chapter 11

1. Michaelfelder and Palmer (1989, pp. 110).

2. For a good discussion of what it means to belong to a political community which, though articulated in the language of nationhood, is largely free of nationalism, see Canovan (1996, chs 4, 6).
3. The Indian poet Tagore coined the evocative term *swadeshchintā* to describe this sentiment. Roughly it would translate as 'anxious or loving concern for the well-being of one's country'. He vehemently rejects all forms of nationalism, calling it *bhowgolic apdevatā* roughly 'evil gods of geography' demanding worship even at the cost of human lives.
4. Fraser (1995a) argues this point very well. See also Kiss (1990).
5. Taylor is fully aware of this but does not give it adequate importance in his theory of recognition.

Bibliography

Ackerman, B. (1989) 'Why Dialogue?', *Journal of Philosophy*, vol. 86.
— (1980) *Social Justice in the Liberal State* (New Haven: Yale University Press).
Ames, R. T. (1997) 'Continuing the Conversation on Chinese Human Rights', *Ethics and International Affairs*, vol. 11.
Anderson, B. (1983) *Imagined Communities: Reflections on the Origin and Spread of Nationalism* (London: New Left Books).
An-Na'im, A. (ed.) (1992) *Human Rights in Cross-Cultural Perspectives: A Quest for Consensus* (Philadelphia: University of Pennsylvania Press).
Appadurai, A. (1990) 'Disjuncture and Difference in the Global Cultural Economy', *Theory, Culture and Society*, vol. 7, pp. 295–310.
Appiah, K. A. (1994) 'Identity, Authenticity, Survival', in A. Gutmann (ed.), *Multiculturalism* (Princeton, NJ: Princeton University Press).
— (1996) 'Against National Culture', in L. Garcia-Moreno and P. C. Pfeiffer (eds), *Text and nation: Cross Disciplinary Essay on Cultural and National Identities* (Columbia: Camden House).
Appignanesi, L. and Maitland, D. (eds) (1989) *The Rushdie File* (London: Fourth Estate).
Appleby, R. S. (2000) *The Ambivalence of the Sacred* (Lanham: Rowman & Littlefield).
Aquinas, T. (1952) *The Summa Theologica of St. Thomas Aquinas*, 2 vols, tr. Fathers of the English Dominican Province (Chicago: Encyclopaedia Britannica).
— (1995) *On the Truth of the Catholic Faith: Summa Contra Gentiles*, 4 vols, tr. A. C. Pegis (New York: Image Books).
Archard, D. (ed.) (1996) *Philosophy and Pluralism* (Cambridge: Cambridge University Press).
Ariarajah, W. (1991) *Hindus and Christians – A Century of Protestant Ecumenical Thought* (Amsterdam: Editions Rodopi).
Aristotle (1955) *The Ethics of Aristotle*, tr. J. Thomson (Harmondsworth, Penguin Books).
— (1988) *The Politics*, ed. S. Emerson (Cambridge: Cambridge University Press).
Audi, R. (1989) 'The Separation of Church and State and the Obligation of Citizenship', *Philosophy and Public Affairs*, vol. 18, no. 2.
Augustine, St (1967) *The City of God*, 2 vols (London: J. M. Dent & Sons).

Barber, B. (1995) *Jihad vs. McWorld* (New York: Random House).

Barry, B. (1991) *Liberty and Justice: Essays in Political Theory 2* (Oxford: Clarendon Press).

Bauböck, R. (ed.) (1994a) *From Aliens to Citizens: Redefining the Status of Immigrants in Europe* (Aldershot: Avebury).

— (1994b) *Transnational Citizenship: Membership and Rights in International Migration* (Aldershot: Edward Elgar).

— (1996) 'Social and Cultural Integration in a Civil Society', in R. Bauböck, A. Heller and A. Zolberg (eds), *The Challenge of Diversity: Integration & Pluralism in Societies of Immigration* (Aldershot: Avebury).

Beetham, D. (1991) *The Legitimation of Power* (London: Macmillan).

Beilin, Y. (1992) *Israel: A Concise Political History* (New York: St Martin's Press).

Beiner, R. (1992) *What's the Matter with Liberalism* (Oxford: University of California Press).

Bell, D. (1999) *East Meets West: Human Rights and Democracy in Asia* (Oxford: Clarendon Press).

Bellamy, R. (1999) *Liberalism and Pluralism: Towards a Politics of Compromise* (London: Routledge).

Benhabib, S. (ed.) (1996) *Democracy and Difference: Contesting the Boundaries of the Political* (Princeton: Princeton University Press).

Berger, P. and Luckmann, T. (eds) (1966) *The Social Construction of Reality* (Harmondsworth: Penguin).

Berlin, I. (1969) *Four Essays on Liberty* (London: Oxford University Press).

— (1991) *Against the Current: Essays in the History of Ideas* (Oxford: Clarendon Press).

Bhabha, H. K. (ed.) (1993) *Nation and Narration* (London: Routledge).

Bloom, A. (1987) *The Closing of the American Mind* (New York: Simon & Schuster).

Boddy, J. (1989) *Wombs and Alien Spirits* (Madison: University of Wisconsin Press).

Brown, D. G. (1999) 'Millian Liberalism and Colonial Oppression', in Wilson, C. (ed.) *Civilisation and Oppression*, Supplementary vol. 25 of *Canadian Journal of Philosophy*.

Brown, P. (1967) *Augustine of Hippo – A Biography* (London: Faber & Faber).

Cairncross, J. (1974) *After Polygamy was made a Sin: The Social History of Christian Polygamy* (London: Routledge).

Cairns, A. (1991) 'Constitutional Change and the Three Equalities', in R. Watts and D. Brown (eds), *Options for a New Canada* (Toronto: University of Toronto Press).

— (1993) 'The Fragmentation of Canadian Citizenship', in W. Kaplan (ed.), *Belonging: The Meaning and Future of Canadian Citizenship* (Montreal: McGill-Queen's Press).

Canovan, M. (1996) *Nationhood and Political Theory* (Cheltenham: Edward Elgar).

Carens, J. (1992) 'Democracy and Respect for Difference: The Case of Fiji', *University of Michigan Journal of Law Reform*, vol. 25, no. 3.

— (1994) 'Cultural Adaptation and Integration: Is Quebec a Model for Europe?' in R. Bauböck (ed.), *From Aliens to Citizens: Redefining the Status of Immigrants in Europe* (Aldershot: Avebury).

— (1996) 'Dimensions of Citizenship and National Identity in Canada', *The Philosophical Forum*, vol. xxvii, nos 1& 2.

— (1997) 'Liberalism and culture', *Constellations*, vol. 4, no. 1.

— (2000) *Culture, Citizenship and Community* (Oxford: Oxford University Press).

Carrithers, M. (1992) *Why Humans Have Cultures: Explaining Anthropology and Social Diversity* (Oxford: Oxford University Press).

Carter, S. (1993) *The Culture of Disbelief: How American Law and Politics Trivialise Religious Devotion* (New York: Basic Books).

Casanova, J. (1994) *Public Religions in the Modern World* (Chicago: Chicago University Press).

Clark, R. T. (1969) *Herder: His Life and Thought* (Berkeley: California University Press).

Cligent, R. (1970) *Many Wives, More Powers: Authority and Power in Polygamous Families* (Evanston: North Western University Press).

Cohen, J. (1989) 'Deliberation and Democratic Legitimacy', in A. Hamlin (ed.), *The Good Polity* (New York: Blackwell).

— (1998) 'Democracy and Liberty', in J. Elster (ed.), *Deliberative Democracy* (Cambridge: Cambridge University Press).

Colley, L. (1992) *Britons: Forging the Nation 1707–1837* (New Haven: Yale University Press).

Connolly, W. (1987) *Politics and Ambiguity* (London: University of Wisconsin Press).

— (1991) *Identity/Difference: Democratic Negotiations of Political Paradox* (Ithaca: Cornell University Press).

— (1996) 'Pluralism, Multiculturalism and the Nation-State: Rethinking the Connexions', *Journal of Political Ideologies*, vol. 1, no. 1.

Constable, M. (1994) *The Law and the Offer* (Chicago: Chicago University Press).

Coward, H. (1989) *Hindu–Christian Dialogue: Perspectives and Encounters* (New York: Orbis Books).

Cowell, F. R. (1959) *Culture in Private and Public Life* (London: Thames & Hudson).

Crawford, J. (ed.) (1988) *The Rights of Peoples* (Oxford: Clarendon Press).

Dallmayr, F. (1998) *Alternative Visions: Paths in the Global Village* (Lanham: Rowman & Littlefield).

Deane, H. A. (1963) *The Political and Social Ideas of St. Augustine* (New York: Columbia University Press).

D'Costa, G. (1986) *Theology and Religious Pluralism: The Challenge of Other Religions* (Oxford: Blackwell).

Dorkenoo, E. and Elworthy, S. (1992) *Female Genital Mutilation: Proposals for Change* (London: Minority Rights Group).

Douglas. R., Mara, G. and Richardson, H. (eds) *Liberalism and the Good* (London: Routledge).

D'Souza, D. (1992) *Liberal Education* (New York: Vintage Books).

Dummett, M. (1990) 'Open Letter to Rushdie', *Independent*, February, 1990.

Dunne, M. and Bonazzi, T. (eds) (1995) *Citizenship and Rights* (Stoke-on-Trent: Keele University Press).

Dworkin, R. (1985) *A Matter of Principle* (Cambridge: Harvard University Press).

Eck, D. (1993) 'In the Name of Religions' *World Quarterly*, Autumn, 1993.

El Dareer, A. (1983) 'Attitudes of Sudanese People to the Practice of Female Circumcision', *International Journal of Epidemiology*, vol. 12, pp. 138–44.

Elis, N. (1982) *The Civilizing Process: State Formation and Civilisation*, tr. E. Jephcott (Oxford: Oxford University Press).

Eliot, T. S. (1948) *Notes Towards the Definition of Culture* (London: Faber & Faber).

Elster, J. (ed.) (1998) *Deliberative Democracy* (Cambridge: Cambridge University Press).

Enright, S. (1991) 'Multi-Racial Juries', *New Law Journal*.

Falk, R. (1988) 'The Rights of Peoples (in Particular Indigenous People)', in J. Crawford (ed.), *The Rights of People* (Oxford: Oxford University Press).

Fleras, A. and Elliott, J. L. (1992) *The Nations Within: Aboriginal–State Relations in Canada, The United States and New Zealand* (Toronto: Oxford University Press).

Fletcher, G. (1997) 'The Case for Linguistic Self-Defence', in R. McKim and J. McMahan (eds) *The Morality of Nationalism* (Princeton: Princeton University Press).

Forst, R. (1997) 'Functions of a Theory of Multicultural Justice', in *Constellations*, April (1997) vol. 4, no. 1.

Fraser, N. (1995a) 'From Redistribution to Recognition? Dilemmas of Justice in a "Post-Socialist" Age', *New Left Review*, no. 212, pp. 68–93.

— (1995b) 'Recognition and Redistribution: A Critical Reading of Iris Young's Justice and the Politics of Difference', *Journal of Political Philosophy*, vol. 3, no. 2.

Fullinwider R. K. (ed.) (1996) *Public Education in a Multicultural Society: Policy, Theory, Critique* (Cambridge: Cambridge University Press).

Fukuyama, F. (1999) *The Great Disruption: Human Nature and the Reconstitution of Social Order* (London: Profile Books).

Gadamer, H. G. (1989) *Truth and Method* (2nd edn) tr. J. Weinsheimer and D. Marshall (New York: Crossroad).

Gagnon, A. G. and Garcea, J. (1988) 'Quebec and the Pursuit of Special Status', in R. D. Olling and M. W. Wesmacott (eds), *Perspectives on Canadian Federalism* (Scarborough: Prentice-Hall).

Galeotti, A. (1993) 'Citizenship and Equality: The Place for Toleration', in *Political Theory* vol. 21, no. 4.

Galston, W. A. (1991) *Liberal Purposes: Goods, Virtues, and Diversity in the Liberal State* (Cambridge: Cambridge University Press).

Garver, E. (1994) *Aristotle's Rhetoric: An Art of Character* (Chicago: University of Chicago Press).

Gbadegesin, S. (1993) 'The Ethics of Polygyny', *Quest*, vol, 7, no. 2.

Geertz, C. (1973) *The Interpretation of Cultures* (New York: Basic Books).

Gerth, H. and Mills, C. (1948) (eds) *From Max Weber* (London: Routledge).

Gilbert, P. (1998) *The Philosophy of Nationalism* (Boulder: Westview Press).

Gilson, E. (1959) *The Christian Philosophy of Saint Augustine* (London: Gollancz).

Glazer, N. (1997) *We Are All Multiculturalists Now* (Cambridge, Mass.: Harvard University Press).

Goldberg, D. T. (1993) *Racist Culture: Philosophy and the Politics of Meaning* (Oxford: Basil Blackwell).

Goodwin, J. (1995) *Price of Honour: Muslim Women Lift the Veil of Silence on the Islamic World* (London: Werner Books).

Grass, G. (1959) *Tin Drum* (London: Faber & Faber).

Gray, J. (1993) *Post-Liberalism: Studies in Political Thought* (London: Routledge).

— (1995a) *Enlightenment's Wake: Politics and Culture at the Close of the Modern Age* (London: Routledge).

— (1995b) *Isaiah Berlin* (London: HarperCollins).

Greenawalt, K. (1996) *Private Consciences and Public Reasons* (Oxford: Oxford University Press).

Grillo, A. (1998) *Pluralism and the Politics of Difference: State, Culture, and Ethnicity in Comparative Perspective* (Oxford: Clarendon Press).

Gutmann, A. (1993) 'The Challenge of Multiculturalism to Political Ethics', *Philosophy and Public Affairs*, vol. 22, no. 3.

Gutmann, A. and Thompson, D. (1997) *Democracy and Disagreement* (London: The Belknap Press).

Gutmann, E. (1988) 'Israel: Democracy Without a Constitution', in V. Bogdanor (ed.), *Constitutions in Democratic Polities* (Aldershot: Gower).

Habermas, J. (1993) 'Struggles for Recognition in Constitutional States', *European Journal of Philosophy*, vol. 1, no. 2.

Halbfass, W. (1990) *India and Europe: An Essay in Philosophical Understanding* (Delhi: Motilal Banarsidass).

Hall, S. (1993) 'Culture, Community, Nation', *Cultural Studies*, vol. 7, no. 3.

— (1996) *Critical Dialogues in Cultural Studies*, ed. Morley, D. and Chen K–H. (London: Routledge)

Hampshire, S. (1983) *Morality and Conflict* (Oxford: Basil Blackwell).

— (1989) *Innocence and Experience* (Harmondsworth: Penguin).

Hansen, T. B. (1999) *The Saffron Wave: Democracy and Hindu Nationalism in Modern India* (Delhi: Oxford University Press).

Hart, H.L.A. (1961) *The Concept of Law* (Oxford: Clarendon Press).

Hastings, A. (1974) *Christian Marriage in Africa* (London: SPCK).

Hegel, G. (1960) *The Phenomenology of Mind*, tr. J. Baillie (London: Allen & Unwin).

Herder, J. G. (1800) *Outlines of a Philosophy of the History of Man*, tr. T. Churchill (London: Trubner).

— (1968) *Reflections on the Philosophy of the History of Mankind*, F. Marvel (ed.) (Chicago: University of Chicago Press).

— (1969) *Herder on Social and Political Culture*, tr. & ed. F.M. Barnard (Cambridge: Cambridge University Press).

Herzog, H. (1984) 'Ethnicity as a Product of Political Negotiation: The Case of Israel', *Ethnic and Racial Studies*, vol. 7.

Hick, J. (1973) *God and the Universe of Faiths* (London: Macmillan).

— (1985) *Problems of Religious Pluralism* (London: Macmillan).

Hillman, E. (1975) *Polygamy Reconsidered* (New York: Orbis Books).

Hood, J. (1995) *Aquinas and the Jews* (Philadelphia: University of Pennsylvania Press).

Honig, B. (1993) *Political Theory and the Displacement of Politics* (Ithaca: Cornell University Press).

Hosking, G. and Schopflin, G. (eds) (1998) *Myths of Nationhood* (New York: Routledge).

Ignatieff, M. (1993) *Blood and Belonging: Journey into the New Nationalism* (New York: Farrar Straus & Giroux).

Inglehart, R. (1990) *Cultural Shirt* (Princeton, N.J.: Princeton University Press).

Ingram, A. (1994) *A Political Theory of Rights* (Oxford: Clarendon Press).

Isaac, J. C., Filner, M. F. and Bivins, J. C. (1999) 'American Democracy and the New Christian Right: a critique of liberalisms', in I. Shapiro and C. Hacker-Cordon (eds), *Democracy's Edges* (Cambridge: Cambridge University Press).

Iyer, R. (ed.) (1986) *The Moral and Political Writings of Mahatma Gandhi*, 3 vols. (Oxford: Clarendon Press).

Jaffrelot, C. (1996) *The Hindu Nationalist Movement and Indian Politics: 1925 to 1990s* (London: Hurst & Co.).

Jones, P. (1980) 'Blasphemy, Offensiveness and Law', *British Journal of Political Science*, vol. 10, no. 2.

— (1990) 'Respecting Beliefs and Rebuking Rushdie', *British Journal of Political Science*, vol. 25.

— (1995) 'Two Conceptions of Liberalism, Two Conceptions of Justice', *British Journal of Political Science*, vol. 25.

— (1999) 'Group Rights and Group Oppression', *Journal of Political Philosophy*, vol. 7, no. 4.

Kallen, H. (1924) *Culture and Democracy in the United States* (New York: Boni & Liveright).

Kant, I. (1996), *Political Writings*, ed. H. Reiss (Cambridge: Cambridge University Press).

Kekes, J. (1993) *The Morality of Pluralism* (Princeton: Princeton University Press).

Kimball, R. (1990) *Tenured Radicals: How Politics has corrupted Higher Education* (New York: HarperCollins).

Kiss, E. (1998) 'Saying We're Sorry: Liberal Democracy and the Rhetoric of Collective Identity', *Constellations*, vol. 4, no. 3.

— (1990) 'Democracy and the Politis of Recognition', in I. Shapiro and Hacker-Cordon (eds), *Democracy's Edges* (Cambridge: Cambridge University Press).

Koso, T. O. (1987) *The Circumcision of Women* (London: Zed Books).

Kukathas, C. (1992a) 'Are there any Cultural Rights', *Political Theory*, vol. 21, no. 1.

— (1992b) 'Cultural Rights Again: A Rejoinder to Kymlicka', *Political Theory*, vol. 20, vol. 4.

Kymlicka, W. (1989) *Liberalism, Community, and Culture* (Oxford: Clarendon Press).

— (1992) 'Two Models of Pluralism and Tolerance', *Analyse und Kritik*, vol. 14, no. 1.

— (1995) *Multicultural Citizenship: A Liberal Theory of Minority Rights* (Oxford: Clarendon Press).

— (1999) *Finding Our Way: Rethinking Ethnocultural Relations in Canada* (Toronto: Oxford University Press).

Larmore, C. (1987) *Patterns of Moral Complexity* (Cambridge: Cambridge University Press).

Levinson, M. (1997) 'Liberalism versus Democracy? Schooling Private Citizens in the Public Square', *British Journal of Political Science*, vol. 27, pp. 333–60.

Levinson S. (1992) 'Religions, Language and the Public Square', *Harvard Law Review*, vol. 105. pp. 2061–79.

Lilla, M. (1993) *G. B. Vico: The Making of An Anti-Modern* (Cambridge: Harvard University Press).

Locke, J. (1963) *Two Treatises of Government*, ed. P. Laslett (Cambridge: Cambridge University Press)

Lovejoy, A. (1961) *The Great Chain of Being: A Study of the History of an Idea* (Cambridge: Harvard University Press).

Lucien, J. (1997) *L'Individu Effacé ou le paradoxe du libéralism français* (Paris: Fayard).

Lukes, S. (1982) 'Relativism in its Place', in M. Hollis and S. Lukes (eds) *Rationality and Relativism* (Oxford: Clarendon Press).

Macedo, S. (1995) 'Liberal Civic Education and Religious Fundamentalism: The Case of God v. John Rawls?', *Ethics*, vol. 105, no. 3. pp. 468–96.

— (1998) 'Transformative Constitutionalism and the Case of Religion: Defending the Moderate Hegemony of Liberalism', *Political Theory*, vol. 26, no. 1.

MacIntyre, A. (1990) *After Virtue: A Study in Moral Theory* (London: Duckworth).

Mahajan, G. (1998) *Identities and Rights: Aspects of Liberal Democracy in India* (New Delhi: Oxford).

Mandel, R. (1989) 'Turkish Headscarves and the "Foreigners Problem": Constructing Difference Through Emblems of Identity', *New German Critique*, vol. 46.

Margalit, A. and Halbertal, M. (1994) 'Liberalism and the Right to Culture', *Social Research*, vol. 61, vol. 3.

Mason, A. (1999) 'Political Community, Liberal Nationalism and the Ethics of Assimilation', *Ethics*, no. 109.

McKim, R. and McMahan, J. (eds) (1997) *The Morality of Nationalism* (Oxford: Oxford University Press).

Mehbubani, L. (1999) 'An Asian Perspective on Human Rights', in P. van Nees, (ed.) *Debating Human Rights* (London: Routledge).

Mehta, U. (1999) *Liberalism and Empire: A Study in Nineteenth-Century British Liberal Thought* (Chicago: University of Chicago Press).

Melzer, A., Weinberger, J. and Zinman, R. (eds) (1998) *Multiculturalism and American Democracy* (Kansas: University of Kansas Press).

Mendus, S. (1989) *Toleration and the Limits of Liberalism* (Atlantic Highlands: Humanities Press).

Michaelfelder, D. and Palmer, R. E. (eds) (1989) *Dialogue and Deconstruction: The Gadamer–Derrida Encounter* (Albany: State University of New York Press).

Mill, J. S. (1964) *Utilitarianism, Liberty, Representative Government* (London: Everyman's Library)

Miller, D. (1995) *On Nationality* (Oxford: Oxford University Press).

Modood, T. (1992) *Not Easy Being British: Colour, Culture and Citizenship* (Stoke-on-Trent: Trentham Books).

— (1993) 'Establishment, Multiculturalism, and British Citizenship', *Political Quarterly*, vol. 65, no. 1.

— (ed.) (1997) *Church, State and Religious Minorities* (London: Policy Studies Institute).

Modood, T. and Werbner, P. (eds) (1997) *The Politics of Multiculturalism in the New Europe: Racism, Identity and Community* (London: Zed Books).

Montesquieu, B. (1959) *The Spirit of the Laws*, tr. T. Nugent (New York: The Hafner Library of Classics).

— (1961) *The Persian Letters*, tr, J. R. Loy (New York: Basic Books).

Morley, D. and Chen, K. (1996) *Stuart Hall: Critical Dialogues in Cultural Studies* (London: Routledge).

Moruzzi, N. C. (1994) 'A Problem with Headscarves', in *Political Theory*, vol. 22, no. 2.

Mulhall, S. and Swift, A. (1996) *Liberals and Communitarians* (Oxford: Basil Blackwell).

Nimni, E. (1994) *Marxism and Nationalism: Theoretical Origins of a Political Crisis* (London: Pluto Press).

— (1999) 'Nationalist Multiculturalism in late Imperial Austria as a Critique of Contemporary Liberalism: The Case of Bauer and Renner', *Journal of Political Ideologies*, vol. 4, no. 3.

Nozick, R. (1974) *Anarchy, State, and Utopia* (Oxford: Blackwell).

Nussbaum, M. (1993) 'Non-relative Virtues: An Aristotlean Approach' in M. Nussbaum and A. Sen (eds), *The Quality of Life* (Oxford: Clarendon Press).

Oakeshott, M. (1972) *On Human Conduct* (Oxford: Clarendon Press).

— (1993) *Morality and Politics in Modern Europe: The Harvard Lectures* (New Haven: Yale University Press).

One Nation, Many Peoples: A Declaration of Cultural Interdependence (1991)
The Report of the New York State Social Studies Review and Development
Committee.

Okin, S. (with respondents) (1999) *Is Multiculturalism Bad for Women?*
(Princeton: Princeton University Press).

O'Sullivan, N. K. (ed.) (2000) *Political Theory in Transition* (London:
Routledge).

Pagden, A. (1991) *European Encounters with the New World* (New Haven:
Yale University Press).

— (1995) *Lords of All the World: Ideologies of Empire in Britain, France and
Spain 1400–1800* (New Haven: Yale University Press).

Paled, Y. (1992) 'Ethnic Demand and the Legal Constructive of Citizenship:
Arab Citizens of the Jewish State', *American Political Science Review*,
vol. 86, no. 2.

Pangle, T. (1973) *The Political Philosophy of Montesquieu* (Chicago: Chicago
University Press).

Parekh, B. (1982) *Contemporary Political Thinkers* (Baltimore: The Johns
Hopkins University Press).

— (ed.) (1990a) *Law, Blasphemy and the Multi-Faith Society* (London:
Commission for Racial Equality).

— (ed.) (1990b) *Free Speech* (London: Commission for Racial Equality).

— (1992) 'A Case for Positive Discrimination', in B. Hepple and E. Szyszczak
(eds) *Discrimination: The Limits of Law* (London: Mansell).

— (1993) 'The Cultural Particularity of Liberal Democracy', in D. Held (ed.)
Prospects for Democracy (Cambridge: Polity Press).

— (1994a) 'Discourses on National Identity', *Political Studies*, vol. 42, no. 3.

— (1994b) 'Decolonizing Liberalism' in A. Shtromas (ed.) *The End of 'Isms'?*
(Oxford: Blackwell)

— (1995a) The Concept of National Identity', *New Community*, vol. 21, no. 2.

— (1995b) 'Oakeshott's Theory of Civil Association', *Ethics*, vol. 106, no. 2.

— (1997a) *Gandhi* (Oxford: Oxford University Press)

— (1997b) 'Is There a Human Nature?' in L. Rouner (ed.), *Is There A Human
Nature?* (Notre Dame: University of Notre Dame Press).

— (1997c) 'Rethinking Humanitarian Intervention', *International Political
Science Review*, vol. 18, no. 1.

Pearson, K., Parry, B. and Squires, J. (eds) (1997) *Cultural Readings of
Imperialism: Edward Said and the Gravity of History* (London: Lawrence
& Wishart).

Phillips, A. (1991) *Engendering Democracy* (University Park: Pennsylvania
University Press).

— (1993) *Democracy and Difference* (Philadelphia: Pennsylvania University
Press).

— (1995) *The Politics of Presence: Issues in Democracy and Group
Representation* (Oxford: Clarendon Press).

Pieterse, J. (1990) *Empire and Emancipation: Power and Liberation on a
World Scale* (London: Pluto Press).

Pieterse, J. and Parekh, B. (eds) (1995) *The Decolonization of Imagination: Culture, Knowledge and Power* (London: Zed Books).

Popper, K. (1945) *The Open Society and its Enemies* (London: Routledge).

Poulter, S. (1998) *Ethnicity, Law and Human Rights: The English Experience* (Oxford: Clarendon Press).

Rajchman, J. (ed.) (1995) *The Identity in Question* (London: Routledge).

Ramanujan, A. K. (1990) 'Is There an Indian Way of Thinking? An Informal Essay' in M. McKim (ed.), *India Through Hindu Categories* (Delhi: Sage).

Ravich, D. (1990) 'Multiculturalism', *American Scholar*, Summer issue.

Rawls, J. (1971) *A Theory of Justice* (London: Oxford University Press).

— (1993a) *Political Liberalism* (New York: Columbia University Press).

— (1993b) 'The Law of Peoples', in S. Shute and S. Hurley (eds), *On Human Rights: The Oxford Amnesty Lectures*. (New York: Basic Books).

Raz, J. (1986) *The Morality of Freedom* (Oxford: Oxford University Press).

— (1994) *Ethics in the Public Domain: Essays in the Morality of Law and Politics* (Oxford: Clarendon Press).

Rex, J. (1996) *Ethnic Minorities in the Modern Nation State* (London: Macmillan).

Richter, M. (1977) *The Political Theory of Montesquieu* (Cambridge: Cambridge University Press).

Ridge, M. (ed.) (1981) *Bilingualism: An American Dilemma* (Los Angeles: University of Southern California Press).

Ross, D. (1956) *Aristotle* (London: Methuen).

Rouner, L. (ed.) (1999) *Religion, Politics and Peace* (Notre Dame: University of Notre Dame Press).

Rushdie, S. (1981) *Midnight's Children* (London: Jonathan Cape).

— (1983) *Shame* (London: Jonathan Cape).

— (1988) *The Satanic Verses* (London: Viking).

Safran, W. (1989) 'The French Left and Ethnic Pluralism', *Ethnic and Racial Studies*, vol. 7.

Said, E. (1993) *Culture and Imperialism* (London: Chatto & Windus).

Sandel, M. (1982) *Liberalism and the Limits of Justice* (Cambridge: Cambridge University Press).

— (1990) 'Freedom of Conscience or Freedom of Choice', in J. Hunter and O. Guiness (eds) *Articles of Faith, Articles of Peace* (Washington: Brookings Institute).

— (1994) 'Political Liberalism: Review of Rawls', *Harvard Law Review*, vol. 107. no.7.

— (1996) *Democracy's Discontent* (Cambridge, Mass.: Harvard University Press).

Schlesinger, A. M. (1991) *The Disuniting of America: Reflections on a Multicultural Society* (New York: Whittle Communications).

Sedgelow, P. (1997) 'Reply to Tyler', *Politics*, vol. 17.

Seminar (December 1999) Special Issue on Indian Debates on Multiculturalism.

Shachar, A. (1998) 'Group Identity and Women's Rights in Family Law: The Perils of Multicultural Accommodation', *The Journal of Political Philosophy*, vol. 6, no. 3.

Shapiro, I. and Hacker-Cordon, C. (eds) (1999) *Democracy's Edges* (Cambridge: Cambridge University Press).

Sharp, A. (1990) *Justice and the Maori: Claims in New Zealand Political Arguments in the 1980s* (Auckland: Oxford University Press).

— (1999) ' "What if Value and Right lie Foundationally in Groups?": The Maori Case', *Critical Review of International Social and Political Philosophy*, vol. 2, no. 2, pp. 1–28.

Shklar, J. (1987) *Montesquieu* (Oxford: Oxford University Press).

Shute, S. and Hurley, S. (1993) (eds) *On Human Rights* (New York: Basic Books).

Skinner, Q. (1978) *The Foundations of Modern Political Thought*, 2 vols. (Cambridge: Cambridge University Press).

— (1989) 'The State', in T. Ball, J. Farr and R. L. Hansin (eds) *Political Innovation and Conceptual Change* (Cambridge: Cambridge University).

Smith, A. (1991) *National Identity* (Harmondsworth: Penguin).

Spinner, J. (1994) *The Boundaries of Citizenship: Race, Ethnicity, and Nationality in the Liberal State* (Baltimore: The Johns Hopkins University Press).

Spruyt, H. (1994) *The Sovereign State and its Competitors* (Princeton: Princeton University Press).

Stone, J. (1985) *Radical Conflict in Contemporary Society* (Cambridge: Harvard University Press).

Tamir, Y. (1993) *Liberal Nationalism* (Princeton: Princeton University).

Tang, J. T. H. (ed.) (1995) *Human Rights and International Relations in Asia Pacific* (London: Pinter).

Taylor, C. (1989) *Sources of the Self* (Cambridge: Cambridge University Press).

— (1993) *Reconciling the Solitudes: Essays on Canadian Federalism and Nationalism* (Montreal: McGill–Queen's University Press).

— (1994) 'The Politics of Recognition' in A. Gutmann (ed.), *Multiculturalism* (Princeton, NJ: Princeton University Press).

Timms, N. (1992) *Family and Citizenship: Values in Contemporary Britain* (Dartmouth: Aldershot).

Todorov, T. (1993) *On Human Diversity: Nationalism, Racism and Exociticism in French Thought* (Cambridge: Harvard University Press).

Tuck, R. (1994) 'Rights and Pluralism', in J. Tully (ed.), *Philosophy in an Age of Pluralism: The Philosophy of Charles Taylor in Question* (Cambridge: Cambridge University Press).

— (1999) *The Rights of War and Peace* (Oxford: Oxford University Press).

Tully, J. (1993) *An Approach to Political Philosophy: Locke in Contexts* (Cambridge: Cambridge University Press).

— (1995) *Strange Multiplicity: Constitutionalism in an Age of Diversity* (Cambridge: Cambridge University Press).

Tyler, C. (1996) 'The Democratic Implications of Parekh's Cultural Pluralism', *Politics*, vol. 16, no. 3.

— (1998) 'Cultural Pluralism: A Response to Sedgelow's Critique', *Politics*, vol. 18, no. 2.

Varshney, A. (2001) *Ethnic Conflict and Civic Life: Hindus and Muslims in India* (New Haven: Yale University Press).

Vertovec, S. (1996) 'Multiculturalism, Culturalism and Public Incorporation', *Ethnic and Racial Studies*, vol. 19, no. 1, January 1996.

Vico, G. (1984) *The New Science of Giambattista Vico*, trs. T. Bergin and M. Fisch (Ithaca: Cornell University Press).

Viroli, M. (1995) *For Love of Country: An Essay on Patriotism and Nationalism* (Oxford: Clarendon Press).

Waldron, J. (1990) *The Law* (London: Routledge).

— (1995) 'Minority Cultures and the Cosmopolitan Alternative', in W. Kymlicka (ed.), *The Rights of Minority Cultures* (Oxford: Oxford University Press).

— (1996) 'Multiculturalism and Melange', in R. K. Fullinwider (ed.), *Public Education in a Multicultural Society* (Cambridge: Cambridge University Press).

Walzer, M. (1983) *Spheres of Justice: A Defense of Pluralism and Equality* (New York: Basic Books).

— (1992a) 'The Civil Society Argument', in C. Mouffe (ed.), *Dimensions of Radical Democracy: Pluralism, Citizenship and Community* (London: Routledge).

— (1992b) *What it Means to Be An American* (New York: Marasilio).

— (1992c) 'Moral Minimalism', in W.R. Shea and A. Spadafova (eds), *From the Twilight of Probability: Ethics and Politics* (New York: Science History Publications).

— (1994) *Thick and Thin: Moral Arguments at Home and Abroad* (Cambridge: Harvard University Press).

— (1997) *On Toleration* (New Haven: Yale University Press).

Webber, J. (1994) *Reimagining Canada: Language, Culture, Community, and the Canadian Constitution* (Montreal: McGill–Queen's University Press).

Weinstock, D. (1994) 'The Political Theory of Strong Evaluation', in J. Tully (ed.) *Philosophy in an Age of Pluralism* (Cambridge: Cambridge University Press).

— (1998) in R. Bauböck and J. Randall (eds), *Blurred Boundaries: Mitigation, Ethnicity and Citizenship* (Ashgate: Aldershot).

Werbner, P. and Modood, T. (eds) (1997) *Debating Cultural Hybridity: Multi-Cultural Identities and the Politics of Anti-Racism* (London: Zed Books).

Willet, C. (1998) *Theorizing Multiculturalism: A Guide to the Current Debate* (Oxford: Basil Blackwell).

Williams, M. (1995) 'Justice Toward Groups: Political not Juridical', *Political Theory*, vol. 23.

Williams, R. (1980) *Problems in Materialism and Culture* (London: Verso).

Young, I. M. (1989) 'Policy and Group Difference: A Critique of the Ideal of Universal Citizenship', *Ethics*, vol. 99, no. 2.

— (1990) *Justice and the Politics of Difference* (Princeton: Princeton University Press).

Index